SOCCERNOMICS

REVISED AND EXPANDED EDITION
OF *WHY ENGLAND LOSE*

SOCCERNOMICS

WHY SPAIN, GERMANY AND BRAZIL WIN, AND WHY THE USA, JAPAN, AUSTRALIA – AND EVEN IRAQ – ARE DESTINED TO BECOME THE KINGS OF THE WORLD'S MOST POPULAR SPORT

SIMON KUPER & STEFAN SZYMANSKI

HarperSport
An Imprint of HarperCollinsPublishers

HarperSport
an Imprint of HarperCollins*Publishers*
77–85 Fulham Palace Road,
Hammersmith, London W6 8JB

www.harpercollins.co.uk

First published as *Why England Lose* in 2009
This revised and updated edition 2014

4

A catalogue record of this book
is available from the British Library

ISBN 978-0-00-758652-3

Printed and bound in Great Britain by
Clays Ltd, St Ives plc

MIX
Paper from
responsible sources

FSC
www.fsc.org

FSC˙ C007454

CONTENTS

SECTION II: THE FANS: LOYALTY, SUICIDES, HAPPINESS, AND THE COUNTRY WITH THE BEST SUPPORTERS

SECTION III: THE COUNTRIES: RICH AND POOR, TOM THUMB, SPAIN, GHIDDINK, SADDAM, AND THE CHAMPIONS OF THE FUTURE

DRIVING WITH A DASHBOARD: IN SEARCH OF NEW TRUTHS ABOUT FOOTBALL

A few years ago, the data department at Manchester City carried out a study of corner-kicks. City hadn't been scoring much from corners recently, and the analysts wanted to find out the best way to take them. They watched more than 400 corners, from different leagues, over several seasons, and concluded: the most dangerous corner was the inswinger to the near post.

The beauty of the inswinger was that it sent the ball straight into the danger zone. Sometimes an attacker would get a head or foot to it and divert it in from point-blank range. Sometimes the keeper or a defender stopped the inswinger on the line, whereupon someone bashed it in. And occasionally the ball just swung straight in from the corner. All in all, the analysts found, inswingers were better than outswingers.

They took their findings to the club's then manager, Roberto Mancini, who like almost all managers is an ex-footballer. He heard the analysts out. Then he said, in effect: 'I was a player for many years, and I just *know* that the outswinger is more effective.' He was wrong, but we can understand why he made the mistake: outswingers tend to create beautiful goals (ball swings out, player meets it with powerful header, ball crashes into net) and beautiful goals stick in the memory. The messy goals generally produced by inswingers don't.

It's a story that captures where soccer is today. On the one hand, the March of the Geeks has advanced fast since 2009 when we first published *Why England Lose* (now renamed, updated and expanded as *Soccernomics*). Football is becoming more intelligent. The analysts who now crunch 'match data' at almost all big European clubs (and at many smaller ones) are just one symptom of the shift. Today's plugged-in clubs know stats like 'pass-completion rates in the final third of the field', kilometres run in each phase of the game, and pace of sprints for all their players. These numbers increasingly inform decisions on which players to buy and sell.

On the other hand, as Mancini's certainty about corner-kicks shows, there is still widespread suspicion of numbers in football. John Coulson of the data provider Opta told us: 'There are still maybe a lot of teams that view data as a threat rather than as a tool.' Baseball has had its *Moneyball* revolution, but in football the transformation has only just begun. This new edition of our book – *Soccernomics 3.0*, as we think of it – uses data to clarify thinking on topics ranging from tackles through transfers to the rise of Spain.

This book began in the Hilton in Istanbul. From the outside it's a squat and brutalist place, but once the security men have checked your car for bombs and waved you through, the hotel is so soothing you never want to go home again. Having escaped the 13-million-person city, the only stress is over what to do next: a Turkish bath, a spot of tennis or yet more overeating while the sun sets over the Bosphorus? For aficionados, there was also a perfect view of the Beşiktaş football stadium right next door. And the staff were so friendly they were even friendlier than ordinary Turkish people.

The two authors of this book, Stefan Szymanski (a sports economist) and Simon Kuper (a journalist), met here. Fenerbahçe football club was marking its centenary by staging the '100th Year Sports and Science Congress', and had flown us both in to give talks.

Over beers in the Hilton bar we found that we thought much the same way about football. Stefan as an economist is trained to torture the data until they confessed, while Simon as a reporter tends to go around interviewing people, but those are just surface differences. We both think that much in football can be explained, even predicted, by studying data – especially data found outside football.

For a very long time football escaped the Enlightenment. Football clubs are still mostly run by people who do what they do because they have always done it that way. These people used to 'know' that black players 'lacked bottle', and they therefore overpaid for mediocre white players. Today they discriminate against black managers, buy the wrong players, and then let those players take penalties the wrong way. (We can, incidentally, explain why Manchester United won the penalty shootout in the Champions League final in Moscow. It's a story involving a secret note, a Basque economist, and Edwin van der Sar's powers of detection.)

Entrepreneurs who dip into football also keep making the same mistakes. They buy clubs promising to run them 'like a business', and disappear a few seasons later amid the same public derision as the previous lot. 'I screwed up,' Tony Fernandes, chairman of Queens Park Rangers, told us. Fans and journalists aren't blameless either. Many newspaper headlines rest on false premises: 'Sunderland Land World Cup Star', or 'World Cup Will Be Economic Bonanza'. The game is full of unexamined clichés: 'Football is becoming boring because the big clubs always win', 'Football is big business', and, perhaps the greatest myth in the English game, 'The England team should do better'. None of these shibboleths has been tested against the data.

Most male team sports are pervaded by the same overreliance on traditional beliefs. American baseball, too, was until quite recently an old game filled with old lore. Since forever, players had stolen bases, hit sacrifice bunts, and been judged on their batting averages. Everyone in baseball just *knew* that all this was right.

But that was before Bill James. Like Dorothy in *The Wizard of Oz*, James came out of rural Kansas. He hadn't done much in life beyond keeping the stats in the local Little League, and watching the furnaces in a pork-and-beans factory. However, in his spare time he had begun to study baseball statistics with a fresh eye, and discovered that 'a great portion of the sport's traditional knowledge is ridiculous hokum'. James wrote that he wanted to approach the subject of baseball 'with the same kind of intellectual rigor and discipline that is routinely applied, by scientists great and poor, to trying to unravel the mysteries of the universe, of society, of the human mind, or of the price of burlap in Des Moines'.

In self-published mimeographs masquerading as books, the first of which sold 75 copies, James began demolishing the game's myths. He found, for instance, that the most important statistic in batting was the rarely mentioned 'on-base percentage' – how often a player managed to get on base. James and his followers (statisticians of baseball who came to be known as sabermetricians) showed that good old sacrifice bunts and base-stealing were terrible strategies.

His annual *Baseball Abstracts* turned into real books; eventually they reached the bestseller lists. One year, the cover picture showed an ape, posed as Rodin's *The Thinker*, studying a baseball. As James wrote in one *Abstract*: 'This is *outside* baseball. This is a book about what baseball looks like if you step back from it and study it intensely and minutely, but from a distance.'

Some Jamesians started to penetrate professional baseball. One of them, Billy Beane, general manager of the little Oakland A's, is the hero of Michael Lewis's earth-moving book *Moneyball* and of the film starring Brad Pitt. In recent years Billy Beane, like so many Americans, has become a soccer nut. He now spends a lot of time thinking about how his insights into baseball might apply to soccer. (We'll say more later about Beane's brilliant gaming of baseball's transfer market and its lessons for football.)

Eventually even the people inside baseball started to get curious about James. In 2002 the Boston Red Sox actually appointed him 'Senior Baseball Operations Adviser', his first regular job since the pork-and-beans plant. That same year, the Red Sox hired one of James's followers, the 28-year-old Theo Epstein, as the youngest general manager in the history of the major leagues. In 2004 the 'cursed' club won its first World Series in 86 years. In 2007 they won another. Today large statistical departments are the norm at Major League Baseball clubs.

In 2006 *Time* magazine named James in its hundred most influential people in the world. Now football is due its own Jamesian revolution.

A NUMBERS GAME

It's strange that football has been so averse to studying data, because one thing that attracts many fans to the game is precisely a love of numbers.

The man to ask about that is Alex Bellos. He wrote the magnificent book *Futebol: The Brazilian Way of Life,* but he also has a maths degree, and his *Alex's Adventures in Numberland: Dispatches from the Wonderful World of Mathematics* appeared in 2010.

'Numbers are incredibly satisfying,' Bellos tells us. 'The world has no order, and maths is a way of seeing it in an order. League tables have an order. And the calculations you need to do for them are so simple: it's nothing more than your three times table.'

Though most fans would probably deny it, a love of football is often intertwined with a love of numbers. There are the match results, the famous dates, and the special joy of sitting in a pub with the newspaper on a Sunday morning 'reading' the league table. Fantasy Football Leagues are, at bottom, numbers games. And

James Alexander Gordon's incantation of the British football results on Saturday afternoons ('Cow-den-BEATH 1, Sten-house-MUIR [pause] 1') was part timeless ritual, part romance of place names, and part poem of numbers.

In this book we want to introduce new numbers and new ideas to football: numbers on suicides, on wage spending, on countries' populations, on anything that helps to reveal new truths about the game. Though Stefan is a sports economist, this is not a book about money. The point of football clubs is not to turn a profit (which is fortunate, as almost none of them does) and nor are we particularly interested in any profits they happen to make. Rather, we want to use an economist's skills (plus a little geography, psychology and sociology) to understand the game on the pitch, and the fans off it.

Some people may not want their emotional relationship with football sullied by our rational calculations. On the other hand, the next time England lose a penalty shootout in a World Cup quarter-final these same people will probably be throwing their beer glasses at the TV, when instead they could be tempering their disappointment with some reflections on the nature of binomial probability theory.

We think it's a good time to be rewriting this book. The world has entered the era of 'big data'. The phrase describes the unprecedented mountain of information that is now collected every day. This information comes mostly from the internet (from innumerable search terms, Facebook pages and emails), and from sensors that are attached to ever more physical objects – among them, footballers during training sessions. By one estimate, the daily amount of data generated worldwide doubles approximately every 40 months.

Big data has reached football too. For the first time in the sport's history, there are a lot of numbers to mine. Traditionally, the only data that existed in the game were goals and league tables. (Newspapers published attendance figures, but these were unreliable.) Now clubs are ceasing to rely on gut alone. Increasingly they work with data companies such as Prozone and Opta to analyse games and players. Every day, data analysts collect ever more information about every player's every move on the pitch or the training ground.

Academics are pitching in as well. At the end of the 1980s, when Stefan went into sports economics, only about 20 or 30 academic articles on sport had ever been published. Now there are countless. Many of the new truths they contain have not yet reached most fans.

Another new source of knowledge is the bulging library of football books. When Pete Davies published his *All Played Out: The Full Story of Italia '90,* there were probably only about 20 or 30 good football books in existence. Now – thanks partly to Davies, who has been described as John the Baptist to Nick Hornby's Jesus – there are thousands. Many of these books (including Bellos's *Futebol*) contain truths about the game that we have tried to present here.

So unstoppable has the stream of data become that even people inside the game itself are finally starting to sift it. Michael Lewis, the author of *Moneyball*, wrote in the *New York Times* in February 2009:

> The virus that infected professional baseball in the 1990s, the use of statistics to find new and better ways to value players and strategies, has found its way into every major sport. Not just basketball and football, but also soccer and cricket and rugby and, for all I know, snooker and darts – each one now supports a subculture of smart people who view it not just as a game to be played but as a problem to be solved.

This statistical virus has even spread from baseball to more serious activities. Look at the career of Nate Silver. In childhood he was an obsessive fan of the Detroit Tigers baseball team. Soon after leaving college, he developed a statistical method to forecast performance and career development for baseball players. He also dabbled in soccer: during the World Cup of 2010, he correctly predicted the outcome of 13 of the 16 games in the knockout stages. But the one-time sabermetrician is best known as a political analyst. In the US presidential elections in 2008, Silver correctly called the winner in 49 states. In 2012 he got all 50 plus the District of Columbia. In other words: Nate Silver won the US election. Afterwards he returned to sport, joining the ESPN TV network as an all-purpose guru. Silver stands for the March of the Geeks. Smart people like him are on the rise inside sport and beyond.

In football, these smart men (it's part of the game's own 'ridiculous hokum' that they have to be men) have even begun gaining key roles at some of Europe's biggest clubs. English football, professional on the field since the late nineteenth century, is finally creaking into professionalism off the field too. Given the global obsession with the game, there could come a time when some of the best and brightest young people are working as executives of football clubs. Already, the rising generation of club executives understands that in football today, you need data to get ahead. If you study figures, you will see more and win more.

Yet another harbinger of the impending Jamesian takeover of football is the Milan Lab. Early on, AC Milan's in-house medical outfit found that just by studying a player's jump, it could predict with 70 per cent accuracy whether he would get injured soon. Later it began testing, almost day by day, each player's muscle weaknesses, the movement of his eyes, the rise and fall of his heart rate, his breathing, and many other obvious and less obvious indicators. Jean-Pierre Meersseman, the Lab's cigarette-puffing director, was given power of veto over the club's prospective signings. 'The last signature on the contract before the big boss signs is mine,' he told us in 2008. By 2013 the Lab had performed 1.2 million physical tests on Milan's players, collected millions of pieces of data on computers, logged even the slightest injury to every player, and in the process stumbled upon the secret of eternal youth. (It's still a secret: no other club has a Milan Lab, and the Lab hasn't divulged its findings, which is why players at other clubs are generally finished by their early thirties.)

Most of Milan's starting 11 that beat Liverpool in the Champions League final of 2007 were 31 or older; Paolo Maldini, the captain, was 38, and Filippo Inzaghi, scorer of both Milan's goals, 33. In large part, that trophy was won by the Milan Lab and its database. It is another version of the Triumph of the Geeks story.

In recent years, cash-strapped AC Milan has reduced the lab's funding and power. However, other big clubs all over Europe are now crunching data to find out how to reduce injuries, and how to predict which 12-year-old will grow into the next Xavi. Meersseman says the Lab's data-driven scientists seem to be better than experienced youth coaches at making these predictions. He told us: 'In soccer, they say, "You know about soccer or you don't." And when you go and test the ones who "know", it's surprising how little they know. It's based on the emotion of the moment.'

As Stefan and Simon talked more, and began to think harder about football and data, we buzzed around all sorts of questions. Could we find figures to show which country loved football most? Might the game somehow deter people from killing themselves? And perhaps we could have a shot at predicting which clubs and countries – the US most likely; perhaps even Iraq – would dominate the football of the future. Stefan lived in London, and Simon in Paris, and so we spent a year firing figures, arguments and anecdotes back and forth across the Channel.

What started as a book turned into a long-term collaboration. Together with the journalist Ben Lyttleton we founded the Soccernomics consultancy. On its website, soccernomics-agency.com, we began publishing an occasional blog with our thoughts on football. And we kept rewriting and updating this book, through about 20 different foreign editions and three British versions so far.

For this latest edition, our contact was transatlantic: Stefan is now at the University of Michigan in the US. This edition of *Soccernomics* comes with a new chapter on how UEFA's 'financial fair play' rules might change the game for the worse, and an afterword arguing that football has never had it so good. We have also expanded our thoughts on some mystifying questions, such as: how do clubs use data to judge, buy and sell players? And we've watched fans and media shift to our point of view on certain issues: most people now recognise that hosting World Cups doesn't make you rich, and that England shouldn't expect to win trophies. (We wish we could claim responsibility for moving global opinion, but we can't.) In every chapter in the book we found analyses to update, and new stories and thoughts to add.

All the while, we distrusted every bit of ancient football lore, and tested it against the numbers. As Meersseman says: 'You can drive a car without a dashboard, without any information, and that's what's happening in soccer. There are excellent drivers, excellent cars, but if you have your dashboard, it makes it just a little bit easier. I wonder why people don't want more information.' We do.

SECTION I

SECTION 1

THE CLUES:

GENTLEMEN PREFER BLONDS: HOW TO AVOID SILLY MISTAKES IN THE TRANSFER MARKET

In 1983 AC Milan spotted a talented young black forward playing for Watford. The word is that the player they liked was John Barnes, and that they then confused him with his fellow black team-mate Luther Blissett. Whatever the truth, Milan ended up signing Blissett for £1 million. As a player Blissett became such a joke in Italy that the name 'Luther Blissett' is now used as a pseudonym by groups of anarchist writers. He spent one unhappy year in Milan, before the club sold him back to Watford for just over half the sum they had paid for him. However, that year did give football one of its best quotes. 'No matter how much money you have here,' Blissett lamented, 'you can't seem to get Rice Krispies.' More on Rice Krispies later.

In 2013 clubs around the world paid each other about £2.2 billion in transfer fees. Unfortunately, much of the money thrown around in the transfer market is wasted. Newcastle United were for years perhaps the most humorous example, but in fact, the net amount that almost any club spends on transfer fees bears little relation to where it finishes in the league. We studied the spending of 40 English clubs between 1978 and 1997, and found that their net outlay on transfers (i.e each club's transfer fees paid minus transfer fees received) explained only 16 per cent of their total variation in league position. In other words, taken over many years, the mere fact of being a 'buying club' in the transfer market didn't help you perform significantly better than a 'selling club'.[1]

By contrast, clubs' spending on salaries was extremely telling. The size of their wage bills explained a massive 92 per cent of variation in their league positions, if you took each club's average for the entire period. That correlation shows little sign of going away. We show the same result below using data for the Premier League and the Championship for the decade up to 2012 (see figures opposite). In that period, wage spending still explained more than 90 per cent of the variation in league position. It seems that over the long term, high wages help a club much more than do spectacular transfers.

Obviously we don't believe that if you took a random bunch of players and doubled their salaries they would suddenly play twice as well. It's not that high pay *causes* good performance. Rather, we think that high pay *attracts* good performers. Manchester United can afford to pay Wayne Rooney's wages, whereas Norwich City cannot. And if you have Rooney and other good players, you will win lots of matches. Rich clubs pay high salaries to get good players to win trophies.

It must be said that, for any one given season, the correlation between salaries and league position is weaker. That's because in such a short period, luck plays a big role in performance. Injuries, dodgy referees, poor form and any host of other factors cause significant swings in performance from year to year. For any one season, spending explains only about 70 per cent of the variation in league position.* But true luck (i.e., statistical randomness) tends to even

* In statistics the measure of correlation can be squared in order to derive a percentage of the variation that is explained. Thus if the correlation (called 'r') between league position and wages is +0.84, then the 'r squared' is 0.7 or 70 per cent.

out over the years. So if you track each club's performance over a longer period – 15 or 20 years, say – then salaries explain about 90 per cent of the variation in league position.

The ranking of English clubs below and overleaf shows the generally iron link between wages and league position. It seems that high wages help a club much more than do spectacular transfers.

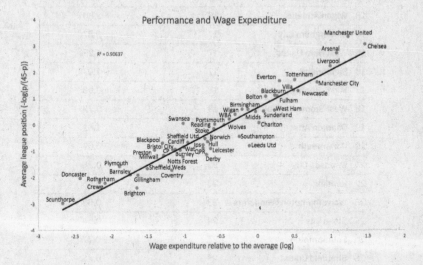

Premier League and Championship teams 2003–2012

THE MORE YOU PAY YOUR PLAYERS, THE HIGHER YOU FINISH (2003–2012)

Club	Average league position	Wage spending relative to the average spending of all clubs
1 Manchester United	2	3.37
2 Chelsea	2	4.23
3 Arsenal	3	2.89
4 Liverpool	5	2.65
5 Tottenham Hotspur	8	1.63

6	Everton	8	1.33
7	Manchester City	9	2.21
8	Aston Villa	10	1.61
9	Newcastle United	11	1.71
10	Fulham	12	1.29
11	Blackburn Rovers	12	1.25
12	Bolton Wanderers	12	1.10
13	Wigan Athletic	16	0.80
14	Birmingham City	17	0.87
15	West Ham United	17	1.25
16	Sunderland	17	1.07
17	Middlesbrough	18	0.96
18	West Bromwich Albion	19	0.73
19	Charlton Athletic	20	1.01
20	Portsmouth	20	0.67
21	Swansea City	22	0.36
22	Reading	23	0.55
23	Wolverhampton Wanderers	23	0.63
24	Stoke City	24	0.54
25	Southampton	25	0.77
26	Sheffield United	27	0.48
27	Norwich City	27	0.53
28	Hull City	28	0.50
29	Leeds United	28	0.89
30	Blackpool	29	0.27
31	Cardiff City	30	0.38
32	Ipswich Town	30	0.47
33	Leicester City	31	0.52
34	Queens Park Rangers	31	0.47
35	Watford	31	0.36
36	Crystal Palace	31	0.34
37	Preston North End	31	0.24
38	Burnley	32	0.32
39	Bristol City	32	0.31

40	Derby County	33	0.49
41	Millwall	33	0.27
42	Nottingham Forest	33	0.36
43	Plymouth Argyle	36	0.15
44	Sheffield Wednesday	37	0.22
45	Colchester United	37	0.15
46	Coventry City	37	0.31
47	Doncaster Rovers	38	0.09
48	Gillingham	38	0.19
49	Rotherham United	39	0.11
50	Barnsley	39	0.17
51	Brighton & Hove Albion	39	0.19
52	Walsall	40	0.19
53	Crewe Alexandra	40	0.12
54	Bradford City	41	0.12
55	Peterborough United	41	0.06
56	Southend United	42	0.14
57	Scunthorpe United	42	0.07
58	Grimsby Town	44	0.14

In short, the more you pay your players in wages, the higher you will finish; but what you pay *for* them in transfer fees doesn't seem to make much difference. While the market for players' wages is pretty efficient – the better a player is, the more he earns – the transfer market is inefficient. Much of the time, clubs buy the wrong players. Even now that they have brigades of international scouts, they still waste fortunes on flops like Blissett. (The transfer market is also of dubious legality – do clubs really have a right to 'buy' and 'sell' employees? – but that's another matter.)

As a case study of bad transfer policy, let's take Liverpool from 1998 to 2010. The club's managers in this period, Gérard Houllier and Rafael Benítez, kept splashing out on big transfer fees, yet Liverpool hardly ever even threatened to win the league. Jamie Carragher, a Liverpool stalwart throughout these years, provides a dolefully comic commentary on some of the club's signings in his excellent autobiography *Carra*:

- ⚽ 'Sean Dundee was not a Liverpool footballer.'
- ⚽ 'The signing I didn't rate was Sander Westerveld ... I thought he was an average goalkeeper who seemed to think he was Gordon Banks.'
- ⚽ 'What about Josemi? He struggled to find a teammate six yards away. Djimi Traoré had the same weakness.'
- ⚽ 'To be blunt, [Christian] Ziege couldn't defend.'
- ⚽ 'The names El-Hadji Diouf and Salif Diao now make the legs of the toughest Liverpudlians shudder in fear ... The first concern I had with Diouf is his pace. He didn't have any ... Do you remember being at school and picking sides for a game of football? We do this at Liverpool for the five-a-sides. Diouf was "last pick" within a few weeks. "You paid ten million for him and no one wants him in their team," I shouted to Gérard ...'
- ⚽ 'If Diouf was a disappointment, Diao was a catastrophe.'
- ⚽ 'But even he wasn't the worst arrival of this hideous summer [of 2002]. Houllier also signed Bruno Cheyrou ...'
- ⚽ On Djibril Cissé, who cost Liverpool £14 million in 2004, then the club's record transfer fee: 'He was supposed to be a strong, physical target man who scored goals. He was neither one nor the other.'
- ⚽ 'The greatest disappointment was Fernando Morientes ... he was a yard off the pace.'

When Benítez replaced Houllier in 2004, writes Carragher, the Spaniard encountered 'a host of poor, overpaid players and expectations as great as ever'. But the new man didn't do much better than his predecessor. Carragher's book is gentler with Benítez than with Houllier, presumably because the Spaniard was still his boss when he wrote it, but the waste of the Benítez years is remarkable. Most strikingly, perhaps, in 2008 Benítez handed

Tottenham £20 million for the 28-year-old forward Robbie Keane. The much-touted fact that Keane was a lifelong Liverpool fan turned out not to help much. Six months after buying the player, Benítez decided that Keane wasn't the thing after all, and shipped him back to Tottenham (who themselves would soon regret buying him) at a loss of £8 million. Virgin Trains placed newspaper advertisements that said, 'A Liverpool to London return faster than Robbie Keane.'

For all the spending, most of Liverpool's best performers during the Houllier–Benítez years were homegrown players who had cost the club nothing: Steven Gerrard, Michael Owen and Carragher himself. Another stalwart for a decade, centre-back Sami Hyppiä, had come for only £2.6 million from little Willem II in the Netherlands. In short, there didn't seem to be much correlation between transfer spending and quality.

In October 2009, after Benítez's sixth and last summer masterminding Liverpool's transfers, the *Sunday Times* totted up the damage. It found that in those six years at Anfield, Benítez had spent £122 million more than he had received in transfer fees. Alex Ferguson's net spend at Manchester United in the same period was only £27 million, yet in those years United had won three titles to Liverpool's none. Arsène Wenger at Arsenal had actually received £27 million *more* in transfer fees than he had spent during the period, the newspaper estimated. From 2005 to 2009, Benítez had even outspent Chelsea on transfers. Yet at the end of this period he had the nerve to complain: 'It is always difficult to compete in the Premier League with clubs who have more money.'

Ferguson later commented that he hadn't been able to see any 'strategy' in Benítez's buying. 'It amazed me that he used to walk into press conferences and say he had no money to spend,' Ferguson wrote in his 2013 autobiography. 'He was given plenty. It was the quality of his buys that let him down. If you set aside Torres and Reina, few of his acquisitions were of true Liverpool standard. There were serviceable players – Mascherano and Kuyt, hard-working players – but not real Liverpool quality.'

Benítez's failure at Liverpool was partially disguised by one night in Istanbul: the victory in the Champions League final of 2005, after having been 3–0 down to Milan at half-time. However, as we'll discuss later in the book, there is a large chunk of luck involved in winning knockout competitions – even leaving aside the fact that Benítez got his tactics wrong going into the game and had to turn his team upside down at half-time. The most reliable gauge of a team's quality is its performance in the league, and here Houllier and Benítez failed. Their expensive transfers didn't bring commensurate results. If you add in agents' fees, taxes on transfers, and the constant disruption to the team, all this wheeling and dealing helps explain how Liverpool got left behind by Manchester United. To quote Carragher: 'As I know to my cost at Anfield, having money is no guarantee of success. The skill is spending it on the right players.'

The question then is what clubs can do to improve their status. If you are Liverpool now, run by a man like John Henry, who understands statistics, and you have this knowledge of the relative importance of wages and unimportance of transfers, how can you win more matches? The obvious answer is to spend less of your income on transfers and more of it on wages. In general, it may be better to raise the pay of your leading players than to risk losing a couple of them and have to go out and buy replacements. Benítez had a net transfer spend of minus £122 million in six years. If he had merely balanced his transfer budget in that period, let alone made a profit as Wenger did, he could have raised his team's salaries by £20 million a year. In the 2008–09 season, that boost would have given Liverpool a slightly larger wage bill than United. United, of course, won the title that year.

Football clubs need to make fewer transfers. They buy too many Dioufs. But they will keep buying players, and the transfer market is probably the area in which clubs can most easily improve their performance. They need to learn from the few clubs and managers who have worked out some of the secrets of the transfer market.

Any inefficient market is an opportunity for somebody. If most clubs are wasting most of their transfer money, then a club that spends wisely is going to overperform. In fact, a few wise buyers have consistently outperformed the transfer market: Brian Clough and his assistant-cum-soulmate Peter Taylor in their years at Nottingham Forest, Arsène Wenger during his first decade at Arsenal, and, most mysteriously of all, Olympique Lyonnais, who progressed from obscure provincial club, a sort of French Southampton, to a period of dictatorial rule over French football. From 2002 to 2008, Lyon won the French league seven times running. That era is now over, and the club has made mistakes since, as it has tried and failed to compete with clubs with much higher revenues, like Real Madrid or Manchester United. Lyon got tempted into paying big transfer fees for supposed 'stars' – for instance, gambling £18 million on the slow French playmaker Yoann Gourcuff in 2010. Nonetheless, its seven-year reign remains an extraordinary feat. The usual way to win things in football is to pay high salaries. These clubs found a different route: they worked out the secrets of the transfer market.

There is a fourth master of the transfer market who is worth a look, even if he works in a different sport across an ocean: Billy Beane, general manager of the Oakland A's baseball team. Michael Lewis's book *Moneyball* explains how Beane turned one of the poorest teams in baseball into one of the best by the simple method of rejecting what everyone in the sport had always 'known' to be true about the transfer market. Lewis writes, 'Understanding that he would never have a Yankee-sized chequebook, Beane had set about looking for inefficiencies in the game.' It's odd how many of the same inefficiencies exist in soccer too.

If we study these masters of transfers, it will help us uncover the secrets of the market that all the other clubs are missing.

First of all, though, here are a few of the most obvious inefficiencies in the market. Although it doesn't take a Wenger or a Beane to identify these, they continue to exist:

⚽ A new manager wastes money.

Typically, the new manager wants to put his mark on his new side. So he buys his own players. He then has to 'clear out' some of his predecessor's purchases, usually at a discount.

Strangely, it's Alan Sugar's tight-fisted Tottenham that provides the worst example. In May 2000 the club's manager George Graham paid Dynamo Kiev £11 million – nearly twice Spurs's previous record fee – for the Ukrainian striker Sergei Rebrov. Clearly, Rebrov was meant to be a long-term investment.

But nine months later, Sugar sold his stake in Tottenham, whereupon the new owners sacked Graham and replaced him with Glenn Hoddle. Hoddle didn't rate Rebrov. The record signing ended up on the bench, was sent on loan to Turkey, and in 2004 moved to West Ham on a free transfer.

This form of waste is common across football: a new manager is allowed to buy and sell on the pretence that he is reshaping the club for many years to come, even though in practice he almost always leaves pretty rapidly. A terrible example was Paolo di Canio at Sunderland in 2013: in the six months and 13 games that he managed the club, he spent £23.5 million on transfers, brought in 14 players and let 15 leave. When he was sacked, he left his successor, Gus Poyet, a team in last place in the Premier League. Tony Fernandes, the Queens Park Rangers chairman who spent a net £40 million on transfer fees while getting relegated from the Premier League in 2012/13, told us mournfully: 'Sunderland's going through, in some ways, what we went through. The manager comes in, he changes everyone. If you change a manager, I don't care who they are, they're going to have a different opinion, right? Mark Hughes liked a certain player, Harry [Redknapp] doesn't like a certain player.'

But why couldn't a chairman just say no to a shopaholic new manager? 'You yourself see the results,' replied Fernandes, 'and you think, "God, we need some change."'

A manager typically doesn't care how much his wheeler-dealing costs: he doesn't get a bonus if the club makes a profit. Billy Beane told us: 'When you think of the structure of most sports teams, there is no benefit to a head coach in the NFL or a soccer manager to think years ahead. The person who has access to the greatest expenditure in the business has no risk in the decision-making.'

He added that the exception to this rule was Wenger. Beane said, 'When I think of Arsène Wenger, I think of Warren Buffett. Wenger runs his football club like he is going to own the club for 100 years.'

Other inefficiencies of the market:

⚽ **Stars of recent World Cups or European championships are overvalued.**

The worst time to buy a player is in the summer when he's just done well at a big tournament. Everyone in the transfer market has seen how good the player is, but he is exhausted and quite likely sated with success. As Ferguson admitted after retiring from United:

> I was always wary of buying players on the back of good tournament performances. I did it at the 1996 European Championship, which prompted me to move for Jordi Cruyff and Karel Poborský. Both had excellent runs in that tournament, but I didn't receive the kind of value their countries did that summer. They weren't bad buys, but sometimes players get themselves motivated and prepared for World Cups and European Championships and after that there can be a levelling off.

Moreover, if you buy a player because of a good tournament, you are judging him on a very small sample of games. Take for instance Arsenal's purchase of the Danish midfielder John Jensen in July 1992. The previous month, Jensen had scored a cracking long-range goal in the European Championship final against Germany. George Graham, then managing Arsenal, told the media that Jensen was a goal-scoring midfielder.

But he wasn't. The goal against Germany had been a one-off. Jensen would go years without scoring for Arsenal. Over time this failing actually turned him into a cult hero: whenever he got the ball, even in his own penalty area, the crowd at Highbury would joyously shout, 'Shoot!' By the time Jensen left Arsenal in 1996, he had scored one goal in four years. (Arsenal fans printed T-shirts saying, 'I was there when John Jensen scored.') Graham's mistake had been to extrapolate from that single famous goal against Germany. This is an example of the so-called 'availability heuristic': the more available a piece of information is to the memory, the more likely it is to influence your decision, even when the information is irrelevant.

Overpaying for these shooting stars fits what *Moneyball* calls 'a tendency to be overly influenced by a guy's most recent performance: what he did last was not necessarily what he would do next.'

Real Madrid are of course the supreme consumer of shooting stars. This is largely because the club's fans demand it. Madrid (or Newcastle, or Marseille in France) probably aren't even trying to be 'rational' in the transfer market. The club's aim is not to buy the best results for as little money as possible. When their president Florentino Pérez handed over a combined total of £136 million for Cristiano Ronaldo and Kaka in 2009, he probably suspected he was paying more for the duo than the benefit he was likely to get in results or higher revenues. But big signings of this type (like Newcastle buying fragile Michael Owen from Madrid for £17 million) are best understood as marketing gifts to a club's fans, sponsors and the local media. (It's hugely in the interest of *Marca*, the Spanish sports newspaper, for Real always to be buying players, or else hardly anyone would bother reading the paper over the three-month summer break.)

As Ferguson explained Real's purchase of Ronaldo: 'Madrid paid £80 million in cash for him, and do you know why? It was a way for Florentino Pérez, their president, to say to the world, "We are Real Madrid, we are the biggest of the lot." Four years later, Madrid's purchase of Gareth Bale made the same statement. Probably nobody at Madrid believed that the Welshman was twice as good a

player as Mesut Özil – sold to Arsenal for half Bale's transfer fee –
but he was deliciously new. His record fee only enhanced his glam-
our. The £85 million is unlikely to bring commensurate reward, but
Real probably doesn't care very much. The club is not a business.
It's a populist democracy. Few football clubs pursue bean-counting
quests for return on investment.

Buying a big name is a way of saying, 'Yes, we are a big club.' It
makes every person in the club feel bigger. Christoph Biermann, in
his pioneering German book on football and data, *Die Fussball-
Matrix*, cites the president of a Bundesliga club who said his coach
got very excited whenever the club paid a large transfer fee. Biermann explains: 'For this coach it was a status symbol to be allowed
to buy players who cost many millions of euros. My car, my house,
my star signing!'

Buying names also gives supporters the thrill of expectation, a
sense that their club is going somewhere, which may be as much
fun as actually winning things. Buying names is how these clubs
keep their customers satisfied during the summer shutdown. (And
some managers buy players in order to make themselves some illicit
cash on the side, as Graham did when he signed Jensen, but that's
another story.)

⚽ **Certain nationalities are overvalued.**

Clubs will pay more for a player from a 'fashionable' football country. The American goalkeeper Kasey Keller says that in the transfer
market, it's good to be Dutch. 'Giovanni van Bronckhorst is the best
example,' Keller told Christoph Biermann. 'He went from Rangers to
Arsenal, failed there, and then where did he go? To Barcelona! You
have to be a Dutchman to do that. An American would have been
sent straight back to DC United.'

More recently, Belgian players have come into fashion. But the
most enduringly fashionable nationality in the transfer market is
Brazilian. As Alex Bellos writes in *Futebol: The Brazilian Way of Life*:
'The phrase "Brazilian footballer" is like the phrases "French chef" or

"Tibetan monk". The nationality expresses an authority, an innate vocation for the job – whatever the natural ability.' A Brazilian agent who had exported very humble Brazilian players to the Faroe Islands and Iceland told Bellos: 'It's sad to say, but it is much easier selling, for example, a crap Brazilian than a brilliant Mexican. The Brazilian gets across the image of happiness, party, carnival. Irrespective of talent, it is very seductive to have a Brazilian in your team.'

A wise club will buy unfashionable nationalities – Bolivians, say, or Belorussians – at discounts.

And, lastly, a less obvious inefficiency:

⚽ Gentlemen prefer blonds.

At least one big English club noticed that its scouts who watched youth matches often came back recommending blond players. The likely reason: when you are scanning a field of 22 similar-looking players, none of whom yet has a giant reputation, the blonds tend to stand out (except, presumably, in Scandinavia). The colour catches the eye. So the scout notices the blond player without understanding why. The club in question began to take this distortion into account when judging scouting reports. We suspect the bias towards blonds disappears when scouts are assessing adult players who already have established reputations. Then, the player's reputation – 'World Cup hero', say, or simply 'Brazilian' – guides the scout's judgement.

Similarly, Beane at the Oakland A's noticed that baseball scouts had all sorts of 'sight-based prejudices'. They were suspicious of fat guys or skinny little guys or 'short right-handed pitchers', and they overvalued handsome strapping athletes of the type that Beane himself had been aged 17. Scouts look for players who *look* the part. Perhaps in soccer, blonds are thought to look more like superstars.

This taste for blonds is an example of the 'availability heuristic': the more available a piece of information is to the memory, the more likely it is to influence your decision, even when the information is irrelevant. Blonds stick in the memory.

The inefficiencies we have cited so far are so-called 'systemic failures': more than just individual mistakes, they are deviations from rationality. All this is what you might call 'transfer market 101'. To learn more about how to play the market, we need to study the masters.

DRUNKS, GAMBLERS AND BARGAINS: CLOUGH AND TAYLOR AT FOREST

'Cloughie likes a bung,' Alan Sugar told the High Court in 1993. Sugar's former manager at Spurs, Terry Venables, had told him so. The court heard that when Clough bought or sold a player for Nottingham Forest, he liked to receive a personal bonus, which in a perfect world would be handed over in a motorway service café. Clough denied everything – 'A bung? Isn't that something you get from a plumber to stop up the bath?' – and was never prosecuted. Yet what seems likely is this: 'Old Big Head' was so good at transfers, making profits even while turning a little provincial club into European champions, that he felt he deserved the odd bonus. More than anyone else in his day, Clough and his right-hand man Peter Taylor had succeeded in gaming the transfer market.

Clough and Taylor met while playing in a 'Probables versus Possibles' reserve game at Middlesbrough in 1955. They seem to have fallen in love at first sight. Pretty soon they were using their free time to travel around the north watching football and coaching children together. Taylor never became more than a journeyman keeper, but Clough scored the fastest 200 goals ever notched in English football until, at the age of 27, he wrecked his right knee skidding on a frozen pitch on Boxing Day 1962. Three years later he phoned Taylor and said: 'I've been offered the managership of Hartlepool and I don't fancy it, but if you'll come, I'll consider it.' He then immediately hung up. Taylor took the bait, though to get in he had to double as Hartlepool's medical department, running on with the sponge on match days. It was the prelude to their legendary years together at Derby and Nottingham Forest.

David Peace's novel *The Damned United* – and Tom Hooper's film of it – is in large part the love story of Clough and Taylor. The men's wives only have walk-on parts. As in all good couples, each partner has his assigned role. As Peace's fictional Clough tells himself: 'Peter has the eyes and the ears, but you have the stomach and the balls.' Taylor found the players, and Clough led them to glory.

The relationship ended in 'divorce' in 1982, with Taylor's resignation from Forest. It seems that the rift had opened two years before, when Taylor published his excellent but now forgotten memoir *With Clough by Taylor*. More of this in a moment, because it is the closest thing we have to a handbook to the transfer market.

But clearly the couple had other problems besides literature. Perhaps Clough resented his partner because he needed him so badly – not the sort of relationship Clough liked. Indeed, the film *The Damned United* depicts him failing at Leeds partly because Taylor is not there to scout players, and finally driving down to Brighton with his young sons to beg his partner's forgiveness. He finds Taylor doing the gardening. At Taylor's insistence, he gets down on his knees in the driveway, and recites: 'I'm nothing without you. Please, please, baby, take me back.' And Taylor takes him back, and buys him the cut-price Forest team that wins two European Cups. Because, whatever their precise relationship, the duo certainly knew how to sign footballers. Here are a few of their coups:

⚽ Buying Gary Birtles from the non-league club Long Eaton for £2,000 in 1976, and selling him to Manchester United four years later for £1.25 million. A measure of what a good deal this was for Forest: United forked out £250,000 more for Birtles than they would pay to sign Eric Cantona from Leeds 12 years later, in 1992. Birtles ended up costing United about £86,000 a goal, and after two years was sold back to Forest for a quarter of the initial fee.

⚽ Buying Roy Keane from an Irish club called Cobh Ramblers for £47,000 in 1990, and selling him to Manchester United three years later for £3.75 million, then a British record fee.

⚽ Buying Kenny Burns from Birmingham City for £145,000 in 1977. Taylor writes in *With Clough by Taylor* that Burns was then regarded as 'a fighting, hard-drinking gambler ... a stone overweight'. In 1978, English football writers voted Burns Footballer of the Year.

⚽ Twice buying Archie Gemmill cheaply. In 1970, when Gemmill was playing for Preston, Clough drove to his house and asked him to come to Derby. Gemmill refused. Clough said that in that case he would sleep outside in his car. Gemmill's wife invited him to sleep in the house instead. The next morning at breakfast Clough persuaded Gemmill to sign. The fee was £60,000, and Gemmill quickly won two league titles at Derby. In 1977 Clough paid Derby £20,000 and the now forgotten goalkeeper John Middleton to bring Gemmill to his new club, Forest, where the player won another league title.

If there is one club where almost every pound spent on transfers bought results, it was Forest under Clough. In the 1970s the correlation must have been off the charts: they won two European Cups with a team assembled largely for peanuts. Sadly there are no good financial data for that period, but we do know that even from 1982 to 1992, in Clough's declining years, after Taylor had left him, Forest performed as well on the field as clubs that were spending twice as much on wages. Clough had broken the usually iron link between salaries and league position.

Clough himself seemed to think that what explained Forest's success was his and Taylor's eye for players, rather than, say, any motivational gift or tactical genius. Phil Soar, the club's chairman and chief executive for four years at the end of the 1990s, told us: 'In hours of musings with Clough (I had to try to defend him from the bung charges) I obviously asked him what made this almost absurdly irrelevant little provincial club (my home town of course) into a shooting star. And he always used to say, "We had some pretty good players you know ..."'

It's hard to identify all of the duo's transfer secrets, and if their rivals at the time had understood what they were up to, everyone would simply have imitated them. Taylor's book makes it clear that he spent a lot of time trying to identify players (like Burns) whom others had wrongly undervalued owing to surface characteristics; but then everyone tries to do that. Sometimes Forest did splash out on a player who was rated by everybody, like Trevor Francis, the first 'million-pound man', or Peter Shilton, whom they made the most expensive goalkeeper in British history.

Yet thanks to *With Clough by Taylor*, we can identify three of the duo's rules:

⚽ Be as eager to sell good players as to buy them.

'It's as important in football as in the stock market to sell at the right time,' wrote Taylor. 'A manager should always be looking for signs of disintegration in a winning side and then sell the players responsible before their deterioration is noticed by possible buyers.' (Or in Billy Beane's words: 'You have to always be upgrading. Otherwise you're fucked.')

The moment when a player reaches the top of his particular hill is like the moment when a stock market peaks. Clough and Taylor were always trying to gauge that moment, and sell. Each time they signed a player, they would give him a set speech, which Taylor recorded in his book: 'Son, the first time we can replace you with a better player, we'll do it without blinking an eyelid. That's what we're paid to do – to produce the best side and to win as many things as we can. If we see a better player than you but don't sign him then we're frauds. But we're not frauds.' In 1981, just after Kenny Burns had won everything with Forest, the club flogged him to Leeds for £400,000.

⚽ **Older players are overrated.**

'I've noticed over the years how often Liverpool sell players as they near or pass their thirtieth birthday,' notes Taylor in his book. 'Bob Paisley [Liverpool's then manager] believes the average First Division footballer is beginning to burn out at thirty.' Taylor added, rather snottily, that that was true of a 'running side like Liverpool', but less so of a passing one like Forest. Nonetheless, he agreed with the principle of selling older players.

The master of that trade today is Wenger. Arsenal's manager is one of the few people in football who can view the game from the outside. In part, this is because he has a degree in economic sciences from the University of Strasbourg. As a trained economist, he is inclined to trust data rather than the game's received wisdom. Wenger sees that in the transfer market, clubs tend to overvalue a player's past performance. That prompts them to pay fortunes – in transfer fees and salaries – for players who have passed their prime. Fifa TMS (the department of Fifa that oversees international transfers) analysed the pay of players who moved to Brazil, Argentina, England, Germany, Italy and Portugal in 2012, and found, remarkably, that the average man earned his peak fixed salary at the ripe old age of 32.

All players are melting blocks of ice. The job of the club is to gauge how fast they are melting, and to get rid of them before they turn into expensive puddles of water. Probably because Wenger was one of the first managers to use statistics to assess players, he spotted that older players declined sooner than was conventionally realised. When Dennis Bergkamp was in his early thirties, Wenger began to substitute him late in games. If Bergkamp complained about it afterwards, Wenger would simply produce the match statistics: 'Look, Dennis, after 70 minutes you started to run less. And your speed decreased.'

Wenger often lets defenders carry on until their mid-thirties, but he usually gets rid of his midfielders and forwards much younger. He flogged Thierry Henry for £16 million aged 29, Patrick Vieira for £14 million aged 29, Emmanuel Petit for £7 million aged 29 and Marc Overmars for £25 million aged 27, and none of them ever did as well again after leaving Arsenal. (Wenger's uncharacteristic decision at the very end of August 2011 to sign 28-year-old André Santos, 29-year-old Mikel Arteta and 31-year-old Yossi Benayoun shows his pressing need at that moment for quick success. In any case, he had built up the cashbox to afford it. It didn't work out well.)

Curiously, precisely the same overvaluation of older players exists in baseball too. The conventional wisdom in the game had always been that players peaked in their early thirties. Then along came Bill James from his small town in Kansas. In his mimeo-graphs, the father of sabermetrics showed that the average player peaked not in his early thirties, but at just 27 years old. Beane told us: 'Nothing strangulates a sports club more than having older play-ers on long contracts, because once they stop performing, they become immoveable. And as they become older, the risk of injury becomes exponential. It's less costly to bring a young player in. If it doesn't work, you can go and find the next guy, and the next guy. The downside risk is lower, and the upside much higher.'

Finally, Clough and Taylor's third rule:

✪ **Buy players with personal problems (like Burns, or the gambler Stan Bowles) at a discount. Then help them deal with their problems.**

Clough, a drinker, and Taylor, a gambler, had empathy with troubled footballers. While negotiating with a new player they would ask him a stock question, 'to which we usually know the answer', wrote Taylor. It was: 'Let's hear your vice before you sign. Is it women, booze, drugs or gambling?'

Clough and Taylor believed that once they knew the vice, they could help the player manage it. Clough was so confident of his psychological skills that he even thought he could handle Manches-ter United's alcoholic genius George Best. 'I'd sort George out in a week,' he boasted. 'I'd hide the key to the drinks cabinet and I'd make sure he was tucked up with nothing stronger than cocoa for the first six months. Women? I'd let him home to see his mum and his sisters. No one else in a skirt is getting within a million miles of him.'

Taylor says he told Bowles, who joined Forest in 1979 (and, as it happens, failed there): 'Any problem in your private life must be brought to us; you may not like that but we'll prove to you that our way of management is good for all of us.' After a player confided a problem, wrote Taylor, 'if we couldn't find an answer, we would turn to experts: we have sought advice for our players from clergymen, doctors and local councillors.' Taking much the same approach, Wenger helped Tony Adams and Paul Merson combat their addictions.

All this might sound obvious, but the usual attitude in football is, 'We paid a lot of money for you, now get on with it,' as if mental illness, addictions or homesickness should not exist above a certain level of income.

RELOCATION, RELOCATION, RELOCATION: THE RICE KRISPIES PROBLEM

Clough and Taylor understood that many transfers failed because of a player's problems off the pitch. In a surprising number of cases, these problems are the product of the transfer itself. Moving to a job in another city is always stressful; moving to another country even more so. Yet clubs who pay millions of pounds for foreign players are often unwilling to spend a few thousand more to help the players settle in their new home. Instead the clubs typically tell them: 'Here's a plane ticket, come over, and play brilliantly from day one.' The player fails to adjust to the new country, underperforms, and his transfer fee is wasted. 'Relocation', as the industry of relocation consultants call it, is one of the biggest inefficiencies in the transfer market.

All the inefficiencies surrounding relocation could be assuaged. Most big businesses know how difficult relocation is, and do their best to smooth the passage. When a senior Microsoft executive moves countries, a 'relocation consultant' helps his family find schools, a house, and learn the social rules of the new country. If Luther Blissett had been working for Microsoft, a relocation consultant could have found him Rice Krispies. An expensive relocation might cost £15,000, or 0.1 per cent of a largish transfer fee, but in football, the most globalised industry of all, spending anything at all on relocation is regarded as a waste of money.

Boudewijn Zenden, who has played in four countries, for clubs including Liverpool and Barcelona, told us during his stint in Marseille:

It's the weirdest thing ever that you can actually buy a player for 20 mil, and you don't do anything to make him feel at home. I think the first thing you should do is get him a mobile phone and a house. Get him a school for the kids, get something for his missus, get a teacher in for both of them straight away, because obviously everything goes with the language. Do they need anything for other family members? Do they need a driving licence? Do they need a visa? Do they need a new passport? Sometimes even at the biggest clubs it's really badly organised.

Milan: best club ever. AC Milan is organised in a way you can't believe. Anything is done for you. You arrive, you get your house, it's fully furnished, you get five cars to choose from, you know the sky's the limit. They really say: we'll take care of everything else, you make sure you play really well. Whereas unfortunately in a lot of clubs, you have to get after it yourself ... Sometimes you get to a club and you've got people actually at the club who take profit from players.

For any foreign player, or even a player who comes in new, they could get one man who's actually there to take care of everything. But then again, sometimes players are a bit – I don't want to say abusive, but they might take profit of the situation.

They might call in the middle of the night, just to say there's no milk in the fridge. You know how they are sometimes.

In football, bad relocations were historically the norm. In 1961, two 15-year-olds from Belfast took the boat across the Irish Sea to become apprentices with Manchester United. George Best and Eric McMordie had never left home before. When they landed at Liverpool docks, they couldn't find anyone from the club to meet them. So they worked out for themselves how to get a train to Manchester, eventually found the stadium, and wound up so lonely and confused that on their second day they told the club: 'We want to go back on the next boat.' And they did, recounts Duncan Hamilton in his biography of Best, *Immortal*. In the end, Best decided to give Manchester one last try. McMordie refused. He became a plasterer in Belfast after leaving school, though he did later make a respectable playing career with Middlesbrough. Just imagine how the botched welcome of Best might have changed United's history.

Yet bad relocations continued for decades, like Chelsea signing cosmopolitan Ruud Gullit in 1996 and sticking him in a hotel in Slough, or Ian Rush coming back from a bad year in Italy marvelling, 'It was like another country.' Many players down the decades would have understood that phrase. But perhaps the great failed relocation, one that a Spanish relocation consultant still cites in her presentations, was Nicolas Anelka's to Real Madrid in 1999.

Half an hour of conversation with Anelka is enough to confirm that he is self-absorbed, scared of other people, and not someone who makes contact easily. Nor does he appear to be good at languages, because after well over a decade in England he still speaks very mediocre English. Anelka is the sort of expatriate who really needs a relocation consultant.

Real had spent £22 million buying him from Arsenal. They then spent nothing on helping him adjust. On day one the shy, awkward 20-year-old reported at the club, and found that there was nobody to show him around. He hadn't even been assigned a locker in the changing-room. Several times that first morning he would take a locker that seemed to be unused, only for another player to walk in and claim it.

Anelka doesn't seem to have talked about his problems to anyone at Real. Nor did anyone at the club ask him. Instead he talked to *France Football,* a magazine that he treated as his newspaper of record, like a 1950s prime minister talking to *The Times.* 'I am alone against the rest of the team,' he revealed midway through the season. He claimed to possess a video showing his teammates looking gloomy after he had scored his first goal for Real after six months at the club. He had tried to give this video to the coach, but the coach hadn't wanted to see it. Also, the other black Francophone players had told Anelka that the other players wouldn't pass to him. Madrid ended up giving him a 45-day ban, essentially for being maladjusted.

Paranoid though Anelka may have been, he had a point. The other players really didn't like him. And they never got to know him, because nobody at the club ever seems to have bothered to introduce him to anyone. As he said later, all Real had told him was, 'Look after yourself.' The club seemed to have taken the strangely materialistic view that Anelka's salary should determine his behaviour. But even in materialistic terms, that was foolish. If you pay £22 million for an immature young employee, it is bad management to make him look after himself. Wenger at Arsenal knew that, and he had Anelka on the pitch scoring goals.

Even a footballer with a normal personality can find emigration tricky. Tyrone Mears, an English defender who moved to Marseille, where his best relocation consultant was his teammate Zenden, says: 'Sometimes it's not a problem of the player adapting. A lot of the times it's the family adapting.' Perhaps the player's girlfriend is unhappy because she can't find a job in the new town. Or perhaps she's pregnant and doesn't know how to negotiate the local hospital, or perhaps she can't find Rice Krispies. ('Or beans on toast,' adds Zenden, when told about the Blissett drama.) The club doesn't care. It is paying her boyfriend well. He simply has to perform.

Football clubs never used to bother with anything like an HR department. As late as about 2005, there were only a few relocation consultants in football, and most weren't called that, and were not hired by clubs. Instead, they worked either for players' agents, or for sportswear companies. If Nike or Adidas is paying a player to wear its boots, it needs him to succeed. If the player moves to a foreign club, the sportswear company – knowing that the club probably won't bother – sometimes sends a minder to live in that town and look after him.

The minder gives the player occasional presents, acts as his secretary, friend and shrink, and remembers his wife's birthday. The minder of a young midfielder who was struggling in his first weeks at Milan said that his main task, when the player came home from training frustrated, lonely and confused by Italy, was to take him out to dinner. At dinner the player would grumble and say, 'Tomorrow I'm going to tell the coach what I really think of him,' and the minder would say, 'That might not be such a brilliant idea. Here, have some more *linguine alle vongole*.' To most players, this sort of thing comes as a bonus in a stressful life. To a few, it is essential.

Years after international transfers became standard, most clubs still did nothing about relocation. Didier Drogba in his autobiography recounts joining Chelsea from Olympique Marseille in 2004 for £24 million. He writes, 'I plunged into problems linked to my situation as an expatriate. Chelsea didn't necessarily help me.'

Nobody at the club could help him find a school for his children. All Chelsea did to get him a house was put him in touch with a real estate agent who tried to sell him one for £10 million. For 'weeks of irritation' the Drogba family lived in a hotel while Drogba, who at that point barely spoke English, went house-hunting after practice.

All Chelsea's expensive foreign signings had much the same experience, Drogba writes. 'We sometimes laughed about it with Gallas, Makelele, Kezman, Geremi. "You too, you're still living in a hotel?" After all these worries, I didn't feel like integrating [at Chelsea] or multiplying my efforts.'

Chelsea was no worse than other clubs. The same summer Drogba arrived in London, Wayne Rooney moved 35 miles up the motorway from Everton to Manchester United and had an almost equally disorienting experience. United had paid a reported £25.6 million for him, but then stuck their 18-year-old star asset in a hotel room. 'Living in such a place I found horrible,' reports Rooney in his *My Story So Far*. The nearest thing to a relocation consultant he found at United seems to have been a teammate: 'Gary Neville tried to persuade me to buy one of his houses. I don't know how many he has, or whether he was boasting or winding me up, but he kept telling me about these properties he had.'

At a conference in Rome in 2008, relocation consultants literally queued to tell their horror stories about football. Almost all of them had tried to get into the sport and been rebuffed. A Danish relocator had been told by FC Copenhagen that her services weren't required because the players' wives always helped each other settle. Many clubs had never even heard of relocation. Moreover, they had never hired relocation consultants before, so given the logic of football, not hiring relocation consultants must be the right thing to do. One Swedish relocator surmised: 'I guess it comes down to the fact that they see the players as merchandise.'

The only relocation consultants who had penetrated football happened to have a friend inside a club or, in the case of one Greek woman, had married a club owner. She had told her husband: 'All these guys would be happier if you find out what their needs are, and address their needs.'

Another relocator had entered a German club as a language teacher and worked her way up. She said, 'I was their mother, their nurse, their real estate agent, their cleaning lady, their everything. They didn't have a car, they didn't speak the language.' Did her work help the players play better? 'Absolutely.' The club was happy for her to work as an amateur, but as soon as she founded a relocation company, it didn't want her any more. She had become threatening.

And so countless new signings continued to flop abroad. Clubs often anticipated this by avoiding footballers who seemed particularly ill-equipped to adjust. For instance, on average Brazilians are the world's best footballers. Yet historically English clubs rarely bought them, because Brazilians don't speak English, don't like cold weather, and don't tend to understand the core traditions of English football, like drinking 20 pints of beer in a night. Few Brazilians adjust easily to English football.

Instead of Brazilians, English clubs traditionally bought Scandinavians. On average, Scandinavians are worse footballers than Brazilians, but they are very familiar with English, cold weather and 20 pints of beer. Scandinavians adapted to England, and so the clubs bought them. But the clubs were missing a great opportunity. Anyone who bought a great Brazilian player and hired a good relocation consultant to help him adjust would be onto a winner. Yet few clubs did. Years used to go by without any English club buying a Brazilian.

In 2008 Manchester City took the gamble on Robinho. As a Brazilian forward who had had his moments in the World Cup of 2006, he was bound to be overvalued, and was also very likely to relocate badly. So it's little wonder that City paid a British record transfer fee of £32.5 million for him, nor that 18 months later they gave up on him and sent him home to Santos on loan. Robinho never returned to English football. The experience obviously taught City a lesson, because for the next two years the club switched to a policy of buying players who had already established themselves in England. It also finally began to take relocation seriously.

Bit by bit in recent years, the football business has started to become smarter. Way back in the mid-1990s, Liverpool had become one of the first clubs to hire some sort of employee to help new players settle. Ajax Amsterdam was another pioneer. The woman who first handled relocations at Ajax found that some of the problems of new players were absurdly easy to solve. When Steven Pienaar and another young South African player came to Amsterdam, they were teenagers, had never lived on their own before, and suddenly found themselves sharing an apartment in a cold country at the other end of the earth. Inevitably, they put their music speakers on the bare floor and cranked up the volume. Inevitably, the neighbours complained. The South Africans had a miserable time in their building, until the woman from Ajax came around to see what was wrong and suggested they put their speakers on a table instead. They did. The noise diminished, their lives got easier, and that might just have made them better able to perform for Ajax.

Most clubs in the Premier League now have 'player liaison officers' – football code for 'relocation consultants'. Some of these officers are full-timers, others not. Some do a serious job. Manchester City in particular learned from Robinho's failure. When we visited the club's training ground in 2012, on a wall just behind reception we saw a map of Manchester's surroundings, designed to catch the eyes of passing players. The map highlighted eight recommended wealthy towns and suburbs for them to live; not on the list was Manchester's city centre, with its vibrant nightlife.

These recommendations are just the start. City's 'player-care department' aims to take care of almost every need a new immigrant might have, whether it's a nanny or a 'discreet car service'. Even before a new player signs, the club has already researched not only his off-duty habits, but also, rather spookily, his partner's. When he arrives for pre-season training, the club might say to him, 'Well, you're going to be busy for a couple of weeks, but here's a little restaurant your girlfriend might like.' It's not true that behind every successful footballer there is a happy woman, but it probably does help. Any Latin players needing additional help could consult City's Argentine full-back Pablo Zabaleta, who after four Mancunian years was considered practically English by his teammates.

In 2011 City signed Zabaleta's compatriot Sergio Agüero. Nobody doubted the young striker's talent. But many doubted whether he would adapt to English football and rainy provincial life. His transfer fee of £38 million seemed a gamble, even for Manchester City. But Agüero scored twice on his debut. He finished his first English season with 30 goals, including the last-second strike in the last game of the season against QPR that won City their first league title since 1968. In part, Agüero succeeded thanks to City's excellence at relocation. Gavin Fleig, the club's head of performance analysis, told us: 'The normal transition time for a foreign player is considered in the industry to be about a year. Normally those players are in a hotel for the first three months. We were able to get from agreeing a fee to Sergio living in his house within two weeks, with a Spanish sat-nav system in his car, linked to the Spanish community in Manchester. We had our prize asset ready to go from day one.'

Still, a few clubs continue to neglect relocation. One player liaison officer in the Premier League told us: 'Some very well-known managers have said to me they can't understand why you would possibly need it. They have said, "Well, when I moved to a foreign country as a player I had to do it myself." Well, yes, but that doesn't mean it's right. You probably had to clean boots too, but nobody does that now.'

THE NICEST TOWN IN EUROPE: HOW OLYMPIQUE LYONNAIS BOUGHT AND SOLD THEIR WAY TO THE TOP

If you had to locate the middle-class European dream anywhere, it would be in Lyon. It's a town the size of Leeds, about two thirds of the way down France, nestled between rivers just west of the Alps. On a warm January afternoon, drinking a coffee outside in the eighteenth-century Place Bellecour where the buildings are as pretty as the women, you think: nice. Here's a wealthy town where you can have a good job, nice weather, and a big house near the mountains.

Lyon also has some of the best restaurants in Europe, known locally as *bouchons*, or 'corks'. Even at the town's football stadium you can have a wonderful three-course pre-game meal consisting largely of intestines or head cheese, unless you prefer to eat at the local-boy Paul Bocuse's brasserie across the road and totter into the ground just before kick-off. And then, for a remarkable decade or so, you could watch some very decent football too.

Until about 2000 Lyon was known as the birthplace of cinema and *nouvelle cuisine,* but not as a football town. It was just too bourgeois. If for some reason you wanted football, you drove 35 miles down the motorway to gritty proletarian Saint-Étienne. In 1987 Olympique Lyonnais, or 'OL', or *'Les Gones'* ('The Kids'), were playing in France's second division on an annual budget of under £2 million. They were like any old backwater provincial club in Europe. From 2002 to 2008 they ruled French football, before they started to make mistakes in the market, and Qatari-funded Paris Saint-Germain began their rise. Their ascent was in large part a story of the international transfer market. Better than any other club in Europe, Lyon worked out how to play the market.

In 1987 Jean-Michel Aulas, a local software entrepreneur with the stark grooved features of a Roman emperor, became club president. Aulas had played fairly good handball as a young man, and had a season ticket at OL.

'I didn't know the world of football well,' he admitted to us in 2007, over a bottle of 'OL' mineral water in his office beside the stadium (which he was aiming to tear down and replace with a bigger one). Had he expected the transformation that he wrought? 'No.'

Aulas set out to improve the club step by step. 'We tried to abstract the factor "time",' he explained. 'Each year we fix as an aim to have sporting progress, and progress of our financial resources. It's like a cyclist riding: you can overtake the people in front of you.' Others in France preferred to liken Aulas to *'un bulldozer'*.

In 1987 even the local Lyonnais didn't care much about *Les Gones.* You could live in Lyon without knowing that football existed. The club barely had a personality, whereas Saint-Étienne were the 'miners' club' that had suffered tragic defeats on great European nights in the 1970s. Saint-Étienne's president at the time said that when it came to football, Lyon was a suburb of Saint-Étienne, a remark that still rankles. At one derby after Lyon's domination began, the *Gones* fans unfurled a banner that told the Saint-Étienne supporters: 'We invented cinema when your fathers were dying in the mines.'

Aulas appointed the local boy Raymond Domenech as his first coach. In Domenech's first season, OL finished top of the second division without losing a game. Straight after that they qualified for Europe. Aulas recalled: 'At a stroke the credibility was total. The project was en route.'

It turned out that the second city in France, even if it was a bit bourgeois, was just hungry enough for a decent football club. The Lyonnais were willing to buy match tickets if things went well; but if things went badly, they weren't immediately waving white handkerchiefs in the stands and demanding that the president or manager or half the team be got rid of. Nor did the French press track the club's doings hour by hour. It's much easier to build for the long term in a place like that than in a 'football city' like Marseille or Newcastle. Moreover, footballers were happy to move to a town that is hardly a hardship posting. Almost nothing they got up to in Lyon made it into the gossip press. Another of Lyon's advantages: the locals had money. 'It allowed us to have not just a 'popular clientele', but also a 'business clientele', said Aulas.

Talking about money is something of a taboo in France. It is considered a grubby and private topic. Socially, you're never supposed to ask anyone a question that might reveal how much somebody has got. Football, to most French fans, is not supposed to be about money. They find the notion of a well-run football club humourless, practically American.

It therefore irritated them that Aulas talked about it so unabashedly. He might have invented the word 'moneyball'. Aulas's theme was that over time, the more money a club makes, the more matches it will win, and the more matches it wins, the more money it will make. In the short term you can lose a match, but in the long term there is a rationality even to football. (And to baseball. According to Michael Lewis's *Moneyball*, Billy Beane believes that winning 'is simply a matter of figuring out the odds, and exploiting the laws of probability ... To get worked up over plays, or even games, is as unproductive as a casino manager worrying over the outcomes of individual pulls of the slot machines.')

In Aulas's view, rationality in football works more or less like this: if you buy good players for less than they are worth, you will win more games. You will then have more money to buy better players for less than they are worth. The better players will win you more matches, and that will attract more fans (and thus more money), because Aulas spotted early that most football fans everywhere are much more like shoppers than like religious believers: if they can get a better experience somewhere new, they will go there. He told us, 'We sold 110,000 replica shirts last season. This season we are already at 200,000. I think Olympique Lyonnais has become by far the most beloved club in France.'

Polls suggested he was right: in a 2008 survey of European supporters by the market research company Sport+Markt, Lyon emerged as the country's most popular club, just ahead of Olympique Marseille. This popularity was a new phenomon. In 2002, when Lyon first became champions of France, the overriding French emotion towards the club had still been: 'Whatever.' The editor of *France Football* magazine complained around that time that when Lyon won the title, his magazine didn't sell. But from 2002 to 2008 the club won the title every year – the longest period of domination by any club in any of Europe's five biggest national leagues ever – and many French fans began to care about them.

With more fans, Lyon made more money. On match days you could get a haircut at an official OL salon, drink an OL Beaujolais at an OL café, book your holiday at an OL travel agency, and take an OL taxi to the game – and many people did. Lyon used that money to buy better players.

But for all Aulas's 'OL mineral water', what made the club's rise possible was the transfer market. On that warm winter's afternoon in Lyon, Aulas told us, 'We will invest better than Chelsea, Arsenal or Real Madrid. We will make different strategic choices. For instance, we won't try to have the best team on paper in terms of brand. We will have the best team relative to our investment.' Here are Lyon's rules of the transfer market:

⚽ Use the wisdom of crowds.

When Lyon were thinking of signing a player, a group of men would sit down to debate the transfer. Aulas would be there, and Bernard Lacombe, once a bull-like centre-forward for Lyon and France, and for most of the last 25 years the club's 'technical director'. Lacombe is known for having the best pair of eyes in French football. He coached Lyon from 1997 to 2000, but Aulas clearly figured out that if you have someone with his knack for spotting the right transfer, you want to keep him at the club for ever rather than make his job contingent on four lost matches. The same went for Peter Taylor at Forest.

Whoever happened to be Lyon's head coach of the moment would sit in on the meeting too, and so would four or five other coaches. 'We have a group that gives its advice,' Aulas explained. 'In England the manager often does it alone. In France it's often the technical director.' Lacombe told us that the house rule was that after the group had made the decision, everyone present would then publicly get behind the transfer.

Like Lyon, the Oakland A's also sidelined their manager. Like Lyon, the A's understood that he was merely 'a middle manager' obsessed with the very short term. The A's let him watch baseball's annual draft. They didn't let him say a word about it.

Lyon's method for choosing players was so obvious and smart that it's surprising all clubs don't use it. The theory of the 'wisdom of crowds' says that if you aggregate many different opinions from a diverse group of people, you are much more likely to arrive at the best opinion than if you just listen to one specialist. For instance, if you ask a diverse crowd to guess the weight of an ox, the average of their guesses will be very nearly right. If you ask a diverse set of gamblers to bet on, say, the outcome of a presidential election, the average of their bets is likely to be right too. (Gambling markets have proved excellent predictors of all sorts of outcomes.) The wisdom of crowds fails when the components of the crowd are not diverse enough. This is often the case in American sports. But in European football, opinions tend to come from many different countries, and that helps ensure diversity.

Clough and Taylor at least were a crowd of two. However, the typical decision-making model in English football is not 'wisdom of crowds', but short-term dictatorship. At most clubs the manager is treated as a sort of divinely inspired monarch who gets to decide everything until he is sacked. Then the next manager clears out his predecessor's signings at a discount. Lyon, noted a rival French club president with envy, never had expensive signings rotting on the bench. They never had revolutions at all. They understood that their coach was only a 'temp'. OL won their seven consecutive titles with four different coaches – Jacques Santini, Paul Le Guen, Gérard Houllier and Alain Perrin – none of whom, judging by their records in Britain, was exactly a Hegelian world-historical individual. When a coach left Lyon, not much changed. No matter who happened to be sitting on the bench, the team always played much the same brand of attacking football (by French standards).

Emmanuel Hembert grew up in Lyon supporting OL when they were still in the second division. Later, as head of the sports practice of the management consultancy A.T. Kearney, he was always citing the club as an example to his clients in football. 'A big secret of a successful club is stability,' explained Hembert over coffee in Paris a few years ago. 'In Lyon, the stability is not with the coach, but with the sports director, Lacombe.'

Another Lyon rule:

⚽ **The best time to buy a player is when he is in his early twenties.**

Aulas told us: 'We buy young players with potential who are considered the best in their country, between 20 and 22 years old.' It's almost as if he had read *Moneyball*. The book keeps banging on about a truth discovered by Bill James, who wrote: 'College players are a better investment than high-school players by a huge, huge, laughably huge margin.'

Baseball clubs traditionally preferred to draft high-school players. But how good you are at 17 or 18 is a poor predictor of how good you will become as an adult. By definition, when a player is that young there is still too little information to judge him. Billy Beane himself had been probably the hottest baseball prospect in the US at 17, but he was already declining in his senior year at school, and he then failed in the major leagues. Watching the 2002 draft as the A's general manager, he 'punches his fist in the air' each time rival teams draft schoolboys.

It's the same in soccer, where brilliant teenagers tend to disappear soon afterwards. Here are a few winners of the Golden Ball for best player at the Under-17s' World Cup: Philip Osundo of Nigeria, William de Oliveira of Brazil, Nii Lamptey of Ghana, the Scottish goalkeeper James Will, and Mohammed Al Kathiri of Oman. Once upon a time they must all have been brilliant, but none of them made it as adults. (Will ended up a policeman in the Scottish Highlands playing for his village team.) The most famous case of a teenager who flamed is the American Freddy Adu, who at 14 was the next Pelé and Maradona.

Only a handful of world-class players in each generation, most of them creators or goalscorers – Pelé, Maradona, Wayne Rooney, Lionel Messi, Cesc Fàbregas – reach the top by the age of 18. Most footballers get there considerably later. Almost all defenders and goalkeepers do. You can be confident of their potential only when they are more mature.

Beane knows that by the time players are in college – which tends to put them in Lyon's magical age range of 20 to 22 – you have a pretty good idea of what they will become. There is lots of information about them. They have grown up a bit. They are old enough to be nearly fully formed, but too young to be expensive stars. Fifa TMS analysed international transfers to England in 2013, and found that players moving aged 20 to 22 were 18 per cent cheaper than players aged 25 to 27. Better yet, the younger players tended to have lower salaries, and higher future resale values.

Lyon always tried to avoid paying a premium for a star player's 'name'. Here, again, they were lucky to be a club from a quiet town. Their placid supporters and local media didn't demand stars. By contrast, the former chairman of a club in a much more raucous French city recalls: 'I ran [the club] with the mission to create a spectacle. It wasn't to build a project for 20 years to come.' A team from a big city tends to need big stars.

Soccer being barely distinguishable from American baseball, the same split between big and small towns operates in that sport too. 'Big-market teams', like the Boston Red Sox and the New York Yankees, hunt players with names. Their media and fans demand it. In *Moneyball*, Lewis calls this the pathology of 'many foolish teams that thought all their questions could be answered by a single player'. (It's a pathology that may sound strangely familiar to European soccer fans.) By contrast the Oakland A's, as a small-market team, were free to forego stars. As Lewis writes: 'Billy may not care for the Oakland press but it is really very tame next to the Boston press, and it certainly has no effect on his behavior, other than to infuriate him once a week or so. Oakland A's fans, too, were apathetic compared with the maniacs in Fenway Park or Yankee Stadium.'

But as Beane told us, English soccer is 'even more emotional' than baseball. 'It's the biggest sport in the world,' he said. 'And that's the biggest league in the world, and then you put in 60 million people and a four-hour drive from north to south, and that's what you have.'

That's why most English clubs are always being pushed by their fans to buy stars. Happy is the club that has no need of heroes. Lyon were free to buy young unknowns like Michael Essien or Mahamadou Diarra just because they were good. And unknowns accept modest salaries. According to the French sports newspaper *L'Equipe,* in the 2007–08 season Lyon spent only 31 per cent of its budget on players' pay. The average in the English Premier League was about double that. Like Clough's Forest, Lyon performed the magic trick of winning things without paying silly salaries.

Here are a few more of Lyon's secrets:

✪ Try not to buy centre-forwards.

Centre-forward is the most overpriced position in the transfer market. (Goalkeeper is the most underpriced, even though keepers have longer careers than outfield players; in baseball, the most overpriced position is pitcher.) Admittedly Lyon 'announced' itself to football by buying the Brazilian centre-forward Sonny Anderson for £12 million in 1999, but the club mostly scrimped on the position afterwards. Houllier left OL in 2007 grumbling that even after the club sold Florent Malouda and Eric Abidal for a combined total of £23 million, Aulas still wouldn't buy him a centre-forward.

✪ Help your foreign signings relocate.

All sorts of great Brazilians have passed through Lyon: Sonny Anderson, the current club captain Cris, the future internationals Juninho and Fred, and the world champion Edmilson. Most were barely known when they joined the club. Aulas explained the secret: 'Ten years ago we sent one of our old players, Marcelo, to Brazil. He was an extraordinary man, because he was both an engineer and a professional footballer. He was captain of Lyon for five years. Then he became an agent, but he works quasi-exclusively for OL. He indicates all market opportunities to us.' As a judge of players, Marcelo is clearly in the Lacombe/Peter Taylor class.

Marcelo said he only scouted 'serious boys'. Or as the former president of a rival French club says: 'They don't select players just for their quality but for their ability to adapt. I can't see Lyon recruiting an Anelka or a Ronaldinho.'

After Lyon signed the serious boys, it made sure they settled. Drogba noted enviously: 'At Lyon, a translator takes care of the Brazilians, helps them to find a house, get their bearings, tries to reduce as much as possible the negative effects of moving ... Even at a place of the calibre of Chelsea, that didn't exist.'

Lyon's 'translator', who worked full-time for the club, sorted out the players' homesickness, bank accounts, *nouvelle cuisine*, etc. Other people at the club taught the newcomers Lyon's culture: no stars or show-offs. By concentrating on Brazilians, the club could offer them a tailor-made relocation service. Almost all the other foreign players Lyon bought were French-speakers.

⚽ **Sell any player if another club offers more than he is worth.**

This is what Aulas means when he says, 'Buying and selling players is not an activity for improving the football performance. It's a trading activity, in which we produce gross margin. If an offer for a player is greatly superior to his market value, you must not keep him.' The ghost of Peter Taylor would approve.

Like Clough and Taylor, and like Billy Beane, Lyon never got sentimental about players. In its annual accounts, the club booked each player for a certain transfer value. (Beane says: 'Know exactly what every player in baseball is worth to you. You can put a dollar figure on it.') Lyon knew that sooner or later its best players would attract somebody else's attention. Because the club expected to sell them, it replaced them even before they went. Ferguson at United also pursued a strategy of early replacement: 'I did feel sentimental about great players leaving us. At the same time, my eye would always be on a player who was coming to an end. An internal voice would always ask, "When's he going to leave, how long will he last?" Experience taught me to stockpile young players in important positions.'

Bringing in replacements before they are needed avoids a transition period or a panic purchase after the player's departure. Aulas explained: 'We will replace the player in the squad six months or a year before. So when Michael Essien goes [to Chelsea for £24 million], we already have a certain number of players who are ready to replace him. Then, when the opportunity to buy Tiago arises, for 25 per cent of the price of Essien, you take him.'

Before Essien's transfer in 2005, Aulas spent weeks proclaiming that the Ghanaian was 'untransferable'. He always said that when he was about to transfer a player, because it drove up the price. In his words: 'Every international at Lyon is untransferable. Until the offer surpasses by far the amount we had expected.'

✪ Abstinence: Just say no to transfers

There's one other kind of mastery of the transfer market: abstinence. Some clubs – notably Barcelona for most of this century – understand the inefficiencies of the transfer market and therefore avoid buying players wherever possible. These clubs try to just say no.

One Saturday lunchtime in July 2009 we caught up with Joan Oliver in his office at the Nou Camp. Barcelona's then CEO had escaped there for a rare bit of peace and quiet, away from the madness of the summer transfer market.

Barça's aim, Oliver told us, was 'to have one of the best, perhaps the best, team in the world, without having to spend x-million on players. The image of that is the final in Rome this year [against Manchester United], with a team of seven players from our academy. The total acquisition cost of our team has been – I don't remember, but something below €70m.' (In 2011, Barça again won the Champions League final, starting the game with seven homegrown players. In 2014 Barcelona had the most stable squad of any European top-division club: the average player had been with Barça for 5.5 years, calculated the CIES Football Laboratory in Lausanne, Switzerland.)

It may seem odd that a big-city club like Barcelona can mostly abstain from the market – buying one great player for a large fee every year or so rather than constantly overhauling its team. After all, we have seen that other big clubs with a frenzied local fan base and media are practically forced to keep buying 'stars'. Barcelona for decades did the same thing. But then, under President Joan Laporta from 2003, the club began to make greater use of its peculiar profile. Barça presents itself as 'the unarmed army of Catalonia'. That image means a lot to the club's fans. It means they are as happy to see local boys like Sergio Busquets (son of a terrible Barça goalkeeper) or Gerard Piqué (grandson of a Barça director) break into the team as they are to see a foreign star brandishing his new shirt at the flashbulbs of the local newspapers. And so Barcelona discovered that it could please its fans by avoiding transfers and bringing in kids instead. The club's most successful coach, Josep Guardiola, was praised for his willingness to throw teenagers into the first team, but he could do it because the crowd supported the policy. Oliver said of the reliance on the club's academy, the Masia: 'It's not only an economic strategy. It's part of the identity of the club.' Growing its own players boosts Barcelona's brand, and the brand makes the club money.

There's another advantage to shunning the transfer market, Oliver added. He called it the 'one-second rule'. The success of a move on the pitch is decided in less than a second. If a player needs a few extra fractions of a second to work out where his teammate is going, because he doesn't know the other guy's game well, the move will usually break down. You can therefore lose a match in under a second. A corollary of that, thought Oliver, is that a new signing is likely to underperform in his first season. The new man is still working out what his role in the team is, and what everyone else is trying to do. That means that if you do buy a player, it's only worth it if you keep him around for the longer term.

All this sounds worthy, and easy to say when things are going well. However, Barcelona in recent years have largely stuck to these principles even in bad times. After the failed 2007–08 season, when another club might have loaded up on stars, Barcelona did buy Dani Alves for £28 million, but they also sold two of their biggest names, Ronaldinho and Deco. When the club does buy, it rightly tends to focus on 'top ten' players: men who are arguably among the ten best footballers on earth, like Zlatan Ibrahimović, David Villa, Fàbregas, Alves or Neymar. Those players cost a lot, but the risk of their failing is small (unless you buy them when they are getting old, like Thierry Henry). Part of being one of the ten best footballers on earth is that you perform almost whatever the circumstances.

Oliver and Laporta have since been ousted, but Barcelona still try to field an unchanging homegrown core supplemented only by rare transfers. Abstinence works for Barça. Other big clubs like Manchester United and Chelsea have also recently tried to keep the cores of their teams together for years at a time. This may be a new trend in football. Nonetheless, many other clubs are still with St Augustine: 'Give me chastity and continence, Lord, but not yet.'

'The problem with the football business,' said Oliver, 'is that usually it is managed with very very short-term goals. After a bad year, it's very difficult not to fall into the temptation of buying a lot of people. Clubs spend irrationally and compulsively on players. And that's very difficult to restrain. You have always the temptation of thinking that if you buy two or three players, perhaps you will reverse the situation. That was perhaps the case of Chelsea in the past, and the case of Manchester City or, I think, of Real Madrid now.'

As a free service to clubs, here are the 12 main secrets of the transfer market in full:

1. A new manager wastes money on transfers; don't let him.
2. Use the wisdom of crowds.
3. Stars of recent World Cups or European championships are overvalued; ignore them.
4. Certain nationalities are overvalued.

5. Older players are overvalued.

6. Centre-forwards are overvalued; goalkeepers are undervalued.

7. Gentlemen prefer blonds; identify and abandon 'sight-based prejudices'.

8. The best time to buy a player is when he is in his early twenties.

9. Sell any player when another club offers more than he is worth.

10. Replace your best players even before you sell them.

11. Buy players with personal problems, and then help them deal with their problems.

12. Help your players relocate.

Alternatively, clubs could just stick with the conventional wisdom.

NOTE

Our view of transfers was recently challenged in the book *Pay as You Play*, written by three Liverpool fans, Paul Tomkins, Graeme Riley and Gary Fulcher. The book is a treasure trove of interesting financial facts, with the added benefit that the authors are donating all their royalties to the children's charity Postpals.

Pay as You Play uses data on transfer fees put together by Riley, by day a senior accountant at Adecco, by night an accomplished football statto. He collected figures for transfer fees paid by Premier League clubs since 1992–93 from newspapers and any other sources he could find. It's a true labour of love.

The authors' approach to transfers is very reasonable. As they point out, adding up the total transfer fees paid for all the players in a squad over many years is misleading because of inflation in transfer fees – the average spend per player has roughly doubled in a decade. The authors therefore convert past transfer fees into the 'current transfer fee purchase price' (CTPP), using average transfer fees as an index. For example, Thierry Henry cost Arsenal an estimated £10.5 million in 1999, which converts to a CTPP of £24.6 million. By giving every transferred player a value, they can compare a team's spending on transfers to performance in the league.

When Tomkins then published a blog by Zach Slaton headlined '*Soccernomics* was wrong: transfer expenditures matter', naturally we sat up and took notice.

Slaton argued that transfer fees were just as good a predictor of league position as is wage spending. One of us (Stefan) contacted Slaton and the authors to find out a bit more about what was going on. Riley kindly showed us the data he had used to calculate his index.

It then became clear where the differences lay. The *Pay as You Play* index refers only to transfer fees paid. But when we said that spending on transfers bears little relation to where a club finishes, we were referring to *net* transfer spending – i.e. transfer fees paid minus transfer fees received. (We have clarified that point in this edition.) The net figure is the crucial one, because hardly any clubs can just keep buying players without occasionally selling some to stop their spending going too far out of whack. The only free-spending exceptions in English football are Manchester City since 2008, and Chelsea. Once you look at net spending, it's clear that very few clubs run successful transfer policies: their net spending barely predicts where they finish in the league. If managers and clubs were valuing players accurately, you'd expect to see a significant correlation between net spending and perform- ance, at least over time.

The reliability of the *Pay as You Play* data is also doubtful. Data on wages are pretty accurate: they are drawn from each club's audited financial accounts, which are publicly available in England. But transfer fees quoted in the media are less trustworthy. Take the following comparison of transfer fees paid for members of Arsenal's 2008/09 squad from *Pay as You Play* data and from another reputable source, transfermarkt.co.uk

Player	Pay for play (£)	Transfermarkt.co.uk (£)
Mannone	350,000	440,000
Almunia	500,000	0
Silvestre	750,000	836,000
Song	1,000,000	3,520,000
Eboue	1,540,000	1,936,000
Fabiański	2,000,000	3,828,000
Vela	2,000,000	2,640,000
Fàbregas	2,250,000	2,816,000
Van Persie	3,000,000	3,960,000
Denilson	3,400,000	4,400,000
Diaby	3,500,000	2,640,000
Gallas	5,000,000	0
Ramsey	5,000,000	5,632,000
Sagna	6,000,000	7,920,000
Adebayor	7,000,000	8,800,000
Walcott	12,000,000	9,240,000
Nasri	12,800,000	14,080,000
Arshavin	15,000,000	14,520,000

There are clearly some big differences here. No wonder, as transfer fees are almost never officially disclosed, only leaked to the media by the club or the player's agent, generally with a spin. Nonetheless, and given these caveats, the Pay as You Play index does quite well at explaining the variation in team performance in the Premier League for the years covered.

That's hardly surprising. A club that spends a big transfer fee buying a player will almost always also spend a big sum on his wages, so in this sense, in the very short term transfer fees can be almost as good an explanation of success as wages. However, real success in the transfer market means buying cheap and selling dear. For that you need to know a club's net spending, which shows very little correlation with team performance. The transfer market remains far from efficient.

THE WORST BUSINESS IN THE WORLD: WHY FOOTBALL CLUBS DON'T (AND SHOULDN'T) MAKE MONEY

A man we know once tried to do business with a revered institution of English football. 'I can do business with stupid people,' he said afterwards, 'and I can do business with crooks. But I can't do business with stupid people who want to be crooks.'

It was a decent summary of the football business, if you can call football a business. People often do. William McGregor, the draper who founded the Football League in 1888, was p̶ first person to say 'Football is a big business', but the since become one of the game's great clichés.

In fact McGregor was wrong. Football is neither good business. It arguably isn't even business at

'BIG BUSINESS'

Few people have heard of a British company called BBA Aviation. It started out in 1879 making conveyor belts in Dundee, but over time it morphed into a supplier to the aeroplane industry. Mostly it now helps fuel, clean, repair and maintain planes. This is pretty unglamorous work, and BBA is an unglamorous company. It's in the FTSE 250, meaning that it ranks as one of the 250 biggest companies on the London stock market. In 2012 it had revenues of £1.34 billion, and pre-tax profits of £80 million. BBA, whose headquarters are on a quiet street in Mayfair, is not big business. For comparison: in 2012 the biggest company on the London market, Royal Dutch Shell, had revenues that were over 200 times bigger.

But compared with any football club, BBA is a behemoth. In September 2013 Real Madrid reported record revenues of €520.9 million (or £445 million) for the fiscal year 2012/13. That's a tidy sum, more than any other club in any sport has ever achieved. However, it's just a third of BBA's revenues, and barely 0.2 per cent of the size of Shell's. To put it very starkly: the Finnish financial analyst Matias Möttölä calculates that in terms of revenue, Real Madrid would still only be the 120th largest company in Finland.

It's worth noting, too, that Deloitte's respected Football Money League ranks clubs based on how much they sell. When business analysts judge normal companies they usually focus on profits, or the company's value if it were sold on the market. However, neither of those methods works with football clubs. Because hardly any clubs are quoted on the stock market anymore, for extremely good reasons, it is hard to work out their value. We can certainly say that not even Real or Manchester United would get anywhere near the FTSE 250.

And if Deloitte ranked clubs by their profits, the results would be embarrassing. Not only do most clubs make losses and fail to pay dividends to their shareholders, but many of the 'bigger' clubs would rank near the bottom of the list. Chasing prizes, they spend themselves into the red.

Whichever way you measure it, no football club is a big business. Even Real Madrid, Barcelona and Manchester United are dwarfed by BBA Aviation. As for all the rest, the author Alex Fynn noted in the 1990s that the average Premier League club had about the same turnover as a British supermarket – not a chain of supermarkets, but one single out-of-town Tesco. True, football clubs have grown since then: by 2012 the average club in the Premier League had a turnover of £125 million. However, Tesco has around 20 superstores that each generate more revenue than this. Remember also that Premier League clubs are the giants of global football. UEFA's most recent annual club licensing report found that the average revenue of the 235 clubs that play in UEFA competitions was a mere €33 million (£28 million).

A good way to visualise the size of the football industry is to visit UEFA's HQ in the Swiss town of Nyon. The building has a lovely view of Lake Geneva, but it looks like the offices of a small insurance company. Football is small business.

This feels like a contradiction. We all know that football is huge. Some of the most famous people on earth are footballers, and the most watched TV programme in history is generally the most recent World Cup final. Nonetheless football clubs are puny businesses. This is partly a problem of what economists call appropriability: football clubs can't make money out of (can't appropriate) more than a tiny share of our love of football.

It may be that season tickets are expensive, and replica shirts overpriced, but buying these things once a year represents the extravagant extreme of football fanaticism. Most football is wa⌐⌐ᵈ not from £1,000-seats in the stadium but on TV – sometime⌐ price of a subscription, often at the price of watching a few⌐ or for the price of a couple of pints in the pub. Compare t'⌐ watching a game in a pub with the cost of eating out, or⌐ movie, let alone going on holiday.

Worse still, football generates little income from repeat showing of matches, transfers to DVD, or re-runs on ITV4. And watching football (even on TV) is only a tiny part of the fan's engagement with the game. There are newspaper reports to be read, internet sites to be trawled, and a growing array of computer games to keep up with. Then there is the football banter that passes time at the dinner table, work, or the bus stop. All this entertainment is made possible by football clubs, but they cannot appropriate a penny of the value we attach to it. Chelsea cannot charge us for talking or reading or thinking about Chelsea. As the Dutch international Demy de Zeeuw says: 'There are complaints that we [footballers] earn too much, but the whole world earns money from your success as a footballer: newspapers, television, companies.' In fact the world earns more from football than the football industry itself does.

BAD BUSINESS

Football is not merely a small business, it's also a bad one. Until very recently, and to some degree still today, anyone who spent any time inside football soon discovered that just as oil was part of the oil business, stupidity was part of the football business.

This became obvious when people in football encountered people in other industries. Generally, the football people got exploited, because people in other industries understood business better. In 1997 Peter Kenyon, then chief executive of the sportswear company Umbro, invited a few guests to watch a European game at Chelsea, the club he would end up running a few years later. After the game, Kenyon took his guests out for dinner. Over curry he reminisced about how the sportswear industry used to treat football clubs. In the 1970s, he said, big English clubs used to *pay* companies like Umbro to supply their kit. It was obviously great advertising for the kit-makers to have some of England's best footballers running around in their clothes, but the clubs had not yet figured that out. And so sportswear companies used to get paid to advertise themselves.

In fact, when England hosted the World Cup in 1966, the FA hoped merely that its usual supplier would give it a discount on boots and shirts ... 'particularly in the opening ceremony of the World Cup with the Queen present,' writes Mihir Bose in *The Spirit of the Game*. As it happened, the English did even better: Umbro offered to supply the kit for free. The company must have been pleased when England won the tournament.

Ricky George saw the ignorance of football in those days from point-blank range. In 1972, when George scored the legendary goal for non-league Hereford that knocked Newcastle out of the FA Cup, he was working for Adidas as a 'soccer PR'. His job was to represent Adidas to England players, former world champions like Bobby Moore, Bobby Charlton and Gordon Banks. There was little need to persuade them to choose Adidas. Most of them wore the three stripes for free anyway.

George says: 'It is quite a fascinating thing if you compare it with today. There were no great sponsorship deals going on. All that happened is that you would give the players boots. But even then, at the beginning of every season the clubs would go to their local sports retailer and just buy 20, 30 pairs of boots and hand them out. For a company like Adidas, it was the cheapest type of PR you could imagine.'

Only on special occasions did George have to pay players. 'When it came to a big international, and the game was going to be televised, my job was to go to the team hotel, hang around there, make myself known, and a couple of hours before the game I would go into the players' rooms and paint the white stripes on their boots with luminous paint so it was more visible. My bosses used to be keenly watching the television to make sure the stripes were visible, and if they weren't I would be in for a bollocking.'

For this service, an England player would receive £75 per match – not a princely sum even in 1972. George recalls: 'Bobby [Moore], the most charming of people, didn't take the money on the day of the game. He just used to say to me, "Let it build up for a few games, and I'll ring you when I need it." And that's what he did.' Then the most famous defender of the era would pocket a cumulative few hundred quid for having advertised an international brand to a cumulative audience of tens of millions.

Only in the late 1980s did English football clubs discover that some people were willing to buy replicas of their team shirts. That made it plain even to them that their kit must have some value. They had already stopped paying sportswear companies for the stuff; now they started to charge them.

Gradually over time, football clubs have found new ways of making money. However, the ideas almost never came from the clubs themselves. Whether it was branded kit, or the Pools, or television, it was usually people in other industries who first saw there might be profits to be made. It was Rupert Murdoch who went to English clubs and suggested putting them on satellite TV; the clubs would never have thought of going to him. In fact, the clubs often fought against new money-making schemes. Until 1982 they refused to allow any league games to be shown live on TV, fearing that that might deter fans from coming to the stadium. They couldn't grasp that games on TV meant both free money and free advertising. There is now a good deal of research into the question of how many fans are lost when a game is shown on TV. Almost all the evidence shows that the number is tiny, and that the gate revenue that would be lost is usually well below the amount that would be made from selling extra matches for television coverage.

It took clubs a long time to realise just how much football was worth to television. When Greg Dyke was chairman of ITV Sport in the 1980s, he offered five big clubs £1 million each for the TV rights for English football. Dyke, who today chairs the FA, fondly recalls: 'It's funny now, when you look at the money that's involved: these chairmen had eyes bulging. They couldn't believe it.' In total, Dyke bought the entire TV rights for English professional football for £12 million a year. Soon afterwards, he went up to Nottingham to try to talk Brian Clough, Forest's then manager, into returning to the screen as a pundit. When Dyke arrived at the club, Clough came up to him and said: 'Thank you. I want to shake your hand, Mr Dyke, because you're the first person that's given football what it's due: 12 million quid.'

In 1992 Rupert Murdoch began paying about £60 million a season for the television rights to the new Premier League. Now the league gets nearly 30 times as much a season from worldwide television. 'I've been screwed by television,' admitted Sir John Hall, then the Newcastle chairman, one rowdy night at Trinity College Dublin in 1995. 'But I'll tell you one thing: I won't be screwed again.'

Or take the renovating of English stadiums in the early 1990s. It was an obvious business idea. Tesco doesn't receive customers in sheds built in the Victorian era and gone to seed since. It is forever doing up its stores. Yet football clubs never seem to have thought of spending money on their grounds until the Taylor Report of 1990 forced them to. They did up their stadiums, and bingo: more customers came.

All this proves how much like consumers football fans are. It's not that they come running when a team do well; rather, it seems that football can quickly become popular across a whole country. All teams then benefit, but particularly those that build nice new stadiums where spectators feel comfortable and safe. That would explain why the three English clubs whose crowds grew fastest over the 1990s were Manchester United, Sunderland and Newcastle. (The club that lost most spectators was Sheffield Wednesday, which shed 8,953 from its average gate during the decade.) In other leagues, clubs such as Juventus, Ajax and Celtic have also drawn big new crowds to their new grounds. There is such a close link between building a nice ground and drawing more spectators that the traditional fans' chant of 'Where were you when you were shit?' should be revised to 'Where were you when your ground was shit?'

Yet like almost all good business ideas in football, the Taylor Report was imposed on the game from outside. Football clubs are classic late adopters of new ideas. Several years after the internet emerged, Liverpool, a club with millions of fans around the world, still did not have a website. No wonder that from 1992 through to May 2008, even before the financial crisis struck, 40 of England's 92 professional clubs had been involved in insolvency proceedings, some of them more than once.

HOW THE TRIBE CHOOSES ITS CHIEFS

Rather than stack up endless examples of the dimness of football clubs, let's take one contemporary case study: how clubs hire their key employee, the manager. English fans are still asking themselves how Steve McClaren ever got to be appointed England manager in 2006, but in fact it is unfair to single him out. The profusion of fantasy football leagues, in which office workers masquerade as coaches, indicates the widely held suspicion that any fool could do as well as the people who actually get the jobs. The incompetence of football managers may have something to do with the nonsensical and illegal methods by which they are typically recruited.

Football 'is a sad business', says Bjørn Johansson, who runs a headhunting firm in Zurich. Like his colleagues in headhunting, Johansson is never consulted by clubs seeking managers. Instead, this is how a club typically chooses its man:

⚽ **The new manager is hired in a mad rush.**

In a panel at the International Football Arena conference in Zurich in 2006, Johansson explained that in 'normal' business 'an average search process takes four to five months'. In football, a club usually finds a coach within a couple of days of sacking his predecessor. 'Hesitation is regarded as weak leadership,' explained another panellist in Zurich, Ilja Kaenzig, then general manager of the German club Hannover 96. Brian Barwick, the Football Association's former chief executive, has noted that McClaren's recruitment 'took from beginning to end nine weeks', yet the media accused the FA of being 'sluggish'. If only it had been more sluggish.

A rare slow hire in football became perhaps the most inspired choice of the last two decades: Arsenal's appointment of Arsène Wenger in 1996. Wenger, working in Japan, was not free immediately. Arsenal waited for him, operating under caretaker managers for weeks, and were inevitably accused of being sluggish. Similarly, in 1990 Manchester United's chairman Martin Edwards was derided as sluggish when he refused to sack his losing manager Alex Ferguson. Edwards thought that in the long term, Ferguson might improve.

⚽ **The new manager is interviewed only very cursorily.**
In 'normal' business, a wannabe chief executive writes a business plan, gives a presentation and undergoes several interviews. In football, a club calls an agent's mobile and offers the job.

⚽ **The new manager is always a male ex-player.**
The entire industry discriminates illegally against women. He is also almost always white, with a conservative haircut, aged between 35 and 60, and a former professional footballer. Clubs know that if they choose someone with that profile, then even if the appointment turns out to be terrible they won't be blamed too much, because at least they will have failed in the traditional way. As the old business saying went: 'Nobody ever got fired for buying IBM.'

The idea is that there is something mystical about managing a team, something that only former players can truly understand. Naturally, former players like this idea. Once in the 1980s, when Kenny Dalglish was in his first spell managing Liverpool, a journalist at a press conference questioned one of his tactical decisions. Dalglish deadpanned, in his almost impenetrable Scots accent: 'Who did you play for, then?' The whole room laughed. Dalglish had come up with the killer retort: if you didn't play, you couldn't know.

A former chairman of a Premier League club told us that the managers he employed would often make that argument. The chairman (a rich businessman who hadn't played) never knew how to respond. He hadn't played, so if there really was some kind of mystical knowledge you gained from playing, he wouldn't know. Usually, he would back down.

'Who did you play for then?' is best understood as a job protection scheme. Ex-players have used it to corner the market in managerial jobs. But in truth, their argument never made sense. There is no evidence that having been a good player (or being white and of conservative appearance) is an advantage for a football manager. Way back in 1995 Stefan Szymanski did a study of 209 managers in English football from 1974 to 1994, and looked at which ones consistently finished higher in the league than their teams' wage bills predicted. He reported:

> I looked at each manager's football career, first as a player (including number of games played, goals scored, position on the field, international appearances, number of clubs played for) and then as a manager (years of experience, number of clubs played for and age while in management). Playing history provides almost no guide, except that defenders and goalkeepers in particular do not do well (most managers were midfielders, forwards are slightly more successful than average).

Dalglish finished top of Stefan's sample of 209 managers, just ahead of John Duncan, Bob Paisley, George Curtis, Ken Furphy and Bill Shankly. (Clough wasn't in the sample because no good financial data existed for his clubs, Derby County and Nottingham Forest, or else he'd have surely won.) Dalglish was a great player and an overperforming manager. However, Bobby Moore, another great player, was 193rd on the managers' list. Taken overall, a good career as a player predicted neither success nor failure as a manager. The two jobs just didn't seem to have much to do with each other. As Arrigo Sacchi, a terrible footballer turned great manager of Milan, phrased it: 'You don't need to have been a horse to be a jockey.'

A horse's knowledge doesn't help a jockey. Here is one player-turned-manager testifying anonymously in *Football Management*, an insightful book by Sue Bridgewater of Warwick Business School:

> I got the job and on the first day I showed up and the secretary let me into my office, the manager's office with a phone in, and I didn't know where I was supposed to start. I knew about football, I could do the on-pitch things, but I had never worked in an office and I just sat there and I waited for something to happen but no one came in so after a while I picked up the phone and rang my mum.

Even this man's claim that 'I knew about football, I could do the on-pitch things' is dubious. Does Diego Maradona know more about the game than José Mourinho? Did Roy Keane's knack for geeing up teammates on the field translate once he had become a jockey?

Playing and coaching are different skill sets. Mourinho, who barely ever kicked a ball for money, is match for match among the most successful coaches in football's history. When Carlo Ancelotti noted Mourinho's almost nonexistent record as a player, the Portuguese replied, 'I don't see the connection. My dentist is the best in the world, and yet he's never had a particularly bad toothache.' Asked why failed players often become good coaches, Mourinho said, 'More time to study.'

The problem with ex-professionals may be precisely their experience. Having been steeped in the game for decades, they just *know* what to do: how to train, who to buy, how to talk to their players. They don't need to investigate whether these inherited prejudices are in fact correct. Rare is the ex-pro who realises, like Billy Beane at the Oakland A's, that he needs to jettison what he learnt along the way. Michael Lewis writes in *Moneyball:* 'Billy had played pro ball, and regarded it as an experience he needed to overcome if he wanted to do his job well. "A reformed alcoholic," is how he described himself.'

Even Ancelotti seems to have changed his mind about the usefulness of a playing career. Once a canny midfielder with Milan, and now coach of Real Madrid, he told us in 2013: 'Experience as a player can help you just in one situation: I can understand what the players are thinking. But the job is different. You have to study to be a manager.'

There are some recent signs that ex-players are losing their monopoly on managerial jobs. By January 2014, three men who didn't have professional playing careers were managing Premier League clubs: Mourinho at Chelsea, Brendan Rodgers at Liverpool and René Meulensteen at Fulham. The Premier League's historical average is just one non-playing manager out of 20. Moreover, Roy Hodgson – whose playing career peaked in Crystal Palace's youth team – was the England manager. Meanwhile, former great players like Roy Keane, Ruud Gullit, Marco van Basten, Paul Ince, Tony Adams and Diego Maradona no longer seem to be in demand as managers of serious clubs. This looks like another indication that football is slowly becoming less stupid.

⚽ Managers don't need professional qualifications.

Only in 2003 did UEFA insist that new managers in the Premier League must have passed the 'Pro Licence' course. In England's lower divisions this remains unnecessary. Yet Sue Bridgewater showed that managers with the Pro Licence won significantly more matches than managers without it. She also showed that experienced managers outperformed novices. That qualifications and experience are useful is understood in every industry except football, where a manager is expected to work the magic he acquired as a superhero player.

⚽ The new manager is often under-qualified even if he has qualifications.

Chris Brady, a business-school professor, teaches finance and accounting on the Pro Licence course. He says his entire module takes half a day. No wonder some English managers mismanage money: they don't understand it. Clubs are ceasing to entrust their finances to managers, giving them instead to more qualified executives like Hannover 96's Ilja Kaenzig, who guarantee stability by staying longer than the club manager's average two-year tenure. That at least is the theory: the week after that conference in Zurich, Hannover released Kaenzig.

⚽ **The new manager is appointed either because he is able to start work immediately (often as a result of having just been sacked), or because he has achieved good results over his career, or, failing that, because he achieved good results in the weeks preceding the appointment.**

McClaren became England manager only because his team, Middlesbrough, reached the UEFA Cup final in 2006 and avoided relegation just as the FA was deciding who to pick. By the time Middlesbrough were tonked 4–0 by Seville in the final, McClaren already had the job.

His period under review was so short as to be a random walk. The same went for the main candidates to manage England in 1996: Bryan Robson, Frank Clark, Gerry Francis and the eventual choice Glenn Hoddle. Today none of them works as a manager (Francis and Clark haven't for many years), none had his last job in the Premier League, and none will probably work at that high a level again. They were in the frame in 1996 because they had had good results recently and were English – another illegal consideration in hiring.

⚽ **The new manager is generally chosen not for his alleged managerial skills, but because his name, appearance and skills at public relations are expected to impress the club's fans, players and the media.**

That is why no club hires a woman – stupid fans and players would object – and why it was so brave of Milan to appoint the unknown Sacchi, and Arsenal the unknown Wenger. Tony Adams, Arsenal's then captain, doubted the obscure foreigner at first sight. In his auto-biography *Addicted*, the player recalls thinking: 'What does this Frenchman know about football? He wears glasses and looks more like a schoolteacher. He's not going to be as good as George. Does he even speak English properly?'

A manager must above all look like a manager. Clubs would rather use traditional methods to appoint incompetents than risk doing anything that looks odd.

BAD STAFF

The most obvious reason why football has long been such an incom-petent business is that football clubs have historically tended to hire incompetent staff. The manager is only the start of it. Years ago one of us requested an interview with the chairman of an English club quoted on the stock market. The press officer asked me to send a fax (a 1980s technology revered by football clubs well into the twenty-first century). I sent it. She said she never got it. On request I sent three more faxes to different officials. She said none arrived. This is quite a common experience for football journalists. Because football clubs are the only businesses that get daily publicity without trying to, they treat journalists as humble supplicants instead of as unpaid marketers of the club's brand. The media often retaliate by being mean. This is not very clever of the clubs, because almost all their fans follow them through the media rather than by going to the stadium.

A month after all the faxes, I was granted permission to send my request by email. When I arrived at the club for the interview, I met the press officer. She was beautiful. Of course she was. Tradition-ally, football clubs recruit the women on their office staff for their looks, and the men because they played professional football or are somebody's mate.

If football clubs wanted to, they could recruit excellent executives. Professors at business schools report that many of their MBA students, who might be paying £30,000 a year in tuition fees, dream of working in football for a pitiful salary. Often the students beg clubs to let them work for free as summer interns. The clubs seldom want them. If you work for a football club, your goal is to keep working there, not to be shown up by some over-educated young thing who has actually learnt something about business.

In part this is because much of the traditionally working-class football industry distrusts education. In part, says Emmanuel Hembert of A.T. Kearney, it is because many clubs are dominated by a vain owner-manager. Hembert says: 'Lots of them invested for ego reasons, which is never a good thing in business. They prefer not to have strong people around them, except the coach. They really pay low salaries.'

Historically only Manchester United recruited respected executives from normal industries (such as Peter Kenyon from Umbro), though now a few other big clubs like Barcelona have started to do so too.

Baseball for a long time was just as incompetent. In *Moneyball* Lewis asked why, among baseball executives and scouts, 'there really is no level of incompetence that won't be tolerated'. He thought the main reason was 'that baseball has structured itself less as a business than as a social club ... There are many ways to embarrass the Club, but being bad at your job isn't one of them. The greatest offense a Club member can commit is not ineptitude but disloyalty.' Club members – and this applies in soccer as much as in baseball – are selected for clubbability. Clever outsiders are not clubbable, because they talk funny, and go around pointing out the things that people inside the Club are doing wrong. 'It wasn't as simple as the unease of jocks in the presence of nerds,' wrote Lewis – but that unease did have a lot to do with it.

The staff of football clubs tend not merely to be incompetent, they are also often novices. This is because staff turnover is rapid. Whenever a new owner arrives, he generally brings in his cronies. The departing staff rarely join a new club, because that is considered disloyal (Kenyon, an exception, was persecuted for moving from

United for Chelsea), even though footballers change clubs all the time. So football executives are always having to reinvent the wheel.

Worse, the media and fans often make it impossible for clubs to make sensible decisions. They are always hassling the club to do something immediately. If the team loses three games, fans start chanting for the club to sack the coach, buy a new player, in short, tear up the plans it might have made a month ago.

Tony Fernandes, the Malaysian businessman who had run a tight ship at his airline AirAsia, couldn't do the same after taking over QPR in 2011. 'Two things are different from AirAsia,' he told us in 2013. 'One is I can control almost everything in AirAsia. You can do whatever you want in football, but it's up to the 11 guys on the pitch at the end of the day, right? The second thing is, you have a very vocal bunch of shareholders – called fans. Everyone has an opinion. The plans get thrown out of the window when you start losing. The excitement you get when you win a football game is unbelievable. The downside is that when you lose you want to kill yourself.'

'Consumer activism in this industry is extreme,' agreed A.T. Kearney in its report *Playing for Profits.* Hembert says: 'As soon as you sign a player for £10 million, you blow up your business plan. Commercial employees have to fight for £100,000 of spending here or there, but then suddenly the club spends £10 million.'

Or more. Sven-Göran Eriksson once flew into Zurich to tell the International Football Arena a 'good story' about his time managing Lazio.

'The chairman I had was very good,' Eriksson recalled for an audience of mostly Swiss businessmen. 'If I wanted a player, he would try to get that player. One day I phoned him up and I said: "Vieri".'

Christian Vieri was then playing for Atlético Madrid. Eriksson and Lazio's chairman Sergio Cragnotti flew to Spain to bid for him. Atlético told them Vieri would cost 50 billion Italian lire. At the time, in 1998, that was about £17 million. Eriksson reminisced: 'That was the biggest sum in the world. No player had been involved for that.'

He says the talks then went more or less as follows:

Cragnotti: 'That's a lot of money.'
Eriksson: 'I know.'

Atlético said they might accept some Lazio players in part-payment for Vieri.

Cragnotti: 'Can we do that?'
Eriksson: 'No, we can't give away these players.'
Cragnotti: 'What shall we do then?'
Eriksson: 'Buy him.'
Cragnotti: 'OK.'

Eriksson recalled in Zurich: 'He didn't even try to pay 49. He just paid 50.'

Nine months after Vieri joined Lazio, Inter Milan wanted to buy him. Once again, Eriksson reports the conversation:

Cragnotti: 'What shall I ask for him?'
Eriksson: 'Ask for double. Ask 100.'
Cragnotti: 'I can't do that.'

Eriksson recalled: 'So he asked 90. And he got 90. That's good business.' (Or the ultimate example of the greater-fool principle.)

Someone in the audience in Zurich asked Eriksson whether such behaviour was healthy. After all, Lazio ran out of money in 2002 when Cragnotti's food company Cirio went belly-up. Cragnotti later spent time in prison, which even by the standards of Italian football is going a bit far.

Eriksson replied, 'It's not healthy. And if you see Lazio, it was not healthy. But we won the league. And we won the Cup-Winners' Cup. We won everything.'

The point is that football clubs, prompted by media and fans, are always making financially irrational decisions in an instant. They would like to think long-term, but because they are in the news every day they end up fixating on the short term. As Arthur Hopcraft wrote in *The Football Man* in 1968: 'It is the first characteristic of football that it is always urgent.' An executive with an American entertainment company tells a story about his long-arranged business meeting with Real Madrid. His company was hoping to build a relationship with the club. But on the day of the meeting, Real ritually sacked their manager. The usual chaos ensued. Two of the club officials scheduled to attend the meeting with the American executive did not show up. That's football.

NOT BUSINESSES AT ALL

When business people look at football, they are often astonished at how unbusinesslike the clubs are. Every now and then one of them takes over a club and promises to run it 'like a business'. Alan Sugar, who had made his money in computers, became chairman of Tottenham Hotspur in 1991. His brilliant wheeze was to make Spurs live within their means. Never would he fork out 50 billion lire for a Vieri. After Newcastle bought Alan Shearer for £15 million in 1996, Sugar remarked, 'I've slapped myself around the face a couple of times but I still can't believe it.'

He more or less kept his word. In the 10 years that he ran Spurs, they lived within their means. But most of their fans hated it. The only thing Spurs won in that decade was a solitary League Cup. They spent most of their time in mid-table of the Premier League, falling far behind Arsenal. Nor did they even make much money: about £2 million a year in profits in Sugar's first six years, which was much less than Arsenal and not very good for a company their size. Sugar's Spurs disappointed both on and off the field, and they also illustrated a paradox: when business people try to run a football club as a business, then not only does the football suffer, but so does the business.

Other businessmen pursue a different strategy from Sugar's. They assume that if they can get their clubs to win prizes, profits will inevitably follow. But they too are wrong. Even the best teams seldom generate profits. Below, we plotted the league positions and profits of all the clubs that have played in the Premier League from its inaugural season of 1992–93 until the 2011–12 season.

Pre-tax profits/loss of Premier League clubs by league position 1993–2012

The chart shows how spectacularly unprofitable the football business is. Each point on the chart represents the combination of profit and position for a club in a particular year. One obvious point to note is that most of the dots fall below zero on the profits axis: these clubs were making losses. But the chart also shows that there was barely any connection between finishing high and making money. While there is some suggestion that a few clubs at the top of the table make more money than other clubs, the chart also shows that other clubs in these positions can make huge losses. Manchester United's profitability is clearly the exception. In the 13 years before being taken over by the Glazer family in 2005 the club generated over £250 million in pre-tax profits while also winning eight league titles. Indeed, other American owners might never have bothered buying into English football without United's example. But no other club could replicate their success.

For most English clubs, our chart shows that there is not even a connection between changing league position and changing profits. In 45 per cent of all cases, when a club changed its league position, its profits moved in the opposite direction: either higher position, lower profits or lower position, higher profits. Only 55 per cent of the time did profits and position move in the same direction. Had there been no correlation at all between winning and making profits, that figure would have been much the same, namely 50 per cent. Clearly, winning games is not the route to making money. As Francisco Pérez Cutiño noted, it's not that winning matches can help a club make profits; rather, the effect works the other way around: if a club finds new revenues, that can help it win matches.

It has in fact so far proved almost impossible to run a football club like a profit-making business. This is because there are always rival owners – the Cragnottis, the Abramoviches, or the Gaddhafis, who owned a chunk of Juventus – who don't care about profits and will spend whatever it takes in the hope of winning prizes. All other club owners are forced to keep up with them. If one owner won't pay large transfer fees and salaries, somebody else will, and that somebody else will get the best players and win prizes. The consequence is that the biggest slice of money that football makes gets handed over to the best players. As A.T. Kearney says, you could even argue that football clubs are nothing more than vessels for transporting football's income to footballers. 'The players are completely free to move,' explains Hembert. 'They are a key factor in winning, and also in the ego, in pleasing the fans. And they all have pretty savvy agents who are able to maximise their bargaining power.'

It means that even the cautious Sugar type cannot make decent profits in football. In fact, because his team will win fewer matches than its free-spending rivals, some fans will desert him. That will eat further into his profits. From 1991 to 1998 average attendances in the Premier League rose 29 per cent, but Tottenham's crowds fell 5 per cent.

'I thought we could make it [QPR] profitable, definitely,' Fernandes admitted to us. 'I haven't yet,' he added, laughing. Even in the 2011–12 season, when the club survived in the Premier League, it lost £22.6 million. The next season, when it kept buying players but got relegated regardless, it lost a lot more. 'On the pitch it was just a disaster,' said Fernandes. He mused: 'Football has survived on benefactors. Shareholders coming in and pumping money in, and then the next sucker comes in and pumps money in.' Did he consider himself a sucker, a benefactor or a businessman in football? 'Now I would define myself as a sucker,' he replied. 'And benefactor. And I hope I will become a benefactor-stroke-businessman.'

Good luck to him. So far in football's history, running a club as a profit-making business has looked like a lost cause.

Stefan and the Spanish economist Pedro García del Barrio (of the Universidad Internacional de Cataluña) were curious to know whether anyone even aspired to do it. They studied the behaviour of Spanish and English clubs between 1993 and 2005, to see whether the clubs were chiefly pursuing profits off the field or victories on it.

If a club wanted to make profits, clearly it would have to spend less than it earned. That would mean limiting its players' wages. Any club that paid players less would suffer on the field, because as we have seen, paying high wages wins you football matches. It's a tradeoff: if you want glory, you have to forget maximising profits. If you want maximum profits, give up hope of glory. Stefan and Pedro estimated, for instance, that if Barcelona wanted to maximise profits, they would have to aim to finish 15th in the league, because they would need to slash their wages. A profit-driven Real Madrid should expect to finish a mere 17th, just above the relegation spots. Most other teams – like Atlético Madrid, Athletic Bilbao, Sevilla or Villarreal – would maximise their profit potential by playing in the second division. There they could save a lot of money on players' wages.

On the other hand, if a club's main aim was to win matches, then it would have to spend every cent it earned (and borrow more besides). So what were clubs chasing: profits or wins?

Stefan and Pedro estimated how each club in the top two Spanish divisions would have behaved on average in the 1994–2005 period if it were pursuing profits, and how it would have behaved if it wanted wins. Then they looked at how clubs behaved in real life. Their unambiguous finding: clubs didn't care about profits. They were spending what it took to win games. 'On average,' Stefan and Pedro concluded, looking at ten years of league tables, 'the Spanish teams were 12 places *above* their profit-maximising position over the sample period, but less than half a place *below* their win-maximising position.' In short, club presidents were spending way more than they would have done if they were hard-headed businessmen out to make profits. Though many of the presidents were in fact hard-headed businessmen in real life, they weren't treating their football clubs as businesses. Nor was there any sign that any other parties – lending banks, say – were pressuring them to make profits.

Building magnates like Florentino Pérez and Jesús Gil y Gil seemed especially prone to blowing what looked like absurd sums of money on players. Possibly they were pursuing a business logic after all: they may have reasoned that making a name in local football would help them befriend bankers and get planning permission from local government for their construction projects. That would have boosted their non-football businesses. Fred Wilpon, the real-estate developer who took over the New York Mets, discovered that a similar effect operated in baseball. Jeffrey Toobin wrote in a profile of Wilpon in the *New Yorker* magazine:

... he didn't anticipate that owning the Mets would boost his seemingly unrelated business interests. 'No one had heard of us before we bought the Mets, and afterward the change was dramatic,' Wilpon told me. 'I don't think someone has not returned one of my telephone calls in thirty years. It's a small club, owning a baseball team, and people want to be near it.'

Owning a football team might help the owner's other businesses. But all Spanish football clubs tended to pursue wins rather than profits. In a sense, they had to. If your rivals are spending whatever it takes to win, then you must as well. Any club that pursued the highest possible profits would probably end up being relegated, because it wouldn't be spending enough to hire good players. And if the club got relegated, it would lose much of its revenues. So football becomes an arms race: every club overspends for fear of the neighbours.

No matter how much money Spanish clubs got their hands on, they spent it. In the decade that Stefan and Pedro studied, the average revenues of a club in the Spanish first division (Primera División) rose nearly fourteen-fold, from €4.3 million in 1994 to €59 million in 2004. (By 2011 the figure was €85 million.) Yet the share of revenue that clubs spent on player wages didn't drop much throughout the period: in that decade, first-division clubs gave over an average of 62 per cent of their revenues to their players. In other words, the clubs weren't able to save all the additional income, or do much else with it, like building new stadiums or cutting ticket prices. Most of the money that came in just went straight out again into players' bank accounts. In the second division, a whopping 93 per cent of clubs' revenues went to the players. These clubs really were just vessels for transporting money to players.

The clubs weren't content with giving the players what money they had. They also gave them money they didn't have. According to the Spanish economists Angel Barajas Alonso and Plácido Rodriguez Guerrero, in the 2007–08 season clubs including Real Murcia, Real Zaragoza, Real Betis, Valencia, La Coruña and Atlético Madrid were spending *more than their entire annual operating revenues* on players. The consequences of this sort of arms race, pursued over many years, are predictable. Professor José María Gay de Liébana of the University of Barcelona compiled this authoritative list of the debts of clubs in the Primera División at the end of the 2009–10 season:

CLUB – TOTAL DEBT IN MILLIONS OF EUROS

Club	Debt	Club	Debt
FC Barcelona	548.6	Real Madrid	659.9
Valencia	470.6	Sevilla FC	112.3
RCD Mallorca	85.2	Getafe	51.9
Villarreal	267.4	Athletic Bilbao	51.2
Atlético Madrid	452.0	Deportivo La Coruña	107.0
Espanyol	173.7	Osasuna	59.2
Almería	27.3	Real Zaragoza	142.2
Sporting Gijón	28.8	Racing CS	74.8
Málaga	37.5	Real Valladolid	48.5
Tenerife	31.0	Xerez CD	0.0

All this added up to a total debt of €3.43 billion, or about £3 billion. It must be said that this figure includes a lot of unpaid inter-club debt, which therefore inflates the data. Still, it's an astonishing figure. Clearly Atlético Madrid and Valencia, in particular, are never going to repay their creditors. In effect, banks and local governments and therefore the poor Spanish treasury are subsidising these clubs. Ordinary taxpayers are paying for the centre-forward's Ferrari.

By the standards of a normal business, this sort of debt spending is barmy. But for football clubs, it makes sense: the only way to win matches is to overspend. Nobody runs a football club in order to turn a tidy annual profit.

Nor, it might be argued, should anyone attempt it. Most of a club's customers (its fans) and employees (its players and coaches) and even usually its owners would say that the club exists to play good football and win things, not to turn profits. That's why a report by the UK's Commission on Industrial Relations in 1974 quoted an anonymous club chairman as saying, 'Any club management which allows the club to make a profit is behaving foolishly.' Traditionally, football clubs have behaved more like charitable trusts than like businesses. In the not-so-distant past the FA used to forbid club owners to profit from their investment. Directors couldn't get paid, and dividends were capped. The aim was to ensure that clubs were run by 'the right class of men who love football for its own sake'. These rules were abolished in the early 1980s. If they still existed, they might have stopped the businessmen Tom Hicks and George Gillett at Liverpool and the Glazer family at Manchester United from burdening these clubs with a combined debt of nearly £1 billion simply to finance their takeovers.

Making profits deprives a club of money that it could spend on the team. The business of football is football. Almost all football clubs that are not Manchester United should ditch the fantasy of making profits. But that doesn't mean that they should continue to be badly run. The weight of money that now washes through football demands a more businesslike approach to managing cash. Bungs might have been no big deal when transfer fees were measured in the hundreds of thousands of pounds, but become a problem when they run into the tens of millions.

Football clubs need to know what they are. They shouldn't kid themselves that they are BBA Aviation. Rather, they are like the British Museum: public-spirited organisations that aim to serve the community while remaining reasonably solvent. It sounds like a modest goal, but few of them achieve even that.

SAFER THAN THE BANK OF ENGLAND: WHY FOOTBALL CLUBS ALMOST NEVER DISAPPEAR

On 15 September 2008, the investment bank Lehman Brothers collapsed, followed almost immediately by the world's stock markets.

Any football club on earth was a midget next to Lehman. In the year to September 2007, the bank had income of $59 billion (148 times Manchester United's at the time), profits of $6 billion (50 times Manchester United's) and was valued by the stock market at $34 billion. If United's shares had still been traded on the market, they would probably have been worth less than 5 per cent of Lehman's. Yet Lehman no longer exists while United very much does.

In the years before the global economic crisis, people worried a lot more about the survival of football clubs than of banks. Yet it was many of the world's largest banks that disappeared. Then, after the recession began, worries about football clubs increased again. Many people pointed out that when Chelsea met Manchester United in the final of the Champions League in 2008, the two clubs had had a combined net debt of more than £1.3 billion. Michel Platini, president of UEFA, warned in 2009 that half of Europe's professional clubs had financial troubles of some kind. 'If this situation goes on,' he added, 'it will not be long before even some major clubs face going out of business.'

Yet the notion that football clubs are inherently unstable businesses is wrong. They virtually never go bust. Despite being incompetently run, they are exceptionally stable businesses. Not only do the football authorities worry far too much about clubs going out of business; they worry about the wrong clubs.

First, some facts. In 1923 the English Football League consisted of 88 teams spread over four divisions. In the 2011–12 season, 85 of these clubs still existed (97 per cent),* and 80 remained in the top four divisions (91 per cent). Forty were in the same division as they had been in 1923. And only six teams still in the top four divisions were two or more divisions away from where they had been in 1923. (No team that was in the First Division in 1923 was placed lower than the third tier in 2012.)

It is a history of remarkable stability. You would have expected the Great Depression of the 1930s, in particular, to pose the clubs something of a threat. After all, the Depression bit deepest in the North, where most English clubs were based, and all romantic rhetoric aside, you would have thought that when people cannot afford bread they would stop watching football.

Crowds in the Football League did indeed fall 12 per cent between 1929 and 1931. However, by 1932 they were growing again, even though the British economy was not. And clubs helped each other through the hard times. When Orient hit trouble in 1931,

---

* The three lost clubs are Aberdare (disbanded 1928), New Brighton (which folded in 1983, was reborn but folded again in 2012) and South Shields (taken over by Gateshead in 1930). Several other clubs have folded and been reborn, e.g. Accrington Stanley, Bradford Park Avenue, Durham City, Halifax Town, Merthyr Town, Nelson and Newport County.

Arsenal wrote its tiny neighbour a cheque for £3,450 to tide it over. Clubs know they cannot operate without opponents, and so unlike in most businesses, the collapse of a rival is not a cause for celebration.

The Depression culled only a couple of clubs. Merthyr Town, after failing to be re-elected to the league in 1930, folded a few years later, the victim of economic hardship in the Welsh valleys (as well as competition from far more popular rugby union). Wigan Borough went bankrupt a few games into the 1931–32 season. It left the league, and its remaining fixtures were never played. Aldershot was elected to replace it, and sixty years later, in another recession, it became only the second English club in history to withdraw from the league with fixtures unplayed.

Almost equally hard as the Depression for English clubs was the 'Thatcher recession' of the early 1980s. Again, many working-class fans lost their factory jobs. The league's attendances dropped from 24.6 million to 16.5 million between 1980 and 1986. Football seemed to be in terminal decline. As Ken Friar, then managing director of Arsenal, put it: 'Football is the oddest of industries. It sells one product and has 92 outlets for it. In any other business, if not all 92 outlets were doing well, there would be talk of closing some of them down. But in football, all 92 outlets claim an equal right to survive.'

Many clubs in the early 1980s seemed to be dicing with death. If we look at one of the diciest, Bristol City, it will help us understand just how football clubs almost always survive.

Bristol City got into trouble in the same way that a lot of clubs do. In 1976 it had been promoted to the old First Division, then the highest tier in English football, a status the club had last enjoyed before World War One. The fans were excited: attendance jumped from 14,000 per game in 1974/75 to 24,500 in 1976/77. The average ticket then cost less than £1, but the higher ticket sales still boosted the club's income from around £250,000 per year to £665,000. City survived three seasons in the top flight. As we've already seen, that took money. The club paid handsomely in the transfer market, and its wage bill doubled: all City's extra income was channeled straight to players.

The money didn't do the trick. In the 1979/80 season, the club was relegated just as Britain, in the first year of the new Thatcher government, was entering recession. First Division attendances dropped five per cent that season, but Bristol City's gates fell 15 per cent, while its wage costs rose 20 per cent.

Clearly the club needed to lose some of its expensive players. Unfortunately, the manager, Alan Dicks, who had just overseen the most successful period in Bristol City's modern history, had signed many of them on extraordinarily lengthy contracts – some as long as 11 years. Soon after relegation, Dicks was sacked. But by the end of the next season, 1980–81, City's average attendance had collapsed to 9,700 per game (half the level of the previous season) and the club was relegated to Division Three. Income was tumbling, yet most of the squad were still drawing First Division wages. When City's accounts were published on 15 October 1981 it was apparent that the club was in deep trouble, but the best that the new chairman could say in his report was that 'so much of this depends on success on the playing field'.

It is doubtful that promotion back to Division Two would have improved the club's financial position materially in 1981–82, but that's a purely academic question since by the end of 1981 Bristol City were heading for the fourth division. By now only 6,500 fans were showing up each week, about a quarter the number of four years earlier. An independent financial report produced that December showed that the club owed far more (over £1 million) than it could realistically repay in the foreseeable future. Early in 1982 Bristol City Football Club PLC – the limited company that owned the stadium at Ashton Gate, the players' contracts, and a share in the Football League – was on the verge of appointing an official receiver to liquidate the company. That would have meant the end. In a liquidation all the players' contracts would have been void, the share in the League would have been returned to the League, the stadium sold, probably to a property developer, and any proceeds used to pay the creditors. Like so many British companies at the time, Bristol City seemed headed for extinction.

But football clubs command more love than widget-makers. Just before Bristol City could fold, Deryn Coller and some other local businessmen who were also fans offered to take over the club. It was at this point that the 'phoenixing' plan emerged.

Coller and his associates created a new company: BCFC (1982) PLC. It was to be a 'new' Bristol City: a phoenix from the ashes of the old club. The Coller group aimed to sell shares in the new company to fans. With the money, the group would buy Ashton Gate from the receiver. The group also asked the Football League for permission to acquire the old club's share in the League. Then the new Bristol City could 'replace' the old one in Division Four. In short, the new company would take over almost everything of the old club – except, crucially, its debts and unaffordable players. Collier's group intended to ask City's most expensive players, left over from Division One days, to tear up their contracts. You can see the appeal of the plan, as long as you were not one of the players.

The Football League said the plan was fine as long as Gordon Taylor, the head of the Professional Football Association (PFA), would agree the deal on the players. Taylor was by no means sure that things were as bad at Bristol City as the directors said (after all, directors are always complaining about wages), but eventually he was convinced that the deal was the only way to save the club. No union wants to see an employer go bust, especially not an ancient employer loved by thousands of people.

The final decision was down to the players. Naturally, they were reluctant martyrs. But the pressure on them was intense, including some threats from fans. In the end, after some sweeteners were thrown in, the players agreed. Peter Aitken, Chris Garland, Jimmy Mann, Julian Marshall, Geoff Merrick, David Rodgers, Gerry Sweeney and Trevor Tainton are not the biggest names in football's history, but few players can claim to have given more for their clubs. On 3 February 1982 the 'Ashton Gate Eight' agreed to tear up contracts worth £290,000 and accept redundancy in order to save their employer. By the standards of the time, they were on very good pay. Most of them, nearing the end of their careers, would never earn as much again. They got a miserly payoff of two weeks' wages, and afterwards they had to choose between retiring from football, moving abroad or joining lower-division clubs. The eight really deserve statues outside Ashton Gate. They gave Bristol City a future.

The phoenix rose from the ashes: the club was transferred from the ownership of Bristol City PLC, a company heading for liquidation, to BCFC (1982) PLC. The directors of the new business still faced the formidable task of finding the money to buy Ashton Gate. They had agreed a price with the receiver of just over £590,000. They raised £330,000 by selling shares in the new club to fans and well-wishers. They might have raised more, but they felt obliged to close the share offer early when rumors emerged that an unknown bidder was considering buying a majority of the shares on offer, possibly with the aim of selling off the ground to property developers. (Ashton Gate is handily located near the city centre.) The rest of the cash was raised from short-term loans.

Today Bristol City still play at Ashton Gate in League One. (And Ashton Gate is now much more than a mere stadium. 'Ashton Gate Stadium, Bristol's premier conference and events venue, features a wide range of function rooms available for both corporate and private hire,' proclaims Ashtongatestadium.co.uk.) The 'phoenixing' of Bristol City was the first of its kind in English football, and established a template that, like the club itself, survives to this day.

Other clubs quickly cottoned onto the joy of 'phoenixing'. Between 1982 and 1984 Hereford, Hull, Wolves, Derby, Bradford and Charlton went through much the same experience as Bristol City. They all survived, either by creating a new 'phoenix' company (Wolves, Bradford and Charlton) or by getting creditors to agree to suspend their claims (a moratorium), under the threat that a phoenix might be the alternative. In all cases, the bankrupt company was ditched, but the immortal club inside it salvaged.

'Phoenixing' – the creation of a new company – turned out to be a brilliant way to escape creditors. Clearly, there is something unfair about the method. Phoenixing allowed some disastrous directors to escape the consequences of their bad decisions. Their clubs survived, but at a cost to creditors (often players, banks and the taxman) who never saw their money again.

Still, this was just what hapless football clubs needed. Many of them struggled during the Thatcher recession, and several survived only thanks to a 'sub' from the PFA. Charlton and Bristol City's neighbours, Bristol Rovers, had to move grounds because they could not pay the rent. However, nobody resigned from the league.

Soon after that recession, a new law made it even easier for British clubs to survive. The UK's traditional method of liquidation – the bankrupt company's assets got sold, the debts repaid as far as possible and the company wound up – had become discredited. Critics said it gave stricken companies little chance to recover. They praised the American approach, which treated failure as a frequently necessary precursor to eventual success. In 1979 the US had introduced the now famous 'Chapter XI' provisions. These protect a firm from winding up by its creditors, while it tries to work out a solution that saves the business. Britain – where insolvencies had hit an all-time high during the Thatcher recession – wanted some of that.

The British Insolvency Act of 1986 introduced a new procedure called 'administration'. Now, when a company went into administration, an independent insolvency practitioner was called in, and charged with finding a way to keep the business running while repaying as much money as possible to the creditors. After the new law came in, stricken football clubs typically entered administration, struck deals with creditors, and then swiftly emerged from administration. That's what Tranmere and Rotherham did in spring 1987, for instance. For most clubs, financial collapse was becoming something of a breeze.

True, Aldershot FC was liquidated in 1992, but supporters simply started a new club almost identical to the old one. The 'new' Aldershot Town AFC has a badge that shows a phoenix rising from the ashes. Aldershot re-entered the Football League in 2008. Other tiny clubs that folded – Maidstone United, Newport County, Accrington Stanley – were also eventually resuscitated and now stumble on somewhere in the semi-professional or professional game. Accrington Stanley's rebirth was surely the most drawn-out: it resigned from the Football League in 1962 with debts of £63,000, got liquidated in 1966, was newly created by fans in 1968, and returned to the Football League in 2006, its brand still very much alive, probably even enhanced by the drama. 'Above the turnstiles now the welcoming sign is, "The Club that Wouldn't Die",' Accrington's then chairman, Ilyas Khan, told us proudly in 2012.

The new British law was so kind to insolvent companies that ever more companies decided to enter insolvency. Some did it just to wipe off their debts. The method became ever more popular even as the economy improved. Company insolvencies in the recession of the early 1980s had run at an average of around 10,000 per year. In the boom period between 1994 and 2001 they ran at 16,000 per year. Football clubs, too, loved the new law: more of them went insolvent in the 1990s' boom than in the early 1980s' bust. They rarely even needed to bother to create a new 'phoenix' company anymore. Clubs with unpayable debts would go insolvent, and hey presto, months later would be fine and signing expensive players again. Better-run rivals complained that insolvency and 'phoenixing' were giving the culprits an unfair advantage. In 2004 this argument prompted the League to introduce a ten-point penalty for clubs that went into administration. Still, it hasn't proved a huge deterrent.

There's something else to note about these near-death experiences: they almost only happen to small clubs. There was a great kerfuffle in England in early 2010 when Portsmouth of the mighty Premier League entered administration. The club had been on much the same journey as Bristol City thirty years earlier, just with larger sums. It had overspent on good players, won an FA Cup and ended up in trouble.

On the one hand, Portsmouth's story was all too familiar: football club goes bust, and after many premature reports of its demise, is reborn. The shared fan angst about their club disappearing has a useful psychological function: it's a communal ritual that gives people a chance to join together to affirm their love of the club. As we write, Portsmouth is bumping along in League Two. It has had a miserable few years, but like every other professional club in England, it's still around.

Yet in another way, Portsmouth's story was exceptional. No club in the Premier League had ever gone into administration before. The other 66 cases of insolvency in English football from 1982 to 2010 involved teams in the lower divisions. That is something that doomsayers like Platini should note. They often complain about the debts of rich clubs: the hundreds of millions of pounds owed by the likes of Real Madrid, Barcelona and Manchester United. They ask how Chelsea would survive if Roman Abramovich falls under a bus.

In fact, though, big clubs are not the problem. Across Europe, lower-tier teams live on the edge of insolvency, while the top-tier teams, even though they mostly lose money too, seldom become insolvent. The highest risk of all is for recently relegated teams. We have been able to identify about a dozen European clubs that have disappeared since the start of the economic crisis in 2008: UD Salamanca, Lorca and CD Badajoz in Spain, Haarlem, Veendam, AGOVV and RBC Roosendaal in Holland, Beerschot in Belgium, Gretna in Scotland, Arsenal Kyiv in Ukraine and Unirea Urziceni in Romania. There is not a single big name among them. Admittedly, Unirea played in the Champions League in 2009–10, but historically it was a tiny club from a small town. It owed its brief rise to a passing sugar daddy. When he lost interest, Unirea expired.

None of these clubs got into trouble by gambling tens of millions to compete with the big boys. Rather, they were tiny outfits (Badajoz in its 107 years of existence never once made it to Spain's top division) that had soldiered on gamely through the years. When the crisis hit, their relatively puny debts overwhelmed them. Haarlem, for instance, owed a fairly manageable £1.5 million. It's just that hardly anybody was interested enough to fight for the club's life. Anyway, several of the defunct clubs were immediately refounded in a slightly different form. Gretna 2008 now plays amateur football in Scotland, as do RBC and AGOVV in Holland. Early in 2014, some Dutch businessmen were also attempting to revive Haarlem as a professional club. Salamanca actually has three successor clubs, each claiming the mantle.

Perhaps because English professional clubs are older established brands than most continental teams, even the littlest among them survived the crisis. But if Platini is determined to worry about clubs going bust, it's the Salamancas he should worry about, not the Real Madrids. And he probably shouldn't worry too much about the issue at all. If European football clubs really did collapse beneath their debts, there would now be virtually no European football clubs left. 'We must be sustainable,' clubs say nowadays, parroting the latest business cliché. In fact they are fantastically sustainable. They survive even when they go bust. You can't get more sustainable than that. Match-fixing (say) is a much bigger problem for European football than bankruptcy.

Platini worries about clubs' debts. But it's precisely because clubs are practically immortal that they run up such large debts. They know from experience that they can take on vast debts and survive. If things go wrong the debt simply does not get repaid, the old directors leave and new ones come in promising to sweep up the mess (while also buying shiny new Brazilian centre-forwards). A club like Bayern Munich, which shuns debt, is in fact missing a trick. Bayern could easily borrow a few hundred million euros to make itself invincible against human opposition in the long term. Even if it flushed the money down the toilet and then said 'Nananananana' to the lenders, the club would survive. Right now, Bayern is a marvellous self-sustaining debt-free business whereas most English clubs aren't. But the point of a football club isn't to have nice accounts – after all, the clubs with horrible accounts survive too. The point of a football club is to win trophies. Bayern won the Champions League in 2013, but in the previous 36 years it had won the trophy only once. That's a meagre return for the biggest club of western Europe's biggest country.

Once again, the comparison between football clubs and 'real' businesses breaks down. When clubs get into trouble, they generally 'do a Leeds': they cut their wages, get relegated and compete at a lower level. Imagine if other businesses could do this. Suppose that Ford could sack skilled workers and hire unskilled ones to produce worse cars, or that British Airways could replace all its pilots with people who weren't as well qualified to fly planes. The government would stop it, and in any case, consumers would not put up with terrible products.

Football clubs have it easy. Recall that almost every English professional club has survived the Great Depression, the Second World War, recessions, corrupt chairmen, appalling managers and the current economic crisis. By contrast, economic historian Les Hannah made a list of the top 100 global companies in 1912, and researched what had become of them by 1995. Nearly half the companies – 49 – had ceased to exist. Five of these had gone bankrupt, six were nationalised and 38 were taken over by other firms. Even among the businesses that survived, many had gone into new sectors or moved to new locations.

What made these non-football businesses so unstable was, above all, competition. There is such a thing as brand loyalty, but when a better product turns up most people will switch sooner or later. So normal businesses keep having to innovate or die. They face endless pitfalls: competitors pull ahead, consumers' tastes change, new technologies make entire industries obsolete, cheap goods arrive from abroad, government interferes, recessions hit, companies over-invest and go bust, or they simply get unlucky. By contrast, football clubs are immune from almost all these effects:

- A club that fails to keep up with the competition might get relegated, but it can always survive at a lower level.
- Some fans lose interest, but clubs have geographical roots. A bad team might find its catchment area shrinking, but not disappearing completely.
- The 'technology' of football can never become obsolete because the technology is the game itself. At worst football might become less popular.
- Foreign rivals cannot enter the market and supply football at a lower price. The rules of football protect domestic clubs by forbidding foreign competitors from joining their league. English clubs as a whole could fall behind foreign competitors and lose their best players, but foreign clubs have financial problems and incompetent management of their own.
- The government is not about to nationalise football.
- Clubs often over-invest, but this almost never destroys the club, only the wealth of the investor. At worst, the club gets relegated.
- A club's income might decline in a recession, but it can always live with a lower income.

In most industries a bad business goes bankrupt, but football clubs almost never do. No matter how much money they waste, someone will always bail them out. This is what is known in finance as 'moral hazard': when you know you will be saved however much money you lose, you are free to lose money.

There is a strange parallel here between professional football and communism. When we ask, 'Why do football clubs almost always survive?' we are echoing the great question asked about communism by one of our favourite economists, the Hungarian János Kornai. He had grown up in Hungary, briefly worked for a communist newspaper despite knowing that the system was all nonsense, and after making his way to the west tried to answer the question: why *exactly* did communism not work?

Kornai's answer could be summed up in four words: 'the soft-budget constraint'. Imagine that you are a tractor factory in communist Hungary. Each year the state gives you a budget. But if at the end of the year you've overspent the budget, and lost money, the state just gives you a bit more money to make up the difference. In communism, bad companies were propped up forever. In other words, the 'budget constraint' on communist firms was soft. If they wanted to overspend their budgets, they could. The obvious consequence: unprofitable overspending became rife.

As scholars such as Wladimir Andreff and Rasmus Storm have noted, Kornai's 'soft-budget constraint' applies beautifully to football clubs. Like tractor factories in communism, clubs lose money because they can. They have no need to be competent. The professional investors who briefly bought club shares in the 1990s got out as soon as they discovered this.

Luckily, as we've seen, society can keep unprofitable football clubs going fairly cheaply. The total revenues of European professional clubs for the 2011–12 season were €15.7 billion, according to Deloitte. Tesco's revenues were more than four times higher. The tinpot losses of football clubs hardly matter when set beside the enormous love they command. These tiny businesses are great enduring brands. Creditors dare not push them under. No bank manager or tax collector wants to say, 'The century-old local club is closing. I'm turning off the lights.' Society swallows the losses and lets even a Bristol City soldier on. In a sense, these clubs are too small to fail.

Football clubs, unlike most businesses, survive crises because some of their customers stick with them no matter how lousy the product. Calling this brand loyalty is not quite respectful enough of the sentiment involved. To quote Rogan Taylor, the Liverpool fan and Liverpool University professor: 'Football is more than just a business. No one has their ashes scattered down the aisle at Tesco.'

IN PRAISE OF SUGAR DADDIES: WHY 'FINANCIAL FAIR PLAY' IS BAD FOR FOOTBALL

When Roman Abramovich decided to buy a football club, he had a look around in Spain and Italy. But ownership there seemed complicated. In Italy, many of the families who owned clubs had been doing business with each other for generations. In Spain, horror of horrors, the fans themselves owned the biggest clubs. As for the Bundesliga, Abramovich seems never to have considered it.

And so in April 2002 he flew to Manchester to watch United. After the game, write Dominic Midgley and Chris Hutchins in their biography *Abramovich*, Rio Ferdinand drove him to Manchester airport, and the Russian charmed the player by joining in a singalong with a fellow passenger, Ferdinand's four-year-old half-brother.

Not long after that, the story goes, Abramovich was flying in a helicopter over London when he spotted a football stadium handily located near his mansion. 'What's that?' he reportedly asked. It was Chelsea. He bought the club, sealing the deal with the departing owner Ken Bates over a bottle of Evian water in London's Dorchester

Hotel. The Russian was then still happy to talk to journalists. When the *Financial Times* rang to ask about his purchase, he revealed that his favourite player was Thierry Henry (then at Arsenal), and explained why he had bought Chelsea: 'I'm looking at it as something to have fun with rather than having to realise a return. I don't look at this as a financial investment.' He has barely spoken another word in public since, but two things have become clear: (1) Buying a football club made this unknown billionaire world-famous. (2) As he predicted, the purchase hasn't been a 'financial investment'. In his first eight years as owner, Chelsea lost a total of over £630 million.

Despite the losses, he seems to have inspired the era of billionaire sugar daddies in global football. Men like him have taken over Manchester City, Paris Saint-Germain, Monaco and most big Russian clubs. Sugar daddies in football aren't like investors in normal businesses. They are willing to lose money just to be part of the game. They have helped drive up wages and salaries for the best players to unprecedented levels. Now UEFA is trying to end that. In 2010 the European football association introduced a set of rules on 'financial fair play' (FFP). These aim, above all, to stop clubs spending more than they earn. If a club's annual revenues are £300 million, say, it won't be able to spend £400 million even if an Abramovich wants to give it the money. Any offending club can be banned from European competition.

The 'FFP rules' are full of loopholes, and only take full effect in 2018, but they do appear to be aimed at the sugar daddies. The idea seems to be, if not to drive the Abramoviches out of football, at least to curb their spending. That would allow rival clubs to spend less, and let them make profits at last. Arsène Wenger, for one, has welcomed the new rules. 'Financial fair play will make a big difference,' he says, 'because you cannot imagine the world will go on just splashing money out without any return.' Many fans, too, seem to regard FFP as football's long-needed dose of sanity. We disagree. We don't think financial fair play will be fully implemented, but if it is, we think it will be bad for football. We don't think clubs should make profits. On balance, we think the Abramoviches are good for the game.

FFP itself has two dimensions, one of which is uncontroversial: that every club must be solvent. Solvency means the capacity to pay your debts – that is, the reasonable expectation that your future income will be enough to pay what you owe. In most European countries, solvency is a basic requirement for doing business. If the directors of a company know it is insolvent, then legally they should stop doing business until either solvency is restored or the company is shut down. Solvency can be restored if the creditors agree to write off some of their debts. If the creditors won't do that, then the business can be closed, the assets sold and the creditors paid off to the greatest extent possible.

Insolvency is a very common business problem. There are thousands of cases across Europe every year. Generally the problem affects small businesses, and so these events go unnoticed by most of us. Occasionally, though, very large companies go insolvent, and it becomes headline news. But as we've already shown, football clubs almost never close down. They are practically always bailed out. This appears to be one reason why European clubs seem forever to be in financial trouble: they overspend because they can. In the past many clubs have restored their finances by refusing to pay small creditors, banks and the taxman – daring any of them to take on the label of the creditor that destroyed a football club. Very few creditors have chosen to tread this path. And perhaps, in the days when there was almost no money in football, it didn't matter. Local banks can usually write off a debt that might be no more than a few tens of thousands of pounds (a lot to an individual perhaps, but not much for a modestly sized bank).

Now, though, the income generated by European football is starting to add up to something. These days, when a club can't pay, a lot of creditors get hurt. Often the victims are small local businesses, or even charities – notably St John's Ambulance, which provides emergency medical aid to fans in British football grounds. Clearly it's wrong for a club to pay its players millions and then try to get out of paying its creditors. So we applaud FFP for demanding solvency. The solvency rule mostly affects smaller clubs – which, as we have seen, are the ones that tend to become insolvent. In the big countries smaller clubs tend to play in the lower divisions, which means UEFA's rules are irrelevant to them anyway. Financial fair play only applies to teams entering UEFA competitions. The requirement for solvency would therefore mostly impact clubs qualifying for European competitions from smaller or poorer countries – Finland, Romania and the like. It shouldn't affect the Chelseas and Real Madrids.

The second, controversial element of FFP is the break-even rule. This requires that, averaged over a three-year period, a club's 'relevant income' must match its 'relevant expenses'. In other words, clubs can only spend what they earn. This rule will only impact big clubs. That is because the break-even rules allow a financial loss of €5 million (a bit over £4 million). According to UEFA, in 2011 only 77 out of 726 top-division clubs in Europe had an annual income over €50 million, and were therefore likely to make losses of over €5 million. Hardly any club outside the elite will notice the impact of break-even.

The chief target of break-even seems to be the sugar daddies. This is because UEFA's definition of 'relevant income' includes gate money, broadcast income, and income from sponsorship and merchandising, but excludes the owner's own money. Break-even is not a solvency issue – it's not as if Chelsea faces any real risk that Abramovich will be unwilling or unable to cover losses as long as he owns the club. Indeed, in 2009 he converted the hundreds of millions of pounds that Chelsea theoretically owed him into shares in the club. That means that if he walks away tomorrow, he can't ask Chelsea for his money back.

UEFA presumably isn't worried about Chelsea's solvency. Rather, it seems to think that money from an owner somehow gives a club an unfair competitive advantage. The FFP rules allow a club owner to put money into the stadium or youth academy, but not into buying stars for the first team.

The break-even rules shouldn't hurt the old 'aristocrats' of football, the likes of Manchester United, Arsenal and Bayern Munich. These clubs generate plenty of income from 'relevant' sources – chiefly fans, sponsors and TV companies. No wonder, then, that the aristocrats support financial fair play. FFP would tend to weaken their rivals, who can compete with the aristocrats only by borrowing fortunes (something banned under the insolvency rule) or by getting fortunes from a sugar daddy (something banned under the break-even rule). If FFP works, the aristocrats will celebrate.

Break-even caps each club at the level of its own resources – a lot for the larger clubs, not so much for the smaller clubs. That means UEFA's rules cement inequality by making it harder for smaller clubs to compete with the aristocrats. This hardly seems fair, unless by 'fair' you mean the idea that big clubs should be protected from competition from upstarts.

Jean-Louis Dupont, a lawyer who helped bring about the Bosman ruling in 1995, decided in 2013 to challenge the FFP rules under European competition law. His main argument was not that FFP is unfair on smaller clubs. Rather, he said it was unfair on players and their agents. FFP will surely put downward pressure on players' salaries, since it aims to stop at least some clubs (such as Chelsea and Manchester City) from spending as much as they want. Stefan and the Flemish economist Thomas Peeters developed a model to estimate the effect the break-even rule will have. Note that the rule puts indirect as well as direct downward pressure on wages. The direct pressure would work like this: Manchester City complies with break-even by spending less on players' salaries. But on top of that comes the indirect effect: by spending less, City becomes less of a competitive threat to other clubs. The cost of winning for these other clubs falls, and so they need to spend less on wages to achieve success.

If the FFP rules have enough bite, clubs will be able to choose their strategy. Either they can continue to spend the same proportion of their 'relevant income', even though they need to spend less now to win; or they can aim for the same level of on-field performance as before FFP, and pocket the surplus as profits. Either way, Stefan and Thomas predicted a very large fall in spending on players as a result of FFP. Using 2010 as a benchmark, and using data from the top divisions of England, France, Italy and Spain (financial data for individual German clubs are not available), the model suggests that player spending would have been €400–800 million lower in those four leagues had the FFP rules applied. That would represent a fall in wage spending of up to 15 per cent. The higher-spending the league, the larger the fall in wages – so FFP would be worst news of all for players trying to earn a crust in the Premier League.

Some people might think lower players' wages would be justification enough for FFP. But remember two things: first, FFP makes football at the top less competitive. Imagine if FFP had been in force since 2003, and Abramovich at Chelsea and Sheikh Mansour at Manchester City hadn't been allowed to spend their fortunes to buy English titles. What would have happened instead? Quite likely, Manchester United would have won the Premier League ten years running. With FFP, as Gabriele Marcotti warned in the *Wall Street Journal*: 'Instead of football having a 1 per cent lording it over everyone else, it could become a 0.1 per cent.'

Second, if FFP does cut players' wages, there is no promise that the money saved will go back into football. More probably, the money will go into the pockets of billionaire owners.

We should say at this point that FFP might not actually take force as planned. More likely, clubs and UEFA will both give a bit. UEFA's main concern will be to stop penniless clubs risking insolvency, and so it will enforce the solvency rule hard. Any Bulgarian club that has lost over €5 million in three years will find itself chucked out of European competition. By contrast, big clubs with sugar daddies may be cut more slack if they fail to break even. In any case, some of these clubs appear to already be finding ways around FFP. Manchester City, for instance, has signed a ten-year deal believed to be worth a flabbergasting £350 million with Etihad Airways for stadium-naming rights and shirt sponsorship. Sceptics note that Etihad, like City's owners, comes from Abu Dhabi. They hint that the deal would enable City to effectively bypass the rules, allowing them to receive a very significant injection of outside (and potentially, related) money, that artificially boosts their 'relevant income'.

If such a deal were ever challenged in the courts on the basis it was believed to be flouting the spirit of the FFP rules, UEFA might struggle to prove that the £350 million was excessive, or that Etihad's owners had anything to do with City's owners (beyond both sets of people coming from the elite of the same tiny emirate). The sugar daddy clubs will hire expensive lawyers to defend them, and will dare UEFA to ban teams full of great players from the Champions League. That will give UEFA pause. It doesn't want to stage a Champions League without Paris Saint-Germain's Zlatan Ibrahimović or Manchester City's Sergio Agüero. It must also worry that any excluded clubs might try to start their own rival competition. UEFA's president Michel Platini sounded cautious when telling the *London Evening Standard* in 2013: 'Sanctions will be decided upon. Do not think we are going to take five to ten clubs out of the European competition. Definitely that would be the very, very last straw. If we have repeat offenders, OK, yes, they will have to be punished severely – possibly. We are not out to kill the clubs.'

Presumably, then, deals like City's with Etihad will be left to stand (even if UEFA believes that it effectively amounts to a breach of the rules). FFP may not transform football. Ivan Gazidis, chief executive of Arsenal, told us: 'Are there loopholes in the way FFP works? Quite possibly. FFP is not part of our strategy.'

Still, our question is: what if FFP actually happens, and works? If UEFA does manage to force clubs to spend only what they earn, then sugar daddies would drift out of the game. After all, there wouldn't be much point in buying Chelsea if you couldn't spend any money to win trophies. You might still want to buy a huge club like Manchester United that can challenge for trophies without your cash, but there aren't many clubs like that. If FFP triumphs, the Abramovich era ends. We think that would be bad news for football.

Sugar daddies are often depicted as a curse on the game. It's easy to see why a Manchester United fan, or an Arsenal fan, would dislike Manchester City or Chelsea. Setting aside local rivalry, it's the age-old disdain of the aristocracy for the *nouveaux riches*. City and Chelsea are upstarts who have used wallets full of foreign currency to barge their way onto the top table. When City won the Premier League in 2012, it did so with several players bought from Arsenal, and at the expense of United. Of course United fans oppose sugar daddies.

What's less clear is why fans of smaller clubs should care. It's not as if the sugar daddy clubs are taking *their* places. Smaller clubs never win anything these days anyway. In 20-plus years of the Premier League, only the sugar daddy clubs Manchester City, Chelsea and Blackburn (when funded by Jack Walker in 1995) have wrested titles from the vice-like grip of Manchester United and Arsenal. Sugar daddies threaten the strong, but they hardly threaten the already weak.

In most other walks of life we welcome the outsider who comes in and shakes up the existing order. Taking the aristocrats down a notch is the plot of endless feelgood movies. Why should it be different for football? It certainly seems that when fans of a particular club learn that a sugar daddy is in the offing, they perk up. Soon after Abramovich bought Chelsea, and began buying expensive players, the club's fans came up with a song in his honour (more or less):

> He's got Verón in his pocket
> We got Johnson from West Ham
> If you want the best
> Then don't ask questions
> 'Cos Roman, he's our man
> Where it all comes from is a mystery.

The sentiment of the song is clear: finding a sugar daddy is like winning the lottery. For most clubs, it's their only hope of competing with the aristocrats.

Some argue that the 'excessive' spending of sugar daddies drives smaller clubs into bankruptcy. In fact, if anything, the opposite is true. Sugar daddies buy players in the transfer market and then pay them very high wages. The usual argument is that this forces other clubs to pay their players higher salaries to stay. However, (a) this will only apply to a small number of players, and (b) no club can be forced to pay more than it can afford. Certainly, if clubs without a sugar daddy try to match the ambitions of the sugar daddies, that will end in tears, but then that must also be the case for clubs that try to compete with the aristocrats. Whether you want to be a Manchester United or an Abramovich-funded Chelsea, if you have no sugar daddy you will fail. The problem for small clubs is that they just don't have the resources to compete with the dominant clubs, and have not had them for half a century or more. This has very little to do with sugar daddies.

But sugar daddies are good for the football economy for one big reason: the cash they inject supports other clubs. In Sheikh Mansour's first five years of owning Manchester City, from 2008 to 2013, the club spent £505 million *net* on acquiring players. This money was pumped into a European market where top-division clubs in 2011 alone lost a cumulative €1.6 billion (then about £1.4 billion). Some of the sheikh's money ended up with agents, but by far the biggest chunk of transfer fees went to clubs. Deloitte calculates that the Premier League benefited from a total of £2 billion of additional finance coming from wealthy owners from 2006 to 2013. And, of course, the new transfer spending didn't all go to other Premier League clubs. Some of it went to clubs playing in lower divisions in England, or in leagues abroad. Some of that money was spent on players, and some on improving training facilities or building better stadiums.

We lament the seizing of so much of the world's wealth by a small number of billionaires but it has been good news for football. After someone becomes a billionaire, he tends to want to convert some of that money into excitement and prestige. Perhaps the best way to do that is by buying a football club. If Abramovich ever wanted to sell

Chelsea, sugar daddies would probably be lining up trying to buy it from him. Ehud Olmert, the former Israeli prime minister who has supported Manchester United since the Munich air crash of 1958, told us a story about the 'eastern investor' who sent him to visit the Glazer family with an offer to buy United. For the many people wanting to buy United, an early obstacle is the difficulty of actually meeting the Glazers. They don't get out much. But they are great friends of Israel, and were delighted to meet Olmert. At their country club in Palm Beach, he handed them a very large cheque to take over United. The Glazers said no straight away. 'This is the strongest brand name in the sports world,' they explained. Still, if they ever decide to sell, we think that a few of the 1,426 billionaires on *Forbes* magazine's list for 2013 might be interested.

To understand how sugar daddies help football, it's instructive to study the Glazers, because they are the opposite of sugar daddies. Most United fans blame them for sucking cash out of the club. The net cost of the Glazers to the club since their takeover in 2005 is probably somewhere over £500 million. So if sucking money out of clubs is a bad thing, then putting money into clubs is surely a good thing.

If FFP succeeds, sugar daddies might fade out of football. If that happens, there must be a real danger that investment in European clubs will dry up. If so, more clubs will probably go insolvent. In the nightmare scenario, the sugar daddies' money might be channelled into emerging leagues elsewhere (the US, China, the Gulf?). That could undermine Europe's dominance. It's hard to think of any other activity in which organisations actively seek to stop wealthy people from investing. Not many universities, art galleries, opera houses or aid agencies say no to sugar daddies.

HORROR OF HORRORS: MIGHT BIG FOOTBALL CLUBS BECOME PROFITABLE?

We've shown in the previous chapter that football clubs almost never make profits. However, in part because of FFP, that may soon change, at least for some of the biggest clubs. It's often said, in current jargon, that a profitable football club is 'sustainable'. We disagree. Fans shouldn't want their clubs to make profits.

Losses were always a fact of life in football, and as more money came into the game, the losses just kept growing. Every year, UEFA's 'club licensing benchmark report' summarises financial information for around 650 clubs playing in the top divisions of Europe's national leagues. Between the financial year 2008 and 2012 revenues grew by 15 per cent (pretty impressive in an economic crisis), yet the number of clubs declaring an operating loss rose from 54 per cent to 63 per cent.

Then something changed. Late in 2013, UEFA trailed some figures from its as yet unpublished report for the financial year 2012. The message: losses were down by 36 per cent. In January 2014 UEFA said that revenue growth was outpacing wage growth at European clubs for the first time since the association began collecting the numbers in 2006. Various factors probably contributed to this financial turnaround. FFP may already have been starting to curb clubs' spending. The jump in global broadcast income for Bundesliga and Premier League clubs presumably helped too. And with the widespread panic about clubs' losses, the Spanish government in particular had cracked down on clubs' spending.

All this may sound like good news. The opposite of a loss is a profit, so if losses are bad then profits must be good, right? But that takes us back to the Glazers: they make sure United makes a very large profit. Yet that profit represents money that the owners can then take out of the business. That's precisely why most United fans resent the Glazers. United's profits would have been more welcome had they been reinvested in buying players, or enlarging Old Trafford, or even funding a cut in ticket prices – but then of course they would have ceased to be profits.

We expect more owners of European clubs to follow the Glazers' lead. Six of the 20 Premier League clubs are now owned by Americans. These people come from a country where many sports franchises actually make money. Most of these people bought into soccer not because they love the game, but as a business proposition. They think European football has the power to capture foreign markets in a way that American sports don't. They see the ceaseless rise in the Premier League's broadcast income. They believe FFP will stop sugar daddies from driving up wages and transfer fees. No doubt egged on by the American owners, the Premier League has backed FFP, and is even considering introducing its own version of FFP in England. In the end, these profit-driven owners hope to take money out of football.

To imagine what that future might look like, think of Arsenal. Wenger, the club's manager, doesn't like spending money. His austerity won zero trophies from 2006 to 2013, but it probably pleased Arsenal's American majority owner, Stan Kroenke. From 2002 to early 2013, Arsenal's share price jumped nearly 1,200 per cent, while British shares in general rose just 60 per cent.

Arsenal hasn't been a great football club lately, but it has been a good business. This is what a football club run as a business looks like: high ticket prices, little desire to win trophies, and big profits. If FFP takes force, and other big clubs end up being run like Arsenal rather than like Abramovich's Chelsea, then we predict:

- ⚽ A fall in players' wages
- ⚽ A fall in transfer fees, which would mean less money trickling down from big clubs to the rest
- ⚽ A rise in club profits, which would mean more money being taken out of the game by people like the Glazers

If football becomes a hardnosed profit-making industry, fans may end up pining for the days when it was the worst business in the world.

NEED NOT APPLY: DOES ENGLISH FOOTBALL DISCRIMINATE AGAINST BLACK PEOPLE?

In 1991 Ron Noades, chairman of Crystal Palace, popped up on Channel Four talking about blacks.

'The problem with black players,' explained Noades, whose heavily black side had just finished third in the old first division, 'is they've great pace, great athletes, love to play with the ball in front of them ... When it's behind them it's chaos. I don't think too many of them can read the game. When you're getting into the mid-winter you need a few of the hard white men to carry the athletic black players through.'

Noades's interview was one of the last flourishes of unashamed, overt racism in British football. Through the 1980s racism had been more or less taken for granted in the game. Fans threw bananas at black players. Pundits such as Emlyn Hughes explained the curious absence of black players at Liverpool and Everton by saying, 'They haven't got the bottle.' The writer Dave Hill summed up the stereo-types:

'No bottle' is a particular favourite, lack of concentration another. 'You don't want too many of them in your defence,' one backroom bod told me, 'they cave in under pressure.' Then there is the curious conviction that blacks are susceptible to the cold and won't go out when it rains.

It's clear that English football in those days was shot through with racism: prejudice based on skin colour. But what we want to know is whether that racism translated into discrimination: unfair *treatment* of people. People like Noades may have been prejudiced against black players, but did they make it harder for these players to get jobs in football? The black striker Garth Crooks, who played in the 1980s, thought they did: 'I always felt I had to be 15 per cent better than the white person to get the same chance,' he said.

Yet the notion of discrimination against blacks clashes with something we think we know about football: that on the field at least, the game is ruthlessly fair. In football good players of whatever colour perform better than bad ones. Fans and chairmen and managers may walk around with Noadesesque fantasies in their heads, but when a black player plays well, everyone can see it. Nick Hornby writes in *Fever Pitch*, in his famous riff on Gus Caesar: 'One of the great things about sport is its cruel clarity; there is no such thing, for example, as a bad one-hundred-metre runner, or a hope-less centre-half who got lucky; in sport, you get found out. Nor is there such a thing as an unknown genius striker starving in a garret somewhere.'

In short, it would seem that in football there is no room for ideolo-gies. You have to be right, and results on the field will tell you very quickly if you are. So would clubs really discriminate against blacks at the cost of winning matches? After all, even Ron Noades employed black players. (He knew something about football too:

after leaving Palace he bought Brentford, appointed himself manager, won promotion and was voted manager of the year in Division Two.) In fact, the very success of blacks on the field might be taken as evidence that the opportunities were there.

It's also often hard to prove objectively that discrimination exists. How can you show that you failed to get the job because of prejudice, rather than just because you weren't good enough? Liverpool and Everton might argue that they employed white players in the 1980s simply because the whites were better.

Luckily, there is no need to get into a 'he said, she said' argument. We have data to prove that English football discriminated against black players. We can show when this particular kind of discrimination ended. And we can predict that the new forms of discrimination that pervade English football today will be harder to shift.

The first black person to set foot in the British Isles was probably a soldier in Julius Caesar's invading army, in 55 BC. The 'indigenous' English themselves only arrived about 400 years later, during the collapse of the Roman empire.

Much later, under Victoria, Britain's own empire ruled a large share of the world's black people. A few of the better educated or entrepreneurial ones made their way from the Raj, the Caribbean or Africa to Britain. Arthur Wharton, born in 1865 in the Gold Coast (now Ghana), became the world's first black professional footballer. As well as keeping goal for Preston, he set the world record of 10 seconds for the 100-yard sprint.

But until the 1950s most Britons had probably never seen a black person. Unlike Americans, they never developed any kind of relationship with blacks, whether positive or negative. Then, after the Second World War, hundreds of thousands of colonial immigrants began arriving. The influx was small enough – less than 5 per cent of Britain's total population, spread over a quarter of a century – to pose little threat to the concepts of Englishness, Scottishness or

Welshness. Nonetheless, the signs went up in the windows of bedsits: 'No Coloureds'.

One of the authors of this book, Stefan Szymanski, is the son of an immigrant from Poland who had escaped to London in 1940 and joined the British army to fight the Nazis. Stefan remembers his father telling him about looking for lodgings in London in the early 1950s, and finding signs in the windows saying 'Rooms to let – no Poles, no Hungarians'. Not only was this kind of discrimination legal, but Stefan's father accepted it. In his mind, he was the immigrant, and it was his job to fit in. Luckily for him (and for Stefan) he was an educated man, able to find a reasonable job and make a reasonable living. He was also a racist. This might sound harsh, but by today's standards most adults seemed to be racist in the 1970s, when Stefan was growing up. In the popular comedy series of the time, *Till Death Us Do Part*, the hero Alf Garnett was a ludicrously prejudiced East Ender who favoured labels like 'Coon', 'Nig-nog', 'Darky', 'Paki' and 'the Jews up at Spurs' (Garnett supported West Ham). Not only were these words used on the BBC, but they were accompanied by canned laughter.

Admittedly, the joke of the series was ultimately on Garnett, who was regularly exposed to the falsity of his own prejudices. But Stefan used to argue that these labels were offensive. His father took this as evidence of a lack of sense of humour.

It was against this 1970s background of instinctive racism that black players began arriving in English football. Most were children of immigrants, like Garth Crooks (born in Stoke), Chris Kamara (Middlesbrough) or Vince Hilaire (Forest Hill). That didn't stop them being treated to monkey noises and bananas. (As Hornby noted in *Fever Pitch*, 'There may well be attractive, articulate and elegant racists, but they certainly never come to football matches.') For a while, neo-Nazi parties even imagined that they could lead a revolution from the football terraces.

Given the abuse the early black players received, it would have been easy for them to give up on football. It was thinkable that they would be driven out of the game. Instead they stayed, played and triumphed. In 1978, when Viv Anderson became the first black player to be capped for England, it became apparent that children of Caribbean migrants might have something of a role to play in English football. Still, even after John Barnes scored his solo goal to beat Brazil at the Maracanã in 1984, the FA's chairman was harangued by England fans on the flight back home: 'You fucking wanker, you prefer sambos to us.'

As late as 1993 you could still witness the following scene: a crowd of people in a pub in the City of London is watching England–Holland on TV. Every time Barnes gets the ball, one man – in shirt-sleeves and a tie, just out of his City office – makes monkey noises. Every time, his workmates laugh. If anyone had complained, let alone gone off to find a policeman and asked him to arrest the man, the response would have been: 'Where's your sense of humour?' (Hornby's line on this sort of problem: 'I wish I were enormous and of a violent disposition, so that I could deal with any problem that arises near me in a fashion commensurate with the anger I feel.')

Whenever people reminisce about the good old days, when ordinary working people could afford to go to football matches, it's worth scanning the photographs of the cloth-capped masses standing on the terraces for the faces you *don't* see: blacks, Asians, women. It's true that today's all-seater grounds in the Premier League exclude poor people. However, the terraces before the 1990s probably excluded rather more varieties of people. In the 1970s and 1980s, when football grew scary, the violence forced out even many older white men.

In the late 1980s Stefan Szymanski began thinking about the economics of football. He was then working for the Centre for Business Strategy at London Business School. Everyone in the Centre was an economist, and therefore tempted to think that markets, more or less, 'worked'. The theory was that any business person who came up with a brilliant innovation – inventing the telephone, say –

would not keep his advantage for long, because others would imitate him and compete.

But the economists were interested in the few companies that stayed successful despite competition. Clearly there must be something to learn from them. Stefan suggested looking for these paragons in football. It was evidently a highly competitive industry, and yet some clubs succeeded in dominating for years on end. How did they manage to stay ahead for so long?

Stefan enlisted the support of Ron Smith, who had taught him when he was writing his PhD. Smith, as well as being an expert on Marxist economics and the economics of defence, is a well-known econometrician. Econometrics is essentially the art of finding statistical methods to extract information from data; or, as a lawyer friend of Stefan's likes to put it, taking the data down into the basement and torturing it until it confesses. Studying the accounts of football clubs, Stefan and Smith could see how much each club spent on salaries. The two discovered that this spending alone explained almost all the variation in positions in the English Football League. When Stefan analysed the accounts of 40 clubs for the period 1978–97, he found that their wage spending accounted for 92 per cent of the variation in their league positions.

Clearly the market in players' pay was highly efficient: the better a player was, the more he earned. And this made sense, because football is one of the few markets that indisputably meet the conditions in which competition can work efficiently: there are large numbers of buyers and sellers, all of whom have plenty of information about the quality of the players being bought and sold. If a player got paid less than he was worth, he could move to another club. If he got paid more, he would soon find himself being sold off again.

But what about the variation in league position that remained unexplained after adjusting for players' pay? If buying talent was generally enough to win titles – as Jack Walker at Blackburn Rovers and Abramovich at Chelsea would soon demonstrate – what else accounted for a team's success? If it was something that was easy to copy – a new tactic, for instance – then other teams would copy it, and the advantage would disappear. That got Stefan thinking about discrimination. What if owners were simply not willing to copy the secret of others' success, because they didn't want to hire the kinds of players that brought that success? He began to search for discrimination against black players.

In most industries, there is a way to demonstrate that discrimination exists. Suppose you could construct a sample of all applicants for a job, and also of all their relevant qualifications. If you then found that a much larger proportion of relevantly qualified white applicants received job offers than relevantly qualified black applicants, you could reasonably infer the presence of discrimination. For example, if 50 per cent of white applicants with a first-class honours degree in philosophy got job offers from university philosophy departments, but only 10 per cent of equally high-achieving black applicants did, then you should suspect discrimination.

This is essentially how economists have tried to identify job discrimination. The method also works for wage discrimination. If equivalently qualified blacks (or women, or left-handers, or whoever) get lower wages for equivalent jobs, then there is probably discrimination going on. Researchers have put together databases of thousands of workers, each identified by dozens of relevant qualifications, to test whether discrimination exists. When it comes to ethnic minorities and women, the evidence usually shows that it does.

The problem is that there are few measurable qualifications that make someone a great footballer. When a company is accused of racism, it often says that while the black (or purple, or female) candidates may possess some of the relevant characteristics, there are other, less quantifiable characteristics that they don't have. Intellectually this point is hard to overturn. Hundreds of cases of racial discrimination have been fought out in American courts, and evidence based on the kinds of studies we have mentioned has often run into trouble.

Happily, there is another way to test for discrimination in football. Once again, it relies on evidence from the market. As a general rule, the best way to find out what people are up to is to see how they behave when faced with a price. Don't know if you prefer Coke to Pepsi? Well, let's see what you choose when they both cost the same. (Most people choose Coke.) Don't know if you prefer watching the FA Cup or the league? Let's see what you do when tickets cost the same. Do managers prefer white players to blacks? Well, let's see how they spend their club's money.

If clubs discriminate, then they will prefer to hire a white player to an equivalently talented black player. If they do that, then blacks will find it harder to get jobs as professional footballers. The blacks will then be willing to accept lower wages than equivalently talented whites. After all, when demand for what we sell is lower, we tend to lower our asking price. So black players become cheaper than white players.

If black players are being discriminated against, that creates an economic opportunity for unprejudiced clubs. By hiring black players they can do just as well in the league as an equivalently talented (but more expensive) team of whites.

That means that a simple experiment will reveal whether discrimination exists: *If teams with more black players achieve higher average league positions for a given sum of wage spending, then the teams with fewer black players must have been discriminating.*

Otherwise, the 'whiter' teams would have seen that black players were good value for money, and would have tried to hire them. Then black players' wages would have risen due to increased competition for their services, and the relative advantage of hiring black players would have disappeared.

Note that the argument is not that some teams hire more black players than others. That could happen for many reasons. Rather, we can infer discrimination if (a) some teams have more black players than others and (b) those same teams outperform their competitors for a given level of wage spending.

After Stefan figured this out, he had the luck of running into just the right person. Around that time, he was also researching the relationship between the pay of senior executives in FTSE 100 companies and the performance of their companies. (Very unlike footballers' wages, there turned out to be almost no correlation between the pay of senior executives and the performance of a company's share price, until share options became common in the 1990s.) Stefan was interviewed for the BBC *Panorama* programme by the political journalist Michael Crick. Over time he and Crick got talking about football.

Crick is a famously thorough researcher. Book reviewers delight in finding errors, no matter how trivial, but they never succeed with Crick's political biographies. And as it happens, Crick supports Manchester United. In 1989 he wrote a fascinating history of the club with David Smith, describing how United packaged their legend for commercial gain. About this time Crick became interested in whether football clubs discriminated in their hiring. Everyone knew of the suspicious cases of the day, chiefly Liverpool and Everton.

Crick began collecting data from the 1970s onwards to see which clubs had hired black players. This was no easy task. How do you decide who is 'black'? Crick took a commonsense approach. He started with the old Rothmans Football Yearbooks, which published a photograph of every league team. From this he made a judgement as to which players 'looked black'. He then followed up by asking clubs and supporters' clubs to fill any gaps. It took him months to come up with a list of players who, to most fans, would have appeared to be black. This sounds arbitrary, but it is precisely what was required. Prejudice is based on appearances. For example, several years after Crick did his research, it emerged that Ryan Giggs's father was black. Giggs even spoke publicly about his pride in his African ancestry. However, until that point, most people would not have considered Giggs a black player. He didn't *look* black, and for that reason he would have been unlikely to face discrimination. So Crick was right not to count Giggs as black.

When Crick told Stefan about his list of black players, it was a cinch to create a test for discrimination. All that was necessary was to count how many times each black player had played for his club in a given season. It would then be clear which teams hired a larger share of black players.

Stefan then matched this data with figures on each team's league position, and its spending on wages. If there were no discrimination in the market, then wages alone would almost entirely explain league performance. Everything else would just be random noise – 'luck'. But if black players were systematically being paid less than equally talented white players, then logically the teams which hired an above average proportion of black players would do systematically better than their wage bill alone would predict.

Back in the 1970s, there were very few black players in English football. Combining our data on wages with Crick's database had given us a sample of 39 out of the 92 professional league teams. In the 1973–74 season only two of these clubs had fielded any black players at all. By 1983–84, there were still 20 teams in our sample that did not a field a black player all season. However, at this point there seems to have been a major breakthrough. By 1989 every team in the sample had fielded at least one black player at some point during these years. By 1992, when the Premier League was founded, only five teams in the sample did not field a black player that season. This implied that about 90 per cent of clubs were putting blacks in the first team. Attitudes were changing. Bananas left the game. When Noades voiced his theories on black players in 1991, he was widely mocked.

It is interesting to look at the characteristics of the black players in the English game in these years. For purposes of comparison, Stefan constructed a random sample of an equal number of white players with similar age profiles. Almost all the black players (89 per cent) were born in Britain, not very different from the white players (95 per cent). However, the blacks were more likely to have been born in the South (46 per cent compared with only 26 per cent of white players) than the North (22 per cent of blacks, compared with 54 per cent of whites). Most of the black players were strikers (58 per cent) compared with only 33 per cent of white players. There were no black goalkeepers at the time. Noades would have noted the fact that black players seemed under-represented in defence. But then strikers always carry a premium in relation to defenders in the market: it takes more talent to score than to stop other people from scoring.

Certain facts about the sample stood out: the careers of the black players averaged more than six years, compared with less than four for the whites. And 36 per cent of the blacks had represented their country, compared with only 23 per cent of the whites. On this evidence, it looked suspiciously as if the black players were better than the whites.

The proof came when Stefan deployed the economist's favourite tool, the regression analysis. He used it to isolate the distinct effects of wages and the share of black players on each club's league performance. What he found was discrimination. The data showed that clubs with more black players really did have a better record in the league than clubs with fewer blacks, after allowing for wage spending. If two teams had identical annual wage budgets, the team with more blacks would finish higher in the league.

The test implied that black players were systematically better value for money than whites. Certain teams of the 1980s such as Arsenal, Noades's Palace and Ron Atkinson's West Bromwich Albion (this was years before Atkinson called Marcel Desailly 'a fucking lazy thick nigger' on air) benefited from fielding blacks.

The clubs with fewer blacks were not suffering from a lack of information. Anyone who knew football could judge fairly easily how good most players were just by watching them play. So the only credible reason why clubs would deny themselves the opportunity to hire these players was prejudice. Clubs didn't like the look of black players, or they thought their fans wouldn't, either simply because of skin hue, or because they perceived weaknesses that were just not there. By testing the behaviour of managers against the market, it proved possible to uncover evidence of discrimination.

In football, you can judge someone's performance only against other competitors. This means that I lose nothing by being inefficient if my competitors are inefficient in the same way as me. I can go on hiring mediocre players as long as other clubs do so too. As long as all clubs refused to hire talented black players, the cost of discriminating was low. What the data showed was that by the beginning of the 1980s, so many teams were hiring talented blacks that the cost of discriminating had become quite high. Teams that refused to field black players were overpaying for white players and losing more matches as a consequence. Yet some level of discrimination persisted. Even by the end of the 1980s, an all-white team such as Everton would cost around 5 per cent more than an equally good team that fielded merely an average proportion of black players. As Dave Hill wrote in the fanzine *When Saturday Comes* in 1989: 'Half a century after Jesse Owens, a quarter of a century after Martin Luther King, and 21 years after two American sprinters gave the Black Power salute from the Olympic medal rostrum, some of these dickheads don't even know what a black person is.'

But by the time he wrote that, precisely because football is so competitive, more and more clubs had begun to hire black players. In 1995 even Everton signed the Nigerian Daniel Amokachi. The economic forces of competition drove white men to ditch their prejudices.

Quite soon, so many clubs were hiring blacks that black players came to be statistically over-represented in football. Only about 1.6 per cent of people in the British census of 1991 described themselves as black. Yet in the early 1990s, about 10 per cent of all players in the Football League were black. By the end of the decade, after the influx of foreign players, the share was nearer 20 per cent.

So did clubs learn to overcome their prejudices? A few years after Stefan ran his first test for discrimination, he badgered some students who were looking for undergraduate projects into compiling a list of black players for another six seasons. That took the dataset up to the 1998–99 season. Once again Stefan merged the data with figures on wages and league performances. Now he could run the regression to the end of the 1990s. For these six additional years, there was no evidence that the share of black players in a team had any effect on team performance, after allowing for the team's wage bill. In other words, by then, black players were on average paid what they were worth – judged, at least, by their contribution to winning football matches.

Perhaps the best witness to the acceptance of blacks in football is Lilian Thuram. A black man born on the Caribbean island of Guadeloupe, and raised in a small town outside Paris, he played professionally from 1991 to 2008 and became France's most capped player. Thuram is also a French intellectual, possibly the only footballer ever to have spoken the words, 'There's an interesting young ethnographer at the Musée de l'Homme ...'

He is acutely sensitive to racism. He now runs an anti-racism foundation. Nonetheless, he feels football is innocent of the sin. Over late-night pasta in an Italian restaurant in Barcelona, he told us: 'In football it's harder to have discrimination, because we are judged on very specific performances. There are not really subjective criteria. Sincerely, I've never met a racist person in football. Maybe they were there, but I didn't see it.'

In fact, he adds: 'In sport, prejudices favour the blacks. In the popular imagination, the black is in his place in sport. For example, recently in Barcelona, the fitness coach said about Abidal [a black French defender]: "He's an athlete of the black race." It's not because he stays behind after training to run. No, it's because he's black.'

So by the 1990s discrimination against black players had disappeared. Gradually they came to feel at home in the industry. Here is a scene from inside the marble halls of Highbury, after a game in 1995: Arsenal's black Dutch winger Glenn Helder is introducing his black teammate Ian Wright (one of Ron Noades's ex-players) to some Dutch people. Then Helder says, 'Ian, show these guys what I taught you.' A look of intense concentration appears on Wright's face, and he begins jumping up and down and shouting in Dutch: 'Buzz off! Dirty ape! Dirty ape!' He and Helder then collapse laughing. There was still racism in football, but by then blacks could mock it from the inner sanctums of the game's Establishment.

The story of racism in American sports followed much the same arc. Right through the Second World War, baseball and basketball had segregated blacks into 'negro leagues'. In 1947 Branch Rickey of the Brooklyn Dodgers broke an unwritten rule among baseball owners and hired the black infielder Jackie Robinson to play for his team. Robinson eventually became an American hero. However, the co-star of his story was economics. The Dodgers had less money than their crosstown neighbours the New York Yankees. If Rickey wanted a winning team, he had to tap talent that the other owners overlooked. Racism provided him with an opportunity.

Of course, discrimination against black players persisted in American sports long after Robinson. Lawrence Kahn, an economist at Cornell University, surveyed the data and found little evidence that before the 1990s baseball teams were withholding jobs or pay from blacks. But he did think they were giving black players unduly short careers, and only using them in certain positions. In basketball, Kahn did find wage discrimination. When he repeated his study in 2000, he discovered, like Stefan the second time around, that discrimination was fading. British and American sports were becoming fair to black athletes.

We suspect that discrimination still exists in some other football leagues. In Russia in 2012, for instance, fans from Zenit St Petersburg's largest supporters' group, Landscrona, wrote to their club demanding that black and gay players be excluded from the team. They said that black players were 'forced down Zenit's throat', while gay players were 'unworthy of our great city'. These views are pretty common in Russian football, and in eastern Europe more generally.

In that kind of atmosphere, a club brave enough not to practise racial discrimination can still expect to pick up good players cheaply.

We had thought that in western Europe at least, this kind of discrimination had died out. But there is a strange postscript to our story. In April 2011, long after we had thought discrimination against black players had disappeared, the French website Mediapart leaked the minutes of a secret meeting at the French football federation. The meeting – held in November 2010 – had begun fairly innocuously. At first the officials had mused about admitting fewer youngsters of dual nationality (often French plus African) into the federation's academies. It bothered the officials that some of these youngsters were eventually choosing to play for Algeria (say) rather than France. However, the discussion quickly spread to scarier territory: complaints about black players per se.

France's coach Laurent 'Le Président' Blanc (a French hero who had played alongside Thuram in the black-white-Arab French team of '98) was quoted as telling the meeting: 'You have the feeling that we are producing really only one prototype of player: big, strong, fast ... and who are the big, strong, fast players? The blacks. That's the way it is. That's the way things are today.'

According to the leaked minutes, Blanc continued: 'I think we need to refocus, above all for boys of 13 to 14, 12 to 13 – introduce other parameters, adjusted to our own culture ... the Spanish say to me: "We don't have this problem. We don't have any blacks."' Blanc did add that he was talking about football qualities, not colour. He wouldn't mind if the whole French team was black, he said, as long as there was a balance of size and skill.

Even so, it's difficult to know where to start with a critique of his position. Most obviously, Blanc seemed to be conflating the dull uncreative physical French style of recent years with the presence of black players. Second, the issue of dual nationality scarcely mattered: a player of African origin good enough to play for France, like the Senegalese-born Patrick Vieira, will choose France. It's generally only French-raised players rejected by France who will represent another country.

Yet some inside the French federation seemed to want to let fewer boys of African origin into the academies. Blocking the pipeline to professional football would mean job discrimination against blacks. It would be a return to the practices of the English game of the 1980s. Nobody – we had previously thought – was barred from top-class football in western Europe anymore because of his skin colour. Whereas ordinary Arabs and blacks in France struggled to find jobs, we had imagined that Arab and black footballers in France did not.

But even before the federation's secret meeting, that had started to change. Earlier in 2010, France's then coach Raymond Domenech had omitted three gifted young men of north African origin from his squad for the world cup: Samir Nasri, Karim Benzema and Hatem Ben Arfa. (The squad that Domenech did take to South Africa returned home in disgrace after a players' revolt, a strike and one point from three games.) We are sure that Domenech made his choices without any racist intention. There were footballing arguments against each of the young trio. Nevertheless, says the French sociologist Stéphane Beaud, author of *Traitres de la Nation?* (*Traitors of the Nation?*), a book on *les Bleus* and ethnicity, Domenech seemed unable to deal with a new more assertive generation of north African youth.

When Mediapart leaked the minutes of the federation's meeting, Thuram promptly broke the social code of football to attack his old teammate Blanc. Three years earlier, Thuram had told us that discrimination in football was impossible. Now he argued that Blanc had been guilty at least of 'unconscious racism' and promoting 'racial stereotypes'. If you say that blacks are stronger and faster than whites, Thuram argued, you open the door to then saying that whites are more intelligent than blacks. Vieira, another hero of 1998, complained too. 'I know Laurent Blanc and I don't think he is racist,' he said. 'But I don't understand how any of the officials present at that meeting can stay in their job.'

In the end, Blanc and the others did stay in their jobs, cleared by a government inquiry, to the joy of most French fans. Many supporters had been complaining for years about the number of blacks in *les Bleus*.

The secret meeting, and the scandal that followed it, had changed nothing. Even the black players stayed in the team. They were the best, and that is still (almost always) what matters in football.

DO MANAGERS MATTER? THE CULT OF THE WHITE MESSIAH

Trevor Phillips points a finger at his own shaven black head: 'Excuse me, here I am: bullseye!' The son of an early Caribbean immigrant to Britain, Phillips was raised in London and has supported Chelsea for over 50 years. But in the 1970s, when throwing darts was the favourite sport of the Shed End, he didn't go to matches. His head felt like an obvious target. Hardly any black people went to Chelsea then. 'Now I can take my daughters,' he marvels.

Yet the longtime head of the Equality and Human Rights Commission (he held the post until 2012) doesn't think football has slain discrimination yet. Over breakfast in Norwich one snowy morning a few years ago, he identified an enduring type of discrimination in British football: 'Loads of black players on the field and none in the dugout.'

You might think this form of discrimination would eventually disappear, that just as competition pushed clubs into buying black players, it will push them into hiring black managers. In fact, the prejudice against black managers has proved harder to shift. As soon as you get to thinking about what it will take to get more black people into coaching jobs, you are brought face to face with the great question about the football manager: does he really matter? It turns out that managers or coaches (call them what you like) simply don't make that much difference. Consequently, the market in football managers is much less efficient than the market in footballers. That means blacks will continue to have a hard time finding coaching jobs.

Like discrimination against black players, discrimination against black managers first became visible in American sports. As early as 1969 Jackie Robinson, who had become quite rebellious as he grew older, refused to attend Old Timers' Day at Yankee Stadium, in protest against baseball's shunning of black coaches and managers.

The issue hit Britain only when the first generation of black players began to retire (it being a longstanding article of faith in football that only ex-players had what it took to become managers). The former England international Luther Blissett, who as a player had made that ill-fated transfer to Milan, applied for 22 manager jobs in the 1990s. He did not get a single interview. Stella Orakwue, who recounts his story in her 1998 book, *Pitch Invaders*, concludes, 'I feel a British black managing a Premiership team could be a very long way off.' Indeed, it was not until 2008, ten years after she wrote this, that Blackburn gave Paul Ince a chance. After Ince's appointment, John Barnes, who himself had struggled to get work as a manager, still maintained, 'I believe the situation for black managers is like it was for black players back in the 1970s.' Ince lasted less than six months at Blackburn. He hasn't had a chance in the Premier League since.

Not even good results with Newcastle could save the black manager Chris Hughton in 2010: he had won the club promotion to the Premier League the season before, but four months into the new season, with Newcastle safely in 11th place in the top division, he was sacked. 'Regrettably the board now feels that an individual with more managerial experience is needed to take the club forward,' the club explained. Newcastle finished the season in 12th place.

True, the black managers Ruud Gullit and Jean Tigana did get longer stints in the Premier League. But as Orakwue notes, the crucial point is that they were foreigners. They were perceived in Britain first of all as Dutch or French, and only secondarily as black. Gullit was cast as a typical sophisticated Dutch manager, not as an untried 'black' one.

At the time of writing, in early 2014, Hughton at Norwich is the only black manager in the Premier League. The 'Rooney Rule' in the NFL of American football – which requires teams to interview at least one minority candidate when recruiting a head coach or other senior officials – has no equivalent in European soccer. That's a shame, as the rule has made quite a difference in the NFL.

You would think that, given this discrimination, unprejudiced football clubs could clean up by hiring the best black (or female) managers at low salaries. A small club like Tranmere Rovers, say, could probably take its pick of the world's black managers. It could get the best female manager in history. Yet it probably won't. That's because the market in football managers is so different from the market in players. Markets tend to work when they are transparent – when you can see who is doing what and place a value on it. That is pre-eminently true of footballers, who do their work in public. When you can't see what people do, it's very hard to assign a value to their work. Efficient markets punish discrimination in plain view of everyone, and so discrimination tends to get rooted out. Inefficient markets can maintain discrimination almost indefinitely.

Black footballers became accepted because the market in players is transparent. It is pretty obvious who can play and who can't, who's 'got bottle' and who hasn't. The market in players' salaries, as we have seen, is so efficient that it explains about 90 per cent of the variation in clubs' league positions in the long run. Typically, the club with the best-paid players finishes top, and the one with the worst-paid finishes bottom. However, the market in managers doesn't work nearly as well. If players' salaries determine results almost by themselves, then it follows that the vast majority of managers are not very relevant.

Still, there is an important caveat: players' wages don't explain everything – merely almost everything at most clubs. That leaves some room for a few good managers to make a difference. The question then is: which elite managers finish consistently higher with their teams than their wage bills would predict? In other words, to borrow a phrase from José Mourinho: who are the special ones? For the new edition of this book, Stefan has tried to answer that question.

First, he got hold of the financial accounts of English clubs in all four divisions from 1973–74 up to 2009–10. This is not as hard as it sounds. All clubs except one were limited companies during this period, and therefore obliged by law to file annual accounts with Companies House. You can obtain copies online for a small fee (if you want to buy your club's accounts for last year, it will cost you all of £1). Going back 37 years is a bit more complicated. Five per cent of accounts were missing, while 15 per cent of clubs had filed abbreviated accounts that didn't reveal wage spending. That left Stefan with wage data for 80 per cent of clubs for the 37-year period.

Stefan began by identifying all managers who had been with a club for at least a full season. There were 699 of them in the database. However, it's unfair to judge a manager on just a couple of seasons, because in such a short period, luck plays a big role. So Stefan only ranked managers who had worked in the game for five or more full seasons: 251 men. It must be said that few of the other 448 managers, the ones who worked fewer than five seasons, looked like overachievers. Indeed, most of them had drifted out of the game early because of their poor records. Some of the worst performers exited the profession fastest.

Stefan then examined how our 251 survivors had performed relative to their players' wage bills. The telling stat is the size of a club's wages relative to those of its rivals. There are 20 clubs in the

Premier League, which means that the average club spends five per cent of the league's total wages. If a club spending five per cent finished in the top half of the table, the manager appeared to have been overachieving. If it finished in the bottom half, he appeared to be underachieving. One season of overachievement doesn't make a star. That could be due to any number of things, above all luck. What counted was the manager's record measured over five years or more.

Only a very few of these 251 managers were *underachievers*: men who consistently finished lower with their teams than the players' wage bill would have predicted. Malcolm Allison (a fêted assistant manager with Manchester City in the late 1960s, but a failure as a go-it-alone manager afterwards) made our list of shame, as did Alan Mullery, Harry Gregg and a few lesser-known names whom it would be kindest not to mention. However, even this handful of failures didn't seem to be terrible managers. Their underachievement was not what statisticians call 'statistically significant'. In plain English: it could simply have been due to chance.

Stefan didn't treat all divisions equally. A manager in League Two who has the 90th highest budget in England but manages to finish 80th in the country is doing well. However, a manager with the third highest budget in England who wins the Premier League is probably doing even better. At the top of football, competition is fiercer, the amount of money typically required to jump a place is much higher, and so Stefan's model gave more credit to overachieving managers in the Premier League than to overachievers lower down. Still, his model does allow some lower-division managers to make it to the top of our rankings.

All in all, he estimated that somewhere between 40 and 70 of the managers in our sample made a positive difference: that is, they usually overachieved with their teams. That group, it's worth noting, is at most 28 per cent of the 251 survivors in our database – and these survivors would themselves tend to be the elite, because underachieving managers rarely survive five years in the game. In other words, at best one-tenth of the 699 managers we have observed since 1973 look like overachievers. These managers tend to have stayed in their posts relatively long, which makes sense.

We ended up with two lists of overachievers. For our first list, we put all English clubs together, and ranked each club's wage spending relative to the other 91. The second list separated the clubs into four divisions, and measured each club's spending relative to the other clubs in its division. We mention this, because each method produced a slightly different list of overachieving managers. Here are our two lists:

OVERACHIEVING MANAGERS IN ENGLAND, 1974–2010

	'Total wage' method		'Divisional wage' method
Rank	Manager	Rank	Manager
1	Bob Paisley	1	Bob Paisley
2	Alex Ferguson	2	Bobby Robson
3	Kenny Dalglish	3	Alex Ferguson
4	Arsène Wenger	4	Arsène Wenger
5	Rafael Benítez	5	David Moyes
6	Bobby Robson	6	Kenny Dalglish
7	Gérard Houllier	7	John Beck
8	Steve Parkin	8	Dave Mackay
9	Dave Mackay	9	Howard Kendall
10	Roy Evans	10	Steve Tilson
11	Howard Kendall	11	Rafael Benítez
12	Steve Tilson	12	Ronnie Moore
13	George Graham	13	Lou Macari
14	Martin Allen	14	Paul Sturrock
15	Martin Ling	15	Steve Coppell
16	Paul Simpson	16	George Graham
17	Ronnie Moore	17	Martin Allen
18	David Hodgson	18	Ray Mathias
19	Steve Wignal	19	Dave Stringer
20	Ian Atkins	20	Sam Allardyce

21	John Beck	21	Martin O'Neill
22	Sean O'Driscoll	22	Mel Machin
23	Leroy Rosenior	23	Jimmy Sirrel
24	Brian Clough	24	Keith Peacock
25	David Moyes	25	Tony Pulis
26	Russell Slade	26	Dave Smith
27	Steve Cotterill	27	Jack Charlton
28	Gary Peters	28	Paul Simpson
29	Micky Adams	29	Bobby Gould
30	Brian Laws	30	Gary Megson
31	Kevin Keegan	31	Terry Venables
32	Ron Atkinson	32	Danny Wilson
33	Dave Stringer	33	David O'Leary
34	David O'Leary	34	Trevor Francis
35	Paul Sturrock	35	Joe Kinnear
36	Keith Alexander	36	Graham Taylor
37	Gary Johnson	37	John Neal
38	Terry Neill	38	Steve Parkin
39	Barry Fry	39	Mike Buxton
40	Roy McFarland	40	Dave Bassett

It should be noted that Brian Clough, who appears on one of our lists, would undoubtedly have ranked somewhere in the top on both if only we had had financial data for his glory years with Nottingham Forest in the 1970s. But uniquely within the (then) Football League, Forest was not a limited company at the time. It was a members' club, and therefore didn't lodge annual accounts at Companies House. Our list shows that even in his declining alcoholic years from 1982 onwards, Clough was among the elite.

Here's our final ranking of managers who made both lists:

THE SPECIAL ONES

Manager	Rank 'Divisional wage' method	Rank 'Total wage' method
Bob Paisley	1	1
Alex Ferguson	3	2
Bobby Robson	2	6
Arsène Wenger	4	4
Kenny Dalglish	6	3
Rafael Benítez	11	5
Dave Mackay	8	9
Howard Kendall	9	11
Steve Tilson	10	12
John Beck	7	21
Ronnie Moore	12	17
George Graham	16	13
David Moyes	5	25
Martin Allen	17	14
Paul Simpson	28	16
Steve Parkin	38	8
Paul Sturrock	14	35
Dave Stringer	19	33
David O'Leary	33	34

This list of 19 names must stand as our best stab at identifying the best managers in England in these years. Paisley is an impressive number one, with his six league titles and three European Cups with Liverpool from 1974 to 1983. Admittedly, though, he inherited Liverpool's dynasty from Bill Shankly, whereas Ferguson created United's.

There are all sorts of other caveats to attach. First, our valuations are by no means precise. Wenger ranks a touch higher than Dalglish in our table, but please don't read that as saying that Wenger is the better manager. Our list cannot be that exact. The two men worked at different clubs at different times, and so they had different experiences. Many other factors besides the manager might have caused each club's overachievement. It's notable that Paisley and Benítez also overachieved with Liverpool relative to wages, and George Graham with Arsenal. Perhaps it was easier to overachieve at Arsenal and Liverpool than at other clubs because these two produced many excellent youth players, allowing managers to do well without spending fortunes on wages. Perhaps Liverpool's 'boot room' of the 1970s and 1980s – the gang of old-time coaches and scouts who would sit around drinking whisky and scheming for games together – gave Paisley and Dalglish the wisdom of crowds. Quite likely Paisley, Dalglish, Wenger and Graham landed in helpful settings. Yet they do seem to have been good managers, too.

There's another caveat to add. Our table measures only spending on wages, not on transfers. We saw in chapter 2 that Wenger and Ferguson had relatively low net spending on transfers, which makes their high rankings in our list even more impressive. But we also saw that Benítez (likewise high on our list) blew fortunes on transfers at Liverpool. So even though he economised on wages, he didn't get his league positions cheaply.

In fact, every manager in this table requires closer analysis. Just as you cannot sign a player simply on the basis of his match data, you cannot simply hire a manager from our list and sit back and wait for the trophies to roll in (although it would certainly be a much better method than hiring a guy because he was a good player). Some managers on our list succeeded in circumstances that might not be repeatable elsewhere. For instance, we suspect Bobby Robson did so well for Ipswich in the 1970s because he was one of the few managers of the time to strive for passing football and to scout on the continent. Today he'd have had to find new tricks.

Critics will ask why such a high proportion of our highest-ranked managers work for giant clubs. Well, for a start, the best managers tend to end up at the best clubs. Arsenal hired Wenger after he'd excelled at Monaco; Manchester United signed Ferguson after he'd broken the Old Firm's duopoly with Aberdeen in Scotland. In fact, Ferguson might have ranked even higher in our table had we been able to include his Aberdeen years. Unfortunately, we had to omit Scottish clubs because the financial data wasn't detailed enough.

A second reason why managers of giant clubs dominate our list: by definition, more overachieving clubs will end up at the top of the league than at the bottom. And thirdly, as we've said, the top of football is more competitive than the bottom, and so we have given extra credit to managers who overachieve at the summit.

Some may wonder whether a manager of Manchester United and Arsenal can overachieve by much. After all, United have the highest revenues in English football, and Arsenal aren't far behind. Surely clubs that rich *ought* to be winning league titles? (Indeed, we must admit that we used to think so ourselves. Simon now blushes with shame to think that he once wrote that if he managed United, with all their money, he would probably do about as well as Ferguson did.)

Certainly, even if United's squad were to operate as an anarchist workers' collective without a manager, it would probably do very well. But Ferguson and Wenger do seem to have added value to their respective clubs. Once you look at the numbers, it turns out that for many years Ferguson's United and Wenger's Arsenal spent little or no more on wages than did some of their frustrated rivals. Both clubs habitually live within their means. Manchester United almost always makes operating profits, used to pay dividends to share-holders, and now forks out large sums each year to repay the debts of its owners, the Glazer family. That didn't leave Ferguson fortunes to spend on players' wages. He didn't seem to need it.

We've seen that the average club in the Premier League spends 5 per cent of the division's total wage bill. Of course Manchester United are always above that 5 per cent line, but especially in the 1990s they weren't above it by very much. In 1995–96, for instance, the club spent just 5.8 per cent of the Premier League's total wages yet won the title. From 1991 to 2000, United's average league position was 1.8 (i.e. somewhere between first and second spot) and yet in that decade the club spent only 6.8 per cent of the Premier League's average on wages. Ferguson was getting immense bang for his buck. In part, he owed this to the Beckham generation. Beckham, the Neville brothers, Paul Scholes, Nicky Butt and Ryan Giggs were excellent players, who were performing with great maturity, but given their youth they would have been earning less than established stars. Furthermore, because Ferguson was at Old Trafford from 1986 until 2013, by the 1990s he had chosen every player at the club himself. He wasn't paying the unwanted signings of his predecessors huge sums to rot in the stands. That helped keep United's wages down.

Ferguson continued to overachieve in the 2000s, even after the Beckham generation had become big names earning top whack. Admittedly his overperformance was less striking than in the 1990s. From 2001 to 2010 United's average league position was again 1.8, but in this decade he spent nearly 9 per cent of the Premier League's total on wages. To put it another way: in the 1990s he spent only 35 per cent more than the division's average, whereas in the 2000s he spent 80 per cent more than the average to achieve the same result. No wonder, because life had become ever more competitive at the top, with Chelsea and Manchester City getting shots of oil money and Arsenal and Liverpool receiving ever more income from the Champions League. None of that had happened in the 1990s.

The amount of money Ferguson required to dominate seemed to keep rising. In 2010, the last year in our database, United's share of the Premier League's wage spending peaked at just over 10 per cent. Yet even that wasn't outsize. Manchester City that year spent about the same proportion, and Chelsea accounted for 14 per cent of the Premier League's total outlay on wages from 2004 to 2010. That's the largest share for any top-division club in the 37 years of our database. Other clubs, too, have exceeded 10 per cent of the division's total spending in the past, notably Leeds United, who were at nearly 12 per cent when Clough spent his infamous 44 days there in 1974. In short, Ferguson was a phenomenon for most of his time at Old Trafford. From 2003 to 2013 he consistently had to compete against clubs with higher wages. Mostly, he won. Even so, it's hard to work out exactly what he was doing right.

Wenger's record is almost as awesome. In his first seven seasons at Arsenal, from 1996–97 onwards, the Frenchman achieved an average league position of 1.6 while accounting for 7.5 per cent of the Premier League's wages. That was a bigger share than Ferguson was spending then, but hardly plutocratic. Admittedly Wenger's performance has declined in recent years. In the six seasons to 2009–10, Arsenal had an average league position of 3.3 while spending 8.8 per cent of the Premier League's wages. That's still overachievement, but less striking than before.

We can explain why he might have declined. When Wenger arrived in insular England in 1996, there were still knowledge gaps to exploit. He brought knowledge that nobody else in the country possessed at that point. He was one of the few managers already using statistics to analyse players' performance; he knew what food footballers should eat; and, above all, he knew foreign transfer markets. He seems to have been the only manager in England to realise that Milan's reserve Patrick Vieira and Juventus's reserve Thierry Henry were great players. Spotting that didn't require mystical insight – Vieira convinced the Highbury crowd of the same fact inside 45 minutes on his debut against Sheffield Wednesday – but none of Wenger's British rivals appeared to have even watched Vieira before. And so Wenger overachieved magnificently.

His problem was that he was too successful for his own good. Other managers began to study what he was doing. They copied his innovations in diet, scouting and statistics. Meanwhile, like many brilliant pioneers, Wenger seems to have fallen into the trap of becoming too sure of himself – less willing to learn new tricks or listen to intelligent criticism – as he got older.

Eventually, when everyone had more or less the same knowledge, Arsenal were overtaken by clubs with bigger wage bills. That is what happens to knowledge gaps inside a league: they close fast. This would explain why Wenger's team won nothing from 2006 to 2013.

Yet during his worst moments, especially after the 8–2 thumping at Old Trafford in August 2011, his critics were much too harsh on him. Given that he was up against several richer clubs, and against another great overachieving manager in Ferguson, it would have been astonishing had Arsenal continued to win titles. It was particularly unfair to castigate Wenger for fielding teams that kept getting out-muscled by Chelsea. There is a common belief that Wenger actively doesn't want players who are both brilliant and strong, such as Didier Drogba, Cristiano Ronaldo and Vieira himself. In fact he built his first Arsenal team around Vieira, and privately regrets that he never managed to sign Drogba and Ronaldo when he could afford them. It's just that he knows that nowadays Arsenal cannot afford players who have it all. The club has to economise on one quality or another; and, forced to choose, Wenger has tended to prefer players who are gifted and fast to those who are strong. Chelsea haven't had to make that choice.

Arsenal's board cannot very well tell the fans, 'Forget it. We probably can't compete with United, Chelsea and City over a whole season.' But the board knows that this is true. It doesn't expect Wenger to win titles any more. That's why, even in the darkest moments of 2011, it never even considered sacking him.

As we've seen, since Abramovich took over Chelsea in 2003 he has thrown money at the problem. In the 1970s Chelsea were still spending a touch less than the average in the top division. Only from the mid-1990s did the club's spending start to rise, and at the end of the 1990s it hit 8 per cent of the Premier League's total. By about 2000 Chelsea's manager Gianluca Vialli was spending more than 10 per cent of the Premier League's wage bill, yet Ferguson repeatedly won the league on less.

When Abramovich bought Chelsea, he gave his manager Claudio Ranieri a mammoth 16 per cent of the Premier League's wage spending for 2003–04. Of course Ranieri ought to have won the league that season. However, we shouldn't be too harsh on him. Even with the highest wage bill, it's tricky to finish top, because you are competing against both bad luck and the fairly well-funded over-achievers Wenger and Ferguson. Though Mourinho's Chelsea outspent their rivals, the Portuguese deserves credit for winning two straight titles. But he spent only three full seasons in England before his return in 2013 and therefore doesn't figure in our rankings. Chelsea were the country's biggest-spending club for six or seven years until the rise of Manchester City, and Abramovich's money bought him three league titles. By 2013, City almost certainly had the highest wage bill in England. Yet Ferguson kept his neighbour from the title, confounding the odds one last time.

So far we've only discussed overperforming managers of giant clubs. However, several of our best managers of the last 37 years – men like Paul Sturrock, Steve Parkin, Ronnie Moore and John Beck – have spent their careers in the lower reaches of the game. As we write, in early 2014, Moore is managing Tranmere in League One, Parkin is assistant manager of Bradford in the same division, while Sturrock and Beck don't have clubs at all. (Beck left non-league Kettering Town in 2012, escorted from the stadium just before a game, and Sturrock was sacked by Southend in 2013.) These men are titans of the lower divisions, but hardly anybody pays attention to titans of the lower divisions. It seems that the market in managers does not work very efficiently: many of the best do not get rewarded, while hundreds of managers who add no value continue to muddle on and get jobs, often good ones.

Admittedly some of our lower-division titans have succeeded by playing a long-ball game that might not work higher up. 'I think my style of play has been successful in the lower leagues,' Sturrock told us cautiously in his bare little office at Southend one winter's night. Yet good managers can surely adjust their methods to better play-ers. We suspect these men are being undervalued because they don't physically look the part, or lack charisma, or have had their reputations unfairly tarnished somewhere along the way. Sturrock thinks this happened to him during his only, brief stint in the Premier League: his 13 matches with Southampton in 2004. He complains, 'Everybody to this day thinks that I was fired. I walked out of the football club. It was an agreement between me and the chairman. It was the best for both of us. So maybe people tagged me that I'd failed in that environment. But if you look at my games ratio to any of the other managers that were round about me at that time, I probably had the most successful 13 games any manager's had there.' Indeed, Sturrock won five of those games – pretty good at a small club – but fell out with Southampton's chairman, Rupert Lowe. He never got a chance at the top level again. In his Southend office, he reflects: 'I've "been to the show", as the Americans would say. The one thing I'll say is that I enjoyed every minute of it.'

We're not telling Manchester City or Newcastle to go and hire Sturrock or one of the other lower-league titans on our list tomorrow morning. But it couldn't hurt to take a look.

We've focused here on overachieving managers. However, the key point is that they are the exceptions. The vast majority of managers appear to have almost no impact on their teams' performance, and do not last very long in the job. They seem to add so little value that it is tempting to think that they could be replaced by their secretaries, or their chairmen, or by stuffed teddy bears, without the club's league position changing. In typical football talk, the importance of managers is vastly overestimated. As Sturrock says: 'Money talks and money decides where you finish up in the leagues.' All in all, Jamie Carragher gets the significance of managers about right in his autobiography:

The bottom line is this: if you assemble a squad of players with talent and the right attitude and character, you'll win more football matches than you lose, no matter how inventive your training sessions, what system you play or what team-talks you give. But anything that can give you the extra 10 per cent, whether that's through diet, your general fitness or the correct word in your ear, also has merit.

Tony Fernandes of QPR insists: 'I think managers do play a big part.' But he adds: 'Ultimately, if you have rubbish players, there's nothing a manager can do.' Perhaps the main service a manager can perform for his club is to avoid spending much money on transfers. After all, transfers usually fail, and they waste funds that could have been spent on boosting the all-determining players' wages. Wenger is a better manager than Benítez in part because he blows less of his budget on transfer fees. But there isn't much else most club managers can do to push their teams up the table. Players matter much more. As Johan Cruijff said when he was coaching Barcelona, 'If your players are better than your opponents, 90 per cent of the time you will win.'

There cannot be many businesses where a manager would make such an extravagant claim. The chairman of General Motors does not say that the art of good management is simply hiring the best designers or the best production managers. Instead he talks about organisation, motivation or building a team. We typically think of businesses as complex organisms. Yet when it comes to football, someone as insightful as Cruijff describes management as little more than assembling the best players. Seldom has a prescription for successful management been so simple.

As we'll argue later in the book, we think that managers of national teams have a better chance of making a difference. A manager can outperform when he brings his team foreign knowledge that it didn't previously have. Fabio Capello arguably did that for England, and Guus Hiddink for most of the foreign countries he managed before his decline from 2008. These men passed on to their players some of the latest western European football know-how. However, it's very rare for such knowledge gaps to exist in a league like England's. All serious English clubs are now stuffed with people from all over the world and have access to current best practice. The Premier League is like a market with almost perfect information. Consequently, very few club managers can make much difference.

The counter-argument to ours would be that the clubs that pay their players the most also tend to pay their managers the most. So the clubs with the best players would also be the clubs with the best managers.

We believe this argument is false in most cases. First, if some managers are good and others are bad, why does the performance of managers over time vary so much more than the performance of players? Wayne Rooney or Frank Lampard are always good players. They will have the odd bad match, but over the years nobody ever thinks they are terrible and in need of sacking. The history of management, by contrast, is littered with blokes appointed as the Messiah and sacked as a loser a few months later. Most managers' careers seem to follow a random walk: some good seasons, some bad ones. And anyway, how can managers make much difference when most of them last such a short time in each job? In 1992 the average manager's tenure in English football was 3.5 years. By the summer of 2013 it was little over a year, and of the 92 managers of English league clubs, only Wenger had held his job for more than seven years.

Chris Anderson and David Sally take on our argument about managers in their book *The Numbers Game*. They say that managers matter rather more than we say, and they point to studies of chief executives making a difference in other industries. However, football isn't like most other industries. For a start, CEOs in other industries tend to stay in their jobs for much longer. In 2011 the average tenure of chief executives of companies ranked in the S&P 500 (the stock-market index of 500 big American companies) was 8.4 years. These people have more time to make a difference than a manager of a football club. Second, although CEOs in all industries like to make speeches about 'the talent of our people', individual talent probably matters more in football than it does at, say, Tesco. For a big retailer, having the right processes and technology is probably what matters most. But if you want to beat Chelsea, you need 11 excellent players. That might help explain the difference in wages between footballers and workers in other industries.

Furthermore, the individual football manager has probably become even less important in recent years. Managers at big clubs now tend to work with dozens of members of staff, ranging from physios to defensive coaches to data analysts. Often these people have been appointed by the club chairman or the technical director, and will stay in their jobs long after the manager leaves. The manager still appears at the post-match press conference, and gets public credit for victory and blame for defeat. Day to day, though, his staff may have a bigger impact on results. Fernandes says these staff are 'underrated ... I think coaching staff make a big difference.'

Most of the media love to focus on great men, but today it probably makes more sense to talk of management teams rather than individual managers. Indeed, you could argue that the main point of the 'top job' now is as a focus of competition for the other members of staff, who can aspire to become manager one day. Brendan Rodgers, André Villas-Boas and Steve Clarke, for instance, all made it from Mourinho's staff at Chelsea to managing big clubs of their own.

It's doubtful anyway whether many clubs or countries choose a manager chiefly because they think he will maximise performance. Often the manager is chosen more for his suitability as a symbolic figurehead than for his perceived competence. In other words, he's more of a monarch, or head of public relations, than an executive.

When a club or country appoints as manager a former iconic player like Maradona or Bryan Robson, it is not simply betting that he will garner more points than some unknown bloke like Avram Grant or Villas-Boas. Performance is only one of the three main criteria used for hiring a manager. That's because a club or country exists only partly to win matches. Its other job is to incarnate the club or country's eternal spirit. So a national team has to be the nation made flesh. Nobody could incarnate Argentina better than Maradona, and so he was made manager. Winning football matches had little to do with it. Whereas players are almost always employed because the club thinks they help win matches, that doesn't go for managers. Popular ex-players often get the job because they are easily accepted by fans, media, players and sponsors. They are hired as much for who they are as for what they can do.

The third criterion in hiring a manager is typically his gift for PR. A manager might not affect his team's result, but after the game he's the person who explains the result at the press conference. He is the club's face and voice. That means he has to look good – which is why so many of them have glossy, wavy hair – and say the right things in public. The forte of most managers is not winning matches – something over which they have little control – but keeping all the interest groups in and around the club (players, board, fans, media, sponsors) united behind them. That's why so many managers are charismatic. Their charisma may not help their teams win matches, but it does help the managers keep support.

The manager's PR role has become ever more important as football has received ever more media coverage. The late Helenio Herrera, Inter Milan's legendary manager in the 1960s, once told us that before his time, managers were unpaid men of low status. 'In those days it was the players who ran the teams. You had the team of Di Stéfano, the team of Mazzola, the team of Sivori, and the trainer was the man who carried the bags,' he said – and mimicked an overburdened porter.

Televised press conferences have probably done more than anything else to create the modern myth of the omnipotent manager. No wonder that the thing Tony Blair seemed to like best about football (according to his former right-hand man, Alastair Campbell) was the post-match press conference. When Blair was prime minister, he'd often spend time on weekends at his country house Chequers slumped on the sofa watching football on TV. He took a mild interest in Burnley, the club Campbell supported. But Campbell tells us that Blair grew fascinated with the then Burnley manager Stan Ternent, a character with a thick Geordie accent and a gift for exuding gloom. After games Blair, a born actor, liked to put on his best Burnley accent and ring Campbell: 'Reet, Ally, 'ow did Burnley get on today, then?'

The general obsession with managers is a version of the Great Man Theory of History, the idea that prominent individuals – Genghis Khan, or Napoleon, or even Stan Ternent – cause historical change. Academic historians, incidentally, binned this theory decades ago.

The myth of managerial omnipotence has been both good and bad for managers. When the manager became the face of the club, his salary and fame rose. On the other hand, he also became more vulnerable. If the team was losing matches, the obvious thing to do was to get rid of its symbolic figurehead.

Sacking the manager has become a ritual, football's version of the Aztec human sacrifice. English clubs spent an estimated £99 million sacrificing their managers in the 2010–11 season, if you add up the cost of compensation, legal fees and 'double contracts' (paying the old and new manager at the same time), according to the League Managers Association. All this money could have been more usefully spent on players' wage bills, or on improving stadiums.

As it happens, after the manager is sacrificed, a team's perform-ance does tend to improve briefly. Sue Bridgewater of Warwick Busi-ness School analysed sackings in the Premier League from 1992 to 2008 and found that 'there is a boost for a short honeymoon period'. For instance, after Manchester City sacked Mark Hughes at Christmas 2009, it won its first four games under Roberto Mancini. However, that's not because Mancini or any other new manager can work magic. The short honeymoon is easy to explain. The average club earns 1.3 points a match. Typically, Bridgewater found, a club sacks its manager when it averages only 1 point a match – that is, at a low point in the cycle. Any statistician can predict what should happen after a low point: whether or not the club sacks its manager, or changes its brand of teacakes, its performance will probably regress to the mean. Simply put, from a very low point you are always likely to improve. The club may have hit the low because of bad luck, or injuries, or a tough run of fixtures, or – as perhaps in Manchester City's case – the time it takes for a largely new team to gel.

Whatever the reason for hitting a low, things will almost inevitably improve afterwards. The new manager rarely causes the pendulum to swing. He's just the beneficiary of the swing. Perhaps some players do briefly work harder to impress him, though on that logic clubs should sack managers even more often.

Eventually results regress to the mean. Bridgewater found that three months after a sacking, the typical club was averaging the standard 1.3 points a game. Sheikh Mansour, City's billionaire owner, should probably have just stuck with Hughes and waited for results to rebound, but in business doing nothing is often the hardest thing. (And not just in business. Harold Macmillan, prime minister during the Cuban missile crisis, mused then 'on the frightful desire to *do* something, with the knowledge that *not* to do anything was prob. the right answer'.)

Inevitably Mancini was credited with City's short honeymoon. 'Mancini really is magic,' proclaimed *The Sun*, and people began to whisper that the Italian might win that season's Premier League. No wonder, because the glossy-haired Italian looks like a manager and boasts a glittering résumé as a player. Those facts reassure owners, fans, media, players and sponsors, even if they don't help City win matches. Mancini's salary – like any manager's – therefore reflected his iconic status and his gift for PR as much as his expected contribution to performance. So it will not always be the case that the best-paid managers are the best performers.

It's different for footballers. They are judged almost solely on results. Very occasionally a player does get bought because he is an icon, or good at PR. However, those qualities in themselves won't sustain him in the team. Any player who doesn't play well will be out the door swiftly, no matter how wavy his hair or how white his skin. As we've just shown, being a player is all about performance. Being a manager isn't. Although clubs pay players only for their contribution to performance, that's not true of how they pay managers.

Perhaps one day clubs will dispense with managers altogether and let a large sample of their fans pick the team instead. In 2007 the non-league side Ebbsfleet United gave their 30,000 fan-owners – who had each paid £35 for the privilege – a vote in player selection. Coincidence or not (and the money the fan-owners put in probably made the biggest difference), Ebbsfleet almost immediately experienced their greatest triumph, victory in the FA Trophy final at Wembley in 2008. Afterwards the club's performance declined, as many of the fans stopped paying, and most of the players had to be let go. Still, it was interesting to see a club select its team using the wisdom of crowds. It would be even more interesting to see what happened if more clubs did this – if they stopped hiring managers and allowed an online survey of registered fans to pick the team. We suspect the club would perform decently, perhaps even better than most of its rivals, because it would be harnessing the wisdom of crowds. And it could use the money it saved on managers to up those crucial players' wages.

None of this is good news for black managers. Because it is so hard to measure a manager's performance without complex grinding of stats over many seasons, it will probably never become painfully obvious that clubs are undervaluing black managers. That means clubs can continue to base their choice of managers on appearance. Any club appointing someone who is not a white male ex-player with a conservative haircut must worry about looking foolish if its choice fails. Hiring a black manager feels risky, because as Barnes says, 'Black guys haven't proved themselves as managers.' White guys have – or at least some of them appear to have.

At last footballers get more or less the jobs they deserve. If only other professions were as fair.

THE ECONOMIST'S FEAR OF THE PENALTY KICK: ARE PENALTIES COSMICALLY UNFAIR, OR ONLY IF YOU ARE NICOLAS ANELKA?

A famous football manager stands up from the table. He's going to pretend he is Chelsea's captain John Terry, about to take the crucial penalty in the Champions League final in Moscow.

The manager performs the part with *Schadenfreude*; he is no friend of Chelsea. He adjusts his face into a mask of tension. He tells us what Terry is thinking: 'If I score, we win the Champions League.' And then, terrifyingly: 'But first I have to score.'

The manager begins pulling at the arm of his suit jacket: he is mimicking Terry pulling at his captain's armband. Terry is telling himself (the manager explains), 'I am captain, I am strong, I will score.'

Still pulling rhythmically at his suit, the manager looks up. He is eyeing an imaginary, grotesquely large Edwin van der Sar who is guarding a goal a very long 12 yards away. Terry intends to hit the ball to Van der Sar's left. We now know that a Basque economist told Chelsea that the Dutch keeper tended to dive right against right-footed kickers. Terry runs up – and here the manager, cackling, falls on his backside.

Van der Sar did indeed dive right, as the Basque economist had foreseen, but Terry slipped on the wet grass, and his shot into the left-hand corner missed by inches.

'This really is football,' the manager concludes. A player hits the post, the ball goes out, and Chelsea's coach, Avram Grant, is sacked even though he is exactly the same manager as if the ball had gone in. By one estimate, Terry's penalty cost Chelsea £85 million.

The penalty is probably the single thing in football that economists have most to say about. The penalty feels cosmically unfair; economists say otherwise. Penalties are often dismissed as a lottery; economists tell both kicker and goalkeeper exactly what to do. (Indeed, if only Nicolas Anelka had followed the economist's advice, Chelsea would have won the final.) And best of all, penalties may be the best way in the known world of understanding game theory.

DIABOLICAL: ARE PENALTIES REALLY UNFAIR?

At first sight, the penalty looks like the most unfair device in all of sport. First of all, it may be impossible for a referee to judge most penalty appeals correctly, given the pace of modern football, the tangles of legs and ball, and the levels of deception by players. When the Canadian writer Adam Gopnik watched the World Cup of 1998 on TV for the *New Yorker* magazine, he as an outsider to football immediately focused on this problem. The 'more customary method of getting a penalty', he wrote,

... is to walk into the 'area' with the ball, get breathed on hard, and then immediately collapse ... arms and legs splayed out, while you twist in agony and beg for morphine, and your team-mates smite their foreheads at the tragic waste of a young life. The referee buys this more often than you might think. After-ward the postgame did-he-fall-or-was-he-pushed argument can go on for hours.

Or decades. The fan at home is often unsure whether it really should have been a penalty even after watching several replays.

And the referee's misjudgements matter, because the penalty probably has more impact than any other refereeing decision in sport. An umpire in baseball or cricket might wrongly call a strike or an lbw, but there are 54 outs in a baseball match, and 40 wickets to fall in a Test match, and so no individual decision tends to make all that much difference. Referees in rugby and American football blunder too, but because these games are higher-scoring than soccer, individual calls rarely change outcomes here either. In any case, officials in all these sports can now consult instant replays.

But football referees cannot. And since important football matches usually hinge on one goal, the penalty usually decides the match. As Gopnik says, the penalty 'creates an enormous dispro-portion between the foul and the reward'.

No wonder the penalty drives managers crazy. As Arsène Wenger lamented at the end of the 2007–08 season: 'Every big game I've seen this year has been decided, offside or not offside, penalty or not penalty.' Indeed, it's now a standard tactic for managers in England, after their team has lost, to devote the post-match press conference to a penalty given or not given. It's a ritual song of lament, which goes like this:

> The penalty completely changed the outcome of the game. We were clearly winning/drawing but lost because of the (diaboli-cal, unjust) penalty.

The manager knows that most of the media prefer covering personality clashes to tactics, and so the 'match' reports will be devoted to the press conference rather than his team's losing performance. Meanwhile, the winning manager, when asked about the penalty, recites:

> It made no difference whatever to the outcome of the game. We were clearly winning and would inevitably have done so without the (entirely just) penalty.

These two ritual managerial chants amount to two different hypotheses about how penalties affect football matches. The first manager is claiming that randomly awarded penalties distort results. The second manager is saying penalties make no difference. On occasion, either manager might be right. But taken over the long term, one of them must be more right than the other. So which is it: do penalties change results, or don't they? We have the data to answer this question.

Our guru is Dr Tunde Buraimo. One of the growing band of sports econometricians – the British equivalent of baseball's sabermetricians – Tunde works, appropriately, in the ancient heartland of professional football at the University of Central Lancashire in Preston. As the saying goes, the plural of 'anecdote' is 'data', and Tunde prefers to work with tens of thousands of pieces of evidence rather than a few random recollections. To help us with our book, he examined 1,520 Premier League games played over four years, from the 2002–03 season until 2005–06. For each game he knew the pattern of scoring and, crucially, which team was expected to win given the pre-match betting odds.

Our test of the two rival hypotheses about penalties is simple. We asked Tunde to divide the games into two groups:

1. Games in which penalties were awarded.
2. Games in which they were not.

We then asked him to compare how often the home team won when there was a penalty, and how often when there wasn't. This is what he found:

PENALTY AWARDED IN MATCH?

Result	No penalty	Penalty	Total
Home win	577	142	719
	46.76%	49.65%	47.30%
Away win	336	80	416
	27.23%	27.97%	27.37%
Draw	321	64	385
	26.01%	22.38%	25.33%
Total	1,234	286	1,520
	100.00%	100.00%	100.00%

Look at the last column first. Taking all games in the database, 47.3 per cent ended in home wins, 27.37 per cent in away wins, and 25.33 per cent in draws. These frequencies reflect the intrinsic advantage of home teams. Now imagine that the first manager is right: penalties change the outcome of the game. How will they do that? It might be that they always favour home teams (because referees are cowards) in which case we would expect the percentage of home wins to be greater when penalties are given. Alternatively, it might be that penalties favour away teams (perhaps enabling a team under the cosh to get off the hook). If so, the proportion of away wins (or draws) would rise with penalties.

But in fact, as the first two columns show, the percentages for all results barely change whether a penalty is given or not. The percentage of home wins is about three percentage points higher when there is a penalty (up from 46.75 per cent to 49.65 per cent) and the percentage of draws is commensurately lower (down to 22.38 per cent from 26.01 per cent). The percentage of away wins remains almost identical (27.97 per cent against 27.23 per cent) with or without penalties. So in games with penalties, there are slightly more home wins and slightly fewer draws.

It's tempting to read significance into this: to think that the rise in home wins when there is a penalty is big enough to show that penalties favour the home team. However, statisticians warn against this kind of intuitive analysis. The absolute number of home wins when there were penalties in the game was 142. Had the frequency of home wins been the same as in games when there no penalty, the number of home wins would have been 134. So the difference (eight extra home wins) is too small to be considered statistically significant. The rise is likely due to chance.

It would have been a different matter had the number of home wins when there was penalty exceeded 150 (or 52 per cent of the games concerned). Then, the increase would have met the standard generally used by statisticians for confidence that there was a statistically reliable difference in outcomes depending on the award of a penalty. As it is, though, the data suggests that the award of a penalty does not affect either home wins, away wins or draws.

But perhaps penalties have a different effect on match results. Perhaps they help favourites (if refs favour the big team). Or do they help underdogs (if penalties truly are given randomly, they should help the worse team more than the better one)? Tunde tested these hypotheses too:

	0	1	Total
Favourite win	633	147	780
	51.30%	51.40%	51.32%
Underdog win	254	67	321
	20.58%	23.43%	21.12%
Draw	347	72	419
	28.12%	25.17%	27.57%
Total	1,234	286	1,520
	100.00%	100.00%	100.00%

It's obvious even to the naked eye that penalties have no impact at all on whether the favourite wins: favourites win 51.3 per cent of games without a penalty, and 51.4 per cent with a penalty. It's true that underdogs win nearly 3 per cent more often when there is a penalty than when there is not, but once again the tests demonstrate that this fact has no statistical significance. We can put the increase down to chance. Match results appear to be the same with or without penalties. Penalties do not matter.

Now, this is a statistical statement that requires a very precise interpretation. Penalties do matter in that they often change the outcome of some individual games. Clearly, a team that scores from a penalty is more likely to win, and so, whatever a manager says, a converted penalty will affect the evolution of almost any game.

However, *on average*, taken over a large sample of games, a penalty does not make it any more likely that home teams or away teams or favourites or underdogs win. If penalties were abolished tomorrow, the pattern of football results would be exactly the same.

This sounds counterintuitive. After all, we argued that penalties look like the most unfair device in sport. They are often wrongly awarded, they cause a lot of goals, and many of these goals decide matches. So surely penalties should make results less fair?

To explain why penalties don't change the pattern of match results, we need to consult Graham Taylor. The retired manager is now remembered as the turnip whose long-ball game cost England qualification for the World Cup of 1994. However, the long-ball game had previously served Taylor very well at Watford and Aston Villa. No wonder, because it rested on one crucial insight into football: that you will only score goals if you get possession in the opposition's final third of the pitch.

Much the same insight applies to penalties: in practice you will only get them if you have possession (or at least a decent chance of winning possession) in the opponent's penalty area. Many a penalty is wrongly given. But it is almost always a reward for deep territorial penetration. That makes it, on average, a marker of the balance of power in the game. That's why good teams get proportionately more penalties than bad teams, and why home teams get more than away teams. On average, a penalty is given with the grain of a game.

RIGHT, LEFT, OR LET VAN DER SAR DECIDE FOR YOU? GAME THEORY IN BERLIN AND MOSCOW

The next question is how to take them. Economists may have no idea when house prices will crash, but they do know something about this one.

A surprising number of economists have thought hard about the humble penalty kick. Even Steve Levitt, author of *Freakonomics* and winner of perhaps the most important prize in economics (the Clark Medal, which some insiders think outranks the Nobel), once co-wrote a little-known paper on penalties. Probably only a trio of economists would have watched videos of 459 penalties taken in the French and Italian leagues. 'Testing Mixed-Strategy Equilibria When Players Are Heterogeneous: The Case of Penalty Kicks in Soccer' is one of those you might have missed, but it always won Levitt handshakes from European economists. Here's an American who *gets it*, they must have thought. Levitt, P.-A. Chiappori and T. Groseclose explain that they wrote the paper because 'testing game theory in the real world may provide unique insights'. Economists revere the penalty as a real-life example of game theory.

Game theory was developed in the 1940s by the likes of John von Neumann, a brilliant mathematician who also helped create the architecture of the modern computer. It is the study of what happens when people find themselves in situations exactly like a penalty-taker facing a goalkeeper: when what I should do depends on what you do, and what you should do depends on what I do.

The American government used game theory extensively during the Cold War, to plan its interactions with the Soviet Union, and to try to predict Soviet moves. (It is said that game-theoretic advice was given during the Cuban Missile Crisis to consider questions like, 'If we bomb Cuba, then the Russians will seize West Berlin, then we'll have to attack Russian troops, then they'll use nuclear bombs and then ...') Today economists use game theory all the time, particularly to plan government policies or analyse business strategy. Game theory even plays a big role in research on biology.

The key to game theory is the analysis of how the strategies of different actors interact. In a penalty kick, for instance, the kicker and the keeper must each choose a strategy: where to kick the ball, and where to dive. But each person's strategy depends on what he thinks the other person will do.

Sometimes in game theory, what's best for the actors is if they both do the same thing – going to the same restaurant to meet for dinner, for instance. Situations of this kind are known as co-ordination or co-operative games. But the penalty kick is a non-cooperative game: the actors succeed by achieving their objectives independently of others. In fact, the penalty is a 'zero-sum game': any gain for one player is exactly offset by the loss to the other side (+1 goal for me is –1 goal for you).

The issue of game theory behind the penalty was best put in 'The Longest Penalty Ever', a short story by the Argentine writer Osvaldo Soriano. A match in the Argentine provinces has to be abandoned seconds before time when a bent referee, who has just awarded a penalty, is knocked out by an irate player. The league court decides that the last 20 seconds of the game – the penalty kick, in effect – will be played the next Sunday. That gives everyone a week to prepare for the penalty.

At dinner a few nights before the penalty, 'Gato Díaz', the keeper who has to stop it, muses about the kicker:

'Constante kicks to the right.'
'Always,' said the president of the club.
'But he knows that I know.'
'Then we're fucked.'
'Yeah, but I know that he knows,' said el Gato.

'Then dive to the left and be ready,' said someone at the table.

'No. He knows that I know that he knows,' said Gato Díaz, and he got up to go to bed.

Game theorists try to work out strategies for players in different types of games, and try to predict which strategy each player will pursue. Sometimes the prediction is easy. Consider the game in which each player has only two choices: either 'Develop a nuclear bomb' or 'Don't develop a nuclear bomb'. To make a prediction, you have to know what the pay-off is to each player depending on the game's outcome. Imagine the players are India and Pakistan (but it could be Israel and Iran, or any other pair of hostile nations). Initially Pakistan does not know if India will or won't develop a bomb, so it figures:

IF INDIA HAS NO BOMB
(a) We don't get a bomb: we can live alongside each other, but there will always be incidents
(b) We get a bomb: India will have to treat us with respect

IF INDIA HAS A BOMB
(c) We don't get a bomb: we can't resist anything India does
(d) We get a bomb: India will have to treat us with respect

Plainly, if you are Pakistan, you will end up developing the bomb, whether India has the bomb or not. Likewise, India will choose the same strategy, and will develop the bomb whether Pakistan does or doesn't. So the *equilibrium* of this game is for both nations to acquire a bomb. This is the gloomy logic of an arms race. The logic of a football match is much the same, and there are many examples of arms races in football, from inflation of players' wages to illegal doping.

PIECES OF PAPER IN STUTTGART, MUNICH, BERLIN AND MOSCOW

The problem for experienced penalty-takers and goalkeepers is that, over time, they build up track records. People come to spot any habits they might have – always shooting left, or always diving right, for instance. Levitt and his colleagues observed 'one goalie in the sample who jumps left on all eight kicks that he faces (only two of eight kicks against him go to the left, suggesting that his proclivity for jumping left is not lost on the kickers).'

There have probably always been people in the game tracking the past behaviour of kickers and keepers. Back in the 1970s, a Dutch manager named Jan Reker began to build up an archive of index cards on thousands of players. One thing he noted was where the player hit his penalties. The Dutch keeper Hans van Breukelen would often call Reker before an international match for a briefing.

Nobody paid much attention to this relationship until 1988. That May, Van Breukelen's PSV reached the European Cup final against Benfica. Before the match in Stuttgart, the keeper phoned Reker. Inevitably, the game went to a penalty shootout. At first Reker's index cards didn't seem to be helping much – Benfica's first five penalties all went in – but Van Breukelen saved the sixth kick from Veloso, and PSV were European champions. A month later, so were Holland. They were leading the USSR 2–0 in the final in Munich when a silly charge by Van Breukelen conceded a penalty. But using Reker's database, he saved Igor Belanov's weak kick.

In Berlin in 2006, the World Cup quarter-final between Germany and Argentina also went to penalties. Jens Lehmann, the German keeper, emerged with a crib sheet tucked into his sock. On a little page of hotel notepaper ('Schlosshotel, Grunewald', it said), the German keeper's trainer Andreas Köpke had jotted down the proclivities of some potential Argentine penalty-takers:

1. Riquelme	left
2. Crespo	long run-up/right short run-up/left
3. Heinze	left low
4. Ayala	2 [His shirt number, presumably given for fear that Lehmann would not recognise him] waits long time, long run-up, right
5. Messi	left
6. Aimar	16, waits long time, left
7. Rodriguez	18, left

Apparently the Germans had a database of 13,000 kicks. The crib sheet might just have tipped the balance. Of the seven Argentines on the list, only Ayala and Rodriguez actually took penalties. However, Ayala stuck exactly to Lehmann's plan: he took a long run-up, the keeper waited a long time, and when Ayala dutifully shot to Lehmann's right, the keeper saved. Rodriguez also did his best to oblige. He put the ball in Lehmann's left-hand corner as predicted, but hit it so well that the keeper couldn't reach it.

By the time of Argentina's fourth penalty, Germany were leading 4–2. If Lehmann could save Esteban Cambiasso's kick, the Germans would maintain their record of never losing a penalty shootout in a World Cup. Lehmann consulted his crib sheet. Sönke Wortmann, the German film director, who was following the German team for a fly-on-the-wall documentary, reports what happened next:

Lehmann could find no indication on his note of how Cambiasso would shoot. And yet the piece of paper did its job, because Lehmann stood looking at it for a long time. Köpke had written it in pencil, the note was crumpled and the writing almost illegible.

Wortmann says that as Cambiasso prepared to take his kick, he must have been thinking: 'What do they know?' The Germans knew nothing. But Cambiasso was psyched out nonetheless. Lehmann saved his shot, and afterwards there was a mass punch-up on the pitch.

Both Van Breukelen's and Lehmann's stories have been told before. What is not publicly known is that Chelsea received an excellent crib sheet before the Champions League final in Moscow in 2008.

In 1995 the Basque economist Ignacio Palacios-Huerta, who was then a graduate student at the University of Chicago, began recording the way penalties were taken. His paper, 'Professionals play Minimax', was published in 2003.

One friend of Ignacio's who knew about his research was a professor of economics and mathematics at an Israeli university. It so happened that this man was also a friend of Avram Grant. When Grant's Chelsea reached the final in Moscow in 2008, the professor realised that Ignacio's research might help Grant. He put the two men in touch. Ignacio then sent Grant a report that made four points about Manchester United and penalties:

1. Van der Sar tended to dive to the kicker's 'natural side' more often than most keepers did. This meant that when facing a right-footed kicker, Van der Sar would usually dive to his own right, and when facing a left-footed kicker, to his own left. So Chelsea's right-footed penalty-takers would have a better chance if they shot to their 'unnatural side', Van der Sar's left.

2. Ignacio emphasised in his report 'that the vast majority of the penalties that Van der Sar stops are those kicked to a mid-height (say, between 1 and 1.5 metres), and hence that penalties against him should be kicked just on the ground or high up.'

3. Cristiano Ronaldo was another special case. Ignacio wrote: 'Ronaldo often stops in the run-up to the ball. If he stops,

he is likely (85%) to kick to the right-hand side of the goalkeeper.'

Ignacio added that Ronaldo seemed able to change his mind about where to put the ball at the very last instant. That meant it was crucial for the opposing keeper not to move early. When a keeper moved early, Ronaldo always scored.

4. The team that wins the toss before the shootout gets to choose whether or not to go first. But this is a no-brainer: it should always go first. Teams going first win 60 per cent of the time, presumably because there is too much pressure on the team going second – the pressure of always having to score to save the game.

Ignacio doesn't know how his research was used, but watching the shootout on TV, he was certain it was. Indeed, once you know the content of Ignacio's note, it's fascinating to study the shootout on YouTube. The Chelsea players seem to have followed his advice almost to the letter – except for poor Anelka.

United's captain Rio Ferdinand won the toss, and turned to the bench to ask what to do. Terry tried to influence him by offering to go first. Unsurprisingly, Ferdinand ignored him. United went first, meaning that they were now likely to win. Carlos Tevez scored from the first kick.

Michael Ballack hit Chelsea's first penalty high into the net to Van der Sar's left. Juliano Belletti scored low to Van der Sar's left. Ignacio had recommended that Chelsea's right-footed kickers choose that side. But at this early stage, he still couldn't be sure that Chelsea were being guided by his report.

He told us later: 'Interestingly, my wife had been quite sceptical about the whole thing as I was preparing the report for coach Grant, not even interested in looking at it. But then the game went into extra time, and then into a penalty shootout. Well, still sceptical.'

At this point Cristiano Ronaldo stepped up to take his kick for United. Watching on TV, Ignacio told his wife the precise advice he had given Chelsea in his report: Chelsea's keeper shouldn't move early, and if Cristiano paused in his run-up, he would most probably hit the ball to the keeper's right. Cristiano did pause in his run-up. To Ignacio's delight, Chelsea's keeper Petr Cech stayed motionless – 'not even blinking', in the Spanish football phrase. Then, exactly as Ignacio had recommended, Cech dived to his right and duly saved Ronaldo's shot. Ignacio recalled later: 'After that, I started to believe that they were following the advice quite closely.' As for his wife, 'I think she was a bit shocked.'

What's astonishing – though it seems to have passed unnoticed at the time – is what happened after that. Chelsea's next four penalty-takers, Frank Lampard, Ashley Cole, John Terry and Salomon Kalou, *all* hit the ball to Van der Sar's left, just as Ballack and Belletti had done. In other words, the first six Chelsea kicks went to the same corner.

Ashley Cole was the only one of the six who partly disregarded Ignacio's advice. Cole was left-footed, so when he hit the ball to Van der Sar's left, he was shooting to his own 'natural side' – the side that Ignacio had said Van der Sar tended to choose. Indeed, the Dutchman chose correctly on Cole's kick, and very nearly saved the shot, but it was well struck, low (as Ignacio had recommended), and it just wriggled out of the keeper's grip. But all Chelsea's right-footed penalty-takers had obeyed Ignacio to the letter and kicked the ball to their 'unnatural side', Van der Sar's left.

So far, Ignacio's advice had worked very well. Much as the economist had predicted, Van der Sar had dived to his natural side four times out of six. He hadn't saved a single penalty. Five of Chelsea's six kicks had gone in, while Terry's, as the whole world knows, flew out off the post with Van der Sar in the wrong corner.

It was Anelka's turn to kick. On United's bench, Alex Ferguson was growing frustrated with his keeper. 'As Anelka jogged to the penalty spot,' Ferguson later recalled, 'I was thinking – dive to your left. Edwin kept diving to the right.'

But after six kicks, Van der Sar, or someone else at Manchester United, had figured out that Chelsea were pursuing a strategy. He had realised that all their penalty-takers were putting their kicks to his left.

As Anelka prepared to take Chelsea's seventh penalty, the gangling keeper, standing on the goal-line, extended his arms to either side of him. Then, in what must have been a chilling moment for Anelka, the Dutchman pointed with his left hand to the left corner. 'That's where you're all putting it, isn't it?' he seemed to be saying. (This is where books fall short as a medium. We urge you to watch the shootout on YouTube.)

Now Anelka had a terrible dilemma. This was game theory in its rawest form. Van der Sar had come pretty close to divining Chelsea's strategy: Ignacio had indeed advised right-footed kickers like Anelka to put the ball to Van der Sar's left side.

So Anelka knew that Van der Sar knew that Anelka knew that Van der Sar tended to dive right against right-footers. What was Anelka to do? He decided to avoid the left corner, where he had presumably planned to put the ball. Instead he kicked to Van der Sar's right. That might have been fine, except that he hit the ball at mid-height – exactly the level that Ignacio had warned against. Watching the kick on TV, Ignacio was 'very upset'. Perhaps Anelka was all at sea because Van der Sar had pressured him to change his plans at the last moment. Van der Sar saved the shot. Ferguson said afterwards: 'That wasn't an accident, his penalty save. We knew exactly where certain players were putting the ball.' Anelka's decision to ignore Ignacio's advice probably cost Chelsea the Champions League.

Clearly there are lessons here for England. The English have exited five major tournaments on penalty shootouts since 1990. Most of the defeated managers seem to have regarded penalties with fatalism, as if they were a lottery that one could not possibly skew in one's favour. Famously, Glenn Hoddle, whose team lost in the shootout to Argentina in 1998, hadn't made his players practise penalties. That World Cup never quite left Hoddle's mind. A decade later, he told us that with hindsight he should have trained his men in visualisation techniques: visualising a penalty going into the net, for instance.

'I think there's certain techniques that you can do,' he said. 'Nine times out of ten if you miss a penalty it's between the walk from the halfway line, in penalty shootouts, and the placing of the ball. So what I'm saying is, it's in your mind where you've missed it. I think nine times out of ten you can tell if a player's gonna miss it. With how he reacts, what his eyes are doing, when he gets the ball on the spot. And that walk between the halfway line to the spot is definitely, definitely the time when you've scored it or you've missed it, in the mind.'

Perhaps visualisation would have helped England. But a database like Ignacio's might have helped too. Certainly the database would need to be something more sophisticated than Jan Reker's index cards, because tips like 'always shoots right' are of limited use.

RANDOMISATION: FRANCK RIBÉRY CRACKS GAME THEORY

Crib sheets like Lehmann's might just work on penalty shootouts. Many of the players who take kicks in a shootout aren't regular penalty-takers. (David Batty's penalty against Argentina in France 98 was the first he had ever taken as a professional.) These inferior penalty-takers are not skilled or steady-headed enough to be able to vary their strategy. Quite likely, they will just aim for their favourite corner, hoping that their lack of a track record means the other side won't know their preference.

But that is not how a good penalty-taker – his team's regular man – thinks.

Suppose the good kicker always chose the same corner for his penalty (game theorists call this a 'pure strategy'). It would be easy to oppose: if the kicker always kicks left then the goalkeeper knows what to do. Pure strategies don't work for penalty-taking. As Levitt and Co. found: 'There are no kickers in our sample with at least four kicks who always kick in one direction.' Take that, Jens Lehmann.

According to the goalkeeper's cribsheet, Messi's penalties tended to go left. In fact, the mini-Argentine randomises his spot kicks almost perfectly. 'He can also change his mind at the very last instant,' adds Ignacio. Sometimes Messi waits for the keeper to shift his weight very slightly to one side, and then shoots to the other corner.

Even a more complicated pure strategy does not work. For example, suppose the kicker always shoots in the opposite corner to the one he chose last time (Diego Forlán tended to do this).

Then a future opponent studying this player would discover the sequence – left, right, left, right, left, right – and with a bit of thought, guess what comes next. The essence of good penalty-taking is unpredictability: a good penalty-taker will be one whose next penalty cannot be predicted with confidence from his history of penalty-taking.

This is a particular kind of unpredictability. It does not mean that the kicker should go left half of the time and right half of the time. After all, most kickers have a natural side, and favouring that side gives them a higher chance of scoring. But even if you naturally shoot to the keeper's right, as most right-footed kickers do, sometimes you have to shoot to his left, just to keep him honest. In fact, if a kicker knows his chances of scoring for either corner of the net (depending also on which way the goalkeeper dives), he can choose the proportion of kicks to his natural side that maximises the probability of scoring. A right-footed kicker won't put 100 per cent of his kicks to his natural 'right' side, because that would give the goalkeeper certainty. Even a small change, like kicking right only 99 per cent of the time, would raise the chances of scoring considerably by creating uncertainty in the goalkeeper's mind.

Kicking to the left half the time would leave the keeper very uncertain. However, it would also entail the kicker hitting many poor shots to his unnatural side. So the kicker does best by hitting somewhere over half his kicks to his natural right side.

Likewise, we can calculate the proportion of times a goalkeeper should dive left or right. (Note that we are assuming the goalkeeper cannot know which way the ball is going before he decides which way to dive.) Kickers and keepers who mix it up like this are pursuing what game theorists call 'mixed strategies'.

Mixed strategies are peculiar because they require the actor to incorporate randomness into decision-making. Should I go to the pub or the cinema? A mixed strategy requires me to toss a coin, which sounds odd, since one might expect that I prefer one to the other. With a mixed strategy, you let the coin make the decision for you.

Game theorists have wondered for years whether people in the real world follow mixed strategies. They have found in tests that people tend not to use mixed strategies even when it is profitable for them to do so. In fact, our behaviour seems to fall short of mixed play in a very specific way: in most cases, our sequence of choices is predictable, because people tend to do the opposite of what they have done in the past. For instance, they choose first left, then right, then left, then right, left, right, left, right, confusing *change* with *randomness*. These guinea pigs would not make good penalty-takers.

Eventually, game theorists began to test mixed strategies in the natural laboratory of penalty-taking. Years before Ignacio Palacios-Huerta advised Chelsea, he collected a database of 1,417 penalties taken between 1995 and 2000. First, he calculated the proportion of successful kicks based on whether the kicker went to his natural side (left or right). The success rate was 95 per cent if the kicker went to his natural side and the goalkeeper went to the opposite side (the remaining 5 per cent of kicks missed the goal). The success rate was 92 per cent if the kicker went to his 'unnatural' side and the goalkeeper went to his own natural side. Obviously the kicker's success rates were lower if the keeper chose correctly:

a scoring rate of 70 per cent if both keeper and kicker went to the kicker's natural side, and 58 per cent if both went to the other side.

Using these figures, Ignacio calculated the optimal mixed-strategy choices for each player. To maximise his chances of scoring, an imaginary penalty-taker would have to hit 61.5 per cent of his kicks to his natural side, and 38.5 per cent to the other side.

In reality, the penalty-takers Ignacio observed got pretty close to this: they hit 60 per cent to their natural side, and 40 per cent the other way.

A keeper's best strategy (if he insists on diving rather than standing still) was to dive to the kicker's natural side 58 per cent of the time and to the other side 42 per cent of the time. The actual figures, Ignacio found, were scarily close: 57.7 per cent and 42.3 per cent. Levitt's team, using a different database of penalties, found that keepers went to the right 57 per cent of the time. So, it looks as if keepers as well as penalty-takers really do follow mixed strategies.

But what we most want to know are the choices of individual kickers and goalkeepers, not the overall averages. Ignacio studied 22 kickers and 20 goalkeepers, each of whom was involved in more than 30 penalties in his database. Again, Ignacio calculated the success rates depending upon the side the kicker and goalkeeper chose, and calculated the frequencies in each direction that would maximise the chances of success for kickers and keepers.

In real life, the actual frequencies the players observed were indistinguishable from the best mixed-strategy choices in over 95 per cent of cases. We can say with a high degree of confidence that penalty-takers and goalkeepers really do use mixed strategies. Levitt's paper found the same thing: except for the bizarre keeper who always dived left, almost all the other kickers and keepers played mixed strategies.

Finally Ignacio tested the most important question of all: are footballers capable of constructing a truly random sequence in their penalty-taking decisions, as the mixed-strategy theory requires? Careful statistical testing showed that indeed they are. In other words, it is impossible to predict which way a regular penalty-taker will kick on the basis of his history of kicks. Each time he chooses his corner without any reference to what he did the last time.

Randomisation of penalties is a completely logical theory that against all odds turns out to be true in practice. As long as the penalty-taker is a pro, rather than some terrified Southgateian inno-cent roped in for a job that he doesn't understand, simple lists like Lehmann's are useless.

All this shows the extraordinary amount of subconscious thought that goes into playing top-level football. Previous studies in game theory had shown that people could construct random sequences if the problem was first explained to them in some detail. Nobody is suggesting that footballers have sat at home ginning up on mixed-strategy equilibria. Rather, the best players intuitively grasp the truth of the theory and are able to execute it. That is what makes them good players.

Franck Ribéry is the designated penalty-taker for Bayern Munich and France. Needless to say, the scar-faced little playmaker places his kicks according to a randomised mixed strategy. But more than that, one of his former managers explains, even once Ribéry has embarked on his jagged hither-and-thither run-up, *he himself* does not know which corner he will choose. When the born economist Arsène Wenger was told this, he gushed with admiration.

Good footballer as Ribéry is, he might do even better as a game theorist.

THE ECONOMIST IN THE WORLD CUP FINAL

Ignacio Palacios-Huerta watched the World Cup of 2010 from his home in the Basque country, in between bouts of childcare. It baffled him, he told Simon over the phone during the tournament, that he probably knew more about the penalty-takers there than did any team in South Africa. 'I have nothing at stake,' he reflected. 'They have lots: the whole nation.'

Four years on from 2006, some teams did have crib sheets more sophisticated than Lehmann's. One team in the quarter-finals told us it had an hour's film of penalties taken by players of the country it was due to face, plus a penalty database. That's why it was silly of Capello to announce England's designated penalty-takers before playing Germany. He potentially gave the opposition time to study their habits.

Still, Ignacio reckoned that even the smartest teams in South Africa probably just counted who shot how often to which corner. 'I would be super-surprised if they do any kind of statistical test,' he said. He himself runs two. The first is: does a particular kicker follow a truly random strategy? If the kicker does randomise, then the direction he chooses for his next kick – right of the keeper, through the middle, or left – cannot be predicted from his previous kicks.

But Ignacio had detected patterns in several of the penalty-takers at the World Cup. Argentina's Gonzalo Higuaín, for instance, before the tournament had been kicking too often to the keeper's right. Germany's keeper Manuel Neuer had also been failing to randomise: too often in club games, Neuer had dived to the opposite corner from his previous dive, going first right, then left, then right, etcetera.

Next Ignacio tests the kicker's success-rate with each strategy. The kicker should have an equally high scoring rate whether he shoots right, middle or left. But going into the World Cup both Argentina's Sergio Agüero and Germany's Miroslav Klose were scoring more often when shooting right of the keeper. That would logically encourage them to aim right if they had to take a kick in South Africa.

Only rarely does Ignacio find a kicker with a very skewed strategy, but England's Frank Lampard was such a man. For years, Lampard had randomised his kicks beautifully. But in the 2009–2010 season, Ignacio noted, 'He kicked 13 out of 15 times to the right of the goalkeeper – and the two lefts were in the same game when he had to retake the same penalty three times.'

No wonder Lampard had developed a habit of missing penalties. Keepers were figuring him out. Portsmouth's David James, for instance, had chosen the correct corner for Lampard's penalty for Chelsea in the FA Cup final a month before the World Cup – perhaps with help from Ignacio, who had sent Portsmouth a briefing note before the game. In the event Lampard's shot went wide. Admittedly, Kevin-Prince Boateng missed his penalty for Portsmouth in the match, but then he had ignored Ignacio's advice to kick left of Petr Cech. It is probably harder for penalty-takers than for goalkeepers to follow someone else's advice.

On the phone Ignacio told Simon, 'I don't think serious analysis of the data has arrived yet in soccer, but it's coming. I think the world will be a different place in a decade or so.'

That phone call got Simon thinking. When Holland and Spain made the World Cup final, Simon, a lifelong fan of the Dutch, emailed an official he knew in Holland's camp. Would the Dutch be interested in a penalty analysis of the Spaniards provided by a specialist? The official said they would. And so Ignacio began pulling all-nighters to draw up a report on his fellow countrymen ready for 11 July 2010. More about this later in the book.

THE SECRET OF CLAUDE MAKELELE: HOW 'MATCH DATA' ARE CHANGING THE GAME ON THE PITCH

Early in 2012, one of us, Simon, visited Manchester City's tranquil training ground in the village of Carrington. It was a glorious sunny winter's morning, and outside the gates hired hands were washing footballers' SUVs and sports cars. The defender Kolo Touré coasted past in a giant black contraption straight out of *The Sopranos*. Carrington is used to cars like that: Manchester United train in the village too.

'Abu Dhabi Travellers Welcome', said the message on the façade of City's sky-blue training centre. Abu Dhabi's ruling family owns Manchester City, and one thing it has done since buying the club in 2008 is hire a large team of data analysts. Inside the building was Gavin Fleig, City's head of performance analysis, a polite sandy-haired man in a neat black City sweater. Hardly anyone outside Carrington has heard of him, and yet Fleig is a prime mover in English football's data revolution. Largely unseen by public and media, data on players have begun driving clubs' decisions –

particularly decisions about whom to buy and sell. At many clubs, obscure statisticians in backrooms are helping shape transfers.

Fleig gave me the sort of professional presentation you'd expect from a 'quant' in an investment bank. Lately, to his excitement, City had acquired stats on every player in the Premier League. Imagine, said Fleig, that you were thinking of signing an attacking midfielder. You wanted someone with a pass completion rate of 80 per cent, who had played a good number of games. Fleig typed the two criteria into his laptop. Portraits of the handful of men in the Premier League who met them flashed up on a screen. A couple were obvious: Cesc Fàbregas and Steven Gerrard. You didn't need data to know they were good. But beside them was a more surprising face: Kevin Nolan, then with Newcastle. The numbers wouldn't immediately spur you to sign him. But they might prompt you to take a closer look.

In recent years, after many false starts, the number-crunchers at big English clubs have begun to unearth the player stats that truly matter. For instance, said Fleig, 'The top four teams consistently have a higher percentage of pass completion in the final third of the pitch. Since the recruitment of Carlos Tevez, David Silva, Adam Johnson and Yaya Touré to our team, in six months, our ability to keep the ball in the final third has grown by 7.7 per cent.'

That stat had not necessarily driven their recruitment, Fleig cautioned. Indeed, some clubs lean far more on stats than Manchester City do. Most of these clubs rarely talk about it, though, for fear of sharing their secrets or getting ridiculed for relying on numbers. Few outsiders know just how far football's data revolution has progressed. 'We've somewhere around 32 million data points over 12 or 13 thousand games now,' said Mike Forde, Chelsea's then director of football operations, one morning in the empty stands of Stamford Bridge in February 2011. Football, it seems, is starting to become clever.

* * *

Charles Reep, a Wing Commander in Britain's Royal Air Force, made possibly the first known attempt to log 'match data' at a football match. He had become interested in the topic in the 1930s, recounts Jonathan Wilson in *Inverting the Pyramid*. In 1950, during the second half of a Swindon Town game, Reep began recording stats. In that one half, he logged 147 attacks by Swindon. Extrapolating from this small sample, he calculated that a typical team had about 280 attacks per match. Given that a team only scored about two goals per game, this meant that 99.29 per cent of attacks in football failed.

He kept logging matches, and over time he developed a theory – based on extremely shaky numbers – that too much passing was a risky waste of time. Most goals came from very short moves, he said. The way to win, he concluded, was long balls forward.

Reep advised the strong Wolves team of the 1950s, and in the early 1980s influenced Graham Taylor, the future England manager, and Charles Hughes, the FA's future director of education and coaching. Using his dodgy stats, Reep encouraged both men to develop the long-ball thinking that would eventually lead to England failing to qualify for the World Cup of 1994.

Reep's crude models probably did more to discredit the project of match data than to further it. However, one of his associates did put data to good use in the lower reaches of English football. Neil Lanham, a tidyily moustachioed auctioneer, had got to know Reep in the Suffolk village where both men lived. In the 1960s Lanham began logging games, but with rather more rigour than the Wing Commander. 'The findings that I talk of,' Lanham wrote in a paper for *Football Journal* in 2008, 'are based on hand-recording every possession for every team in more than 4,000 games ... When you sit in the stands and write down every possession by hand, you see and virtually kick every ball.'

His methods led him to some startlingly exact findings. For instance, Lanham reckoned that teams scored on average once every 180 possessions, a figure that he said was 'near constant' for any division of English football and for the World Cup. This finding, he added, was based on '328,018 hand-noted possessions'.

Lanham came to the same conclusion as Reep: the secret of football was putting the ball near the other team's goal fast. 'Two thirds of goals come from possessions won in the final third of the field,' he pronounced. The great sin, to him, was losing the ball near your own goal.

Some time in the 1980s Lanham wrote to clubs offering his analysis. Many ignored him, but Wimbledon's manager Dave Bassett replied at once. Advised by Lanham, Wimbledon won two promotions and went on to terrorise the top division. Generally, long-ball football seemed to work better at lower levels than it would in the early 1990s for Taylor's England. Lanham, billing himself with the startling twenty-first-century title 'football performance analyst', went on to advise Sheffield United, Crystal Palace and Cambridge United as they used long-ball tactics to climb the divisions. 'Eight promotions,' read the stat on Lanham's letterhead. He also did 'various works for international managers', he told us in a letter in 2011.

Though Lanham was determinedly artisanal, in 1985 he began feeding his shorthand codes into what he called 'a database computer system'. Computers were about to revolutionise match data. In the late 1980s, the young French manager of Monaco, Arsène Wenger, a keen mathematician, began using a computer programme called Top Score, developed by a friend, which gave marks for every act performed during a game. 'Most players who had very high scores had a successful career,' Wenger said later.

A less likely pioneer of match data was the late, great, vodka-sodden Ukrainian manager Valeri Lobanovski. When Simon visited Kiev in 1992, Lobanovski's pet scientist, Professor Anatoli Zelentsov, had him play the computer games that Dynamo Kiev had developed to test players. When Lobanovski said things like, 'A team that commits errors in no more than 15 to 18 per cent of its actions is unbeatable,' he wasn't guessing. Zelentsov's team had run the numbers.

Meanwhile, up in Norway, Reep's disciple Egil Olsen was making great strides. The Norwegian Marxist and the Wing Commander had become unlikely allies. Olsen, too, had a love of stats that went far beyond football. (He can – and sometimes does – name the highest mountain of every country in the world.) As manager of Norway, Olsen would gather his players before games to show them their latest individual stats on a big screen. It got to the point that when the midfielder Lars Bohinen mishit a pass at the World Cup of 1994, he'd instantly think, 'Oh no, I've got an M' – Olsen's code for a misplaced pass. Still, the method seemed to work. Norway briefly rose to second place in FIFA's rankings. When Olsen became Wimbledon's manager in 1999, the 95-year-old Reep – still billing himself as Wing Commander – offered his services as an analyst, writes Jonathan Wilson.

But Olsen, Wenger and Lobanovski were years ahead of their time. The broader breakthrough for stats came in 1996, when Opta Consulting in London began collecting 'match data' for the Premier League. The management consultancy was simply trying to build its brand by creating football rankings. The Premier League's sponsor, Carling, paid for the so-called Opta Index. Clubs and media got the data for free. Each club was sent an Excel report with some basic statistics on passes, tackles and shots. By today's standards, it was primitive. But in football then, it was revolutionary.

Within a few short years, the game moved from paucity of data to a state of too much information. Soon Opta and its rivals were sending out thousands of new data points each week. Clubs learned facts they had never contemplated before: how many kilometres each player ran per match, and how many tackles and passes he made.

Collecting these numbers took – and still takes – meticulous work. Most people know the impact of computers on our lives, but the work of the grunts is often forgotten. They are like the farm labourers of the pre-industrial age who were required to bring in the harvest. Opta's 10th-floor offices next to London's Waterloo Station provide a spectacular view of the city, but the dozens of 'analysts' barely notice.

We visited Opta's offices the day after Manchester City won 6-1 at Old Trafford in October 2011. Two young men were sitting side by side, each in front of a computer, both watching the same images from the game on a screen. One logged all of City's actions, and the other all of Manchester United's. Two other people had logged the game live the day before, with a third person watching for quality control, but Opta like to repeat the process the next day 'with a different set of eyes', said John Coulson, head of professional football services at the company. 'We're collecting 2,000 events a game live as it happens, with every event logged with a time code and a pitch co-ordinate, so you have to keep up with it,' he explained.

Opta's analysts type in the minutiae of every televised game they can find that might interest their clients, from the Premier League to the MLS or the Montenegrin league. Most of the analysts work in London, but others sit in regional offices from just outside Venice to New York. All the ones we saw were men, generally in their twenties, kitted out in regulation grunge and looking wan. Most were university graduates who hadn't been able to resist the temptation of earning pitiful amounts of money to watch football. 'We take on one person of the 20 or 30 who apply for these jobs,' said Coulson. Not that the analysts can really watch the games, as they sit there logging every single event in endless detail (long pass, weight on the ball, origin of the ball, where the ball lands ...). In all, Opta now collects several hundred categories of data. Analysing the games looks like a harder job than playing football. Most of the grunts are burned out after a couple of years, but then there are plenty more people willing to give it a go.

Gradually, managers started to look at the stats being pumped out by the data companies. In 2001 Alex Ferguson suddenly sold his defender Jaap Stam to Lazio Roma. The move surprised everyone. Some thought Ferguson was punishing the Dutchman for a silly autobiography he had just published. Although Ferguson didn't say this publicly, the sale was prompted partly by match data. Studying the numbers, Ferguson had spotted that Stam was tackling less often than before. He presumed the defender, then 29, was declining. So he sold him. It was a milestone in football's history: a major transfer driven largely by stats.

As Ferguson later admitted, it was also a mistake. Like many football men in the early days of match data, the Scot had struggled to identify the right numbers. Stam might have been tackling less, but perhaps that didn't really matter. The player wasn't in decline at all: he would go on to have several excellent years in Italy. Nate Silver points out in his book *The Signal and the Noise* that as more data become available, we become more likely to use them to make mistaken decisions. Often, the masses of data seem to form a pattern that just isn't there. That's why you often see false positives for breast cancer in mammograms, or false assessments of footballers.

Despite the dangers, Ferguson's rival Wenger embraced the new match data. He has said that the morning after the game he's like a junkie who needs his fix: he reaches for the spreadsheets. 'Wenger always used to love the averages, the trends,' Opta's chief executive Aidan Cooney told us. Dennis Bergkamp, in his book *Stillness and Speed*, describes how Wenger 'used statistics on me' during the Dutchman's declining years as a player at Arsenal. Their conversations would go something like this:

BERGKAMP: Where in your statistics does it say that I changed the game with a killer pass?

WENGER: You run less in the last 30 minutes and you're more at risk of getting injured, and your pace is dropping.

Few would suspect it of West Ham's manager 'Big Sam' Allardyce, but his somewhat Neolithic appearance conceals a professorial mind. As a player Allardyce spent a year with Tampa Bay, where he grew fascinated with the way American sports used science and data. In 1999 he became manager of little Bolton. Unable to afford the best players, he hired good statisticians instead. The analysts fixed upon one particular number that enchanted Allardyce. 'The average game, the ball changes hands 400 times,' recites Chelsea's Forde, who got his start in football under Allardyce. 'Big Sam' loved the figure, and would drum it into his players. To him, it summed up the importance of switching instantly to defensive positions the moment the ball was lost.

More concretely, stats led Allardyce to a source of cheap goals: corners, throw-ins and free-kicks. Fleig, another Allardyce alumnus, recalled that Bolton used to score 45 to 50 per cent of their goals from such 'set-pieces', compared with a league average of about a third. Fleig said, 'We would say, "If a defender clears the ball from a long throw, where will the ball land? Well, this is the area it most commonly lands. Right, well that's where we'll put our man."'

In 2003 football's data revolution got a new impetus when Michael Lewis published *Moneyball*. 'I bought 20 copies and sent them out to all the Premier League managers,' said Cooney. He paused, and chuckled: 'Didn't get one response.' Nonetheless, a few people in English football read the book and sat up. They began thinking about doing 'a *Moneyball* of soccer': using stats to find new ways of valuing players.

It so happened that just as football executives were getting interested in *Moneyball*'s hero Billy Beane, Beane was getting interested in football. On a London holiday with his wife, he'd encountered the game and fallen hard for it. Forde, who had studied in Beane's hometown of San Diego and followed American sports, made the pilgrimage to Oakland to quiz Beane about the uses of data. That proved tricky: Beane spent the first few hours of the conversation quizzing Forde about football. 'In the last half an hour I managed to turn it around to talk about his role in baseball,' Forde told us.

Early in 2011, Simon visited Beane in the Oakland Coliseum. The conversation took place in what looked like the junk room, but in fact is the clubhouse. Beane can often be found sprawled on a dilapidated sofa here watching European football matches while sceptical baseball players watch him. When Beane watches football, he sees a game full of emotion, and where there is emotion, he knows people will be making emotional decisions.

Football will follow baseball in turning into 'more of a science', Beane predicted. 'I always say, in a casino there's a reason guys who count cards get kicked out and guys who bet on gut feel don't.' He agreed that data probably wouldn't transform soccer as they had baseball, but then they didn't need to, he said. If using statistics in soccer gave you an edge, then all clubs would end up having to use statistics. Beane explained: 'If somebody's right 30 per cent of the time using gut feel, and you can find a way to be right 35 per cent, you create a 5 per cent arbitrage, and in sports that can make the difference between winning and losing.'

Beane's closest friend in football was the Frenchman Damien Comolli, a former assistant of Wenger's. Comolli had the advantage of having lived in northern California for a year as a teenager. He was a baseball fan, and an A's fan, and the ideal reader of *Moneyball*. When he became director of football at Tottenham in 2005, he began using data to inform the club's decisions on transfers.

The surprise is not that this happened, but that it happened so late. London has long since been taken over by highly educated professionals. Every other serious company in town uses data and computers. It just took London's football clubs a while to catch up.

Yet Comolli's three years at Spurs encapsulated many of the early struggles of football's data revolution. The British game had always been suspicious of educated people. The typical manager was an ex-player who had left school at 16 and ruled his club like an autocrat. He relied on 'gut', not numbers. He would have noticed that in many other industries, lesser-educated working-class men like himself had been replaced by people with degrees or by computers. He wasn't about to obey a bespectacled Frenchman who had never played professionally.

The manager's suspicion might sound perverse: after all, Comolli's numbers might have helped the club win games. However, many people in football clubs are less bothered about winning than about hanging on to their own job and power base.

In fact, the traditionalists shouldn't have been so worried. In football, there will always be a place for gut alongside numbers. Fergus Connolly, a performance consultant whose clients include Premier League football clubs and NBA basketball teams, says: 'Some coaches are afraid that data will tell them what to do. It can never tell them what to do. It can never be black and white.' The work of data companies is 'supplementary', agrees Rob Bateman of Opta. Data can support a decision about a player, but not determine it. As Silver says, an expert needs to use his judgement to interpret the stats, rather than imagine that the stats are speaking an unmistakable truth. No dataset will do away with the need for football managers.

The traditionalists worried nonetheless. Comolli at Spurs was always having to fight 'nerds versus jocks' battles. With hindsight, he unearthed some excellent players for Tottenham: Luka Modrić, Dimitar Berbatov and a 17-year-old left-back from Southampton named Gareth Bale. Some of his choices didn't pay off: using data can only raise your probability of finding the right player, not guarantee success. On balance, Comolli did pretty well. However, he was eventually forced out. The forces of tradition were too strong.

When it comes to knowledge, the world divides into liberals and conservatives. Conservatives tend to believe that we have reached the limits of what we can know, and that delving further is not only futile but immoral – some things are better left unknown. Liberals, on the other hand, tend to believe that even if we don't know how something works, patient analysis will eventually reduce the problem to a manageable set of proven relationships. Ever since Renaissance scholars began figuring out where a cannon ball would land, the conservatives have been on the retreat. So many things that we once thought were beyond analysis are now well understood, from the aerodynamics of flight to the mechanisms of disease. Now neuroscientists are starting to find answers to questions about how we know what we like, how we fall in love, and what we achieve in life. The conservative's ultimate fear is that one day we may know so much about what happens next that there are no choices left to be made; the universe will seem so pre-determined that no one will bother to get out of bed.

In football, the conservatives fought back. There was one question the new nerds kept having to answer. Yes, the conservatives would say, stats may well be useful in a stop-start game like baseball. The pitcher pitches, the batter hits, and that event provides oodles of clear data for nerds to crunch. But surely football is too fluid a game to measure?

Forde responds: 'Well, I think it's a really genuine question. It's one that we ask ourselves all the time.' However, the nerds can answer it. For a start, good mathematicians can handle complex systems. At Chelsea, for instance, Forde employed a statistician who had a past in insurance modelling. Football – a game of 22 men played on a limited field with set rules – is not of unparalleled complexity.

Second, in recent years the fluid game of basketball has found excellent uses for data. Beane said: 'If it can be done there, it can be done on the football field.' And thirdly, a third of all goals in football don't come from fluid situations at all. They come from corners, free-kicks, penalties and throw-ins – stop-start set-pieces that you can analyse much like a pitch in baseball.

The nerds could point to so many obvious irrationalities in football, especially in the transfer market, so many areas where smart clubs could clean up. For instance: goalkeepers have longer careers than forwards, yet earn less and command much lower transfer fees. Clubs often sign large players but actually tend to use the smaller ones, having belatedly realised that they have overvalued size. And few clubs have asked themselves even basic questions such as: do they earn more points when certain players are on the field?

Given that you can hire perhaps 30 statisticians for the approximately £1.5 million that the average player in the Premier League earns, you'd think it might be worth paying some nerds to study these questions. Yet football's suspicion of numbers has not entirely faded. 'Letting even a top-level statistician loose with a more traditional football manager is not really the right combination,' said Forde.

Given the prevailing suspicion, the clubs that have led the data revolution are typically the ones where the manager himself has trusted numbers. By the early 2000s, Wenger's Arsenal and Allardyce's then club Bolton were valuing players in much the way that financial investors value cattle futures. Take Bolton's purchase of the 34-year-old central midfielder Gary Speed in 2004. On paper, Speed looked too old. But Bolton, said Fleig, 'was able to look at his physical data, to compare it against young players in his position at the time who were at the top of the game, the Steven Gerrards, the Frank Lampards. For a 34-year-old to be consistently having the same levels of physical output as those players, and showing no decline over the previous two seasons, was a contributing factor to say: "You know what, this isn't going to be a huge concern."' Speed played for Bolton till he was 38 (and, tragically, committed suicide at 42).

Just when Bolton was buying Speed, Wenger was searching for an heir to Arsenal's all-action midfielder Patrick Vieira. As Christoph Biermann recounts in his German book *Die Fussball-Matrix*, Wenger wanted a player who could cover lots of ground. He scanned the data from different European leagues, and spotted an unknown teenager at Olympique Marseille named Mathieu Flamini who was running 14 kilometres a game. Alone, that stat wasn't enough. Did Flamini run in the right direction? Could he play football? Wenger went to look, established that he could, and signed him for peanuts. Flamini prospered at Arsenal, and after a few years with Milan is now back there prospering again. Wenger, said Beane, 'is undoubtedly the sports executive I admire most'.

Conversely, the clubs that stuck with 'gut' rather than numbers began to suffer. In 2003, Real Madrid sold Claude Makelele to Chelsea for £17 million. It seemed a big fee for an unobtrusive 30-year-old defensive midfielder. 'We will not miss Makelele,' said Madrid's president Florentino Pérez. 'His technique is average, he lacks the speed and skill to take the ball past opponents, and 90 per cent of his distribution either goes backwards or sideways. He wasn't a header of the ball and he rarely passed the ball more than three metres. Younger players will cause Makelele to be forgotten.'

Pérez's critique wasn't totally wrong, and yet Madrid had made a terrible error. Makelele would have five excellent years at Chelsea. There's now even a position in football named after him: the 'Makelele role'. If only Madrid had studied the numbers, they might have spotted what made him unique. Forde explained: 'Most players are very active when they're aimed towards the opposition's goal, in terms of high-intensity activity. Very few players are very strong going the other way. If you look at Claude, 84 per cent of the time he did high-intensity work, it was when the opposition had the ball, which was twice as much as anyone else on the team.'

If you watched the game, you could miss Makelele. If you looked at the data, there he was. Similarly, if you looked at Manchester City's Yaya Touré, with his languid running style, you might think he was slow. If you looked at the numbers, you'd see that he wasn't. Beane said, 'What stats allow you to do is not take things at face value. The idea that I trust my eyes more than the stats, I don't buy that because I've seen magicians pull rabbits out of hats and I just know that rabbit's not in there.'

Yet by the mid-2000s, the numbers men in football were becoming uneasily aware that many of the stats they had been trusting for years were useless. In any industry, people use the data they have. The data companies had initially calculated passes, tackles and kilometres per player, and so the clubs had used these numbers to judge players. However, it was becoming clear that these raw stats – which still often get beamed up on TV during games – mean little.

Forde remembered the early hunt for meaning in the data on kilometres. 'Can we find a correlation between total distance covered and winning? And the answer was invariably no.'

Tackles seemed a poor indicator too. There was the awkward issue of the great Italian defender Paolo Maldini. 'He made one tackle every two games,' Forde noted ruefully. Maldini positioned himself so well that he didn't need to tackle. That rather argued against judging defenders on their number of tackles, the way Ferguson had when he sold Stam. Fleig said, 'Tackles to me are a measure of being under pressure.' Connolly, the performance consultant, added, 'You will find that teams that tackle less win more games. That's related to possession: if you have more possession, you tackle less.'

Forde reflected, 'I sat in many meetings at Bolton, and I look back now and think, "Wow, we hammered the team over something that now we think is not relevant."' Looking back at the early years of data, Fleig said: 'We should be looking at something far more important.'

That is starting to happen now. Almost unseen by fans, some big clubs have arrived at statistical insights that are incrementally changing the game. Especially in England and Germany, where clubs have tended to look more at match data than in Spain or Italy, the 'quants' are isolating the numbers that matter. 'A lot of that is proprietary,' Forde told us. 'The club has been very supportive of this particular space, so we want to keep some of it back.' But the quants will discuss certain findings that are becoming common knowledge in football. For instance, rather than looking at kilometres covered, clubs now prefer to look at distances run at top speed. 'There is a correlation between the number of sprints and winning,' Daniele Tognaccini, AC Milan's chief athletics coach, told us in 2008.

That's why Fleig cares about a player's 'high intensity output'. Different data companies measured this quality differently, he said, 'but ultimately it's a player's ability to reach a speed threshold of seven metres per second.' If you valued this quality, you would probably have never made the mistake Juventus did in 1999 of selling Thierry Henry to Arsenal. 'For Henry to reach seven metres per second, it's a relative coast,' said Fleig admiringly. The Frenchman got there almost whenever he ran.

Equally crucial is the ability to make repeated sprints. Carlos Tevez, Manchester City's star player until he fell out with the club, was a bit like a wind-up doll: he'd sprint, briefly collapse, then very soon afterwards be sprinting again. Fleig said, 'If we want to press from the front, then we can look at Carlos's physical output and know that he's capable of doing that for 90 minutes plus.' Fleig didn't mention it, but the data shows that Tevez's successor at Manchester City, Sergio Agüero, does much less defensive running. The whole team needs to work harder to allow Agüero to score his goals.

The quants have also got better at valuing goalkeepers. They used to rank keepers by what percentage of shots each one stopped. However, that tended to favour keepers from big clubs, who play behind tight defences and therefore see a higher proportion of easy shots from outside the penalty area. Once clubs started counting only shots from inside the area, the rankings became more telling.

By now statisticians have developed endless metrics for judging keepers. Columbia University in New York did a sophisticated analysis of the Premier League's keepers for the 2009–10 season. In the 10th-floor office at Waterloo, the Opta men flashed it up on a screen for us. Columbia had worked out how many shots each goalkeeper faced from different parts of the field, measured the strength of those shots, clocked what proportion each keeper stopped, and ended up with a surprising number one: Craig Gordon of Scotland and Sunderland. Gordon was consistently above average in all areas, while all the other keepers seemed to have at least one significantly weaker spot. Second in the rankings was Liverpool's José

Reina, and third was Heurelho Gomes of Spurs (another of Comolli's signings, later banished by the club into outer darkness). Our eyes flitted down the list, through great keepers from all over the world, until we reached the bottom four in the Premier League rankings: David James, Paul Robinson, Robert Green and Chris Kirkland. All four were recent England goalkeepers. It should be noted that this was only one season of data, but probably English football needs to rethink how it develops goalkeepers.

Of course, not all clubs care about the same stats. Some managers request custom-made numbers from the data companies: how many players each team stations by each post at corner-kicks, for instance. Favoured stats differ per country, too. Italian clubs, said Cooney of Opta, don't use the concept 'tackle'. German clubs love what they call 'duels' between players. They even track duels when there is no ball nearby. And the data providers have made it ever easier for clubs to use the stats. For instance, you can now crunch data in countless categories to identify the right-back in the German second Bundesliga who best meets your specifications, and then click on a button and watch video of every through-ball he has hit in the last month. Or, if you are Liverpool and looking for the next Gerrard, you can ask the computer to find the midfielders in Europe aged under 23 whose attributes most closely resemble his.

Bit by bit, the data revolution in football progresses. Partly because number-crunching succeeded in baseball (the New York Yankees recently hired 21 statisticians), and is now sweeping almost all ballgames, it has arrived in European football larded with prestige. And it keeps getting more useful. Just as clubs have learned to isolate sprints from other running, they have learned to isolate telling passes from meaningless square balls. On the screen in Carrington, Fleig flashed up a list of Manchester City's players, ranked by how many chances each had created. One name stood out: David Silva had passed for a third more goalscoring opportunities (irrespective of whether the goal was actually scored) than any of his team-mates.

THE MONEYBALL OF SOCCER:
A TALE OF ONE CITY AND TWO CLUBS

The most telling statistics in the world aren't much use if you ignore them. At many clubs, the 'data analyst' is just a guy who has branched out from making videos. These clubs find the flood of data that arrives each week overwhelming. They are drowning in information. Opta has video of some games from Liechtenstein, Lesotho and Nicaragua. Who has time to watch that? And even when a club's data analysts do come up with an insight, the manager is liable to ignore them. Knowledge is no use if people in power won't use it.

Manchester United under Ferguson was an example of a club with only limited use for statistics. Ferguson did employ a large data department, but then he was always vacuuming up information from all sources: from ex-managers he spoke to on the phone all day as well as from mathematics graduates. And he couldn't do what Wenger does and crunch numbers himself. 'If you showed him a laptop,' growled an employee of Ferguson's, 'he'd think it was a place-mat.'

It's worse at some other clubs, where analysts get locked in computer-filled backrooms and never meet the manager. A key question in any company is, 'Who controls the budget?' In English football, typically, the manager does. The quants advise, but they almost never make the final decision on who gets bought or sold. Coulson of Opta thought in 2011 that data played a big role in recruitment at only 'four or five teams' in the Premier League. As we described in chapter 2, not all clubs have entirely perfected their transfer policies.

Lately, however, one city appears to have taken over the lead in football's data revolution. In October 2010 the Boston Red Sox's owner John Henry bought Liverpool. Henry, who made his money trading commodities, believes in numbers. In 2002 he had tried to bring Billy Beane to Boston, and subsequently won two world series using *Moneyball* methods. He wanted to do 'a Moneyball of soccer' at Anfield. The only problem was that he knew nothing about soccer. He called Beane to ask for advice. Beane told him to hire Comolli. The Frenchman was made Liverpool's director of football. Often during his time at Anfield he'd exchange ideas with the father of *Moneyball* 5,000 miles away. Beane told us: 'You can call him anytime. I'll email him and it will be two in the morning there and he'll be up, and he'll email me and say, "Hey, I'm watching the A's game," because he watches a lot of A's games on the computer. The guy never sleeps.'

Comolli became the poster-boy for the '*Moneyball* of soccer'. When he was sacked in April 2012, the experiment accordingly appeared discredited. His experience at Anfield tarnished the image of stats in football. But meanwhile, almost unnoticed, just across town, Liverpool's rivals Everton had been playing *Moneyball* quite successfully for years. The story of Liverpool and Everton illustrates both the scope and the shortcomings of *Moneyball* in football.

At Liverpool, Comolli had the power to use data to shape club policy. In January 2011 he bought Andy Carroll and Luis Suárez for a combined £58 million, and sold Fernando Torres to Chelsea for £50 million. 'When you find yourself handling three of the biggest transfers in English football history in the last days of the market,' Comolli said at the time, 'precise figures allow you not to do that blind.' He didn't say much more than that, but before selling Torres, he would undoubtedly have tracked the player's rate of decline. With older players – and at 26 a nippy striker is getting old – the key question is, 'How fast is he fading?' You can measure that by comparing the player's key outputs from year to year. If, for instance, his top sprinting pace, number of shots on goal and number of completed passes in the final third are gradually declining, you can probably see his future. (Comolli presumably knew that Steven Gerrard's number of shots on target – a key stat – had been falling since he was 26. A canny, unsentimental Liverpool might have sold Gerrard at 28, before others noticed his decline.)

Getting a statistical take on Suárez was harder. The forward had never played in the Premier League. What formula do you use to translate goals, shots or assists in the easy Dutch league into their equivalents in tougher England? Luckily, Suárez's Dutch numbers spoke loudly. Beane said, 'He was so dominant there that even though he was jumping into a bigger league, I think they felt like they were going to have at least a certain calibre of player no matter what.' One day there will be so many years of statistical analysis on players from almost every foreign league that English clubs will be much better able to predict how well a newcomer from, say, Norway will make the jump.

In the summer of 2011, numbers guided Comolli again. Few followers of football had identified Stewart Downing as a great talent, but the data showed that he was one of the most prolific dribblers and creators of chances in the Premier League. According to rankings produced by Opta with the CIES Football Observatory in Switzerland, the midfielder had been responsible for 17 per cent of Aston Villa's 'overall club production' in the 2010–11 season, a greater share than any other player at any other club in the Premier League. Comolli bought him and Jordan Henderson, who at the age of just 20 was already Sunderland's link-man, responsible for 13.6 per cent of the team's passing. Together, Henderson and Downing were supposed to provide the crosses for Carroll to head home.

It didn't work out. Just as previous Liverpool managers Gérard Houllier and Rafael Benítez had relied on experience and gut feeling to make bad transfers (as discussed in chapter 2), Comolli's data-driven purchase of the Carroll–Henderson–Downing trio went horribly wrong. It begged the question: can *Moneyball* thinking work in football? Even John Henry has said football is 'too dynamic' to allow stats to guide recruitment.

Yet Comolli's experiences need to be examined more carefully – and then set alongside what Everton's then manager David Moyes was simultaneously doing with stats in the same city.

What the Comolli experiment showed is that the *Moneyball* of football is still in its infancy. He had assembled the best possible players for a crossing strategy. The problem is that as we learn more about match data, we are learning that crosses from open play are a poor way to score goals. Much of the best work on match data is done not in football clubs but by amateurs on the sofa. Many of these amateurs have day jobs in statistics – working in insurance, doing maths PhDs and the like. One excellent blogger, who identifies himself merely as 'a Liverpool supporting atmospheric scientist who spends far too much time looking at numbers' analysed Liverpool's play in the 2011–12 season. He found that Liverpool had hit more crosses than any other team in the Premier League. However, he wrote: 'Their conversion from crosses was simply atrocious. They required a staggering 421 open-play crosses to score a single goal in open-play on average last season. This was the worst rate in the whole league.'

It turns out that crossing is not the way to victory. Comolli had bet the company on a bad strategy. A cross from a free-kick makes sense, because the player hitting it has time and space to achieve precision. But to send a man sprinting down the wing with a defender in his face, and then count on his cross being nodded in, is usually hopeless.

Another problem for football's *Moneyball*ers has to do with the game theory that we discussed in the last chapter. It's one thing to plan a strategy – for instance, of heading in crosses – and to show statistically that this strategy produced goals using historic data. It's quite another to declare that this strategy will keep working in the future. Once you have signed a good crosser and a tall striker, it's perfectly obvious to your opponents what you are going to do and therefore how they should set about defending against your strategy. In some extreme cases (Messi and Cristiano Ronaldo spring to mind) defending may be impossible even if you know what your opponents are planning, but generally this is not the case. Telegraphing your strategy may be the biggest pitfall when it comes to using big data in football.

At least the Liverpool experiment taught us more about which data matter: crosses rarely work. That knowledge is progress of sorts. It's also wrong to write Comolli off as a failure: this, after all, is the man who recruited Bale and Suárez to the Premier League, and sold the declining Torres for the largest fee ever paid by an English club. In part, Comolli got scapegoated because he's exactly the type of person whom media, fans and ex-players-turned pundits are quick to scapegoat: a bespectacled Frenchman who never played professionally and isn't very easy-going or clubbable. His habit of claiming credit for good decisions can also bite him in the leg when there's a bad decision looking for an owner.

But there's more to *Moneyball* in football than Comolli. Everton pay lower wages than Liverpool, yet in both 2012 and 2013 they finished the season above their rivals in the table. In part, at least, this was thanks to data analysis. One day in March 2013, Simon visited Everton's training ground at Finch Farm, on the city's semi-rural outskirts. It was a Monday morning, two days after Everton had beaten Manchester City, possibly the world's richest club, yet there weren't hordes of fans waiting outside. In fact there was nobody waiting there at all.

In the dining room a few players in shorts were eating lunch. At the other end of the room was a table with four members of manager David Moyes's support staff. One of the men, David Weir, a quiet Scotsman in a cardigan, had played for Everton for years before becoming a coach there; but the other three were unknown outside Finch Farm. Steve Brown, James Smith and Dan Hargreaves, in their blue elephant-adorned training kit, were Everton's unheralded assets, who earned dozens of times less than the players they worked with. Yet Moyes obviously took them seriously. Smith and Brown, the club's main performance analysts, weren't hidden away in some back room where nobody could hear them scream. Instead, their offices were on the corridor directly opposite Moyes's.

Often Moyes would march into their rooms firing out questions: how efficient was next Saturday's opponent at scoring from crosses, or throw-ins? What types of passes did their midfielders make? When Everton faced Bale at Tottenham, Moyes wanted 'an assessment of where Bale is actually picking up the ball compared to the areas where you think he is working', said Brown. Smith added: 'He [Moyes] is quite demanding in terms of data. In terms of managers, he is probably as into it as any.' (A measure of the staff's awe for Moyes was that they rarely referred to him by name. What to call him? 'Moyes'? 'Mr Moyes'? 'David'?)

Moyes had no particular ideology of how he wanted to play football. Instead he tailored Everton's style to each new opponent. He worked out what the opposition did, and then tried to stop it. Before facing Manchester City, for instance, he found the positions where City's playmaker Silva usually received the ball, and put men there (this, incidentally, is excellent game theory).

The insights that Moyes and his staff gleaned from video and statistics were constantly transmitted to Everton's players. Brown said: 'There is a post-match data sheet that goes up in the changing-room. Some players will actually sit down and look at the Prozone data with us; they will look at pass-maps and their "receive positions", their crossing data. We have one central midfielder who comes in every week and looks at his pass completion.' The analysts cautioned that you always need to understand the context of any piece of data. For instance, what was a player's role in a particular game? Who was he playing alongside? Match data without context are meaningless.

Weren't some players sceptical of numbers? 'There's a bit of that,' agreed Brown. But mostly, the analysts said, Everton's players appreciated the help. Many players considered stats (about themselves and about opponents) a survival tool that could help keep them afloat a little longer in the lucrative higher reaches of football. Smith said: 'Going out to play in the Premier League is a daunting thing. They want David Moyes to tell them what to do. That's reassuring. One player once said to me: "They might complain about a meeting, but if it wasn't there they would be the first to say, 'Where is the meeting?'"'

The staff noted that most fans and the media seem unaware of all the analysis that went into preparing games. Often, in pubs and TV studios, a game is discussed as if it were a mix of bursts of inspiration, individual blunders and a manager's motivational powers. Hargreaves said: 'What the public sees isn't necessarily what's happening. The level of ex-player punditry doesn't lend itself to what's happening behind the scenes.' In part, that's because managers like Moyes won't reveal their tactical secrets, so journalists end up writing about how a winning manager 'psyched out' his opponent with 'mind games'.

It's not that Moyes at Everton based his every decision on data. Rather, data were one of the things he considered. They made signing a player, for instance, a little less of a leap in the dark. 'Watching players is actually a very subjective thing, an inexact science,' said Smith. 'There are all kinds of inputs: live player reports, extensive video analysis, speaking to people who have worked with them, and data are one of those layers. Data play a role – not a massive role at the moment.'

One occasion when data did matter was in 2008, when Everton was trying to replace midfielder Lee Carsley. Smith said: 'We needed someone to replace things that he had been doing: possession regains, winning tackles and headers, protecting the back four.' The club's eye fell on a 20-year-old Belgian, obscure but for his enormous mane of hair, named Marouane Fellaini. 'We'd followed him at the 2008 Olympics but he didn't have a great tournament, and actually he got sent off quite early on,' Smith recalled. There were few match stats for Fellaini, because at the time there were no data available for Belgian league matches. And so Everton watched videos of him to compile their own set of stats, using key performance indicators that seemed relevant. Smith said: 'Fellaini was one of those where everything said, "Yes, do it": the data, the subjective reports, the age, the fact that he was already playing for Belgium, his size.' Everton gambled £15 million on him – still the club's record transfer fee. It paid off. In September 2013,

after Moyes had moved to Manchester United (undoubtedly bringing his data-driven methods with him), he bought Fellaini for £27.5
million.

Everton's performance analysts wanted to improve their use of
data. They had been picking brains inside and outside football for
new insights. They were painfully aware, for instance, that no one in
their group had so much as a maths degree. Still, football clubs may
now be more advanced than most corporations in using data to
recruit employees. In the typical corporation, very few human-
resources staff have college degrees involving numbers, says Rob
Symes, who made the documentary film *Outside View* on sports and
data. Daniel Kahneman, the psychologist who won the Nobel prize
for economics in 2002, says in the film that a key to good decision-
making is to let statistics, 'not humans make the final decision'.
Increasingly, that is happening in football.

Football's data revolution is only just getting started. Clubs still
have great room for improvement. For instance, you still constantly
see players shoot at goal from outside the penalty area. Yet Opta's
data show that in the Premier League, only 2 per cent of shots from
just outside the area produce goals. Presumably the players have in
their minds images of crackers flying into the top corner: these are
the beautiful goals that stick in the memory long after all the balls
that disappear into the crowd have been forgotten. Statisticians
have a lobbying job to do here.

There's a particular problem with free-kicks. Whenever a team
gets one anywhere near the penalty area, the team's biggest name
generally grabs the ball, makes a great show of placing it, and then
whams it into the crowd. It's a superstar's perk, rather like the film
star's trailer with his name on it in Hollywood. In the 2010–11
season, write Anderson and Sally in *The Numbers Game*, the average team in the Premier League scored from just one of every 35
direct free-kicks. Yet a free-kick should be the perfect opportunity
to pass. Your opponents have to retreat 10 yards, and they need
to put two or three people in the wall in case you shoot. That leaves

vast spaces to pass to runners in the penalty area. Almost inevitably, teams will start to do that instead of shooting from free-kicks.

Someone who has thought harder than most about what shape a *Moneyball* of soccer might take is the director of baseball operations at the Oakland A's. Farhan Zaidi is a little, round MIT economics graduate with a sense of humour. He's the sort of guy you'd expect to meet late one night in a bar in a college town after a gig, not at a professional sports club. For work, Zaidi crunches baseball stats. But he and Beane spend much of their time arguing about their other loves: the band Oasis, and soccer. In 2006, in the middle of the baseball season, he and Beane travelled to the World Cup in Germany together. 'We spend so much time together,' chuckles Zaidi, 'that if all we ever talked about was the numbers on these spreadsheets, we would have killed each other a long time ago.'

Because Zaidi knows where the data revolution in baseball has gone, he can make predictions for football, which lags baseball by perhaps a decade. Football's holy grail, he thinks, is a stat he calls 'Goal Probability Added'. That stat would capture how much each player's actions over his career increased the chance of his team scoring, or decreased it. Zaidi explains: 'With some of the tools that are being created now to track everything that's happening on the football field, I really feel like this is the next frontier: having enough data so that whenever a player advances the ball from point A to point B on the field, you know that play has happened 100 times before, and you know exactly how valuable it is. So if a ball is in grid one of the field, you know that the team over the next five minutes scores a goal 0.5 per cent of the time. Now that player advances it to grid six, say. You know that the team from there scores a goal in the next five minutes with a probability of 2 per cent. He's raised the probability of scoring by 1.5 per cent.'

Does this mean that one day pundits might say things like, 'Luis Suárez has a Goal Probability Added of 0.60, but Carroll's GPA is only 0.56'?

Zaidi replied, 'I tend to think that will happen, because that's what happened in baseball. We talk now about players in ways that we wouldn't have dreamed of 10 or 15 years ago.' In their ancient battle against the jocks, the nerds are finally taking revenge.

THE SUBURBAN NEWSAGENT'S: CITY SIZES AND FOOTBALL PRIZES

The scene: the VIP room at the Athens Olympic Stadium, a couple of hours before the Champions League final of 2007 between Milan and Liverpool kicks off. Michel Platini and Franz Beckenbauer are being buttonholed every couple of yards by other middle-aged men in expensive suits. There is a crush at the buffet, and another across the room, where a familiar silver cup with 'big ears' stands on a dais. You queue up, assume a conquering pose beside the Champions League trophy, and grin. Nice young ladies from UEFA slip the snap into a frame for you.

An Englishman watching the scene, a football official, confides that he first got this close to the cup 30 years ago. Where? In Bramcote, a suburb of Nottingham. One of Brian Clough's brothers ran the local post office-cum-newsagent's, and Clough himself would sometimes pop in and serve customers, or just stand behind the counter reading the papers. One Sunday morning when the future official went in with his grandfather, there was the European Cup freshly won by Forest, plonked on top of a pile of *Nottingham Evening Post*s. Behind it stood Brian Clough, holding an open newspaper in front of his face. He neither moved nor spoke, but he knew the boy would remember the scene for ever. The official remembers: 'I was too young and shy to speak to the man, which I regret to this day.'

It's odd to think of the game's biggest club trophy ending up in a place like Bramcote (population 7,318). Yet it's not that exceptional. Provincial towns like Nottingham, Glasgow, Dortmund, Birmingham or Rotterdam have all won European Cups, while the four biggest metropolitan areas in Europe – Istanbul, Paris, Moscow and London – never had until Chelsea finally got one in 2012. This points to an odd connection between city size, capital cities and footballing success. Here's why London took so long to win the Champions League – and why Europe's biggest cities might now start adding some trophies.

GENERAL FRANCO'S TRANSISTOR RADIO: THE ERA OF TOTALITARIAN FOOTBALL

The best measure of success in club football is a simple list: the names of the clubs that have won the European Cup since the competition began in 1956. Study this list, and you'll see that the history of the European Cup breaks down into three periods.

The first, from 1956 through the late 1960s, is dominated by the capital cities of Fascist regimes. Of the first 11 European Cups, eight were won either by Real Madrid (favourite club of General Franco) or Benfica (from the capital of the Portuguese dictator Salazar). In seven of the first 16 finals, the losing teams also came from Fascist capitals: Real, Benfica and, in 1971, Panathinaikos from the Athens of the colonels' regime.

But by the start of the 1970s, the dominance of Fascist capitals was eroding. Fascist governments seldom outlast their leaders, and Portugal's had entered a twilight after Salazar died in 1970. Meanwhile everyone was waiting for Franco to go too.

Yet even after Fascism disappeared, teams from Europe's remaining dictatorial capitals continued to thrive. Steaua Bucharest, run by Nicolae Ceaucescu's son Valentin, won the cup in 1986. Red Star Belgrade triumphed in 1991 just as Yugoslavia was breaking into pieces. The same phenomenon was at work in the communist countries as in the Fascist capitals before them. Dictators send resources to the capital because that is where they and their bureaucrats and soldiers and secret policemen live. So the dictators do up the main buildings, boost the local economy, and help the football club. That's totalitarian football.

A communist takeover of Britain could have done wonders for a capital side like Arsenal. Just look at the triumphs of Dynamo Berlin, founded in the former East Germany with the express purpose of keeping the league title in the capital. The club president until the Berlin Wall fell was Erich Mielke, feared octogenarian chief of the East German secret police, the Stasi. Mielke loved Dynamo. He made all the best East German players play for them. He also talked to referees, and Dynamo won lots of matches with penalties in the 95th minute. Dynamo were popularly known as '*Die elf Schweine*' (The 11 Pigs), but they did win the East German league title every year from 1979 to 1988. This was possibly Europe's most extreme case of politicians rigging the football market.

Dynamo never got far in the European Cup, but General Franco's local team did. The general made a point of catching Real Madrid's games on the radio, taking a transistor along with him if he was out partridge-shooting, writes Jimmy Burns in his *When Beckham Went to Spain*. It wasn't so much that Franco fixed referees or gave Real money. Rather, he helped the club indirectly, by centralising Spain's power and resources. And he believed that Real's European Cups helped him. Fernando María Castiella, foreign minister under Franco, called Real Madrid 'the best embassy we have ever had'.

DOWN AND OUT, PARIS AND LONDON: THE FAILURE OF DEMOCRATIC CAPITALS

Totalitarian capitals got off to a great start in the European Cup. But for the first 42 years of the trophy's life, the democratic capitals of Europe never won it.

There is only one caveat: Amsterdam is nominally the Dutch capital, and Ajax of that city won the European Cup four times. However, Amsterdam really is only nominally the capital. The government, parliament, the king's palace and the embassies are all in The Hague, a city that at times does not even have a team in the Dutch premier division. The Hague's only professional club, ADO, traditionally play their games in front of a few thousand people, a large proportion of whom are nuts. Little happens on the pitch beyond the occasional smoke-bomb or plague of rabbits. This is the curse of the democratic capital.

Instead of western capitals, provincial western European cities have dominated the competition. The rule of the provinces holds true even in the most obsessively centralised countries. Teams from five provincial British cities won the European Cup before London finally got one. (The town of Nottingham still has more trophies – two – than London, Paris, Istanbul, Berlin and Moscow combined.) Olympique Marseille won the cup in 1993, but Paris Saint-Germain never have. Porto have won it twice since Portugal went democratic, while the Lisbon clubs have been winless since 1962. Clubs from Milan and Turin have won a combined total of 12 trophies; Roman clubs, zero. The cup has gone to Munich and Hamburg, but never to Bonn or Berlin. For many years, in fact, neither of those cities even had a team in the Bundesliga. Hertha Berlin, the only big club in the current capital, have not been champions of Germany since the Weimar Republic.

Capitals – especially London, Paris and Moscow – tend to have the greatest concentrations of national resources. It's therefore striking how badly their clubs seem to underperform. We can speculate about why this is, but perhaps the main reason why teams from democratic capital cities are not up to much is psychological. In capital cities, no football club can matter all that much. There was an instructive sight, some time in the late 1990s, of a group of visiting fans from an English provincial town wandering down London's Baker Street yelling their club songs at passers-by. In their minds, they were shaming the Londoners, invading the city for a day, making all the noise. But the Londoners they were shouting at – many of them foreigners anyway – didn't care or even understand the point they were making.

Capitals simply have less to prove than provincial cities. They have bigger sources of pride than their football teams. Londoners don't go around singing songs about their city, and they don't believe that a prize for Arsenal or Chelsea would enhance London's status. Roman Abramovich and David Dein brought trophies to Chelsea and Arsenal, but neither could ever have been voted mayor of London. Football matters even less in Paris, where it's possible to spend a lifetime without ever knowing that football exists. Paris Saint-Germain, whose ground is only just within the city's Périphérique ring road, are hardly going to become the main focus of Parisian pride.

London, Paris and Moscow don't need to win the Champions League. It is a different type of city where a football club can mean everything: the provincial industrial town. These are the places that have ousted the Fascist capitals as rulers of European football.

DARK SATANIC MILLS: WHY FACTORY TOWNS BECAME FOOTBALL TOWNS

In 1878 a football club started up just by the newish railway line in Manchester. Because the players worked at the Newton Heath carriage works of the Lancashire and Yorkshire Railway Company, their team was called Newton Heath. They played in work clogs against other works teams.

Of course, we know that Newton Heath became Manchester United. What matters here are the club's origins, well recounted in Jim White's *Manchester United: The Biography*. White describes the L&YR's workers, 'sucked in from all over the country to service the growing need for locomotives and carriages'. Life in Manchester then was neither fun nor healthy, he writes. 'In the middle of the nineteenth century the average male life expectancy in Little Ireland, the notorious part of Manchester ... was as low as seventeen.' This was still the same brutal Manchester where a few decades before Karl Marx's pal Friedrich Engels had run his father's factory; the industrial city so awful it inspired communism.

Industrial Manchester had grown like no other city on earth. In 1800 it had been a tranquil little place of 84,000 inhabitants, so insignificant that as late as 1832 it did not even have an MP. It was the Industrial Revolution that changed everything. Workers poured in from English villages, from Ireland, and feeble economies every-where. For instance, the great-grandparents of Simon Kuper, one of the authors of this book, came to Manchester from Lithuania.

By 1900 Manchester was the sixth-biggest city in Europe, with 1.25 million inhabitants, more than Moscow at the time. It was still a hard city. In the early twentieth century Simon's great-grandparents emigrated on to much healthier southern Africa, after two of their children had died in Manchester of scarlet fever.

Inevitably, most 'Mancunians' were rootless migrants. Unmoored in their new home, many of them embraced the local football clubs. Football must have given them something of the sense of commu-nity that they had previously known in their villages.

The same thing happened in Britain's other new industrial cities: the migrants attached themselves to football clubs with a fervour unknown in more established towns. When the Football League was founded in 1888, six of the 12 founding members came from indus-trial Lancashire, while the other six were from the industrial Midlands. Montague Shearman wrote for the Badminton Library that year: 'No words of ours can adequately describe the present popularity [of football] which, though great in the metropolis, is infinitely greater in the large provincial towns ... it is no rare thing in the north and midlands for 10,000 people to pay money to watch an ordinary club match, or for half as many again to assemble for a "Cup Tie".' It helped that workers in the textile industry in the northwest began to get Saturdays off in the 1890s, a luxury that workers elsewhere in Britain did not enjoy.

By 1892, all 28 English professional clubs were from the north or the Midlands. Football was as northern a game as rugby league. The champions in the Victorian era came from northern industrial towns like Preston, Sheffield or Sunderland, then still among the richest spots on earth. When these places became too poor and small to support successful clubs, the league title merely migrated to larger northern cities.

The legacy of the Industrial Revolution still shapes English fandom. Today the combined population of Greater Merseyside, Greater Manchester and Lancashire county is less than 5.5 million, or a little over 10 per cent of the English population. Nonetheless, as we write, in March 2014, four of the top seven clubs in the Premier League table – Liverpool, Everton, and the two Manchester clubs – are based in this region. Their advantage: more than a century of brand-building. Manchester United became arguably the most popular club on earth partly because Manchester had been the first industrial city on earth. The club is only the biggest local footballing relic of that era. The 43 professional clubs within 90 miles of Manchester probably represent the greatest football density on earth.

Almost all Europe's best football cities have a profile like Manchester's. They were once new industrial centres that sucked in hapless villagers. The newcomers cast around for something to belong to, and settled on football. Supporting the club helped them make a place for themselves in the city. So clubs mattered more here, and grew bigger, than in capital cities or ancient cathedral towns with old-established hierarchies.

The market research company Sport+Markt (now part of Repu-com) began studying fandom since 1994. In 2008 it asked 9,600 people interested in football, spread over 16 European countries, to name their 'preferred' club. This was the top 20:

	Club	Estimated number of fans (in millions)		Club	Estimated number of fans (in millions)
1	Barcelona	44.2	11	CSKA Moscow	11.1
2	Real Madrid	41.9	12	Inter Milan	10.3
3	Manchester United	37.6	13	Olympique Lyonnais	9.4
4	Chelsea	25.6	14	Olympique Marseille	9.4
5	Zenit St Petersburg	23.9	15	Galatasaray	9.0
6	Liverpool	23.0	16	Spartak Moscow	8.1
7	Arsenal	21.3	17	Fenerbahçe	7.3
8	AC Milan	21.0	18	Wisła Kraków	6.5
9	Bayern Munich	19.8	19	Ajax Amsterdam	6.5
10	Juventus	17.5	20	Dynamo Moscow	5.7

It would be wrong to treat the results as at all precise. The figures differed significantly from those in Sport+Markt's survey of the previous year. In that one year Chelsea, for instance, had supposedly gained almost six million fans. Enormous numbers of people change their answers to the question, 'Which is your preferred team?' depending on who just won the league or where Cristiano Ronaldo happens to be playing. However, the survey does tell us something. Few would dispute that this top 20 includes most of Europe's best-supported clubs. And there is something remarkable about this list: the biggest clubs are not in the biggest cities. They are in the formerly industrial ones.

Of course some teams from capitals are popular. They would be, given that London, Paris, Rome and Moscow are by far the largest cities in their countries. Clubs in capitals have unparalleled catchment areas, even given the profusion of local teams. But in none of the seven largest European countries surveyed does the best-supported club come from a capital city. Here is the favourite team of each large country, according to Sport+Markt:

BEST-SUPPORTED CLUB

England	Manchester United
France	Olympique Lyonnais
Germany	Bayern Munich
Italy	AC Milan
Poland	Wisła Kraków
Russia	Zenit St Petersburg
Spain	Barcelona

In six out of seven countries, the number one team comes from a provincial town with a strong industrial history. The sole exception is France, where Lyon is a provincial town but was mostly bypassed by the Industrial Revolution. We saw how the club's popularity came from nowhere after 2002, thanks to their brilliant gaming of the transfer market under president Jean-Michel Aulas.

Taken together, the provincial industrial towns in Sport+Markt's top 20 dominate European football. Between them they won 30 out of 51 European Cups from 1963 to 2013. The smaller industrial or port cities Glasgow, Nottingham, Birmingham, Porto, Dortmund, Eindhoven and Rotterdam have won another nine between them. And all these cities have a story much like Manchester's, although their growth spurts happened later. Peasants arrived from the countryside, leaving all their roots behind. Needing something to belong to in their new cities, they chose football. That's why in all these places, the football clubs arose soon after the factories.

In most of the cities on Sport+Markt's list, the industrial migrants arrived in a whoosh in the late nineteenth century. Munich had 100,000 inhabitants in 1852, and five times as many by 1901. Barcelona's population trebled in the same period to 533,000 people. Turin, for centuries a quiet Piedmontese town, began acquiring factories in the 1870s. Milan surged with the new railways that followed Italian reunification.

Once the local merchants had grown wealthy and discovered English ways, they founded football clubs: Juventus in 1897, Barcelona and AC Milan two years later, Bayern in 1900. The clubs then grew with their cities. Newly industrial Milan, for instance, sucked in so many migrants that it could eventually support two of the three most popular teams in the country.

The second stage of the football boom in the continent's industrial cities happened after the war. The 1950s and 1960s were the years of Italy's 'economic miracle', when flocks of poor southern Italian peasants took the 'train of the sun' north. Many of these people ended up in Turin making cars for Fiat. The historian Paul Ginsborg writes: 'So great and persistent was the flow from the South, that by the end of the sixties Turin had become the third largest "southern" city in Italy, after Naples and Palermo.' The migrants found jobs, but not enough schools or hospitals or apartments. Often there was so little space that housemates had to take turns sleeping. Amid such dislocation, football mattered all the more. Goffredo Fofi, author of a study of southern immigration to Turin in the 1960s, said that 'during a Juventus–Palermo match, there were many enthusiastic immigrant Sicilian fans whose sons, by now, like every respectable FIAT worker, backed the home team.'

It's one of the flukes of history that this mass migration to Turin began soon after the Superga air disaster of 1949 had decimated the city's previous most popular team, Torino. The migrants arrived soon after Juve had established itself as the local top dog, and they helped make it a global top dog. For a start, they transmitted the passion to their relatives down south.

Barcelona experienced the same sort of growth spurt at about the same time as Turin. In the 1950s and 1960s perhaps 1.5 million Spaniards moved to the Barcelona area. Entire villages in the country's interior were left almost empty. On wastelands outside Barcelona, self-built shantytowns sprang up – the sort of thing you might now see on the outskirts of Jakarta – packed with peasants who had left behind everything they knew. Many were illiterate, and hardly any spoke the local language, Catalan. A lot of them attached themselves to Barça. In Spain's new Manchester, it was the quickest way to belong.

The link between industry and football is almost universal across Europe. The largest average crowds in Europe in the 2012–13 season were at Borussia Dortmund (average: 80,558), one of many clubs in the industrial German Ruhr region. In France, too, it is the industrial cities that have historically loved their clubs best. The country's few traditional hotbeds of football are the mining towns of Lens and Saint-Étienne, and the port of Marseilles.

All these industrial cities were products of a particular era. In all of them the Industrial Revolution ended, often painfully. But besides the empty docks and factory buildings, the other legacy of industrialisation was beloved football clubs. The quirk of a particular era gave Manchester United, Barcelona, Juventus, Bayern Munich and the Milan clubs enough fans to dominate first their own countries, and then Europe.

If Sport+Markt had polled the popularity of football clubs in Turkey, it would have found the universal principle holding there too. The country's capital of football is not the capital city, Ankara, but the new industrial powerhouse Istanbul. The city is home to all three of Turkey's most popular clubs: Galatasaray, Fenerbahçe, and Beşiktaş.

It's true that Istanbul, like St Petersburg, was once the seat of government, but both cities lost that role more than 90 years ago, long before football amounted to anything in their countries. Even as late as 1950, Istanbul was a sleepy place with barely a million inhabitants. Then it became possibly the last big European city to experience an industrial revolution. Migrants were sucked in from all over Anatolia. Between 1980 and 1985 alone, Istanbul's population doubled. Today it is the largest metropolitan area in Europe with nearly 14 million inhabitants. The rootless peasants needed somehow to belong in their new home, and so they attached themselves to one of the city's great clubs. Often, these were their strongest loyalties in Istanbul.

Admittedly almost all cities in Europe have some experience of industrialisation. But very few have had as much as Manchester, Turin, Milan, Istanbul or Barcelona. These were the European cities with the most flux, the fewest longstanding hierarchies, the weakest ties between people and place. Here, there were emotional gaps to fill. This becomes obvious when we contrast the industrial cities with old towns that have a traditional upper-class streak. In England, Oxford, Cambridge, Cheltenham, Canterbury, York and Bath (including its rural outskirts) are all decent-sized places, with somewhere between 100,000 and 175,000 inhabitants each. Many industrial towns of that size or even smaller – Middlesbrough, Reading, Ipswich, Blackburn, Watford, Burnley – have serious football traditions. Yet Oxford, Cambridge, Bath, Canterbury, York and Cheltenham between them currently have just three small teams in the Football League: Cheltenham Town, which joined it only in 1999, Oxford United, which re-entered the league only in 2010, and York City, which returned in 2012. All three clubs play in League Two. In towns like these, with age-old hierarchies and few incoming peasants, people simply didn't need football clubs to root themselves.

Oxford's face to the world is the university. In industrial cities it is the football club. The clubs of Barcelona, Newcastle and Marseille are the pride of their cities, a symbolic two fingers up at the capital. When Barcelona win something, the president of Catalonia traditionally hoists himself up on the balcony of his palace on the Plaça Sant Jaume, and shouts at the crowds below: 'Barça wins, Catalonia wins!'

These provincial clubs have armies of fans, players who will bleed for the club, and backing from local plutocrats. Bernard Tapie put money into Olympique Marseille, the Agnelli family into Juventus, and Sir John Hall into Newcastle because they wanted to be kings of their town. Local fans and sponsors invest in these clubs partly because they feel civic pride is at stake. In the Middle Ages they would have built a cathedral instead.

Usually, provincial cities such as these only have one major club, which often becomes the only thing that many outsiders know about the place. For instance, there must be many Manchester United fans around the world who don't know that Manchester is a city in England. True, most provincial cities have two teams that compete for top-dog status: United and City in Manchester, Inter and AC Milan in Milan, Torino and Juventus in Turin, United and Wednesday in Sheffield, Celtic and Rangers in Glasgow, Forest and County in Nottingham, Everton and Liverpool, Bayern and 1860 in Munich, Barça and Espanyol in Barcelona. Many of these rivalries have something to do with religion and/or politics. But usually one team struggles. Manchester City, Torino and 1860 Munich have all spent long phases in the lower divisions. City only reached the top thanks to the arrival of a billionaire Arab sheikh in 2008. Everton last won the league in 1987. FC Amsterdam went bust. Mid-sized provincial cities are simply not big enough to sustain two big clubs for long. In the end, one club pulls ahead.

'THEY MOVED THE HIGHWAY': THE RISE AND FALL OF SMALL TOWNS

Provincial industrial towns began to dominate the European Cup in the late 1960s. But their rule breaks down into two main periods. The first, from 1970 to 1981, is the small-town era, when clubs from some very modest places won the European Cup.

Here they are, with the populations not just of the cities themselves but of their entire metropolitan areas, including people in all the local dormitory towns:

Club	Year(s) they won it	Metropolitan area
Feyenoord Rotterdam	1970	1 million
Ajax Amsterdam	1971–1973	1 million
Bayern Munich	1974–1976	2.9 million
Liverpool	1977–1978, 1981	1.4 million
Nottingham Forest	1979–1980	470,000

Note that we are estimating the size of these places very generously, going way beyond the city borders. The figure for Liverpool, for instance, includes all of Merseyside.

The rule of the small is even more striking when you consider some of the losing teams in European Cup finals in this era. In a remarkable four-year period from 1976 to 1979, the towns of Saint-Étienne, Mönchengladbach, Bruges and Malmö all had teams in the final.

Club	Size of town	Size of total metropolitan area
Saint-Étienne	175,000	320,000
Mönchengladbach	260,000	260,000
Bruges	115,000	270,000
Malmö	240,000	600,000

Perhaps the emblematic small-town team of the 1970s is Borussia Mönchengladbach, whose rise and fall encapsulates the story of all these towns.

In that decade Gladbach won five German titles and reached four European finals. The Bökelberg stadium, perched on a hill among the gardens of smart houses, saw the best years of Gunter Netzer, Rainer Bonhof and Alan Simonsen. Fans drove in from neighbouring Holland and Belgium, as well as from the town's British army barracks. Decades later, a German marketing company showed that the knee-jerk response of the country's fans to the word 'counterattack' was still 'Gladbach'.

It was a cosy little club: Berti Vogts spent his whole career there, and when Netzer later played in Zurich he often used to drive up, sometimes to scout players for Spanish clubs, but often just to eat sausages in the canteen.

Like David Cassidy, Gladbach would have done well to combust spontaneously at the end of the Seventies. In 1980 they lost their last UEFA Cup final to Eintracht Frankfurt, and the decades since have been disappointing. There was the spell in 1998, for instance, when they just couldn't stop getting thrashed. 'We can only get better,' announced Gladbach's coach, Friedel Rausch, just before his team lost 8–2 to Bayer Leverkusen. 'I feel I can solve our problems,' he said afterwards. When Gladbach lost their next match 7–1 to Wolfsburg, Rausch was sacked. Gladbach spent time in Germany's second division, and have never regained their former heights.

This upsets leftist, educated 50-somethings all over Germany, who still dislike Bayern, revere the socialist Netzer, and on Monday mornings check the Gladbach result first. But there is nothing to be done. The glory days cannot come back, because what did for Gladbach was the modern era.

In the words of Norman Bates in Hitchcock's *Psycho*: 'They moved the highway.' In the 1970s Gladbach's coach Hennes Weisweiler was able to build a team of boys from the local towns. The part-Dutch Bonhof came from nearby Emmerich, Vogts was an orphan from Neuss-Büttgen, and Hacki Wimmer, who did Netzer's dirty work, spent decades after his playing career running his parents' stationery shop just down the road in Aachen.

These stars stayed at Gladbach for years because there was little more money to be earned anywhere else in football, because most rich clubs were only allowed a couple of foreign players, and because their own club could generally stop them leaving. In short, there were market restraints. That's why Gladbach, Nottingham Forest, Bruges and Saint-Étienne could thrive in the 1970s. Even then big cities had bigger resources, but they had limited freedom, or limited desire, to use them.

The beginning of the end for small towns was the day in February 1979 when Trevor Francis became football's first 'million-pound man'. In fact, Clough agreed a fee of only £999,999 to bring him from Birmingham to Forest, but there were taxes on top. Three months later Francis headed the goal (against Malmö) that gave Forest the European Cup. But the swelling of the football economy that he embodied would eventually do for small clubs like Forest.

In the 1980s TV contracts grew, and Italy opened its borders to foreigners. Later clubs around Europe began redoing their stadiums, which allowed the ones with lots of fans to make more money. After the European Court of Justice's 'Bosman ruling' in 1995, big clubs could easily sign the best players from any country in the European Union. Around the same time, the clubs with most fans began earning much more from their television rights. Big clubs everywhere got bigger. Bayern Munich, previously Gladbach's main rivals, mushroomed into 'FC Hollywood'.

After that, clubs like Gladbach could no longer keep their best players. Lothar Matthäus made his debut for '*Die Fohlen*' (The Foals) at the end of the golden era, but when he was only 23 he graduated to Bayern. The next great white hope, the local lad Sebastian Deisler, left Gladbach for Hertha aged 19 in 1999, as soon he distantly began to resemble Netzer. Small towns couldn't afford the new football.

'THAT'S NOT COCAINE, IT'S SAFFRON': THE DEMISE OF THE CATHEDRAL CITIES

Wandering around Florence, you can still imagine it as the centre of the universe. It is the effect of the great cathedral, the endless Michelangelos, and all the tourists paying seven euros for an orange juice. A Medici ruler returning from the dead, as in one of Florence's umpteen paintings of the Day of Judgement, might feel his city had won the battle of prestige among European city-states.

But he would be wrong. These days a mid-sized city in Europe derives its status less from its cathedral than from its football club.

Here towns the size of Florence (600,000 people in its metropolitan area) have slipped up.

Fiorentina's last flurry came in 1999, when they beat Arsenal in a Champions League match at Wembley thanks to a goal by Gabriel Batistuta, with Giovanni Trapattoni sitting on their bench. In those days the biggest problems facing 'Trap' were his players' insistence on busing the 150 metres from changing rooms to training ground, and the Brazilian Edmundo's ritual late return from the Rio carnival. But those days will never return. In the Champions League, the mid-sized cities are now finished.

Fiorentina's demise can be dated to the day in July 2001 that the Italian police raided the home of their owner, the Italian film baron Vittorio Cecchi Gori. What happened was exactly what should happen when police raid a film baron's home, as if Cecchi Gori had read up on Jackie Collins beforehand.

The police broke into his apartment in the Palazzo Borghese in Rome, but then took 90 minutes to find him. This was because his bedroom door was concealed inside a mirrored wall. Only after the Filipina maid had pointed this out did they enter the bedroom to find Cecchi Gori asleep with his girlfriend, Valeria Marini, a Caprice-like figure who calls herself a singer–actress but in fact can do neither.

The police told Cecchi Gori to open his safe. Donning his silk dressing-gown, he did so. When the police remarked on the stash of cocaine stored inside, Cecchi Gori replied nonchalantly: 'Cocaine? That's not cocaine, it's saffron!'

Meanwhile his business empire was untangling. It should be said that he acquired the empire only by inheritance from his father Mario, who before dying in 1993 had warned his old business partner, Silvio Berlusconi: 'Take care of Vittorio, he is so impulsive and naive.'

Vittorio's problem was that he wanted to be Berlusconi. He bought commercial TV channels (a failure), pumped fortunes into his football team (no titles), dabbled in politics (getting no further than senator), but might have been OK had he not got caught in a divorce expected to be so expensive that it alone could have funded Fiorentina for years. Cecchi Gori remained admirably upbeat even after all this, leaning out of the window of his Mercedes limousine on Rome's Via Veneto to shout '*La dolce vita*!' to friends. However, he ruined Fiorentina.

It was hard to work out which bit of Cecchi Gori's empire owed what to which, but it was clear that he had borrowed tens of millions of pounds from the club. After everything went wrong, he tried the traditional Italian remedy of putting his 82-year-old mother in charge, but even she could not save Fiorentina. A fax from a Colombian bank offering to pay off the club's entire debt proved, amazingly, to be a forgery.

In 2002 Fiorentina went bankrupt, slipping into Italy's fourth division, where they had to visit Tuscan village teams most of whose players were Fiorentina fans. Now they are back in Serie A, but the days of Trap, Batistuta and 'The Animal' Edmundo won't return. Florence is just too small now.

Florence is typical. Mid-sized European cities (between 150,000 and a million inhabitants) have all but dropped off the map of European football. They can no longer afford to compete with clubs from bigger places. In early 2004 it was the turn of Parma, whose owners, the dairy company Parmalat, turned out to have mislaid 10 billion euros. Leeds United are the great English example. In Spain Deportivo La Coruña, pride of a mid-sized Galician city, suddenly discovered that their debt had hit the strictly notional figure of 178 million euros. Valencia followed a few years later. These clubs fell short because they had hardly any supporters outside their own city walls. Other mid-sized cities – Glasgow, Amsterdam, Nottingham – have retreated with less fanfare, but they too must know they will never again produce a European champion. Even Newcastle has slowly emerged from denial.

The third period of the European Cup began in 1982, and hasn't ended yet: rule by sturdy provincial city. There were still a few undersized winners: Porto and Liverpool twice each, and Eindhoven,

Marseille and Dortmund. However, these towns are not exactly midgets. Four of the five are from agglomerations of 1.2 million inhabitants or more. Only Eindhoven has just 210,000 people, and a metropolitan area – if you draw it very generously – of only 750,000. In general, European champions were getting bigger. In modern times, the race has usually gone to the rich.

The swelling of the football economy – the bigger TV contracts, the new stadiums, the freer movement of players and so on – favoured the most popular clubs. For historical reasons, these tended to be the ones in big provincial cities. Their teams came to dominate the Champions League in a sort of endless loop. Every club that won the trophy from 1998 to 2011 had won it at least once before. Most had won it several times before. Are their fans growing blasé? When you have won the thing nine times, the buzz probably starts to fade.

The dominant clubs until now haven't come from the mega-cities of Moscow, London, Paris or Istanbul, but from urban areas with two to five million inhabitants: Milan, Manchester, Munich, Madrid and Barcelona. These cities are big enough to produce the required fan base, yet provincial enough to generate a yearning for global recognition.

Strangely, one of these cities, Madrid, is a democratic capital. How could Real break the golden rule of the Champions League and win the trophy in 1998, 2000 and 2002? Because they had built their mammoth stadium, brand and support in the days when Madrid was the capital of a dictatorship. Spain may have gone social democratic, but Real's players still enter the Santiago Bernabeu in those white 'meringue' shirts as if it were 1955. The club's global standing is a relic of the Fascist era.

GEORGE ZIPF COMES TO LONDON: THE FUTURE METROPOLITAN ERA?

George Kingsley Zipf is an almost forgotten Harvard linguist. Born in 1902, he died in 1950 just as he was starting to make a name, and Zipf is now known only for having formulated a law that explains almost everything. Among other things, Zipf's law tells us that London and Paris should start winning more Champions Leagues soon.

Consider the following: if you rank every American city by the size of its population, the difference in population between two consecutive cities is simply the ratio of their ranks. So if you compare cities number one and two, city two has half (or ½) the population of city one. If you compare cities number two and three, city three has two thirds (⅔) the population of city two. City 100 has 99/100ths the population of city 99, and so on down the list. Statistically speaking, the fit of this relationship is almost as perfect as it is possible to be.

This is a particularly elegant example of a more general relationship known as Zipf's law, and it applies to a lot more than city sizes. For instance, it is also true of the frequency with which words are used in English. 'The' is the most commonly used word in the language, 'of' is second, and so 'of' is used about half (½) as often as 'the'. All in all, Zipf's law has been called possibly 'the most accurate regularity in economics'. (The Nobel prize-winning economist Paul Krugman says, 'Anyone who spends too much time thinking about Zipf's law goes mad,' but we hope that is a joke.)

Zipf's law also works for European cities, though not quite as neatly. City sizes in most European countries are more closely bunched, and so the second city is closer to the first city's size than in the US, the third closer to the second, and so on.

Why might this be? Zipf's law must have something to do with migration. People will always try to migrate to where the money is. In the US, with its open markets and very high mobility of labour, they generally do. But in Europe, political and cultural barriers have curbed migration. That might explain why city sizes are more compressed there. Nonetheless, the academics Matthieu Cristelli, Michael Batty and Luciano Pietronero showed in an article in the prestigious journal *Nature* in 2012 that 'Zipf's Law holds approximately for the city sizes of each European country (France, Italy, Germany, Spain, etc).' They added that the law 'completely falls apart' if you rank them as cities within a single state, i.e. the European Union, but then that is no surprise – these cities grew big in their nation states long before the EU was ever thought of.

For a long time, nobody could understand why Zipf's law should hold for so many different phenomena. Now, though, economists and scientists are starting to generate models of growth in which the natural outcome of a process is distribution obeying Zipf's law. Recently, the New York University economist Xavier Gabaix came up with an explanation for why Zipf's law applies to city sizes. He said Zipf's law emerges when all cities grow at the same rate, regardless of their size and their history, but subject to random variation. This implies that common factors drive the growth of cities within a country, while the differences in growth are due to a series of random events ('shocks' in the economic jargon), like for instance bombing during the war, which in principle could occur anywhere. A story as simple as this is enough to explain the city sizes predicted by Zipf's law.

Two consequences of Zipf's law are crucial to football. First, giants – whether giant cities, giant football clubs, or giants of any other kind – are rare. That is because becoming a giant requires a long sequence of positive shocks, like tossing a coin 50 times and coming up 'heads' every time. It can happen, but it is rare. Second, once a city becomes a giant, it is unlikely to shrink into the middle ranks unless it experiences a long series of repeated misfortunes (50 'tails' in a row). By contrast, small cities are unlikely ever to become giants. In other words, the hierarchy of cities, which has established itself over centuries, probably won't change much in the foreseeable future.

This 'law of proportionate growth' has some other consequences. What's true for cities is also true for many other social phenomena.

For example, if your kid is behind at school, don't worry: he or she will almost certainly catch up, since all children tend to learn at the same rate, plus or minus a few shocks. Likewise, if you think your brilliant six-year-old footballer is going to become another Beckham or Rooney, don't. More likely the boy had a few positive shocks in his early years, which will cancel out. Rooneys and Beckhams almost never happen. The distribution of talent is thus a bit like the distribution of city sizes: a few great talents stand out at the top, the Maradonas and Messis, but as you go down the list the differences become smaller and smaller.

This brings us back to European cities: there are only a few giants, chiefly Moscow, Istanbul, Paris and London. You would expect these giant cities to produce the biggest clubs, and yet they have won just one Champions League between them.

But soon they might win more. Football is changing. It is becoming more of a free market, as Fascist dictators no longer interfere, and the best players are free to move clubs almost as they like. Inevitably, the best players are starting to move to the biggest markets, as happens in American baseball. And so you would expect dominance in European football to move too: after rule by dictatorial capitals, mid-sized provincial towns, and big provincial cities, now London and possibly Moscow and Paris should get in on the act at last.

Moscow might, because it is Europe's last large, non-democratic capital. Russia's resources are being sent to the centre, and with all that oil and gas under the soil, that's a lot of resources. Paris might, because it has nearly 12 million inhabitants, lots of potential sponsors and only one top-division football club, Paris Saint-Germain, which has been appallingly run for years but has now been taken over by Qataris who have converted oil into footballers. And with Chelsea's victory over Bayern on penalties in 2012, London has already got there. (This is one prediction we got right in the 2010 and 2012 editions of *Soccernomics*. We wrote then that 'soon' Arsenal or Chelsea 'could become the first London team to be champions of Europe'.)

It's little surprise that London has finally become a front-rank football city. Even after the implosion of British banks, it has the largest local economy in Europe. It already supports two of Europe's biggest teams, and could probably cope with more. This represents quite a change. In the early 1990s, London rather resembled Moscow *circa* 1973. Tired people in grey clothes waited on packed platforms for 1950s Tube trains. Coffee was an exotic drink that barely existed. Eating a meal outside was forbidden. The city centre was almost uninhabited, and closed at 11pm anyway. There was a sense of permanent decline.

Nor had London ever been even the footballing capital of Britain. Only in 1931 did a southern club – Arsenal – first win the league. Even after that, though, the title generally went north.

But in the 1990s London transformed. Cheap flights from five airports took Londoners around Europe. Trains began running to Paris and Brussels. Today it is quicker to get there than to the shrinking northern cities of Liverpool and Manchester, and less of a culture shock when you arrive. London became a European city, detached from the rest of Britain. The geographer Daniel Dorling said Britain was starting to look like a city-state. Moreover, the city was starting to grow again. Greater London had been losing inhabitants from the Second World War until the 1980s, but boom-time London changed that. Just between 2001 and 2011, the city's population jumped 12 per cent to 8.17 million – the fastest growth of any region of England or Wales in that period.

From the late 1990s until 2008, London offered a technicolour vista of raucous young people from all over the world dressed in weird youth-culture outfits chucking cash at each other. The Tube trains ceased to be antique curios. The place came to smell of money. All this started to give London footballing dominance.

At the same time as the city became fully international, so did the market in footballers. The best ones could now work wherever they wanted. Many of them – like many investment bankers and actors – chose London.

Black and foreign footballers liked living in a city where 95 per cent of inhabitants agree with the statement, 'It is a good thing that Britain is a multicultural society.' When Thierry Henry was spending his best years at Arsenal, he said: 'I love this open, cosmopolitan city. Whatever your race, you never feel people's gaze on you.' In a virtuous cycle, foreigners attract foreigners. The Frenchman Jacques Santini, Tottenham's manager for about five minutes, wanted to come to London because his son Sebastien already lived there – a classic example of chain migration.

Equally to the point, a footballer can still earn a living in London. The capital's clubs have been coining it. In the first place, their customers can still afford to pay exorbitant ticket prices. In 2013–14 Arsenal charged £985 for its cheapest season ticket, which was the highest rate in English – and probably global – football. So many Londoners are happy to fork out this kind of money that Arsenal has been able to build a new stadium with 60,000 seats and sell it out. No club in London's history has drawn such a large regular crowd. In 2012–13 Arsenal and Chelsea achieved revenues per seat per game of over £50, according to the financial analyst Stephen Clapham of the London-based research consultancy Behind the Balance Sheet. These were the highest seat revenues in England, and probably in Europe.

No other European city has as many investors. When Roman Abramovich decided to buy a football club, it was always likely that he would end up owning Chelsea in his adopted city rather than, say, Bolton. When the American billionaire Shahid Khan bought Fulham in 2013, it mattered to him that it was a London club. Even Queens Park Rangers are owned by the Malaysian Tony Fernandes and Indian Lakshmi Mittal, the world's forty-first-richest man, according to *Forbes*, who of course lives around the corner from the club in Kensington. Yes, other rich foreigners have bought Liverpool, Manchester City, Blackburn, and Aston Villa, but London is still a touch more appealing to billionaires.

The handful of the biggest provincial clubs – notably Manchester United, Liverpool, Bayern and Barcelona – have built up such strong brands that they should remain at the top of European football. However, their new challengers will probably not be other provincial clubs but teams from London and Paris. Over the 2012–13 season, the business advisory firm Deloitte ranked Paris Saint-Germain, Chelsea and Arsenal among the eight European clubs with the highest revenues – and that's excluding the extra money put in by Abramovich and PSG's Qataris.

At last, being in a giant capital city is becoming a strategic asset to a football club. No London team had ever reached the Champions League final before 2006. From 2006 to 2012, Arsenal got there once and Chelsea twice, winning one. Soon, if we're not careful, the city will dominate every aspect of British life.

UNFAIR AND UNBALANCED: ARE MANCHESTER UNITED REALLY A PROBLEM?

Kevin Keegan has a knack for phrasing things. In May 2008, at the end of another hopeless season for his club Newcastle, he delivered a 13-minute monologue about the tedium of the Premier League.

'This league is in danger of becoming one of the most boring, but great leagues in the world,' he told a press conference. 'The top four next year will be the same as this year. No manager is going to say what I said 12 years ago, "Watch out, Alex, we are after your title." If they do, they will think they have been drinking something or they are on something.'

He was right about the top four of Manchester United, Chelsea, Arsenal and Liverpool staying the same in 2009. However, the main point about Keegan's monologue is that it phrased so well a new truism of football: that the game is becoming boring because the big clubs win everything.

However, this truism is not true. Fans may say that they wish football were fairer – the Champions League as well as the Premier

League – but the truth is that most of them don't. The majority of supporters prefer unequal leagues. In fact, if football were even less fair, it might become even more popular.

Football stole the idea for a league from baseball. Professional American baseball players had come up with the concept in 1871. The format worked because fans turned out to want a championship in which the winner had played all the other teams. Early championships had involved either, irregular schedules, in which some teams may not have faced all the others, or the knockout cups beloved of English public schoolboys. The all-play-all format of a league has nothing romantic about it, but the winner can justly claim to be the best over a sustained period. No underdog who wins the FA Cup can say the same. Even some world champions can't.

William McGregor proposed the format for his new Football League in 1888, prompted by the musings of several journalists and inspired, according to some contemporaries, by league baseball. His public-school detractors pointed out the idea's American origins as a way of implying that he was only doing it for the money. Yet leagues spread around the world almost as quickly as football did. If cups are high drama, then a league is a soap opera in dozens of episodes with endless crises and some sort of suspense until the very last day. In sports where leagues have traditionally been weak, like rugby union or cricket, fans tend to focus on the national team, and don't follow the sport day-to-day.

The English league has always had strong and weak teams. However, for decades the differences between them had little to do with money. Football was not a free market. Players used to have little freedom to join rich clubs, which is why a small club like Stoke City could hang on to Stanley Matthews for so long. Little clubs were sometimes able to keep a set of good players together for a while. Though Liverpool won the English league from 1982 to 1984, the runners-up were first Ipswich, then Watford, then Southampton. This is no accident. Any rigid labour market will keep talent locked in place.

But we have seen that from the 1980s rich clubs got richer, mostly thanks to new stadiums and TV contracts. As players became freer to change teams, the best went where the money was. In 1995 the Bosman ruling became football's Big Bang: suddenly a European player could join any club in the European Union once his contract had ended. Rich clubs started to gain a monopoly on good players.

In 1992 all the teams in the English top division combined had a total income of £166 million. Over the next 20 years that figure grew by 14 per cent annually – nearly twice as fast as the growth of the British housing bubble in the same period (7.2 per cent a year) – to reach £2.34 billion in 2012.

Meanwhile, in the same period the teams in the second tier of English football raised their revenues by a mere 11 per cent a year. Their total income went from £62 million to about £475 million. (Data are not available for two clubs in 2012.)

Thanks to those three extra percentage points of growth a year, the biggest clubs ran away from the rest. In 1991, remarkably, the English club with the highest income had been Tottenham, with £19 million. Hull City, with £1 million, had the lowest income in the second division. By 2012 the highest revenue of any club in English football was £320 million, and the lowest (known) in the second tier was Doncaster Rovers with £8 million. In other words, the ratio of biggest to smallest in these divisions had jumped from 19:1 to 40:1.

The rich put their money to use. Since the creation of the Premier League in 1992, only very rich clubs have won the title – usually Manchester United, but sometimes Arsenal or a sugar-daddy club.

No wonder Keegan complained about tedium. When he spoke, only four clubs in England had any hope of winning the title. The *Observer* remarked before the 2008–09 season that even though Everton had just finished fifth, you could get odds of 200–1 against their winning the title. Hull were at 10,000–1. The paper noted that fans of most clubs fantasised about finishing fourth; they could imagine nothing grander. Things were similar in the Champions League, where Liverpool and Chelsea flattened tiny foreign clubs like PSV Eindhoven and Bordeaux.

Perhaps the main critic of rule by big clubs is UEFA's president, Michel Platini. The Premier League's lobbyists need to portray the Frenchman as a dangerous enemy, given that nobody with any power in Britain opposes their product, and the old romantic does his best to oblige. Platini is always talking about helping the smaller clubs. Though a former superstar, he even manages to look like a friend of the little man. He is a touch chubby, his suit trousers are too long, and he has the friendly grin of a local grocer.

During an interview in UEFA's headquarters on Lake Geneva, Platini kept grumbling about big money in football. Abu Dhabi's takeover of Manchester City had upset him. Manchester City ought to be a local club, he said. 'Otherwise why should the club call itself Manchester? They should call themselves, I don't know, Coca-Cola.'

Platini has spent a lot of energy trying to limit the disproportionate buying power of English clubs. However, he has had almost no success. 'The English TV rights are very, very, very, very, very significant,' he mused to us. 'So the English league is the richest, so players go to the English league. How to even that out?'

Perhaps it's impossible to even out?

He paused, then admitted: 'Legally it's impossible. You can't stop the foreigners from coming. Financially it's impossible.'

Searching for a way to even things out, in the spring of 2009 Platini put a team of UEFA officials on a plane to the US. Like many others in European football, he had been impressed by the equality in American sports. Perhaps this was something that football could copy? Even Emilio Butragueño, when he was sporting director of plucky little Real Madrid, told the BBC: 'You need uncertainty at the core of every competition ... We may eventually have something similar to the [salary cap] system in the US, to give a chance to all the clubs.'

Andy Burnham, Britain's then culture secretary, warned in 2008 that while the Premier League was 'the world's most successful domestic sporting competition', it risked becoming 'too predictable'. He told the *Guardian*: 'I keep referring to the NFL, which has equal sharing ... In the US, the most free-market country in the world, they understand that equal distribution of money creates genuine competition.'

Indeed, the NFL of American football has been called 'the social-ist league'. Its clubs share TV income equally. Moreover, 40 per cent of each game's gate receipts goes to the visiting team. In the famous slogan promoted by the league, 'On any given Sunday any team can beat any other team.' Baseball, basketball and the US's major league soccer also share far more of their income than European football does. Take the New York Yankees baseball cap, one of the most popular pieces of merchandise in all of sport. Outside of New York, the Yankees receive only one thirtieth of the profit on each cap sold, the same as every other team in baseball. It is as if each Premier League club got one twentieth of the profit every time Manchester United sold a shirt. That's the sort of thing Platini, Burn-ham and Keegan seem to dream of.

Yet their premise is wrong. There is almost no evidence to support their arguments for balance. The data show that, overall, football fans prefer unbalanced leagues.

If predictable results bored fans, then more of them would go to matches where the outcome was very uncertain. How to test whether fans really behave like that? Researchers have tried to gauge expected outcomes of games by using either pre-match betting odds, or the form of both teams over the previous half-dozen games. Studies of football, mostly in England, show mixed results. Some find that more balanced games attract more fans. Others find the reverse.

A moment's thought suggests why some unbalanced games might be very attractive. Often they involve strong home teams play-ing weak away teams (Manchester United v Stoke, say), in which case the home team typically has lots of fans who enjoy watching their heroes score lots of goals; or they are games between weak home teams and strong away teams (Stoke v Manchester United), in which local fans come to see the visiting stars or in the hope of seeing an upset.

The economists David Forrest of Salford Business School and Robert Simmons of Lancaster University have done some of the best work in this field. They found that a balanced game could sometimes increase attendance. However, they also carried out a simulation to show that if the English leagues became more balanced, they would attract *fewer* fans. That is because a balanced league, in which all teams were equally good, would turn into an almost interminable procession of home wins and away losses. By contrast, in real existing football, some of the most balanced games occur when a weak team plays at home against a strong team (again, Stoke v Manchester United).

Forrest and Simmons found that the people who care most about competitive balance are television viewers. Most fans at the ground are the hard core: they simply want to see their team. But TV viewers tend to be 'floating voters'. When the outcome of a game seems too predictable, they switch off. The two economists found that the closer a televised match was expected to be (measured by the form of both teams going into the game), the higher the viewing figures on Sky TV. Yet the size of this effect was modest. Forrest and Simmons said that even if the Premier League were perfectly balanced (in the sense that each team had an equal probability of winning each game) TV audiences would rise by only 6 per cent. That would be a small effect for such a revolutionary change.

Another way of looking at competitive balance is to view the league as a whole, rather than match by match. Do more spectators come when the title race is exciting than when one side runs away with it?

It turns out that a thrilling title race does little to improve attendances. Fans will watch their teams play in the league even when they haven't a hope of winning it (or else dozens of English clubs would not exist).

It is true that a game has to be significant to draw fans, but that significance need not have anything to do with winning the title. A study by Stephen Dobson and John Goddard showed that when a match matters more either for winning the league *or* for avoiding relegation then attendance tends to rise. Trying to qualify for Europe also gives meaning to matches. Most matches in the Premier League are significant for something or other. Given that they can be significant in many different ways, it is unclear why a more balanced league would create more significance. As the Premier League's chief executive Richard Scudamore said, responding to Keegan's lament: 'There are a lot of different tussles that go on in the Premier League, depending on whether you're at the top, in the middle or at the bottom, that make it interesting.'

There is a third way of looking at balance: the long term. Does the dominance of the same teams year in, year out turn fans off? Let's compare a long period with dominance to a long period without dominance: the fairly 'equal' era in English football that ran from 1949 to 1968, and the 'unfair' era of the Premier League from 1993 to 2012.

In the first 20-year period, 11 different teams won the English league. The most frequent winner, Manchester United, won five titles in the period. The second period was far more predictable: only five teams won the title, with United taking it 13 times. And yet during the first, 'equal' period, total annual attendance in the first division fell from an all-time high of 18 million in 1949 to only 15 million in 1968 (and even that figure got a temporary boost from England winning the World Cup). During the second, 'unequal' period, total attendance rose from below 10 million to over 13 million, even though tickets became much more expensive and people had many more choices of how to spend their free time.

Anyone who says that the Premier League has become 'one of the most boring leagues in the world', a closed shop that shuts out smaller clubs from the lower divisions, has to explain why so many people now go to watch all levels of English league football. In the 2009–2010 season, in the pits of recession, over 30 million spectators saw professional games in England, the highest figure since well before all-seater stadiums came in in the early 1990s. The Premier League drew vast crowds despite its intense predictability. Yet more than half of those 30 million-plus watched the Football League, the three divisions below the Premier League. All the clubs in the Championship have supposedly been doomed to irrelevance by the super-rich clubs, and can only dream of clinging on at the bottom of the Premier League, yet their division in 2010–2011 was Europe's fourth-best attended league, ranked by total number of spectators.

Some of English football's critics have not digested these figures. When we pointed out to Platini that English stadiums are full nowadays, he replied: 'Not all. They're full at the teams that win.' Indeed, whenever rows of empty seats appear at struggling teams near the bottom of the table, it is back-page news, and regarded as ominous for the Premier League as a whole. Yet it's natural that some fans should desert disappointing teams, while others flock to exciting ones. Sunderland, Arsenal, Manchester United and other clubs have built bigger stadiums, and filled them. Not every English team has gained spectators since 1992, but most have.

All 20 clubs in the Premier League in 2011–12 had a higher average attendance than in 1992–93. If the team had been in the Premier League in 1992, the average increase was 48 per cent; if it had risen from a lower division, the average increase was an even more handsome 93 per cent. Even teams that were in the Premier League in 1992–93 but not in 2011–12 usually had a higher attendance – only Leeds, Sheffield Wednesday and Oldham Athletic lost spectators. The rising English tide had lifted almost every boat.

Admittedly, today's large crowds don't in themselves prove that dominance attracts fans. After all, many other things have changed since the more equal 1949–68 period. Crucially, the stadiums have improved. However, the rising attendances do make it hard to believe that dominance in itself significantly undermines interest. Indeed, pretty much every football league in Europe exhibits more dominance than the American major leagues, and yet fans still go.

There are good reasons why fans generally prefer inequality to balance. First, most fans in the stadium are fans of the home team, and so they do not really want a balanced outcome. Second, big teams have more fans than small ones, and so if Manchester United beat Stoke more people are happy than if Stoke win. Third, fans are surprisingly good at losing. Psychological studies show that they are skilled at transferring blame: 'We played well, but the referee was rubbish.' This means that fans will often stick with a team even if it always loses. It also explains why, the morning after England get knocked out of a World Cup, people don't collapse into depression but get on with their lives.

Fourth, dominant teams create a special interest of their own. In the 1990s, millions of people supported Manchester United, and millions of others despised them. In a way, both groups were following the club. United were the star of football's soap opera. Every other team's fans dreamt of beating them. Much of the meaning of supporting West Ham, for instance, derives from disliking Manchester United. Keegan thrillingly captured that national sentiment with his famous 'I will love it if we beat them! Love it!' monologue in 1996. Big bad United made the league more fun.

Strangely, it was the fanzine *When Saturday Comes* that put this best. *WSC* is, in large part, the journal of small clubs. It publishes moving and funny pieces by fans of Crewe or Swansea. Few of its readers have much sympathy with Manchester United (though some, inevitably, are United fans). Many have argued for a fairer league. One of the magazine's regular writers, Ian Plenderleith, is fairly typical in being a Lincoln City supporter. Yet in September 2008 Plenderleith, who lived outside Washington DC, argued in *WSC* that American major league soccer, in which 'all teams started equal, with the same squad size, and the same amount of money to spread among its players' wages', was boring. The reason: 'No truly memorable teams have the space to develop.'

'MLS is crying out for a couple of big, successful teams,' Plenderleith admitted. 'Teams you can hate. Dynasties you really, really want to beat. Right now, as LA Galaxy coach Bruce Arena once memorably said: "It's a crapshoot."'

In short, the MLS lacks one of the joys of an unbalanced league: the David v Goliath match. And one reason why fans enjoy those encounters is that surprisingly often, given their respective budgets, David wins.

The economist Jack Hirshleifer called this phenomenon 'the paradox of power'. Imagine, he said, that there were two tribes, one large, one small. Each can devote its efforts to just two activities: farming and fighting. Each tribe produces its own food through farming, and steals the other tribe's food through fighting. Which tribe will devote a larger *share* of its efforts to fighting?

The answer is the small tribe. The best way to understand this is to imagine that the small tribe is very small indeed. It would then have to devote almost all its limited resources to either fighting or farming. If it chose farming, it would be vulnerable to attack. Everything it produced could be stolen. On the other hand, if the tribe devoted all its resources to fighting, it would have at least a chance of stealing some resources. So Hirshleifer concludes – and proves with a mathematical model – that smaller competitors will tend to devote a greater share of resources to competitive activities.

He found many real-world examples of the paradox of power. He liked citing Vietnam's defeat of the US, but one might also add the Afghan resistance to the Soviet Union in the 1980s, the Dutch resistance to the Spanish in the sixteenth century or the American resistance to the British in the War of Independence. In these cases the little guy actually defeated the big guy. In many other cases, the little guy was eventually defeated, but at much greater cost than might have been expected on the basis of their physical resources (the

Spartans at Thermopylae, the Afrikaners in the Boer War, the Texans at the Alamo).

In football, as in war, the underdog tends to try harder. Big teams fight more big battles, and so each contest weighs a little less heavily than it does with their smaller rivals. Little teams understand that they may have few opportunities to compete at the highest level, and so they give it everything. They therefore probably win more often than you would predict on the basis of ability alone.

Fans enjoy unbalanced modern football. Yet the complaints about its imbalance continue. The curious thing is that these complaints are relatively new, a product of the last 20 years or so. Contrary to popular opinion, football was unbalanced in the past too, but before the 1990s fewer people complained.

It is a fantasy that in the past every team had a chance to win, just as it's a fantasy that football used to be more popular. (It is possible that more people are interested today than at any time in the past.) Europe as a whole has never been a very balanced footballing continent. In smaller countries, clubs from the capital tended to rule. Serie A was always dominated by Juventus, Milan and Inter, and the Primera Liga by Barcelona and Real Madrid. By the 1980s Bayern dominated in Germany, and in the post-war era English football has been dominated by Manchester United, Arsenal and Liverpool. United's 13 titles in 21 seasons up to 2013 may sound boring, but Liverpool won 10 in 20 between 1969 and 1988. A handful of sides have dominated for most of English football's history. Even a club as large as Newcastle have not won the title since 1927. The imbalance in England as in all European leagues was reinforced by European competition, which handed the dominant teams more money.

The old European Cup was seldom much fairer than the Champions League is now. We saw in the previous chapter that only between 1970 and 1981 did teams from modestly sized towns regularly win the trophy. Usually the cup went to the biggest provincial cities, or to Madrid. Even Platini admits: 'For 40 years it's been the biggest clubs that won the Champions League; when I played, too. With or without homegrown players, it was Real Madrid, Liverpool, Manchester, Juventus who won. English clubs won the cup 10 times in a row, I think. No? In the 1980s.'

Oh dear. Platini is not going to win any pub quizzes any time soon. In fact English clubs won six European cups from 1977 to 1982. But his point stands: inequality in the European Cup is nothing new.

He smiles, thinking again of that English dominance in the 1980s: 'It's funny. There were no great debates then, saying, "We have to change everything." Today it's the money that makes the difference.'

That is precisely the point. Today's inequality bothers people not because it is unprecedented, but because it is more driven by money than it used to be. In the old days, a middling team could suddenly enjoy years of dominance if it happened to hire an excellent manager who signed excellent players. That's what happened to Liverpool under Bill Shankly, and to Forest under Brian Clough. Today, a middling team can suddenly enjoy years of dominance if it happens to be bought by a billionaire who hires an excellent manager who signs excellent players. That is what happened to Chelsea under Roman Abramovich, and what may happen to Manchester City under Abu Dhabian rule. In short, inequality in football, as well as not being boring, is not even new. The one thing that is new is the money.

Many people tend to feel that inequality becomes unfair when it is bought with money. It disgusts them that Chelsea can sign the best players simply because they are a rich club. This is a moral argument. It's a form of idealistic egalitarianism, which says that all teams should have more or less equal resources. This stance may be morally right (we cannot judge), but it is not a practical political agenda, and it probably doesn't reflect what most football fans want. Spectators vote with their feet. It's certainly not the case that millions of them are abandoning the Premier League because the money offends them. The evidence of what they go to watch suggests that they want to see the best players competing against each other. Many people resent Manchester United. Few seem to find them boring.

SECTION II

THE FANS:
Loyalty, Suicides, Happiness, and the Country
with the Best Supporters

THE COUNTRY
THAT LOVES
FOOTBALL MOST

Which country loves football most?

This might sound like a matter of the heart that is hard to measure, but in fact the data exist. Loving football expresses itself in three main ways: playing the game, going to the stadium, and watching football on TV. We have international figures for all three.

First, a caveat: not all the numbers are reliable. There are lies, damned lies and statistics; and statistics from outside the western world tend to be even worse. We will therefore limit our quest to Europe. Using a bit of judgement, by the end of the chapter we will be able to say with some confidence which European country cares most about the game.

PLAYERS: OH, TO BE A TINY ISLAND

In 2006 FIFA tried to count how many people in the world played football. The 'Big Count' came up with 265 million footballers, more than 90 per cent of them males. Some were registered with proper clubs. The overwhelming majority, though, were 'unregistered occasional players' who kicked around with mates on playgrounds and beaches and five-a-side courts. The only way to find out whether these people played football was by asking them – or at least a tiny representative sample of them.

None of these obstacles put off FIFA. The organisation is a bit vague about exactly how it got hold of the figures, saying it used 'the standard practice of a questionnaire as well as an online tool'. It also threw in its Big Count 2000, plus a UEFA survey and other 'internal analyses', to 'supplement missing data from associations and for plausibility purposes'. Reading between the lines of the survey, it seems that more than a fifth of national FAs didn't even bother to take part. The whole endeavour was 'scientifically observed by Lamprecht & Stamm SFB AG, a social research company based [handily] in Zurich'.

Anyway, the most ambitious survey of football participation in history came up with a list of the keenest football-playing countries. China and the US were found to have the most players (26 million and 24 million respectively), but of course the key question is which countries had the largest percentage of their inhabitants playing. Here is FIFA's list:

1	Costa Rica	27	11	Anguilla	12
2	Germany	20	12	Austria	12
3	Faroe Islands	17	13	Norway	12
4	Guatemala	16	14	Slovakia	11
5	Chile	16	15	Sweden	11
6	Paraguay	16	16	Bermuda	11
7	Aruba	15	17	Iceland	11
8	Barbados	13	18	Netherlands	11
9	Vanuatu	13	19	Ireland	10
10	Mali	12	20	Cook Islands	10

It's striking how many of the keenest footballers live on little islands where there presumably isn't much else to do but play football and watch the waves roll in. The Faroe Islands, Aruba, Barbados,

Vanuatu, Anguilla, Bermuda, Iceland and the Cook Islands (combined population about a million) all make the top 20.

FIFA's list is interesting if true. Let's take the case of Mali, tenth on the list. This is a vast, unstable country with poor or non-existent roads. It stretches much of the way across the Sahara. The average inhabitant has a daily income of about £1. Who worked out that 11 per cent of the 12 million Malians play football?

Even the European figures are dubious. When the Mulier Instituut in the Netherlands set out to collate data on sports participation in the EU, it began its report with a series of caveats. Different countries use different methods to establish how many people play sport, it said. 'Even within a single year, research conducted in one and the same country can result in significant differences in the recorded figures for sport participation for up to 40 per cent.'

Still, when it comes to European countries at least, FIFA's list probably has some value. That's because Europe is an organised sort of continent where a high proportion of the people who play football are actually registered with a club. We have a good idea of how many registered footballers there are, because every one of them belongs to the country's FA. So the number of registered players in a European country is a fair indicator of the total of all its footballers. By way of reality check, let's see whether the European countries on FIFA's overall list of keenest players had lots of *registered* footballers too.

It turns out that Germany, Holland, Austria and Sweden – all in the top 20 of keenest football countries per capita – also figured in FIFA's top 20 countries with the most registered footballers. Furthermore, Slovakia was in the top 20 countries with most registered *male* footballers, even though it has only 5.4 million inhabitants. In the Faroes, Norway and Ireland, also on FIFA's list of keenest countries, a mammoth 10 per cent or so of the population were registered footballers. Of the keenest European countries identified by FIFA, only Iceland lagged a bit in registration: just 7 per cent of Icelanders were registered players. However, as we'll see,

Iceland – with artificial mini-pitches at most of its schools – now seems to harbour an unusually high amount of casual kickaround football.

So it seems that the European countries in FIFA's top 20 per capita might really play a lot of football. Without treating the Big Count as gospel, let's give those nine Europeans countries on FIFA's list a little star each, and continue our quest to find the keenest of them all.

SPECTATORS: GREAT HORDES OF PEOPLE NOT GOING TO FOOTBALL MATCHES

Playing is one way of expressing a love of football. Going to watch matches is another.

When you think of packed football stadiums, you think of England. Visually, football crowds are one of the things that the English do best. And everyone knows that the Premier League has the biggest crowds in the world.

Well, the second-biggest crowds, anyway. The average attendance in the Premier League in 2012–13 (the season for which we have compared attendances around Europe) was 35,921. That was nearly 7,000 fewer than went to see the average Bundesliga game that same year.

This fact comes from a weirdly addictive statistics website. The best thing about www.european-football-statistics.co.uk is its collection of average attendances for almost every football league in Europe. These stats give surprising insights into fandom, and help reveal which European country is maddest about the game.

The first thing you notice on the website is how much attendances fluctuate over time. The data on the site go back decades. Back in the 1980s, when Italian stadiums were as safe as family restaurants and Serie A was the world's best league, Italians watched far more football than the English. In the 1984–85 season the average crowd in Serie A was 38,872. Meanwhile, in the English first division in that year of Bradford and Heysel, only 21,080 braved the average league match.

How times change. By the 2012–13 season, Serie A and the Premier League had pretty much changed places: the average Italian game drew only 23,234 people, a good 12,000 fewer than the Premier League.

Many other European leagues also have sharp trends in attendance over time, further evidence that fans behave much more like consumers than like addicts. French, German and Dutch attendances have soared since the 1990s. In eastern Europe, by contrast, we see what Brian Clough once called the great hordes of people not going to football matches. These empty stadiums are a post-Communist phenomenon. Back in 1989, Nicolae Ceaucescu's last year in power, the average crowd at a Romanian first-division match was officially 17,000, nearly as many as in England at the time. In 2012–13 it was just 5,184.

The least popular league in Europe was Estonia's, with an average attendance in the country's top division of 215 (presumably not so hard to count). And even given that Russian men are dying at such a startling rate, it's disappointing that only 13,180 on average bothered to turn up to premier league matches there. The English Championship (average: 17,488) was more popular, and in fact outdrew every league in Europe east of Germany. The English and Germans are the only Europeans who go to watch lower-division football in numbers.

However, as a friend of ours in Moscow once advised: 'Never believe any Russian statistic.' Paul In 't Hout, longtime boss of european-football-statistics.co.uk, told us he doubted the stats for certain eastern European countries. He got particularly suspicious when the official attendance for a game was reported as a round number – 3,000, for instance – as opposed to a precise one, like 3,142. He emailed: 'In some leagues I found figures for one game of, for example, 2,000 and 5,000.' His doubts recall Benford's law, a theory about the frequency with which digits will appear in data.

One implication of this law is that datasets with lots of zeroes at the end often turn out to be fraudulent.

The western European data on attendances tend to be more reliable. Even there, though, there are doubts. In England, is the attendance the number of people who actually went to the game, or the number who held tickets for it? After all, many season ticket holders skip some matches. At a small club at the end of a disappointing season, they might have trouble passing on their tickets. In countries such as Italy, ticket sellers have been known to wave hundreds of scary-looking away fans through without anyone paying. Some turnstile attendants might slip the odd bribe into their pockets and click somebody through, or let in friends for free. Clubs in some countries might report a lower attendance than the real figure, to reduce the tax they pay on their ticket income. Anyway, there's often nobody assiduously counting bums on seats.

Still, the figures on european-football-statistics.co.uk do tell us something. Most of them are not made up. Especially in western Europe, they probably correlate to a large degree with the number of people who actually went to games. And we can accept the general finding that eastern European crowds are low. A glance at the pictures on TV tells us that. Admittedly we can't make a precise ranking of average crowds in all European countries, but we can identify a few countries where attendances at football seem to be particularly high as a share of their population.

The way to identify these hot spots is first to count the combined average crowds for the main professional divisions in each country. Let's start with the largest European countries, which typically have three serious divisions each. England has four, but so as to compare it with France, Germany, Italy and Spain we will only analyse its top three divisions.

The 68 English league clubs in those three divisions averaged about 1.29 million spectators between them in 2012–13. (The clubs in League Two averaged another 105,000 in total, too few to make much difference to the national total.) That is, over two normal match days, in which every club played at home at least once, you would expect 1.29 million people to show up in England's top three divisions. That is by no means a precise figure, but it is probably a decent indication.

We then divided that spectator average by the country's population. England has 53 million inhabitants. 1.29 divided by 53 = 0.024. That means that the total combined spectator average of English clubs equals 2.4 per cent of the English population.

It turns out the English are the keenest stadium-goers of all the large European countries. Here are the (very rough) stats for the top three divisions of each big country:

TOTAL SPECTATOR AVERAGE AS PERCENTAGE OF POPULATION

1	England	2.4	4	Italy	1.0
2	Spain	1.5	5	France	0.9
3	Germany	1.5			

Spain has experienced a sharp fall since 2007–08, when we last calculated these numbers. Probably because of the recession, its percentage dropped from 1.9 per cent then to 1.5 per cent today. Spain's average in both cases included only the top two divisions – all that european-football-statistics.co.uk had. However, in the other large countries the crowds for the third division added only between 0.1 and 0.2 percentage points to the national total.

So far the English have lived up to their reputation as great consumers (if not players) of football. But when we compare them to the smaller western European nations, their spectating becomes less spectacular. The Scots, for one, are much keener watchers of football. Celtic and Rangers between them drew average crowds of over 92,000 in 2012–13. That's not bad in a nation of 5.3 million, particularly in a season when Rangers were playing in the third division. In a typical fortnight that year, a combined total of 1.7 per cent of Scots watched either Celtic or Rangers play at home. The two most watched clubs in England, Manchester United and Arsenal,

would need home crowds of 450,000 each to draw the same proportion of the English population. You might even say that the English
are somewhat lacklustre fans given that they have the best teams
on earth playing in their local grounds. On the other hand, they also
have to pay the highest ticket prices on earth.

The Scots are among the European spectating elite, if not at the
very top. Here are the European countries whose inhabitants,
according to european-football-statistics.co.uk, are most inclined to
watch professional football:

TOTAL SPECTATOR AVERAGE AS PERCENTAGE OF POPULATION

1	Faroe Islands	10.0	4	Cyprus	3.6
2	Iceland	4.0	5	Norway	2.6
3	Scotland	3.8	6	Netherlands	2.5

For Scotland, Norway and the Netherlands, we counted attendance
figures in the top two divisions; for even smaller Cyprus, Iceland
and the Faroes, only the top one. All 12 clubs in the Icelandic top
division put together had a total average attendance of just 12,684
in 2013, a bit less than Bristol City all by itself. However, that
was pretty good for a country of about 320,000 people who had
just decimated their own economy by buying up half the world's
toxic assets.

But even among these high-flying countries, one stands out: the
freezing, windswept Faroe Islands of the north Atlantic. The Faroes'
10 first-division clubs, staffed mostly by men who work in fishing,
have combined average home crowds of 5,070 people. That figure
may not sound mammoth, but it amounts to a whopping 10 per cent
of the Faroes' population. By tradition, the crowd invades the artificial pitch at half-time and after the game.

International games draw about 5,000 people to the national
stadium (which handily houses a bed-and-breakfast). However,
Virgar Hvidbro, general secretary of the Faroe Islands Football Association, recalls 8,000 cramming in for a game against Malta in the

good old days when regulations were less strict. A rare foreign observer of Faroese football, the British photographer Andrew Tobin, explains: 'Watching the local team is one of the main activities available in the small towns, which, while often very picturesque, lack many other forms of entertainment.' According to Tobin, many Faroese introduce themselves first with their own name, and second with the name of the English club they support.

When it comes to watching live football, no other country in Europe even comes close to the Faroes. We've already seen that 17 per cent of the islanders played the game in 2006. These fishing folk sure do like their football. 'The importance of football to the Faroes is almost the same as it is for the Brazilians,' says prime minister Kaj Leo Johannesen, who is of course a former international goalkeeper.

It would be silly to treat the attendance figures for these top six nations as exact to the decimal point. On the other hand, these are countries that tend to produce fairly reliable statistics. Norway and the Netherlands are wealthy and hyper-organised. Iceland was wealthy until it discovered toxic assets, and remains hyper-organised. The Faroes are fairly well off, and those 5,070 spectators can't be very difficult to count. Scottish football has some modern stadiums and voracious marketing officials, who keep elaborate electronic databases of their supporters. They have a pretty good idea of how many come to matches. In 't Hout told us that he considered the Norwegian, Icelandic and Scottish attendance data quite reliable, because they were reported as exact figures – 3,921 or 5,812 spectators. He was more suspicious of Cyprus, where (as in eastern Europe) the figures were reported as round numbers like 2,000 or 9,000.

Still, we can say with some confidence that all these top six nations love going to watch football. Their position at the top of these rankings is not a one-off. When we did this exercise in 2008, Cyprus, Iceland, Scotland and Norway were all in the top four (the website had no attendance figures for the Faroes back then). People in these countries watch in astonishing numbers, given how poor their leagues are. To quote Nick Hornby, marvelling at the thousands of people who watch even the most pathetic English clubs: 'Why, really, should anyone have gone at all?'

In the case of Norway in particular, it should be noted that Norwegians don't just go to watch their own football. They go and watch England's too. Obsession with English football is now almost a human universal – South African cabinet meetings have occasionally been interrupted by quarrels over the previous night's English games – but Norway got there first. On Saturday 29 November 1969, decades before the Premier League hatched its secret plans for world domination, Norwegian TV broadcast its first-ever live English match: Wolves 1, Sunderland 0. Naturally, the nation was hooked. The Saturday game from England fast became an institution. 'The most important thing in Norway when it comes to affection for soccer is the Saturday TV games,' says Andreas Selliaas, who works for Norsk Tipping, the Norwegian national lottery. 'My father supports Leyton Orient. Why?'

Orient isn't even the worst of it. Tiny British teams like Barnet and Rushden and Diamonds have Norwegian fan clubs (King Harald is an honorary member of the Spurs supporters' club). Then there are the planeloads of Norwegians who commute to Old Trafford. According to the national tourist agency VisitBritain, 80,000 Norwegians came to see a football match in Britain in 2011, more than any other visiting nationality except the Irish. And while doing all this, the Norwegians still find time to lead the world at winter sports.

Norway and the other five leading spectating countries each get a star in our quest to find Europe's most enthusiastic football nation. Four of the top six – the Faroes, Norway, Iceland and the Netherlands – also appeared in our very cautious list of the countries that played the most football. The Faroes were ahead of their nearest rivals in both categories, so they currently lead the European pack. But the Norwegians, Icelanders and Dutch also enter the final round of our contest with two stars each.

NATIONS OF COUCH POTATOES:
THE MOST POPULAR TV PROGRAMMES IN HISTORY

In our quest to establish which country cares most about football, one statistic towers over all the others: TV viewing figures. After all, relatively few people actually play football – seldom more than 10 per cent of a country's inhabitants – and even fewer watch it in stadiums. In any case, we have seen the flaws in the data for playing and spectating. But we do have good figures for the most popular way to consume football: watching World Cups and European Championships on TV. Viewing figures are the final piece of evidence to assess before we can name the most football-mad country in Europe.

TV ratings have plunged over the last 30 years. Once upon a time only the BBC broadcast in Britain, and so every programme the Corporation aired had a market share of 100 per cent of viewers. Then television expanded: first came other free channels like ITV and Channel Four, and later satellite and broadband cable. Audiences in all rich countries splintered between the different channels. The share that any one show could command slumped. In the US for instance, 36 of the top 45 shows ever aired were shown before 1990. No longer does the whole family sit down together to watch *M*A*S*H* or *Cheers*. But here's the thing: all the top nine American programmes from 1990 to 2008 were sports events. Seven were Super Bowls, and the other two were ladies' figure-skating events from the 1994 winter Olympics, which people watched because they knew that one American skater had paid someone to nobble her rival in the national team. Only sport could still unite Americans on the sofa.

It is the same in Germany, where seven out of the eight highest-rated programmes involved the German football team playing in a major tournament. In Britain only the 1966 World Cup final and the 1970 FA Cup final replay between Leeds and Chelsea make the top 10. Still, here too big football tournaments provide some of the communal glue once supplied by trade unions, churches and royal weddings. Possibly the best chance English people get to bond with each other nowadays, unless they are weeping over the passing of Jade Goody, is during a World Cup.

Big football matches have that sort of unifying role in most European countries. Their appeal goes beyond men. Forty per cent of the global audience for Euro 2004 was female. In fact, it is the long-term rise in female viewers that has made televised football more popular than ever before.

Before we can work out which country watches most football on TV, we need to separate the reliable viewing data from the false ones. Organisations like FIFA and the International Olympic Committee report the highest numbers they can. The more TV viewers an event attracts, the more advertising will flow to the event, and the more broadcasters will pay to screen it.

Hence the improbable tallies that organisers sometimes cite for their events. According to FIFA, a cool 715 million people watched the World Cup final in 2006. Even this claim looks modest compared with the 1.5 billion who supposedly saw the opening ceremony of the Commonwealth Games in Melbourne. What to believe?

This is where Kevin Alavy comes in. Alavy is managing director of the Futures Sport + Entertainment consultancy. His job is to sit in London working out how many people really watch different sports events, though in fact he is far more interesting and charming than that description implies. This is how he defines his work: 'Very simply, are these sports events worth the massive investment that they typically cost, and how can my clients get even more value from their association with sport?'

Alavy can explain how the inflated numbers were invented and provide advertisers (and some of the rights-holders) with the more reliable estimates they need. He also extracts trends from the mountains of broadcasting data that exist nowadays. For this book, he gave us an insight into some of the data he has been gathering on World Cups and European Championships since 1998. Using it, we can identify the most fanatical football nation in Europe.

Around the world, TV data are extrapolated from the viewing habits of a sample of the population – in the US, about 10,000 people. Individuals used to get paid a small fee to keep a diary of their TV consumption. Then came the 'people meter': a little electronic box attached to a TV set that allows each person in a household to indicate when they are watching. Invented in Britain, the people meter is now used in most wealthy countries to measure viewing. Alavy calls it 'the gold standard of global media research'.

To see how people meter data differ from the inflated data, consider the Super Bowl. It is indisputably the most watched event in the US. The 10 Super Bowls up to 2008 were the 10 most watched American TV programmes of that decade. But exactly how watched were they? Figures of 750 million to a billion global viewers per game get cited. Instead, using the people meter data, Alavy puts a typical Super Bowl's average live audience in those years at about 100 million viewers, or about one third of all Americans excluding the under-fives. (That is a mammoth figure, except when compared with the viewing figures for big soccer games. For instance, six matches at Euro 2004 drew a larger live global audience than that year's Super Bowl.)

The inflated figure of '750 million to one billion' is not an outright lie. Rather, it is a reasonable guess as to the number of people in the world who could have watched the Super Bowl on TV because they subscribed to the right channels.

Using the people meter, Alavy has collected verifiable viewing figures for sport in 54 countries. Of the countries on his list 31 are in Europe, 12 in Asia, 10 in the Americas, and only one (South Africa) in Africa, a continent where there is almost no serious measurement of viewing habits. Many poorer countries still use diaries rather than people meters. Even so, for 33 of Alavy's 54 countries, we have figures for at least four of the six major football tournaments from the World Cup of 1998 up to Euro 2008.

The viewing figure Alavy uses for any given game or event is the 'average programme audience'. That is the average number of viewers during the entire event, rather than the peak figure, which would typically be 1.5 times higher, or the 'reach', which includes anyone who caught at least three minutes.

The average audience for many TV programmes is frighteningly low. In fact, Alavy estimates that on current trends, over a quarter of sports programmes around the world are now *watched by nobody*. That is, they have no measurable audience.

Happily, big international football tournaments are watched by many people. Almost any game at a world cup and many in the European Championship nowadays will beat the magic mark of 100 million global viewers. Hardly anything else on television can match that, not even iconic events like the Oscars, or President Obama's inauguration, or Princess Diana's funeral, says Alavy.

He reports the viewing figure for any game as a percentage of all the people in each country who live in households with TV sets. In most European nations almost every household has owned a set since the 1970s. However, that is not true in less developed nations. Only about a quarter of India's population of 1.2 billion, for instance, lived in households with TVs in 2008.

Alavy's collection is a treasure chest: thousands of TV ratings covering hundreds of games between national teams screened in 54 countries since 1998. However, there is an obvious problem: Germans probably watch lots of games involving Germany, and Germany has a pretty good record; how to compare the viewing figures of the successful Germans with the not-quite-so-successful English? Indeed, how to compare German viewing of Euro 2008, where their team made the final, to viewing by the English, whose team didn't even qualify? Or to cite another complication: a casual fan who only watches his own national team is surely not to be compared to the fanatic who glues herself to the sofa for every match of the tournament. Going one step further, viewers in Malaysia or Colombia who follow European Championships must surely be considered to have reached the acme of perfection in fandom.

There are other problems. The World Cup in Japan and Korea had disastrous TV ratings in Europe, because most games were played in the European late morning or at lunchtime. That is why FIFA was so keen to keep the World Cup of 2010 in South Africa despite all the problems there: Johannesburg is usually just one hour ahead of Central European Time, making it ideal for European viewers. It's less convenient for Americans. In all the agonising over the refusal of Americans to watch soccer on TV (as opposed to playing it, which American children do in great numbers) an obvious but overlooked explanation is that most of the best games are played in Europe at times when most Americans are working. In 2014, for the first time in 20 years, Americans will have a World Cup more or less in their own time zones (but even then most kick-off times were scheduled to suit Europeans).

We also need to take account of the significance of each match. Obviously some matches will draw more viewers than others, but how many more?

In short, no two of our thousands of ratings are strictly comparable. Happily, there is a way to control for the differences, and so to strip down to the essence of TV fandom. We can expect viewing levels in every country to rise for the final of a tournament. We can also expect an uplift when the country's own national team plays, or when a game is shown in prime time. We need to wheel out the technique of multiple regression. Quite simply, multiple regression is a mathematical formula (first identified by the mathematician Carl Friedrich Gauss in 1801) for finding the closest statistical fit between one thing (in this case TV viewing figures) and any other collection of things (time of match, who is playing and so forth). The idea is beautifully simple. The problem used to be the endless amount of computation required to find the closest fit. Luckily, modern computers have reduced this process to the press of a button (just look up 'regression' on your spreadsheet package).

When you have many observations – like the thousands we have here – the regression technique is extremely powerful. Not only does it give you a precise figure for the influence of one factor on another, but it can also tell you how reliable that statistical estimate is. For example, the regression can show that playing a game in prime time will add, say, 4 per cent to the size of the audience; and it can also reveal that the probability that this estimate is mistaken is less than 1 per cent.

Running a regression will allow us to isolate each contributory factor – such as kick-off time – and measure its impact on attendance. Not only will this tell us a great deal about what attracts viewers to televised football, but the final figure that we are left with after these regressions consists of two parts. One part is what is called a 'random error': that which we cannot explain because we know too little about what happened on the day. The other part, though, is a 'fixed effect': an estimate of the viewing share that a football match will achieve in a given country, stripped of all other characteristics like kick-off time, identity of teams, stage in the tournament etc.

The 'fixed effect' is what we are after. The size of the fixed effect in each country will tell us how keen that country is on watching international football on TV. The method works like this:

Our data show that the 'fixed effect' for the UK is 6.98. This means that just under 7 per cent of all British households with TV sets will watch a World Cup or European championship game, regardless of its characteristics. Seven per cent is the proportion of Brits that we can expect to have watched, say, Tunisia v Saudi Arabia at the World Cup of 2006.

However, if the game is played in the middle of prime time (meaning a kick-off between 7pm and 8.45pm) the total of British viewers rises by about 4.3 per cent. If the game is a semi-final, viewing goes up another 5.6 per cent.

So our regressions would lead us to estimate the British audience for each World Cup semi-final in 2006 at 16.9 per cent. The core audience of 7 per cent would have risen by 4.3 per cent because each game kicked off in prime time, and by another 5.6 per cent because it was a semi-final. (7 + 4.3 + 5.6 = 16.9). The actual viewing figures for each game were within two percentage points of our estimates.

This is by no means perfect, but over the hundreds of games seen in 54 countries, the errors are relatively small. The average rating figure for each game taken across all 54 countries is 8.6 per cent. Again: that is the proportion of households with TV sets that watched the game. For more than three quarters of our estimates, the error was smaller than half this number. So while we should not place too much weight on any single estimate for a particular match seen in a specific country, overall the regression summarises the data pretty well. The regression captures just over two thirds of the variation in viewing figures. The remaining third of the variation is due to unexplained random factors.

Before we ask which countries are the biggest football couch potatoes, let's pick apart the other regression effects for what they tell us about fandom. We found that only two time-of-day effects mattered: games played during 'sleep time' (midnight to 5.40am) reduced the average audience by 3.6 percentage points, while prime time added about 4 percentage points depending on the exact time.

The significance of a match was crucial. In the group stages, if one or both teams playing in the third match were already knocked out, the TV rating fell. If both teams were out, the game lost 4.7 percentage points of its rating – a giant loss, since a rating of 4.7 per cent is usually enough to keep a series on TV in the first place.

Yet when one or both teams in a third group game had nothing much to play for because they had already qualified for the next round, viewing figures barely fell. Football is soap opera. We watch it because of the story that unfolds after the game, not just because of the game itself. As long as a team is still in the tournament, its story continues.

Viewing figures rise steadily for each round of a tournament. The World Cup's round of 16 adds 1.4 per cent to the audience, while quarter-finals add 2.5 per cent, semi-finals 5.6 per cent and the final itself 10.1 per cent. Even the match for third place, often mocked as meaningless, raises audiences by 4.9 per cent – only slightly less than the semi-final effect. UEFA dropped the third place play-off from the European Championship in 1984 because the game was thought to be boring. Perhaps UEFA should reconsider.

Besides time and significance of the match, a third effect sometimes matters: who is playing. Brazil are everybody's 'second team'. Despite getting duller since 1970, they still command a viewing premium of 2.2 per cent whenever they play. Weirdly, only one other team consistently enhanced viewing figures across all 54 nations in Alavy's database: not Italy or Holland or Argentina but, yes, England. Their games boost global TV ratings by 1.4 per cent.

To sum up, imagine a World Cup final played in mid prime time between England and Brazil; this would add 10.1 (the final effect) + 4 (prime-time effect) + 1.4 (England effect) + 2.2 (Brazil effect) = 17.7 per cent to average viewership expected in any country.

There is one last factor to consider: nationalism. Its effect is enormous. For any game, for any country, broadcasting the national team added an average of 17.9 per cent to the audience. It appears that for the average person on earth, simply watching his own national team in a bog-standard group match is more attractive than watching England v Brazil in the World Cup final. People who love football are vastly outnumbered by nationalists who only tune in for 'our boys'.

If England did play Brazil in a World Cup final in prime time, how many Britons would watch? Our model would predict 7 per cent (the core audience) + 17.9 (the nationalist effect) + 16.3 (the prime-time, final and Brazil effects) = 41.2 per cent. That would equal about 25 million viewers. In fact this is almost certainly an underestimate, partly because it wouldn't count the people watching in pubs and other public places. Predictions about events that are both extremely rare and important are inevitably subject to wide margins of error. The same problem afflicts forecasting in financial markets: no statistical model can accurately predict a crash in the stock market. We have a good idea of how regular 'small' factors like the time of day will affect viewing figures. We are much less precise about the effect of big one-offs like the country's own national team playing a final.

Now we can finally open the last door: after correcting for all incidental factors, which country has the highest TV ratings for World Cups and European Championships?

THE BIGGEST FOOTBALL COUCH POTATOES

CORE TV VIEWING RATING FOR FOOTBALL AS PERCENTAGE OF HOUSEHOLDS WITH TV SETS

1	Croatia	12.4	11	Germany	8.6
2	Norway	11.9	12	Hungary	7.9
3	Netherlands	11.5	13	Italy	7.8
4	Uruguay	10.7	14	Argentina	7.4
5	Denmark	9.1	15	Indonesia	7.3
6	Ecuador	9.0	16	Singapore	7.1
7	Serbia	9.0	17	Romania	7.1
8	Brazil	8.8	18	UK	7.0
9	Korea	8.7	19	Lebanon	7.0
10	Sweden	8.6			

And the winner is: Croatia! Alavy notes that Croat passion goes beyond football. 'They also have very high ratings in other major sporting events,' he says. For instance, when Croatia and Spain met in the world handball final in 2005, average ratings in Croatia were nearly four times higher than in Spain. This enthusiasm may stem from having recently fought for independence in a nationalist war; or it may just be because Croatia has very good sports teams.

The other European countries that watch most international football – the Norwegians, Dutch, Danes and Serbs – also have relatively small populations and relatively big football reputations. Quite likely, small nations score high in our rankings because they tend to be more interested in what is going on outside their borders than big nations like France or Mexico. Alavy notes: 'To have high average ratings, it's all about having a high tendency to watch when your local heroes are *not* playing.'

Britain, for all its claims to football obsession, is stuck in what Alavy calls 'a kind of mid-table mediocrity', sandwiched in 18th place between Romania and Lebanon. Germany are the keenest couch potatoes among Europe's big countries. Eleventh in the table, they would be even higher but for their new custom of 'public viewing', as they call it in their impenetrable language. Since 2006, Germans have taken to watching games in huge crowds on big screens outside. About 12 million Germans are estimated to have chosen this method to watch their team lose to Italy in that year's World Cup semi-final. The figure was particularly impressive given that the 30 million other Germans who watched at home were by themselves the country's largest ever TV audience up to that point. At Euro 2008, the 'Fan Mile' by the Brandenburg Gate in Berlin had to be shut nearly three hours before the tournament's final because it was already packed with nearly half a million singing and dancing 'public viewers'. Yet these people do not show up in Germany's 'people meter' data.

Generally, European countries dominate at the top of Alavy's table. Partly this is because most World Cup games are played at times designed to suit them. There is a vicious (or virtuous) cycle here: because Europe has high viewing figures for football, World Cups are often held in Europe, and so European teams do well, and so European viewing figures are high. Only as Asians become richer and keener on football might this change. Chinese prime time could be a very lucrative market one day.

The Asian figures in our table need to be taken with a pinch of salt. The Korean figures are for 2002–08, so they benefited from the 'halo effect' created by South Korea's run to the semi-final in 2002. More-over, in Korea and Indonesia the World Cup is hard to escape because it is often shown 'wall to wall' on several channels simultaneously. By contrast, Singapore scores highly partly because only the best World

Cup matches are shown there – and partly because Singaporeans love betting on football the way other people love football.

And here are Alavy's least enthusiastic nations:

CORE TV VIEWING RATING FOR FOOTBALL AS PERCENTAGE OF HOUSEHOLDS WITH TV SETS

#	Country	Rating	#	Country	Rating
1	Australia	2.7	6	Canada	1.7
2	New Zealand	2.5	7	Latvia	1.6
3	Ukraine	2.1	8	India	1.2
4	Mexico	2.0	9	US	0.6
5	Lithuania	1.8	10	Taiwan	−0.8

The Taiwanese must really not like football. Of course even they cannot achieve a negative rating in practice, but our data combine the actual viewing figures with the specific characteristics of each game (time of day, group match, etc) to produce a final figure. In real life the Taiwanese numbers do not come out far from zero. Nor do the ratings for the US and India, though viewing rose sharply in both countries for the World Cup of 2010. An oddity of the US is that it is the only country where the nominal national team does not draw the highest ratings. At the World Cup of 2006, viewers there preferred watching Brazil, Italy and Mexico. For many people living in the US, of course, these are their true 'home' teams.

Americans, Indians and Taiwanese at least have an excuse for not watching soccer: they prefer other sports. The nations that stand out among Alavy's least enthusastic are Mexico and Ukraine, which both have respectable traditions in football. Indeed, several other countries that haven't historically cared much – Spain, Portugal and France – have some of the best football teams on earth. Alavy notes that Spanish audiences for international sport tend to be relatively low, perhaps because of the country's regional divides. Many Basques, for instance, did not want to follow a Spanish 'national' team. That is now changing: Spanish viewing figures shot up during Euro 2008 even before Spain reached the final, and then again, for obvious reasons, during the World Cup of 2010.

The problem, in terms of our quest for Europe's most football-crazy nation, is that Alavy didn't have TV viewing figures for two of our contenders, Iceland and the Faroe Islands. It may be that the entire population of both countries watches every game of every international tournament, even the goalless draw between Bolivia and South Korea at the World Cup of 1994, but he just doesn't know. We checked with some high-powered Faroes television executives (the place has had TV since the early 1980s), and even they don't have any viewing figures. 'The islands pretty much sit down for World Cup and European finals,' Hvidbro of the Faroes FA assured us. However, in the absence of hard numbers we have to rule the islanders out of our quest. They can content themselves with a very honorable mention.

Iceland is a different matter. It introduced people meters only in 2007, and anyway it is too small a market for Futures Sport + Entertainment to have bothered to track its viewing habits. But we went and found some Icelandic figures. FIFA produced an unprecedentedly rigorous report on worldwide viewing of the 2010 World Cup. The report, written by the research consultancy KantarSport, drew on well-sourced viewing figures from national TV stations around the world. Again, we'll just look at the European figures. The key numbers, for us, are the average TV ratings for live matches – i.e. the percentage of the possible total audience that watched the average match. Here are the leading European countries as ranked by KantarSport and FIFA:

VIEWING OF WORLD CUP 2010 (EUROPEAN COUNTRIES ONLY): AVERAGE LIVE TV RATING AS PERCENTAGE OF POSSIBLE IN-HOME AUDIENCE

1	Iceland	18.8	6	Montenegro	9.7
2	Netherlands	16.1	7	Norway	9.7
3	Germany	12.4	8	Switzerland	9.6
4	Serbia	11.1	9	United Kingdom	9.0
5	Croatia	10.8			

Iceland's first place is impressive given that the country's TV broadcast 250 hours of live matches from South Africa, more than twice
as much as Norwegian TV, and 90 hours more than Dutch TV.
Icelanders did particularly well to out-watch the Dutch, given that
they didn't have a dog in the fight whereas Holland went all the way
to the final.

THE COUNTRY THAT BOUGHT WEST HAM

Iceland, the land of fish, volcanoes and endless winters, is officially
Europe's kookiest nation about football.

Just to recap: here is how it won our award. In our first category,
playing football, Germany and the Faroes scored highest in Europe,
at least according to FIFA. Austria, Norway, Slovakia, Sweden,
Iceland, Holland and Ireland followed at some distance.

Of these enthusiastic playing countries, the most enthusiastic
about spectating was the Faroes, with Iceland a distant second.
Somewhat further behind, the Dutch and Norwegians also went to
lots of games, as did the Scots and Cypriots.

So our third category, TV viewing, had to provide the decider
between the front runners, the Faroes, Norway, the Netherlands and
Iceland. Norway and Holland registered among the continent's leading couch potatoes as compiled by Kevin Alavy, alongside Denmark
and Croatia. (In the previous edition of this book, when we didn't yet
have viewing figures for Iceland, we named Norway as the most foot-
ball-loving country in Europe.)

There are no TV data for the Faroes. But Iceland's viewing of the
2010 World Cup blew away even the Dutch and Norwegians. Given
that the Icelanders also led these two nations in going to the
stadium, they clearly have an unhealthy obsession with football.

In some ways, Iceland's story is very like Norway's or the Faroes'.
Iceland too is a social democracy, whose government does its best
to give all inhabitants the chance to play sport. It's also a cold country, with long winters, which Icelanders tend to spend hunkered

down inside, either working hard or drinking hard while they wait for the summer partying season. What to do while hibernating? Vidar Halldórsson, an Icelandic sports sociologist, says: 'We grew up watching English football on TV, from the 1970s. The only TV station in Iceland showed English games once a week, on Saturdays (not live, but a week later). They were the only professional sports we saw at the time.' In a survey of Icelandic men in 2003, Halldórsson found that 88 per cent could name a favourite English football team. Aron Jóhansson (raised in Iceland but now an American international) recalls boys fighting in the streets of Reykjavik over English football results. 'That passion was very deep,' he says. It's a passion that arguably reached its apogee in 2006 when the billionaire Björgólfur Guðmundsson – then Iceland's second-richest man after his son, Björgólfur Thor – bought West Ham United. After the financial crisis struck Iceland in 2008, *Forbes* magazine revalued Guðmundsson's estimated net worth from $1.1 billion to zero. In 2009 he was declared bankrupt. Still, no doubt the passion remained.

In the twentieth century, Icelanders watched English football but didn't have much opportunity to play or watch their own. Iceland's league runs from May to September – 'the shortest football season in the world', the country's FA proudly calls it. But some time in the late 1990s, Iceland began building an all-weather football infrastructure that may be unparalleled on earth. Over 110 Icelandic schools got artificial mini-fields, and there are now seven heated indoor halls with full-sized football grounds, Nowadays, Icelanders can play all year round, whether they belong to a club or not.

Playing sport is a part of life in Iceland, especially in the villages. Gender barely matters: nearly a quarter of the country's registered football players are girls aged under 18. Even six-year-old kids are trained by qualified paid football coaches. And they usually play other sports besides.

Sport in Iceland is something you do very seriously, for fun, while continuing real life on the side. There can't be many countries where the national team's goalkeeper is also a professional filmmaker.

Hannes Thor Halldórsson actually shot the TV advert for Icelandair that featured his own team. 'It was weird,' he told *Sports Illustrated*. 'I had to act in the commercial as well, so I was directing the commercial in the national kit and boots.' Meanwhile, Iceland's legendary handball captain, Ólafur Stefánsson, seemed to regard himself primarily as an existentialist philosopher. When we asked him during the London Olympics what a handball gold would mean for the little country, he replied that he was unable to answer: 'You have so many different realities. The game is – what is it? A simulacrum of life itself, maybe, in simplified terms.'

In Beijing in 2008, Stefánsson's team had beaten Spain in the Olympic semi-final. During that game, 'there was not a single transaction made on the Icelandic stock exchange,' says the sociologist Halldórsson. Stefánsson's men ended up with silver. No country that small had ever won an Olympic medal in a team sport.

Icelanders excel in many different competitions – they have won Miss World three times – but football is what really does it for them. In November 2013 Iceland only had to beat Croatia in a playoff to become the smallest nation ever to reach the World Cup. Before the home match, the country's federation put the 9,800 tickets available to Icelanders up for sale at 4 am, worried that its website would crash if it opened sales in daytime. The tickets were gone before the sun rose (admittedly not difficult in an Icelandic winter). Sadly, Iceland lost 0–2 over two legs. But if these people ever make it to a tournament, they might really start to like football.

ARE FOOTBALL FANS POLYGAMISTS? A CRITIQUE OF THE HORNBY MODEL OF FANDOM

> Just this one afternoon started the whole thing off – there was no prolonged courtship … In a desperate and percipient attempt to stop the inevitable, Dad quickly took me to Spurs to see Jimmy Greaves score four against Sunderland in a 5–1 win, but the damage had been done, and the six goals and all the great players left me cold: I'd already fallen for the team that beat Stoke 1–0 from a penalty rebound.
>
> NICK HORNBY in *Fever Pitch* (1992)
> on the origin of his lifelong love of Arsenal.

Fever Pitch is a wonderful memoir, the most influential football book ever written, and an important source for our image of the football fan. The 'Fan', as most Britons have come to think of him, is a creature tied for life to the club he first 'fell for' as a child. Hornby says his love of Arsenal has lasted 'longer than any relationship I have made of my own free will'. But is Hornby's 'Fan' found much in real life? Or are most British football supporters much less loyal than is usually presumed?

Let's start with Hornby's version, because it is the accepted story of the British Fan. As far as life allows, the Hornbyesque Fan sees all his club's home games. (It's accepted even in the rhetoric of fandom that travelling to away games is best left to unmarried men under the age of 25.) No matter how bad his team get, the Fan cannot abandon them. When Hornby watches the Arsenal of the late 1960s with his dad, their incompetence shames him but he cannot leave: 'I was chained to Arsenal and my dad was chained to me, and there was no way out for any of us.'

'Chained' is a very Hornbyesque word for a Fan's feelings for his club. Often, the Fan uses metaphors from drugs ('hooked') or romantic love ('relationship', 'fell for'). Indeed, some adult Englishmen who would hardly dare tell their wives that they love them will happily appear in public singing of their love for a club, or for a player who would snub them in a nightclub if they ever managed to sneak past his entourage.

No wonder the Fan's loyalty to his club is sometimes described as a bond stronger than marriage. Rick Parry, as chief executive of the Premier League in the 1990s, recited the then dominant cliché about fandom: 'You can change your job, you can change your wife, but you can't change your football team ... you can move from one end of the country to another, but you never, ever lose your allegiance to your first team. That's what English soccer is all about. It's about fierce loyalty, about dedication.' (The Argentine variant: 'You can change your wife – but your club and your mother, never.') Recently, in more metrosexual times, football officials trying to emphasise the strength of club brands have extended the cliché by one more attachment: you can even change your gender, the officials say, but not your club.

Ideally, the Hornbyesque Fan supports his local side (even if Hornby did not). This gives the Fan roots, a sense of belonging. In a wonderful essay on fandom in the highbrow journal *Prospect*, Gideon Rachman quotes an archetypal declaration of faith from a Carlisle Fan called Charles Burgess, who wrote in the *Guardian*: 'There never was any choice. My dad ... took me down to Brunton Park to watch the derby match against Workington Town just after Christmas 41 years ago – I was hooked and have been ever since ... My support has been about who we are and where we are from.'

In real life Rachman is a commentator on international politics in the *Financial Times,* but his essay in *Prospect* is a key text in the British debate about fandom. It is the anti-*Fever Pitch*. In it, Rachman outs himself as a 'fair-weather fan, an allegiance-switcher', who at different times in his life has supported Chelsea, QPR and Spurs. So casual are his allegiances that he registered with FIFA for the World Cup of 2006 as an Ivory Coast supporter, figuring that that way he wouldn't face much competition for tickets. He got into every round including the final. Rachman attended the World Cup in South Africa as a registered Paraguay fan.

He treats the passions of Hornbyesque Fans as slightly bizarre. After all, in England a Fan's choice of team is largely random. Few clubs have particular religious or class affiliations, and few English people have an attachment dating back generations to any particular location. Some children become fans of their local team, however terrible it might be, but if you live in a rural area like Cornwall you will have no local team, while if you live in London or around Manchester you have many. As Rachman asks: 'Why devote a huge amount of emotion to favouring one part of west London over another?'

Nonetheless, the Hornbyesque Fan is a widely admired figure in Britain, at least among men. Whereas 'fanatic' is usually a pejorative word, a 'Fan' is someone who has roots somewhere. As we will argue later, this respect is connected to the quirks of British history: in this country, roots of any kind are in short supply.

However, our first question is: how true is the Hornby model of fandom? Does it really describe the way most British fans feel about their clubs?

THE CHINESE SERIAL FAN

Very little is known about sports fans who are not hooligans. The academics D.L. Wann and M.A. Hamlet estimated in 1995 that only 4 per cent of research on sport concentrated on the spectator.

So we start our quest into the nature of fandom with only one or two fairly safe premises. One is that foreign fans of English clubs, at least, are not all monogamous in their devotion. Rowan Simons explains in *Bamboo Goalposts*, his book on Chinese football, that many Chinese fans support 'a number of rival teams at the same time', and are always changing their favourite club. Simons adds: 'So dominant is the serial supporter in China that it is quite rare to find a fan with a real unflinching loyalty to one team.'

Stephanus Tekle, who worked for the market researchers Sport+Markt, has polling data to back up Simons's claim. Tekle says that since the late 1990s hordes of new fans around the world – particularly women – have come to football without long-standing loyalties. Many of these people appear to be 'serial supporters' who probably support Manchester United and Liverpool, or Real Madrid and Barcelona, simultaneously. No wonder that clubs like United or Real keep changing their guesses as to how many fans they have worldwide. Here are a few of United's estimates of the last few years:

Year	Estimated Fans	Source
2003	75 million	Mori
2007	About 90 million	Manchester United
2008	333 million (including 139 million 'core fans')	TNS Sport
2011	659 million	Kantar

None of these estimates is necessarily wrong. There may well be 659 million people on earth who have feelings for Manchester United. However, few of these 'fans' are likely to be lifelong Hornbyesque devotees. José Angel Sanchez, now chief executive of Real Madrid, a club with its own share of foreign serial supporters, thought many of these serial fans might eventually evolve into Hornbys. He told us in 2003: 'We used to say that the chances of changing your team is less than changing your partner or even your sex. But the way that people enter football in Asia is different: they enter through the stars. But this will not stay this way, in my opinion.' Well, perhaps.

Still, surely British fans are a lot more loyal than those fickle Chinese? Unfortunately, polling suggests otherwise. In 2008 Sport+Markt (since merged with Repucom) found that Chelsea had 2.4 million 'fans' in Britain. Again according to Sport+Markt, that represented a rise of 523 per cent in the five years since Roman Abramovich had bought the club. Yet even that figure of 2.4 million represented a swift decline: in 2006, when, no doubt coincidentally, Chelsea had just won the league twice running, Sport+Markt credited the club with a mammoth 3.8 million British fans.

Again, we are not saying that Sport+Markt's figures were wrong. Rather, its premise was. To serial supporters, the question 'Which is your preferred football club?' does not make sense. It presumes that everyone who likes football is a one-club Hornby-esque Fan. Instead, researchers should be asking, 'Which *are* your preferred football *clubs*?' After all, a very large proportion of people who like football are polygamous consumers. One of the authors of this book, Stefan, as a Saturday-morning coach of primary-school children, has seen the colour of the shirts switch from red to blue and back again depending upon who last won the league. Newly rising clubs like Chelsea were particularly prone to attracting short-term fans, said Tekle of Sport+Markt. Clubs like Liverpool or Manchester United with stronger brands tended to have more loyal long-term supporters, he added. In fact the likes of Manchester United are likely to have both far more Hornbys *and* far more casual fans than other clubs. But detractors of United tend to seize upon the hordes of casual fans, and don't mention the Hornbys.

Hornby himself recognised the prevalence of casual fans in football. Many of the people who pop up briefly in the pages of *Fever Pitch* enjoy the game but are not wedded to a particular club. Hornby calls this type the 'sod-that-for-a-lark floating punter', and speaks of it with admiration: 'I would like to be one of those people who treat their local team like their local restaurant, and thus withdraw their patronage if they are being served up noxious rubbish.'

SPECTATORS: THE HARD CORE

We know there are broadly speaking two types of football fan: the Hornbys and the sod-that-for-a-lark floating punters. We know that the sod-that-for-a-lark people are heavily represented among foreign fans of clubs like United, and even seem to be pretty common in Britain. By 2006, if we can believe Sport+Markt's figures, about 90 per cent of Chelsea's fans were people who had not supported them in 2003. No doubt a club like Hartlepool has a higher percentage of devoted Hornbys among their fans, but then clubs like Hartlepool don't have many fans full stop.

One might carp that the sod-that-for-a-lark lot are mostly just armchair fans, and that 'real' fans tend to be Hornbys. However, it would be wrong to dismiss armchair fans as an irrelevance. The overwhelming majority of football fans in Britain are armchair fans, in the sense that they hardly ever go to games. In a survey by pollsters Mori in 2003, 45 per cent of British adults expressed an interest in football. But we've seen that the total average weekly attendances of all professional clubs in England and Scotland equal only about 3 per cent of the population. In other words, most of the country's football fans rarely or never enter football stadiums.

Fletcher Research, in one of the first serious market analyses of English football in 1997, found that only about 5 per cent of supporters of Premier League clubs attend even one match in an average season. If only a small minority of football fans get to the stadium at all, even fewer see every single home game for years on end as Hornby did.

Most football fans are armchair supporters. If we want to unearth the Hornbys, we need to concentrate on the elite of fans that actually go to games: the spectators.

We know that, in the Premier League at least, most spectators now watch every home game their club plays. Often they have to: at the most successful clubs, only season-ticket-holders can get seats. Many of these regular spectators may be sod-that-for-a-lark punters at heart, who have been enticed by ticketing policies to show up every week. However, it's among this group of week-in-week-out spectators that we must look for the small hardcore of lifelong Hornbys in English football. At moments of high emotion, the TV cameras like to zoom in on spectators in the stands – heads in hands, or hugging their mates – as if these people incarnated the feelings of the club's millions of supporters. They don't. Rather, they are the exceptions, the fanatical few who bother to go to games. Some of these spectators presumably support their club 'through thick and thin', watching them unto eternity as Hornby does.

At least, that is the theory. But we studied attendances in English football over the last 60 years, and found that even among the actual spectators, a startlingly high proportion appeared to be sod-that-for-a-lark types.

Nobody seems to have tried before to calculate how many British fans are Hornbys. Yet the figures required to make some sort of esti-mate do exist. That marvellous website www.european-football-statistics.co.uk has statistics on attendances and league performance for all clubs in the top four divisions of English football since 1947. Using this data, we can find out (a) the annual mortality rate of football spectators – how many of the people who watched last season don't come back the next? – and (b) the sensitivity of new spectators to the success of teams – do most newcomers flock to Chelsea when Chelsea win the league?

Our model is based on some fundamental truths of football fandom. Generally speaking, teams cannot have very loyal Hornbyesque fans (i.e. a low mortality rate) and at the same time be capable of attracting large numbers of new spectators when they are successful. If most of the crowd consisted of Hornbys who never gave up their seats, then when a team did well, there would be no room in the stadium for all the new fans who wanted to watch them. So floating supporters can only get tickets if the mortality rate of the existing spectators is high enough.

Previous studies have shown that a club's attendance tends to rise and fall with its league position. (The rare exceptions include Newcastle, Sunderland and the Manchester City of the late 1990s.) In our data for the period 1947–2008, there were 4,454 changes in clubs' league position. The average club moves six or seven positions a year. In 64 per cent of the cases where the club rose in the league, its home crowd increased too. In 74 per cent of the 'down' years, home attendance fell. This means that 69 per cent of all cases confirmed the simple hypothesis that fans respond to performance. Simply put: there is a market in football spectators. The few academics who study fandom – most of them in the US – explain the fans' motives through the psychological phenomenon of 'BIRGing', or 'Basking in reflected glory'.

To account for the ebb and flow of English football fans, we have constructed a very simple model. It consists of two elements that are logically connected to one another. First, there are the 'new fans' coming into the game. New fans are estimated as the difference between the total attendance for the season and the number of loyal fans left over from the previous season. We divide new fans into two groups: the BIRGers, who come to watch the team depending on its success; and those who come for reasons we can't explain. We will treat these reasons as random factors, although each person probably had a good reason to come to the game at the time – a friend invited them, a girlfriend left them, etc.

The second element of our model are the 'loyal fans': those who came back from the previous season. Loyal fans are estimated as the difference between the total attendance for the season and the new fans entering the game. Of course, the difference between the loyal fans plus the new fans and last season's attendance is the 'lost fans'. We can think of these lost fans as falling into two groups as well: the BIRGers who were lost to the club because its performance declined, and those who were lost for other reasons that we cannot measure (got back together with girlfriend, took up DIY, etc).

So, total fans = loyal fans from last year + fans sensitive to winning + random fans.

In our model we estimate the shares of loyal fans and fans sensitive to winning by minimising the number of random fans. We minimise random fans precisely because we think most fans go for a reason: either loyalty or BIRGing. Randomness surely plays a relatively small role.

Now, we are not claiming that we can identify new fans, loyal fans and lost fans *individually*. However, we can identify these categories *in a statistical sense*, as groups. We know how many people are in each group, even if we do not know their names.

Our model produces two results. First, it gives us an estimate of the BIRGers: the fraction of new fans that a team can expect to attract as a result of the position it achieves in the league. Looking at the annual changes in attendances, we found that spectators are only mildly sensitive to a team's performance. Our estimates implied that the club that won the Premier League would attract 2.5 per cent of all new spectators entering the league the next season. However, a team that finished at the bottom of the Premier League, or the top of the Championship, does almost as well: it attracts 2 per cent of all the league's new spectators. Teams in the middle of the four divisions (i.e. those ranked around 46th in England) would attract 1 per cent of all new spectators, while teams at the very bottom of the fourth tier would attract almost nobody. In short, while new spectators do like success, the vast majority of them are not simple

BIRGers, glory-hunters. Judging by the ebb and flow of crowds over the 61 years up to 2008, most people seem to go to a plausible club playing near their home.

That is the profile of the newcomers. But how many of last year's crowd do they replace? What is the mortality rate of the existing spectators?

We know how many spectators each club lost or gained, season by season, for 61 years. We also know how many spectators the league as a whole lost or gained. That means that for every club we can calculate the average percentage of spectators at a given game one season who would not attend that same fixture the next season. And the percentage that fits the data best? 50. Yes: on average in the post-war era, half of all spectators in English football did not take their seats again for the equivalent match the next season.

Let's be clear about what exactly we are saying. Imagine that Bristol City play Wolves one season, in front of 15,000 spectators. The next season, for the same fixture, even if there are again 15,000 spectators, half of them would typically be people who had not seen the previous year's match. 7,500 of last year's crowd would be gone. Now, many of those 7,500 people might well see other games in the new season. Many of the 'newcomers' might be people who had seen Bristol City–Wolves two years before, or ten years before, but had then gone missing at that fixture for a while. However, the point still stands: at any given match, half the spectators would be new compared with the same match the season before.

Here's an example of how the model works:

Bristol City finished the 2006–07 season in second place in League One. Their total attendance that season was 295,000. Note that that doesn't mean 295,000 different people. Rather, 295,000 tickets were sold for all City's matches combined. Most fans would have attended multiple matches.

The total attendance for all four divisions was 29.5 million.

The next season,

(a) The total attendance for all four divisions rose by 400,000, to 29.9 million.

(b) Bristol City came fourth in the Championship – a rise of 22 places.

So to calculate Bristol City's expected attendance in 2007–08, we estimate their numbers of loyal 'returning' fans and of new fans:

(c) Loyal fans are 50 per cent of the previous season's total: 148,000.

(d) New fans are calculated by estimating Bristol City's share (based on league performance) of new fans of the entire league:

(e) We predict 15.1 million new spectators for English football as a whole. That equals this year's total attendance (29.9 million) minus loyal fans from last year (50 per cent of 29.5 million = 14.8 million) = 15.1 million (29.9 – 14.8).

(f) Given that Bristol City finished 24th out of 92 clubs, we estimate their share of all new fans in the country at 1.7 per cent. Their number of new fans should therefore equal .017 x 15.1 million = 257,000.

(g) So City's loyal + new spectators = 148,000 + 257,000 = 405,000.

(h) Bristol City's actual number for 2007–08 was 374,000, so our model overestimated their support by 31,000, or 8 per cent.

Obviously the model does not work perfectly for every club. At big clubs like Arsenal or Manchester United, there is very little flux in the stands. Their stadiums are pretty much always full, and total attendance therefore always the same. Most of their spectators are season-ticket holders who see every game. These people generally renew their season tickets each year, because they know that if they don't their seats will be snapped up by others and they might never get back into the ground again. However, taking all 92 clubs together, the estimate that fits the data best is that 50 per cent of the fans who saw a game last season do not see it again the next season. To quote one analysis of the English game:

> One Third Division club in the London area, for example, has an estimated 'hard core' support of about 10,000; this rises to 20,000 according to the team's success and the standing of the visiting team.

These words were written in 1951, in an economic study of football published by the Political and Economic Planning think tank. They remain a good summary of English fandom as a whole since the war.

The discovery that half of all spectators – supposedly the hardest of hardcore fans – are not there when the same fixture rolls around the next season conflicts with the Hornby version of loyal one-club fandom. Yet it has to be true, to explain the churn we see in attendances. Even a club like Leeds, noted for its devoted fans – while stuck in League One it drew significantly larger crowds than Juventus – saw attendance fall from a peak of 755,000 in the 2001–02 season to only 479,000 in 2006–07.

Nor is this high mortality rate a new phenomenon. The 61 years of attendance data suggest that habits of English spectators have changed little over the years. While there has always been a hard core of Hornbys, it seems it has also always been the case that the majority of people who go to English football matches go only once in a while, and are often quite fluid about who they choose to watch. And given that spectators are the fans who commit the most time and money to the game, their devotion is in most cases really rather limited. The long-term devoted spectator of the kind that Hornby described in *Fever Pitch*, far from being typical, is a rare species. Committed one-club lifelong fandom is a beautiful theory – or, as Gandhi supposedly said when asked what he thought of modern civilisation, 'That would be a good idea.' The reality is that in English football, the loyal Hornbys are a small shoal in an ocean of casual Rachmans. England may be a nation of fans, but it's scarcely a nation of Hornbys.

CALL YOURSELVES 'LOYAL SUPPORTERS'

In 1996 Alan Tapp, a professor of marketing at Bristol Business School, started to develop a relationship with a struggling club in the Premier League. Over the next four years he met the club's executives, got to see the data they had on their supporters, and assembled a team of researchers who conducted hundreds of interviews with the club's fans. Tapp eventually published two papers about his work in academic marketing journals. Together they add up to a rare, marvellous study of how the spectators of one club actually behave. Tapp titled his second paper, published in 2004, 'The loyalty of football fans – we'll support you evermore?' – with a very pregnant question-mark. What he found was that fans talk loyal, but don't always act it.

The club Tapp and his colleague Jeff Clowes studied – based in a Midlands town that is quite easy to identify – was not very good. It wasn't the sort of outfit to attract many BIRGing glory-hunters. Most of the club's spectators lived locally. In a survey in 1998, a massive 87 per cent of them agreed slightly or strongly with the phrase, 'I would describe myself as a loyal supporter.'

Well, they would say that, wouldn't they? Tapp cautions that many of those 87 per cent might have been engaging in 'socially desirable responding'. After all, almost nobody in English football calls himself a 'sod-that-for-a-lark floating punter'. That would be socially taboo. Most fans told Tapp and Clowes that they regarded sod-that-for-a-lark types as 'pariahs'. As Rick Parry said, English fans pride themselves on their loyalty.

Yet when Tapp studied how these spectators behaved, he found a peculiar lack of loyalty. To start with the most basic fact: the club's average crowd during the four-year period of study slipped from about 24,000 to just 16,000.

The average across the period was about 21,000, which broke down as follows:

⚽ About 8,000 season ticket holders.

⚽ Another 8,000 places typically filled from a group of 15,000 or so regular attenders.

⚽ 5,000 spectators who came from a 'revolving door' of perhaps 20,000 'casual fans'.

Tapp came up with three labels for the different groups: 'fanatics', 'committed casuals', and 'carefree casuals'.

The 'fanatics', or Hornbys, were mostly season-ticket-holders. Tapp said some of these people were veritable '"football extremists" who had commitment to the sport and the club that is arguably unparalleled in other business or leisure sectors'. There was the man who, when asked by Tapp's team what he would save if there were a fire in his house, replied: 'Oh, my [match] programmes and tapes. No question. And my wife and kids of course.' Many of the fanatics came from the local area, and had supported the club since childhood.

But even some of the fanatics were less fanatical than they claimed to be. Tapp found that each season, on average, 1,000 of the 8,000 season ticket holders did not renew their seats and were replaced by new people. 'Even at the fanatic end, the loyalty bucket had significant leaks,' he remarked.

The team was playing badly. In one season, a mere 2 per cent of fans proclaimed themselves 'very satisfied' with performances. However, it was not the bad football that was driving them away. When Tapp's team asked people why they were letting their season tickets lapse, the lapsers usually talked about their lives away from the stadium. Fans were much more likely to give up their season tickets if they had children aged under five, or if they described their lives as 'complicated'.

So it wasn't that the lapsers felt less loyal to the team than the people who kept going year in, year out. They were simply at different stages in life. Some regular fans admitted that at one point in life 'they had simply lost interest, often in their late teens and early twenties'. Others had been 'triggered' by a son or daughter to return to the stadium. Older people, whose lives were presumably more stable, were the most likely to renew their season tickets. Tapp surmises that they 'have simply settled into some form of auto-repurchase'. In other words, showing up to the stadium year in, year out is not a good marker of loyalty. Rather, it is a good marker of age.

At the far end of the scale from the 'fanatics' were the 'carefree casuals'. Few of the carefree casuals claimed to be 'loyal support-ers'. They were 'football fans' rather than 'club fans', they preferred to see a good game rather than a victory for their team, and they treated football as just one of several possible activities on a Saturday. Tapp noted: 'Being club supporters is not part of their self-image.'

Many of the 'carefree casuals' sometimes went to watch other teams. Tapp reckons that it is probable that some regulars at Derby County, for instance, also occasionally show up at Derby's rivals Nottingham Forest, even if this flies in the face of everything we are always told about English football fans.

Tapp adds that these people are mostly not 'brand-switchers', who switch from supporting one club to supporting another. Very few people love Derby one year, Forest the next, and Carlisle the year after. Rather, these adulterous spectators are engaging in what marketing experts call 'repertoire buying': they purchase different brands at different times. In normal consumer markets in almost every country, 'repertoire buyers' are thought to outnumber both 'brand-loyal' and 'price buyers'. In football too, repertoire buyers seem to be fairly common. Tapp says: 'Repertoire fans took a lot of pleasure from a multiplicity of aspects of the game itself, while single club fanatics were less interested in football, more devoted to the club as an entity.'

Tapp's middle group of spectators at the Midlands club were 'committed casuals'. These people didn't go to every match, but they did tend to describe themselves as 'loyal supporters'. They rarely watched other clubs, and were more interested than the 'carefree casuals' in seeing their team win. However, they too treated football as just one option for their Saturday. Tapp said they 'perhaps have their football support in perspective with the rest of their lives'.

In short, through close-up study very rare in English football, Tapp has got past the cliché of 'We'll support you evermore'. Instead he found the same thing that we did: there are some Hornbys in British football, but even among the self-proclaimed 'loyal supporters' of an inglorious club they are outnumbered by casual fans who can take it or leave it. Tapp ends by cautioning sports marketers that for all the rhetoric of undying love pervading English football, fans' loyalty 'cannot be relied upon'. He urges marketers to 'look under the surface of supporter loyalty', where they will find 'loyalty patterns quite similar to, say, supermarket goods sectors'.

HORNBYS, CLIENTS, SPECTATORS AND OTHERS

It turns out that few British football fans are either Hornbys or BIRGing glory-hunters. Rather, most have a shifting relationship with the club or clubs they support. Of the 50 per cent of spectators who do not show up for the same fixture from one season to the next, the largest group may well continue to be monogamous fans of that club. They just don't watch every game, or can't afford to go any more, or are busy raising children, or have moved to another part of the country, or simply care less than they used to. The object of their love might not have changed, but the intensity has. Many of them may once have been Hornbys who fell for a team as an eight-year-old when their father took them to their first game. However, by the time they are 28 or 88 they are no longer the same fan. For many people, fandom is not a static condition but a process.

Other lapsed fans will have lost interest altogether. Others still might be shifting their allegiances to another club or clubs, either because they have moved to a new town, or have started to follow the team their kids support, or have simply fallen for better football elsewhere. Rachman, for example, explains in his *Prospect* essay that he stopped supporting Chelsea 'because they were a terrible team, followed by violent cretins'.

Instead, he made a 2½-mile journey within west London and became a QPR fan. In the rhetoric of English football, the choice facing the supporter is often presented as stark: either he sticks with his local team or he becomes a BIRGing glory-hunter. However, reality is more nuanced. England is so densely stuffed with professional football clubs – 43 within 90 miles of Manchester, as we saw – that many people can find a new local side without going to the trouble of moving house.

Then there is a dirty secret of English football: many fans support more than one team. If you live in Plymouth, say, you might support Plymouth Argyle, Chelsea and Barcelona, and have a fondness for half a dozen other clubs, even though if Plymouth ever make the FA Cup final you will travel to Wembley decked out as a 'lifelong Plymouth fan'. Hornby himself, in *Fever Pitch*, supports Cambridge United as well as Arsenal. In fact, whereas the usual analogy for football fandom is idealised monogamous marriage, a better one might be music fandom. People are fans of The Beatles, or The Cure, or The Pixies, but they generally like more than one band at the same time, and are capable of moving on when their heroes fade.

As so often, it was Arsène Wenger who put this best. In January 2009 he gave Arsenal's website an untraditional account of how he thought fandom worked:

Football has different types of people coming to the game. You have the client, who is the guy who pays one time to go to a big game and wants to be entertained. Then you have the spectator, who is the guy who comes to watch football. These two categories are between 40 and 60 [years old].

Then you have two other categories. The first is the supporter of the club. He supports his club and goes to as many games as he can. Then you have the fan. The fan is a guy between 15 and 25 years old who gives all his money to his club.

Obviously, Wenger's four categories are not exact. Here and there they even conflict with those of Tapp and Clowes, who found that many fans *lose* interest between 15 and 25. But Wenger agrees with them that there are several different categories of spectator, of varying emotional intensity, and that people move between these categories depending largely on their time in life.

Ties in football fandom are much looser than the rhetoric of 'We'll support you evermore' suggests. In that regard, they resemble ties of real existing marriage in Britain today. People still get married promising 'till death do us part', but in 2011 there were 117,558 divorces in England and Wales, nearly five times as many as in 1960, even though the number of marriages has plummeted. Over half of all adults in England and Wales are not presently married. A lifelong monogamous marriage has become almost as rare as a lifelong monogamous love of a football club.

THE INAUTHENTIC NATION

Against all evidence, the stereotype persists that the typical British football fan is a full-on Hornby. No wonder it does, because the tiny percentage of fans who are Hornbys dominate the national conversation about fandom. Of course they do: they are the people who are most motivated to join the conversation. For them, following football is not just a hobby but an identity. Also, they make up a disproportionately large share of the football economy – 'the most valuable customers', Tapp calls them – and so clubs and media listen to them more than to the sod-that-for-a-lark punters. And the Hornbys have a compelling story to tell. Most of the best stories are about love, and these are people who proclaim their love in public every week.

Yet there is a deeper reason why the Hornby account of fandom has been so easily accepted in Britain. That is because it tells a story of roots, of belonging – a lifelong love of the club your father or grandfather supported before you – in a country that is unusually rootless. In transient Britain, the story of the rooted Fan is especially seductive.

Britain was the first country on earth where peasants left their native villages to go to work in rootless industrial cities. It was among the first countries where the churches began to empty; a tie that helps root people all over the world has long been extraordinarily weak among native Britons.

Even after the Industrial Revolution, the British never settled down much. The average Briton now changes his residence about once every seven years, more often than all other Europeans except the Nordics and the Dutch, according to a Eurobarometer survey for the European Commission in 2005. Many Britons emigrate. About six million of them now live outside Britain, as do another 50 million-odd people with British ancestry. Probably only India and China have produced diasporas that are as large and as widely spread, says the British government.

It is hard for people this transitory to build up deep ties of any kind, even to football clubs. Admittedly Tapp and Clowes found that many of the 'fanatical' supporters of the club they studied had spent their lives in the local town. But it was the club's 'casual' fans, who 'had often moved to the area as adults', who were more typical of British migratory patterns. For instance, Tapp and Clowes identified one group whom they called 'professional wanderers': 'people (mainly managers/professionals) who have held jobs in a number of different places who tended to strike up (weakly held) allegiances with local teams, which they retain when they next move.' Like most Britons, the professional wanderers were too rootless to become Hornbyesque Fans. *None* of the casual fans interviewed by Tapp and

Clowes 'felt a close part of the local community, in contrast to the fanatics'.

And Britons have suffered yet another uprooting: as well as leaving their place of birth, many of them have left their class of birth too. This upheaval began on a large scale in the 1960s. As the economy grew, and more Britons stayed on at school and went to university, a mostly working-class nation turned into a mostly middle-class one. For many people this was a traumatic change. Their fathers had been factory workers, and now they were managers/professionals, with the different set of experiences and attitudes that that entails. They lost touch with their roots. Naturally, many of them began to worry about their authenticity deficits. In the 1990s, when football went upmarket and the proverbial prawn sandwiches replaced the proverbial pies, there were endless laments for a lost cloth-capped proletarian culture from people who themselves somewhere along the way had ceased to be cloth-capped proletarians. They yearned to be authentic.

All this makes the true Fan a particularly appealing character to Britons. He is our version of a blood-and-soil myth. The Fan has roots. Generations may pass, and blue collars turn to white, but he still supports his 'local' team in what is supposed to be the 'working man's game'. Many Britons who aren't Hornbyesque Fans would like to be. The Fan is more than just a compelling character. He is a British national fantasy.

FANS' SUICIDE NOTES: DO PEOPLE JUMP OFF BUILDINGS WHEN THEIR TEAMS LOSE?

It is one of the eternal stories that are told about football: when Brazil get knocked out of a World Cup, Brazilians jump off blocks of flats. It can even happen when Brazil wins. One writer at the World Cup in Sweden in 1958 claims to have seen a Brazilian fan kill himself out of 'sheer joy' after his team's victory in the final. Janet Lever tells that story in *Soccer Madness*, her eye-opening study of Brazilian football culture published way back in 1983, when nobody (and certainly not female American social scientists) wrote books about football. Lever continues:

> Of course, Brazilians are not the only fans to kill themselves for their teams. In the 1966 World Cup a West German fatally shot himself when his television set broke down during the final game between his country and England. Nor have Americans escaped some bizarre ends. An often cited case is the Denver man who wrote a suicide note – 'I have been a Broncos fan

since the Broncos were first organized and I can't stand their
fumbling anymore' – then shot himself.

Even worse was the suicide of Amelia Bolaños. In June 1969 she
was an 18-year-old El Salvadorean watching the Honduras v El
Salvador game at home on TV. When Honduras scored the winner
in the last minute, wrote the great Polish reporter Ryszard Kapus-
cinski, Bolaños 'got up and ran to the desk which contained her
father's pistol in a drawer. She then shot herself in the heart.' Her
funeral was televised. El Salvador's president, ministers and the
national football team walked behind the flag-draped coffin. Within
a month, Bolaños's death would help prompt the 'Soccer War'
between El Salvador and Honduras.

Then there was the Bangladeshi woman who reportedly hanged
herself after Cameroon lost to England in the World Cup of 1990.
'The elimination of Cameroon also means the end of my life,' said
her suicide note. In fact, if *The Hindu* newspaper in India is right,
Bangladeshis have a terrible proclivity for football suicides. After
Diego Maradona was thrown out of the World Cup of 1994 for using
ephedrine, 'about a hundred fans in Bangladesh committed
suicide', said an article in the newspaper in 2006. (It would be fascinating to know *The Hindu*'s source.)

By now the notion that football prompts suicide has become a
truism. It is often cited to show the grip of the game over its devotees, and as one reason (along with heart attacks on sofas during
televised matches) why the average World Cup causes more deaths
than goals.

We found that there is indeed an intimate connection between
suicide and football. However, the connection is the opposite of what
is commonly believed. It's not the case that fans jump off buildings
when their teams lose. Working with a crack team of Greek epidemiologists, we have found evidence that rather than prompting suicide,
football stops thousands of people from killing themselves. The
game seems to be a life-saver.

* * *

Measured suicide rates rose by 60 per cent in the 45 years to 2011, estimates the World Health Organisation. Nearly a million people a year now kill themselves, according to the WHO. That is more than twice as many as died in war worldwide in the average year from 1955 to 2002, and nearly twice the number that die of breast cancer each year. To use Germany as an example: in 2005, a total of 10,260 Germans officially died by suicide, more than died in traffic accidents, illegal drugs, HIV, and murder and other violence put together. For Germans aged under 40, suicide was the second most common cause of death. And the reported figures for suicides are understatements, says the University of Hamburg-Eppendorf, which runs a therapy centre for people at risk of suicide: 'There may be a significant share of unrecognised suicides among the death types labelled "traffic accidents", "drugs" and "causes of death unknown".'

The suicide risk varies depending on who in the world you are. If you are an elderly, alcoholic, clinically depressed, divorced Lithuanian man, be very afraid; but suicide rates are relatively low in Latin America, leaving aside for the moment the issue of World Cups. Globally, women attempt suicide more often than men do, but most 'successful' suicides are males. In the US, for instance, nearly 80 per cent of the 38,364 people who were reported as having killed themselves in 2010 were male. For reasons that nobody quite understands, suicide peaks in spring, when daylight hours are longest. In the northern hemisphere, that means May and June.

The question of why people commit suicide has preoccupied sociologists since sociology began. In 1897 Emile Durkheim, descendant of a long line of French rabbis, published his study *Suicide*. It wasn't just the first serious sociological study of suicide; it was one of the first serious sociological studies of almost anything. Drawing on copious statistics, Durkheim showed that when people lost their connection to wider society because of a sudden change – divorce, the death of a partner, a financial crisis – they sometimes killed themselves. He concluded that this particular form of suicide 'results from man's activities lacking regulation and his consequent sufferings'.

A few decades later, sociologists began to wonder whether man's sufferings might possibly include the results of sports matches. The numbers of suicides this caused might be significant: after all, most suicides are men, and sports give meaning to many men's lives. Frank Trovato, a sociology professor at the University of Alberta in Canada, was among the first to investigate the suicide–sport nexus. He found that when the Montréal Canadiens ice hockey team – once described as the national team of French Canada – got knocked out of the play-offs early between 1951 and 1992, Québecois males aged 15 to 34 became more likely to kill themselves. Robert Fernquist, a sociologist at the University of Central Missouri, went further. He studied 30 American metropolitan areas with professional sports teams from 1971 to 1990, and showed that fewer suicides occurred in cities whose teams made the play-offs more often. Routinely reaching the play-offs could reduce suicides by about 20 each year in a metropolitan area the size of Boston or Atlanta, said Fernquist. These saved lives were the converse of the mythical Brazilians throwing themselves off apartment blocks.

Later, Fernquist investigated another link between sport and suicide: he looked at the suicide rate in American cities after a local sports team moved to another town. It turned out that some of the fans abandoned by their team killed themselves. This happened in New York in 1957 when the Brooklyn Dodgers and New York Giants baseball teams left, in Cleveland in 1995–96 when the Browns American football team moved to Baltimore, and in Houston in 1997–98 when the Oilers American football team departed. In each case the suicide rate was 10 to 14 per cent higher in the two months around the team's departure than in the same months of the previous year. Each move probably helped prompt a handful of suicides. Fernquist wrote: 'The sudden change brought about due to the geographic relocations of pro sports teams does appear to, at least for a short time, make highly identified fans drastically change the way they view the normative order in society.' Clearly none of these people killed themselves just because they lost their team. Rather, they were very troubled individuals for whom this sporting disappointment was too much to bear.

Perhaps the most famous recent case of a man who found he could not live without sport was the Gonzo author Hunter S. Thompson. He shot himself in February 2005, four days after writing the following note in black marker entitled 'Football Season Is Over':

> No More Games. No More Bombs. No More Walking. No More Fun. No More Swimming. 67. That is 17 years past 50. 17 more than I needed or wanted. Boring ...

Thompson, an occasional sportswriter, loved American football. One night during the presidential campaign of 1968, he took a limousine journey through New Hampshire with his least favourite person, the Republican candidate Richard Nixon, and they talked football non-stop on the back seat. 'It was a very weird trip,' Thompson wrote later, 'probably one of the weirdest things I've ever done, and especially weird because both Nixon and I enjoyed it.' The reminiscence, in *Fear and Loathing on the Campaign Trail '72*, segues into an ominous musing on suicide, as a Nixon aide snatches away the cigarette Thompson is smoking over the fuel tank of the candidate's plane. Thompson tells the aide: 'You people are lucky I'm a sane, responsible journalist; otherwise I might have hurled my flaming Zippo into the fuel tank.'

'Not you,' the aide replies. 'Egomaniacs don't do that kind of thing. You wouldn't do anything you couldn't live to write about, would you?'

'You're probably right,' says Thompson. As it later turned out, he was wrong. His ashes were fired from a cannon in Aspen, Colorado.

So much for suicides and North American sports. We know much less about the connection between suicides and European football. In one of the very few European studies done so far, Mark

Steels, a psychiatrist at the University Hospital in Nottingham, asked whether Nottingham Forest's worst defeats prompted local suicides. He looked at admissions for deliberate self-poisoning to his hospital's accident and emergency department on two bad days for Forest: after the team's defeats in the FA Cup final of 1991, and the FA Cup quarter-final of 1992. He found that both games were followed by an increase in self-poisonings. After the Cup final, the rise was statistically significant, meaning that it was unlikely to have happened by chance. Steels concluded 'that a sudden disappointment experienced through an entire community may prove one stress too many for some vulnerable members of this community'.

All this is fascinating but inconclusive. For a start, the sample sizes of all these studies are pretty small. How many people are admitted to a Nottingham hospital for self-poisoning after a football match? (Answer: 10 in the 12 hours after the 1991 Cup final; nine after the 1992 quarter-final.) How many people kill themselves in Cleveland in any given month? The other problem is that almost all these researchers pursued what you might call the Brazilian apartment-building hypothesis: that when people suffer a sporting disappointment, they kill themselves. Mostly, these are studies of the dogs that barked: people who did commit suicide.

But what if the relationship between suicide and sport is deeper than that? If sport gives meaning to fans' lives, if it makes them feel part of a larger family of fans of their team, if fans really do eat and sleep football as in a Coca-Cola ad, then perhaps sport might stop some of these fans from killing themselves. We wanted to find out if there were dogs that didn't bark: people who didn't commit suicide because sport kept them going.

It so happens that we have a case-study. Frederick Exley was a fan of the New York Giants American football team, whose life alternated between incarcerations in mental hospitals and equally unhappy periods spent in the bosom of his family. In 1968 Exley published what he called 'a fictional memoir', *A Fan's Notes*, one of the best books ever written about sport. Nick Hornby gave *Fever Pitch* the subtitle 'A Fan's Life' in part as a tribute to Exley.

The Exley depicted in *A Fan's Notes* is a classic suicide risk. He is an alcoholic loner separated from his wife. He has disastrous relationships with women, alienates his friends, and spends months at a time lying in bed or on a sofa at his mother's or aunt's house. For a while his only friend is his dog, Christie III, whom he dresses in a mini blue sweatshirt like his own, and teaches to stand up like a man. 'Like most Americans,' Exley writes, 'I had led a numbingly chaste and uncommitted existence in which one forms neither sympathies nor antipathies of any enduring consequence.'

Only one thing in life provides him with any community: the New York Giants. While living in New York City he stands on the terraces every home game with a group of Brooklyn men: 'An Italian bread-truck driver, an Irish patrolman, a fat garage mechanic, two or three burly longshoremen, and some others whose occupations I forget ... And they liked me.'

When the Giants are not playing, Exley spends much of his time drinking alone. But when a game is on, he watches – depending on the stage of his life – with his Brooklyn group, or with other people in bars, or with his stepfather at home. Exley is the stepfather's eternal house guest from hell, but 'things were never better between us than on autumn Sunday afternoons':

> ... after a time, hardly noticeable at first, he caught something of my enthusiasm for the beauty and permanent character of staying with someone through victory and defeat and came round to the Giants.

Fittingly, the stepfather dies just before a Giants game: 'Seated on the edge of the davenport watching the starting line-ups being introduced, he closed his eyes, slid silently to the floor, and died painlessly of a coronary occlusion.'

Inevitably, at one point in the memoir, Exley contemplates suicide. He has convinced himself he has lung cancer. Determined to avoid the suffering his father went through, he decides to kill himself instead. Drinking with strangers in bars, he gets into the habit of working 'the conversation round to suicide', and soliciting their views on how best to do it. The strangers are happy to oblige:

> Such was the clinical and speculative enthusiasm for the subject – 'Now, if I was gonna knock myself off ...' – that I came to see suicide occupying a greater piece of the American consciousness than I had theretofore imagined.

Only one thing keeps Exley going. The Giants are 'a life-giving, an exalting force'. He is 'unable to conceive what my life would have been without football to cushion the knocks'. The real-life Frederick Exley lived to the age of 63, dying in 1992 after suffering a stroke alone in his apartment. He might never have got that old without the Giants.

There may be a great many Exleys around. The viewing figures we saw earlier in the book suggest that sport is the most important communal activity in many people's lives. About a third of Americans watch the Super Bowl. However, European football is even more popular. In the Netherlands, possibly the European country that follows its national team most keenly, three quarters of the population watch Holland's biggest football games. In many European countries, World Cups may now be the greatest shared events of any kind. To cap it all, World Cups mostly take place in June, the peak month for suicides in the northern hemisphere. How many Exleys have been saved from jumping off apartment buildings by international football tournaments, the world's biggest sporting events?

This is not just a rhetorical question. A study of football tournaments and suicide would bring together both an incomparably compelling communal event and a sample the size of several countries. So we set about finding the data.

We needed suicide statistics per month over several years for as many European countries as possible. These figures do not seem to be published anywhere. Luckily we found out that the Greek epidemiologists Eleni Petridou and Fotis Papadopoulos had laboriously got hold of these data years earlier by writing to the statistical offices of several countries. A statistician who works with Petridou and Papadopoulos, Nick Dessypris, went through the numbers for us. He found that in almost every country we know about, fewer people kill themselves while the national team is playing in a World Cup or a European Championship. Dessypris said the declines were 'statistically significant' – unlikely to be due to chance.

Let's take Germany, the biggest country in our study and one that always qualifies for big tournaments. Petridou and Papadopoulos had obtained monthly suicide data for Germany from 1991 to 1997. A horrifying total of 90,000 people in Germany officially killed themselves in this period. The peak months for suicides were March through June.

But when Germany were playing in a football tournament – as they did in the Junes of 1992, 1994 and 1996 – fewer people died. In the average June with football, there were 787 male and 329 female suicides in Germany. A lot more people killed themselves in the Junes of 1991, 1993, 1995 and 1997 when Germany were not playing football. In those football-free Junes, there were an average of 817 male and 343 female suicides; or 30 more dead men and 14 more dead women than in the average June with a big tournament. For German men and women alike, the June with the fewest suicides in our seven-year sample was 1996, the month that Germany won Euro 96.

We found the same trend for 10 of the 12 countries we studied. In Junes when the country was playing in a football tournament, there were fewer suicides. These declines are particularly remarkable given how much alcohol gets consumed during football tournaments, because drinking would normally be expected to help prompt suicides. Only in the Netherlands and Switzerland did football tournaments not seem to save lives; these two countries saw very slight increases in the suicide rate during tournaments. In the other countries, the life-saving effect of football was sometimes spectacular. Our data for Norway, for instance, run from 1988 to 1995. The football-mad country played in only one tournament in that period, the World Cup of 1994. The average for the seven Junes when Norway were not playing football was 55 suicides. But in June 1994 there were only 36 Norwegian suicides, by far the lowest figure for all eight Junes in our dataset. Or take Denmark, for which we have suicide tallies from 1973 to 1996, the longest period for any country. In June 1992 the Danes won the European Championship. That month there were 54 male suicides, the fewest for any June since 1978, and 28 female suicides, the joint lowest (with 1991) since the dataset began.

We have tried to make some very rough estimates of how many lives these tournaments saved in each country. 'Lives saved' represents the decline in deaths during the average June when a country's national team is playing in a World Cup or European Championship compared with the average June when the team isn't playing. Here is the tally:

	Male lives saved	Female lives saved
Austria	9	–3
Czech Republic	14	6
Denmark	4	4
France	59	8
Germany	30	14
Greece	0	5
Ireland	2	1
Netherlands	–5	0
Norway*	[19 lives saved spread across both genders]	
Spain	4	1
Sweden	4	15
Switzerland	–1	–2

* The data for Norway were not broken down by gender

The figures are negative for the Netherlands and Switzerland because more people killed themselves when their teams were playing than when there was no football.

The next question is what happens after a team is knocked out. Do all the people who had been saved from suicide by football then fall into a void and jump off apartment buildings? If so, you would expect a rise in suicides in the period after the tournament.

However, we found that in 10 of our 12 countries, suicides *declined* for the entire year when the national team played in a big tournament. Only in the Netherlands did suicides rise in the year when the team played; in Spain the difference was negligible. But in the other 10 countries, even after the team got knocked out and the euphoria ended, there was no compensating rise in suicide. To the contrary: it seems that the uniting effect of the tournament lasted for a while afterwards, continuing to depress the suicide rate. For each of these 10 countries, more lives were saved on average over the entire year than in June alone. Here are our very rough estimates for lives saved over the entire year when the national team plays in a tournament ('lives saved' represents the decline in deaths during a 'football' year compared with the average year):

	Male lives saved	Female lives saved
Austria	46	15
Czech Republic	55	12
Denmark	37	47
France	95	82
Germany	61	39
Greece	9	13
Ireland	19	−10
Netherlands	−10	−1
Norway	[92 lives saved spread across both genders]	
Spain	2	−3
Sweden	44	16
Switzerland	20	2

Very roughly, football tournaments in these periods appear to have helped save several hundred Europeans from suicide.

We couldn't find any monthly suicide data for any of the British nations. However, the only two previous studies on this topic that we know of in Britain suggest that the life-saving effect works there too.

'Parasuicide' is a suicidal gesture in which the aim is not death, but rather self-harm, or a cry for help. One example of parasuicide is taking an insufficient overdose. George Masterton, a psychiatrist in Edinburgh, and his co-author J.A. Strachan studied Scottish parasuicides during and immediately after the World Cups of 1974, 1978, 1982 and 1986. Each time, Scotland had qualified for the tournament. Each time, Masterton and Strachan found a fall in parasuicide for both genders during the tournament 'which has been sustained for at least eight weeks after the last game'. The Scottish case is a pretty strong piece of evidence against the apartment-building theory of football suicides, because if there was ever an excuse for football fans to try to kill themselves, it was Scotland's performance at the World Cup of 1978. (Their fantasist manager, Ally McLeod, had boasted beforehand that they would leave with a 'medal of some sort'.)

Later Masterton and Anthony J. Mander studied the numbers of people who came to the Royal Edinburgh Hospital with psychiatric emergencies during and after the World Cups of 1978, 1982 and 1986. The researchers found 'reductions in all illness categories during and afterwards (with the exception of alcoholism during)'. The decline in emergencies applied to both genders, and was more marked after each World Cup than during it. For instance, there was a 56 per cent fall in admissions of male neurotics in the weeks after a tournament.

The authors then tried to explain what was going on here:

There are few outlets which permit a wide and acceptable expression of Scottish nationhood – sport is perhaps the most powerful, and football is the national game ... We would

speculate that such a common interest and endeavour, fused
with a surge of nationalism, might enhance social cohesion in
the manner proposed by Durkheim to explain the decreased
suicide rates that accompany times of war.

'Social cohesion' is the key phrase here. This is the benefit that
almost all fans – potential suicides and the rest of us – get from
fandom. Winning or losing is not the point. It is not the case that
losing matches makes significant numbers of people so unhappy
they jump off apartment buildings. In the US, fans of longtime losers
like the Chicago Cubs and the Boston Red Sox baseball teams
(Boston only became frequent winners from 2004) have not killed
themselves more than other people, says Thomas Joiner, author of
Why People Die by Suicide, whose own father died by suicide.

Joiner's article 'On Buckeyes, Gators, Super Bowl Sunday, and
the Miracle on Ice' makes a strong case that it's not the winning that
counts but the taking part – the shared experience. It is true that he
found fewer suicides in Columbus, Ohio, and Gainesville, Florida, in
the years when the local college American football teams did well.
But Joiner argues that this is because fans of winning teams 'pull
together' more: they wear the team shirt more often, watch games
together in bars, talk about the team and so on, much as happens
in a European country while the national team is playing in a World
Cup. The 'pulling together' saves people from suicide, not the
winning. Proof of this is that Joiner found fewer suicides in the US on
Super Bowl Sundays than on other Sundays at that time of year,
even though few of the Americans who watch the Super Bowl are
passionate supporters of either team. What they get from the day's
parties is a sense of belonging.

That is the life-saver. In Europe today, there may be nothing that
brings a society together like a World Cup with your team in it. For
once, almost everyone in the country is watching the same TV
programmes and talking about them at work the next day, just as
people used to do 30 years ago before cable TV arrived. Part of the

point of watching a World Cup is that almost everyone else is watching too. Isolated people – the types at most risk of suicide – are suddenly welcomed into the national conversation. They are given social cohesion. All this helps explain why big football tournaments seem to save so many female lives in Europe, even though relatively few women either commit suicide or (before about 2000 at least) watch football. The 'pulling together' during a big football tournament is so universal that it drags many women along in a way that club football does not. It may also be that, during tournaments, some troubled women benefit from a brief holiday from male partners who are distracted by football.

Other than sport, only war and catastrophe can create this sort of national unity. Most strikingly, in the week after John F. Kennedy's murder in 1963 – a time of American sadness but also of 'pulling together' – *not one* suicide was reported in 29 cities studied. Likewise, in the US in the days after the September 11 attacks, another phase of national 'pulling together', the number of calls to the 1-800-SUICIDE hotline halved to about 300 a day, 'an all-time low', writes Joiner. And in Britain in 1997, suicides declined after Princess Diana died.

Joiner speculates that 'pulling together' through sport may particularly suit 'individuals who have poor interpersonal skills (often characteristic of severely depressed or suicidal persons)'. You don't have to be charming to be a fan among fans.

In 1956 Frederick Exley was drunk, unemployed and loveless in Chicago. He writes: 'Though I had completely disregarded football my first year in that happy city, during the autumn of 1956, after losing my job, I once again found that it was the only thing that gave me comfort.' At some point or other in life, we have all known how that feels.

HAPPINESS: WHY HOSTING WORLD CUPS IS GOOD FOR YOU

You don't often see people consciously building a white elephant, but that's what was happening in Brasília in 2012. Smack in the middle of town, on the main avenue of Brazil's tropical capital, workers were finishing off a stadium for 70,000 people. The Estádio Nacional is one of 12 stadiums built for the World Cup in 2014. And even before the tournament ends, it will be redundant. Brasília's tinpot clubs seldom draw 1,000 spectators. Nor will the Rolling Stones regularly be flying into this city in the middle of nowhere to fill the Nacional. Brasília might as well tear down the stadium after the last World Cup game, and save itself a fortune in maintenance costs. Other host cities like Manaus, Cuiabá and Natal could do likewise.

It's this kind of waste that brought Brazilians onto the streets in June 2013, demonstrating against their country's hosting of the World Cup and the Rio Olympics of 2016. 'We have world-class stadiums – now we need a country to go around them,' read one protestors' banner. 'A teacher is worth more than Neymar,' said another. Worldwide, people are starting to reach the same conclusion: hosting sports events doesn't make you rich.

Whenever a country prepares to host a World Cup or an Olympics, its politicians prophesy an 'economic bonanza'. They invoke hordes of shopaholic visitors, the free advertising of host cities to the world's TV viewers, and the long-term benefits of all the roads and stadiums that will get built. No wonder that nowadays almost every government seems to want to host these events. The bidding to stage the World Cups of 2018 and 2022 was the most cut-throat ever. If only the bidding countries could grasp the real reason for wanting to be a host: hosting doesn't make you rich, but it does make you happier. Brazil will benefit from 2014, but not in money.

The 1989 movie *Field of Dreams* is a sentimental redemption story starring Kevin Costner as an Iowa farmer. Growing up the son of a baseball nut, the farmer had dreamt of being a baseball star. As an adult, he hears a voice telling him to build a baseball diamond on his cornfield. 'If you build it, he will come,' is the film's catchphrase. The moral: building stadiums where they do not currently exist is uplifting and good for you. This originally American idea later spread to soccer in Europe.

There is in the US a small industry of 'consultants' who exist to provide an economic rationale for 'If you build it, he will come.' In almost any city in the US at almost any time, someone is scheming to build a spanking new sports stadium. The big prize for most American cities is to host a major-league team; ideally an American football one, but if that can't be had then baseball, basketball or, if nothing else is going, ice hockey or, at worst, soccer. Hosting an American sports 'franchise' has a lot in common with hosting a World Cup. Both the franchise and the World Cup are mobile beasts. Their owners are generally willing to move to whichever city or country offers them the best deal. In the US, owners of sports teams usually demand that the host city's taxpayers stump up for a stadium, with lucrative car parks thrown in. All this is then handed over to the franchise owner, who also gets to keep the money he makes from selling tickets. About 70 major-league stadiums and arenas were built in the US in the 20 years before the crash of 2008. The total cost: $20 billion, about half of which came from the public. In New Orleans, for instance, the taxpayer paid for the Superdome but not for better levees.

In 1989 there was a typical case in which 70 investors, including the son of the then American president George H.W. Bush, paid $83 million for the Texas Rangers baseball club. The Bush group wanted a bigger stadium. Strangely for a phalanx of right-wing millionaires, it decided that local taxpayers should finance it. If that didn't happen, the new owners threatened to move the Rangers elsewhere. The people of the local town of Arlington duly voted to increase the local sales tax by half a per cent, raising the $191 million needed for the ballpark.

Bush Junior became the Rangers' managing director. Mostly, this just meant being the official face of the club. He would sit in the stands during games handing out baseball cards with pictures of himself. When he ran for governor of Texas in 1994, he constantly cited his experience in baseball. There wasn't much else on his CV at the time. He was duly elected, and decorated his Austin office with 250 signed baseballs.

In 1998 the Bush group sold the Rangers to Tom Hicks for $250 million. Most of the value was in the stadium that the taxpayers had built. Bush personally netted $14.9 million. He admitted: 'When it is all said and done, I will have made more money than I ever dreamed I would make.' Meanwhile he was already beginning to parlay his governorship into a bigger political prize.

So the trick for American club owners is to persuade the taxpayer to cough up for stadiums. This is where economists come in handy. Economists like to say that people respond to incentives. Well, economists certainly respond to incentives. Anyone hoping to persuade taxpayers to stump up for a stadium in the US commissioned an economist to write an 'economic impact' study. By a strange coincidence, these studies always showed that the stadium would make taxpayers rich. (One book describing this racket is aptly called *Field of Schemes*.)

The argument typically went as follows: building the stadium would create jobs first for construction workers, and later for people who worked in it. Fans would flock in from all around ('If you build it, he will come'), and they would spend money. New businesses would spring up to serve them. As the area around the stadium became populated, more people would want to live there, and even more businesses (and jobs) would spring up. 'The building of publicly funded stadiums has become a substitute for anything resembling an urban policy,' notes Dave Zirin in his *People's History of Sports in the United States*.

The 'economic impact' study then typically clothes this model with some big numbers. If you put your mind to it, you can think up a total in benefits that runs into the billions, whatever currency you happen to be working in. Best of all, no one will ever be able to prove that number wrong. Suppose you promise that a stadium will bring a city economic benefits of $2 billion over ten years. If the city's income (hard to measure in the first place) rises by only $1 billion over the decade, then, of course, it was something completely different (the world economy, say) that restricted the income. You could only prove the original estimates wrong if you could estimate how much economic growth there would have been had the stadium never been built – but this 'counterfactual' figure is unknowable, precisely because it is a counterfactual. The same economists soon branched out into writing studies that justified ever more extravagant spending on the Olympics.

It would have seemed rude to derail this industry with anything so inconvenient as the truth. But then along came Rob Baade.

The quiet, courteous academic seemed an unlikely figure to be taking on the stadium lobby. After all, he is a former top-class athlete himself: at college, Baade captained the Wisconsin basketball team. When the white coach seemed antagonistic to the majority of black players, Baade found himself championing players against coach in what he describes as one of the most difficult years of his life.

Afterwards he wanted to do graduate work in public finance, a branch of economics that usually involves many equations and few words. But he also wanted to coach basketball, and to apply something of what he had learnt while in the Wisconsin team. A colleague told him about a job at Lake Forest College, an idyllic little place just outside Chicago. To the dismay of some of his purist professors, he went to Lake Forest on a temporary appointment and ended up coaching there for 18 years, while also rising to full professor of economics. He was a good coach, too: the year before he arrived the team had not won a single game, but within four years they were winning 85 per cent of their games.

When you start out as an academic you try to write papers that will grab your colleagues' attention. Baade used his own background to enter the economics of sports, then still almost virgin terrain. At a seminar in New York he presented a paper entitled 'The Sports Tax'. Journalists from the *New York Times* and the *Wall Street Journal* happened to be in the audience, and they zeroed in on what had been almost a throwaway line in his talk: public investment in stadiums does not provide a good return for taxpayers. As a coach himself, Baade might have been expected to join the stadium boosters. Had he done so, he could have earned himself good money in 'consulting'. Instead he went into opposition.

The Heartland Institute, a conservative think tank, asked him to write up his thoughts. There are few issues in American political life where the right joins with an intellectual liberal like Baade, but the paper he published in 1987 laid out the problem clearly: 'Contrary to the claims of city officials, this study has found that sports and stadiums frequently had no significant positive impact on a city's economy and, in a regional context, may actually contribute to a reduction in a sports-minded city's share of regional income.'

Baade had asked the awkward questions that stadium boosters always ignored. For instance, where would all the construction workers for the new stadium come from? Wouldn't they have jobs already, and therefore wouldn't a shortage arise somewhere else? Worse still, as competition for their skills intensified, wouldn't costs rise?

Once you start thinking of people as having alternatives, rather than just standing around waiting for the stadium to arrive, the economics begin to look less appealing. For every dollar going in, there is probably a dollar going out somewhere else. In particular, if a city has to balance its budget, then spending more on stadiums must mean spending less on hospitals and schools. These lost jobs have to be counted against the stadium's benefits. And if the city doesn't balance its budget, isn't it storing up future burdens for taxpayers, who will have to forego something, some day?

That is bad enough, but what if the stadium doesn't produce the promised benefits? After all, most stadiums are only used for a few hours a week, and barely at all in the off-season. Even allowing for the occasional rock concert (and there is a limit to how many times Elton John can play in your town), most of the time the neighbour- hood around the stadium will be deserted. Nobody wants to live in a place like that. The neighbourhoods around Anfield or Old Trafford have hardly become des res, for instance.

Nor did Baade believe that a stadium would draw in much spend- ing from outside the city. Most out-of-town fans would buy a hot dog and beer, watch the game, and leave – hardly an economic bonanza. A mall, or a Cineplex, or even a hospital, would generate more local spending.

Around the end of the 1980s other economists, too, began asking these awkward questions. However, Baade went one better. In order to show that the boosters' numbers didn't add up, he gener- ated some numbers of his own. Perhaps he couldn't measure the counterfactual, but he could get close by comparing economic growth in cities that had major-league teams with those that didn't. After all, he reasoned, if the boosters were right, then over time cities with stadiums must do better than cities without stadiums.

Baade examined data such as income per head, and the numbers of new businesses and jobs created in various cities. The more he looked, the less difference he found between the economic profiles of cities with and without stadiums. All this spending was evidently producing no benefit.

Gradually people took notice. Other economists started to replicate Baade's findings, and to find new ways to test the proposition that stadiums create wealth. 'Anti-stadium movements' began in many American cities.

In the mid-1990s Baade was asked to testify before Congress. On the day of his testimony, Congress was also holding hearings on the Clinton Whitewater affair and on military intervention in Bosnia, but when the stadium hearings started, the other chambers emptied. One of the people in the room was Paul Tagliabue, commissioner of the NFL and someone all the Congressmen wanted to be seen with. Powerful people like Tagliabue were getting quite irritated with Baade's awkward facts.

Academic freedom is a cherished value of American universities, but, as Baade was starting to realise, so is making money. He recalls an old guy coming up to him after one meeting, and saying: 'You might be right, Professor, but if I were you I would watch my back. You're getting in the way of a whole lotta commercial projects.' A university seldom likes seeing its employees upset local politicians and business people. Lake Forest College always supported Baade, but at times it would have been convenient had he thought differently.

He kept on telling the truth regardless. Among economists, often not the sportiest of types, he developed a special credibility as a former athlete. This sometimes came in handy, for example when a questioner in a public debate asked, 'No disrespect, Professor, but what does an economist like you know about athletics?'

Eventually Baade descended on soccer. He and Victor Matheson conducted a study of the impact of hosting the World Cup of 1994 in the US. They looked for evidence of faster economic growth in the host cities, and as usual they found nothing. Meanwhile, the old bogus American arguments for hosting sports had spread to other countries.

The raising and dashing of hopes of an 'economic bonanza' became as integral a part of a modern football tournament as the raising and dashing of hopes that England would win it. A few months after England hosted Euro 96, for instance, a report by a body called Tourism Research & Marketing said that fewer than 100,000 overseas fans had visited England for the tournament, against a forecast – admittedly plucked out of thin air by the FA – of 250,000. Nor had the visitors spent much. Euro 96 generated about £100 million in direct income for Britain. This was peanut dust beside the £12.7 billion spent by all overseas visitors to the country in 1996. Meanwhile, a study by Liverpool University and the city council found that the 30,000 visitors to Liverpool during Euro 96 spent only £1.03 million between them. How many jobs did that create? Thirty, all of them temporary.

A few years later Japanese and Korean government officials were predicting that the World Cup of 2002 could boost their economies by a staggering $26 billion and $9 billion respectively. Of course, after the event there was little sign of any such boost, and indeed some evidence that tourists had stayed away for fear of football hooligans.

Big sports tournaments attract some visitors, and deter many others. Greek tourism officials estimated in late 2004 that there'd been a ten per cent *fall* in tourist arrivals during that year's Athens Olympics, as holiday-goers choosing summer destinations steered clear of the frenzy. Nor did the 22 stadiums built for the Athens Games generate an economic bonanza. In 2010 an analysis by the *Wall Street Journal* found that 21 were unoccupied.

Finally, the weight of this research was starting to stack up. It was becoming obvious that even if you build it, he doesn't necessarily come. The boosters' claims of economic benefits were growing muted. The estimates produced for the World Cup in Germany in

2006 were altogether more sober. Even a study sponsored by the German football federation suggested a mere $2 billion in new benefits. (Similarly in London, estimates of the likely economic benefits from the 2012 Olympics were kept studiously vague.)

Perhaps the best estimate we have of how much visitors to football tournaments actually spend was done at the German World Cup. This was the biggest media event in history, a month-long party (except for the boring football), and yet even here the hosts didn't make much money.

A team of economists, led by Holger Preuss from the University of Mainz, decided to work out how much 'new' money visitors to the World Cup actually spent. In the old days, when boosters estimated economic bonanzas, they simply multiplied the number of seats in stadiums by some imaginary spending number (counting meals, hotels, and transport as well as tickets) to produce an enormous hypothetical sum.

The problem with this method, as serious economists pointed out, is that not every visitor to an event really injects extra spending into the economy. Preuss's team surveyed a large sample of visitors to the World Cup, and found that only about a fifth of them were foreigners who had travelled to Germany specifically for the football. Over half the 'visitors' were in fact Germans. For the most part these Germans would have been in Germany anyway, and had there been no World Cup they would presumably have spent their money on other forms of entertainment (such as going to cinemas or restaurants). If they spent money on the World Cup, they spent less elsewhere in the German economy, which largely offset any economic benefit from the football. Of course, some Germans who might otherwise have been spending their money in Spanish bars stayed home for the football. However, their spending was probably offset by other Germans who went abroad precisely in order to avoid the madness of the World Cup.

The remaining foreign visitors to the World Cup – about a quarter of all visitors – were either 'time-switchers', who would have come to Germany anyway at some point, and simply timed their visit to coincide with the World Cup, or foreigners who would have been in Germany during the World Cup anyway, and just decided to go along and see what all the fuss was about. Preuss's team called this last category 'casuals'.

'Time-switchers' and 'casuals' would have added little to spending, because even without the World Cup they would have spent their money in Germany. Preuss's team asked their respondents detailed questions about their spending plans. They concluded that the World Cup generated spending by visitors of €2.8 billion. That was negligible besides the Paris Hiltonesque €1,000 billion-plus spent annually by consumers in Germany. It was also much less than the German state spent preparing for the tournament. Remarkably, more than a third of that visitor income came from people who never got inside a stadium but merely watched the games on big screens in public places. In short, even the World Cup was barely a hiccup in the German economy.

Almost all research shows the same thing: hosting sports tournaments doesn't increase the number of tourists, or of full-time jobs, or total economic growth. Economists foresaw well in advance that the World Cup of 2010 would not be a sort of aeroplane dropping dollars on South Africa. When the country's finance minister flew three eminent sports economists to Pretoria for a workshop years before the tournament, the trio argued that the best South Africa could hope for was that the World Cup would *not reduce* economic growth. Of course this was not exactly what the South African officials wanted to hear.

None of this is to mention the host's costs. If the economic benefits of putting on these tournaments are muted, the expenses seldom are. The economists Brad Humphreys and Szymon Prokopowicz made some rough estimates of the costs to Poland of hosting just half of Euro 2012. Poland needed to lay on a lot more than just new stadiums, airports, and hotels for fans. UEFA requires, for its own officials and guests, the use of one entire five-star hotel within 45 minutes' drive of every stadium. The teams need another 16 hotels, most of them five-star. The referees have to be in five-star hotels near the stadiums. The doctors who perform the doping controls need five-stars 'in the countryside'. Much of the cost of these hotels came courtesy of the Polish government. Poland also had to put up surveillance cameras all over its stadiums and towns.

In all, Humphreys and Prokopowicz estimated that Poland would have to spend about $10 billion on Euro 2012. With hindsight, this looks like a serious underestimate. True, some of the infrastructure the country bought still has its uses after the tournament. However, much of it doesn't, because the things you need for a football tournament are never quite the same as the things you need for daily life.

Almost all the research points in one direction: hosting doesn't create economic bonanza. And yet South Africa went into its World Cup in 2010 promising its citizens economic bonanza. In a sense, the country had to. When about a third of your population lives on less than $2 a day, the government can hardly say it's blowing billions on a month of fun. It has to argue that the football will benefit the poor. You then end up with people like Irvin Khoza, who chaired the tournament's local organising committee, saying things like, 'The 2010 World Cup will change the face of the country. It may prove a pivotal point in our development as a young democracy.'

The South African ruling class put this message across so energetically that when the country was named host in May 2004, crowds celebrating in the township of Soweto shouted, 'The money is coming!' Half the people you met in South Africa in the years before the tournament had a scheme for 2010: buying apartments just to rent them out during the tournament, selling sausage and maize pudding outside stadiums, corralling peasant women to weave beaded flags in the colours of all the participating teams. Much of South African conversation was about such schemes, and in newspaper profiles, when a celebrity described what he was working on, he would often add, 'The key thing is to be ready for 2010.' The year had become a magic number.

As 2010 approached, the tournament's expected costs inevitably soared. South Africa had initially promised a cheap World Cup. All the stadiums put together, it had said in 2004, would only cost about $170 million. But with Fifa demanding perfection, and every local powerbroker in South Africa wanting his own whizzo stadium, the bill for stadiums ended up about ten times that. This embarrassing overrun may be why copies of South Africa's original bid book were 'disappeared'.

Some of the South African organisers ended their journey in 2010 feeling rather chastened. We witnessed this one chilly winter's Saturday during the World Cup, in a chic convention centre in Johannesburg's business district of Sandton. A few dozen visiting Brazilian officials had taken their seats to listen to South African officials explain what it had really been like to stage the tournament – to hear, in the words of one South African speaker, about 'some of our cuts and bruises'.

The Brazilian guests were mostly cheery, as befits officials on a 'study visit' to a World Cup. But they heard some chilling things. Perhaps the most chilling came from a lady whom we won't name, to keep her out of trouble. She was a senior official for Gauteng, the province that includes Johannesburg.

She told the Brazilians how, in 2009, she had reviewed the projected economic boost that the World Cup would give South Africa. She looked – and found almost nothing. 'It wasn't going to be giving us the benefits that we had told the country the World Cup was going to give us,' she said. True, the tournament would improve Johannesburg's creaky transport links a bit, but: 'It wasn't as much as we had thought.'

And so, over a year before kickoff, Gauteng quietly binned hopes of economic boost. Instead it recast the World Cup as an exercise in branding – 'almost a 30-day advertisement for Gauteng'. That, the lady admitted, was all the tournament had proven to be. 'There are a lot of mistakes we made that you hopefully won't make,' she told the Brazilians.

After her talk, we buttonholed her to ask why the promised economic boost had never happened. 'If you look at all the research about mega-events,' she replied, 'all the findings are that the economic returns are highly inflated by people hoping to profit from the events.'

That's right. For instance, the expected hordes of foreign visitors never reached South Africa. In 2009 the management consultancy Grant Thornton – producer of a stream of upbeat economic forecasts about the World Cup – was predicting 483,000 foreign visitors for the tournament. (Earlier forecasts had been even sunnier.) A retrospective study based on official South African statistics, co-authored by Stefan with Thomas Peeters of the University of Antwerp and Victor Matheson from the College of the Holy Cross in the US, estimates that the number of additional visitors in June and July 2010 was only 220,000, less than half Grant Thornton's prediction. Given that tourist arrivals from countries outside of Africa average about 2 million per year, this represented a boost to tourism, but not a big one. Nor did the economy as a whole see much benefit. John Saker, chief operating officer of KPMG Africa, said: 'The big boost didn't happen.'

There is a vignette of the national disappointment in an email sent by a professor at the University of the Western Cape a month after the World Cup. This man, formerly a very senior government official, wrote that his university had reserved 92,000 'bed-nights' for visitors to the tournament. But shortly before the World Cup began, FIFA's booking agency Match had returned 91,000 nights unused. 'We are still trying to sell off the additional linen we had to purchase,' the professor complained.

Predictably, most of the stadiums that South Africa built for the tournament are now white elephants. The country never had any need for them. The larger hosting cities – Cape Town, Johannesburg, Durban and Pretoria – have for decades possessed large, very decent rugby grounds that can serve the modest needs of local football too. Johannesburg also had the original Soccer City, a stadium rightly touted as the best in Africa when South Africa was bidding for the World Cup.

Very few domestic games outside the Johannesburg region draw more than about 10,000 spectators. Towns like Nelspruit, Polokwane and Port Elizabeth now have World Cup stadiums, but they do not have clubs in the country's Premier Soccer League. (If you are wondering how Port Elizabeth became a host city, it just happens to be the hometown of Danny Jordaan, the World Cup's chief executive.) In October 2010 the French company SAIL Stadefrance said that it was pulling out of its 30-year lease to operate Cape Town's Green Point stadium, even before the lease came into effect. The company admitted it had underestimated the cost of running the venue. Quite likely, in the next few years Cape Town will find better uses for that prime piece of land overlooking the Atlantic Ocean than a redundant football stadium.

BRAZIL 2014: THE HYPE NEVER CEASES

You would have thought that people might have learned from the shame of the South African World Cup; from the way FIFA forced a developing country to build unnecessary stadiums swish enough for sponsors, while a few miles away people lived in corrugated-iron shacks. In 2009, a senior European football official mused to us about putting pressure on FIFA to let Brazil host a cheaper World Cup. It could be done, this man said, if a few powerful national football associations – Germany, France, the US, England, and some others – argued that Brazil needn't build the most expensive stadiums on earth, but just some good solid ones that wouldn't turn into white elephants the day the circus left town.

No such luck, however. One morning in Johannesburg during the World Cup of 2010, one of us, Simon, had breakfast with the Brazilian sports minister, Orlando Silva Junior. The minister was a charming man, wearing the sort of casual clothes we wish our own ministers in Britain would try. And he was really looking forward to hosting the World Cup. 'I guess that the Cup has served as a stimulus for development and infrastructure here in South Africa,' he said, 'and we will follow the same path in Brazil.' He said his country had deliberately chosen 'less developed regions' to host matches, just to give them the chance to develop. Brazil was building airports, ports and stadiums all over. There'd be jobs galore. In short, the World Cup was just what Brazil's economy needed.

Regrettably Silva is no longer in office, having resigned in 2011 over a corruption scandal, despite maintaining his innocence. However, Brazil 2014 is already looking like a rerun of South Africa 2010. There is the ever-rising cost of stadiums: from an initial estimate of under $1 billion, most of which would be paid by private business, to over $3.5 billion (almost entirely funded by the Brazilian taxpayer) by late 2013.

And let's just say the estimated cost (or 'investment', as officials like to call it) is unlikely to fall. The construction companies knew the stadiums had to be ready by June 2014. This meant they could charge almost whatever they liked to build them; the government would just have to pay.

No wonder the construction of stadiums kept hitting delays. This allowed the construction companies to tell the government at the last minute: 'Oops, this is costing more than we thought. Give us more cash or we won't finish on time and you will look stupid in front of the world.' When Silva was asked in August 2011 how much the World Cup would cost Brazil's federal government, he replied: 'The figure has not been decided.'

The Brazilian World Cup is a wonderful thing if you happen to own a construction business; not so wonderful if you pay tax in Brazil, or if you were hoping the government would do something about all the terrible Brazilian roads that don't lead to football stadiums.

We confidently predict that in July 2014, when the last of the party animals has tumbled out of a cupboard and flown home, it will turn out that nobody made much more from the tournament than they would have done in the regular tourist season.

Having said all that, the Brazilian World Cup will probably have a more worthwhile legacy than the South African one did. For a start, if Brazil has its wits about it, it will twin the preparations for the World Cup with the Rio Olympics of 2016. South Africa built infrastructure for one party. Brazil, at least, should be building for two.

More importantly, Brazil has a greater need than South Africa did for the main legacy of a World Cup: football stadiums. Brazil has nearly 200 million inhabitants, almost four times as many as South Africa. It has a much larger football-going public: no club in South Africa has an average attendance of over 20,000, whereas several in Brazil do. And Brazil lacks decent stadiums. When it was named host in 2007, it didn't have a single one good enough for a World Cup. Its football fans were watching – or not watching – in the tumble-down stadiums of a poorer era.

A wealthier Brazil can afford better grounds. During the recent boom years, this became more of a middle-class country. It now has more inhabitants able to pay to watch football in comfort. The World Cup will make that happen. The government's aim, said Silva at our breakfast, is 'to raise the comfort level of our stadiums without excluding the workers'. Once the comfort level rises in the shiny new stadiums, more middle-class Brazilians and their families should start coming to league matches. This is what happened in England after the country raised the comfort level of its stadiums in the early 1990s. True, England then was much richer than Brazil is today. But Brazil today is richer than its rundown stadiums pre-World Cup. Admittedly, six of the host cities for 2014 don't even have teams in the National Championship, but at least the other six stadiums (including a marvellous new Maracanã in Rio) should come in handy after 2014. That's a better ratio than South Africa managed.

If well-off Brazilians start buying expensive tickets to games after 2014, that would make Brazilian clubs richer. An official at Chelsea told us he saw Brazil in future as 'a marketplace of threat for the talent that you have here'. Already, as the country gets richer, Brazilian clubs can afford to keep more of their better players at home.

Brazil has ceded its traditional position of football's biggest exporter of players to neighbouring Argentina. Post-2014, Brazil could have a very good league. After all, the Brazilian economy is bigger than England's, and the country produces some decent players.

If our rosy predictions for Brazilian football come true, then that won't make Brazil as a whole richer. Rather, the Brazilian World Cup is best understood as a series of financial transfers: from women to men (who will have more fun); from Brazilian taxpayers to Fifa and the world's football fans; and from taxpayers to Brazilian football clubs and construction companies. Possibly Brazilian society desires these transfers. Still, we have to be clear that this is what's going on: a transfer of wealth from Brazil as a whole to various interest groups inside and outside the country. This is not an economic bonanza. Brazil sacrificed a little bit of its future to host the World Cup.

Ah, say the boosters, but the biggest economic benefits from these events are intangible. Think of the billions of people seeing the host country on TV every night. Saker of KPMG Africa promised that South Africa would benefit from 'word of mouth and goodwill for years to come' after 2010. Similarly, Silva told us that the 2014 World Cup would promote Brazil's image in the world. Well, maybe. First of all, as the American sports economist Andrew Zimbalist says, 'Brazil is hardly a secret as an international tourist destination.' Rio is already the most visited city in the southern hemisphere, he notes. Furthermore, there's the risk that the World Cup could *damage* Brazil's brand. That has happened to several Olympic hosts: Munich in 1972, Montreal in 1976, and Atlanta in 1996. The 2014 World Cup might persuade people that Brazil is not a crime-ridden country with terrible traffic. Alternatively, it might persuade them that Brazil is precisely that.

It's rare for a truth long known to economists to sink in with the general public, but that is happening on this issue. People everywhere are cottoning on to the truth that building stadiums doesn't bring wealth. In referendums in Europe in 2013, the citizens of Munich voted against bidding for a winter Olympics, and the

Viennese against bidding for a summer Games. In the US, the economic crisis seems to have made taxpayers more sceptical of stadium boondoggles. In 2013 two local US sports teams, in cahoots with local politicians, avoided letting locals vote on funding their planned new stadiums – because they suspected people would vote against. When Insider Advantage–Fox 5 polled 1,698 registered voters in Cobb County, Georgia, in November 2013, 56 per cent opposed spending local tax dollars on one of the stadiums. Yet later that month, Cobb County commissioners voted for it.

Other international sporting bodies don't want to anger taxpayers the way FIFA has in Brazil. That's partly why the IOC gave the 2020 Olympics to Tokyo: the megacity could better afford to stage the Games than its poorer rivals Istanbul and Madrid. In football, UEFA went one step further: it didn't choose a host at all for Euro 2020. The burden would have been too great, explained UEFA's general secretary Gianni Infantino, especially in hard economic times. Instead 13 countries will share the hosting.

FIFA, too, must have learned from its Brazilian experience. It now knows that to ask a democratic country to fund white elephants is to ask for protests. Much easier to give the world cup to dictatorships like Russia or Qatar, where protestors are discouraged. Alternatively, you could choose a host country that doesn't need to build world-class stadiums because it already has dozens. Step forward the US for 2026.

HAPPINESS IS A WORLD CUP

Most people now agree with Rob Baade: hosting a sports tournament doesn't make a place rich. The question then is why countries still bother. Why did so many countries go to such embarrassing lengths to stage the World Cups of 2018 and 2022? The answer has nothing to do with desire for profit. To the contrary: Qatar, chosen as host for 2022, has so much money that it can afford to waste pots of it on a month of fun. However, the frantic bidding by respectable democracies like Australia, the US, England and Spain does reveal something about the new politics of happiness now emerging in the rich world.

In recent years, social scientists have learnt a lot about happiness. Their best source in Europe is the Eurobarometer research programme, which is funded by the European Commission. Each year it asks about 1,000 citizens from each European country how happy they are. To quote the exact question: 'On the whole, are you very satisfied, fairly satisfied, not very satisfied, or not at all satisfied with the life you lead?'

The survey has been conducted for over 40 years. By now, some insights have accumulated. Perhaps the most interesting is that having money in itself doesn't make you happy. 'There is a paradox at the heart of our lives,' is how Richard Layard opens his book *Happiness: Lessons from a New Science*, one of a flood of recent works on the subject. 'Most people want more income and strive for it. Yet as Western societies have got richer, their people have become no happier.' Layard (who under Labour became the British government's 'happiness czar') says that in the US, Britain and Japan, people have got no happier in the last 50 years even as average incomes have more than doubled.

It seems that we humans adapt quickly to our environment. The things we once thought of as luxuries soon become necessities (although, by the same token, our sense of well-being would quickly adapt to losing half our income). What we care about is not our absolute wealth but our rung on the ladder. Ruut Veenhoven, a leading researcher of happiness, says: 'When we have overtaken the Joneses, our reference drifts upward to the Smiths, and we feel unhappy again.'

Only in countries where income per capita is below about £11,000 – countries such as Mexico, the Philippines or India – has increased wealth brought some happiness. Layard writes: 'The reason is clear – extra income is really valuable when it lifts people away from sheer physical poverty.' But that very rarely happens in Europe any more.

Some other truths emerge from the European data. Scandinavians are very happy; eastern Europeans are not. The Irish both north and south of the border are surprisingly happy. Age, sex and social status matter too. In western Europe at least, the average person's happiness tends to decline with age until he is 26 years old, and then starts to rise again. Women seem to be happier than men, which might help account for their much lower rates of suicide. The more educated people are, the happier they tend to be. Married people are generally happier than unmarried ones. What happens around you in society also matters: when unemployment or inflation rises, people tend to grow unhappier. Spending time with friends and family makes people happy.

And, we discovered, so does hosting football tournaments. Staging a World Cup won't make you rich, but it does tend to cheer you up.

The day before the World Cup final of 2006, one of the authors, Simon, visited the street where he used to live in Berlin. Fifteen years before, the Hohenfriedbergstrasse had been a dull-brown place with toilets on the stairwells where nobody ever spoke to anyone else. This time, he had to check the street sign to make sure it was the same place. Flags were flying from every house – German flags made in China, but also flags of many other nations – and everywhere there were children playing, even though they had supposedly gone extinct in Germany. The World Cup seemed to have made a usually gloomy nation happy.

This is typical. Georgios Kavetsos and Stefan Szymanski (with a lot of help from Robert McCulloch, guru of happiness research) took the European Commission's happiness data for 12 western European countries from 1974 to 2004, and checked whether it correlated at all with sports tournaments. The obvious first question was whether people became happier when their national team did well. It turned out that they didn't: there was no visible correlation. Then

Kavetsos and Stefan looked at hosting and happiness, and here they found a link. After a country hosts a football tournament, its inhabitants report increased happiness.

What Kavetsos and Stefan did was to replicate existing studies of happiness using all the measures researchers usually consider (income, age, marital status, etc), and then to see whether living in a host country made a difference as well. Their data on happiness covered eight separate hosts of tournaments: Italy and France for the World Cups of 1990 and 1998; and for the European Championships, Italy (1980), France (1984), West Germany (1988), England (1996) and Belgium and the Netherlands (2000). In all but one of these eight host countries, there was a significant up-tick in self-reported happiness just after the tournament. The only exception was the UK, where happiness fell slightly just after Euro 96, but then we all know that the UK is not England.

The London Olympics do seem to have boosted British happiness. The UK's Office for National Statistics registered a small rise in self-reported 'life satisfaction' from 2011–12 to 2012–13, despite the economic crisis. Of the 165,000 British adults polled, 77 per cent rated their life satisfaction at seven or more out of ten – up a touch from 75.9 per cent in 2011–12. The ONS commented that the Olympics and the Queen's Diamond Jubilee may have 'influenced people's assessment of their ... well-being'.

The mass of evidence is persuasive. However, given that so many other factors influence happiness, we wanted to test whether this effect could be measured even after allowing for the other factors. To do this, several large databases have to be welded together, and in the process the data from some years was lost. For instance, it turns out that the income of respondents was not surveyed in every single year. That left us with data for five hosts: Italia 90, and the Euros of 1984, 1988 and 2000, the last of which had two hosts. Admittedly this is a small sample, but in all five host countries, happiness rose after the tournament, even allowing for all the other effects that influence happiness. The inhabitants reported a higher level of happiness the year after the tournament than they had the year before; and they reported more happiness in the autumn surveys (i.e. after the tournament) than in the spring surveys (held before the tournament). Interestingly, this is just what Arthur Hopcraft observed when England hosted the World Cup in 1966. He wrote two years later:

> ... The competition released in our country a communal exuberance which I think astonished ourselves more than our visitors. It gave us a chance to spruce up a lot, to lighten the leaden character of the grounds where the matches were played, to throw off much of our inhibition of behaviour, particularly in the provinces, so that we became a gay, almost reckless people in our own streets, which is commonly only how we conduct ourselves when we put on our raffia hats in other countries' holiday resorts. Except in the celebrations that greeted the end of the Second World War, I have never seen England look as unashamedly delighted by life as it did during the World Cup.

We found much the same thing in the nations we studied. The jump in happiness was quite large. Citizens of wealthy countries like the Netherlands or France would need to make hundreds of euros more a month to experience a similar leap. One way to express this is that the average person gains twice as much happiness from hosting a football tournament as from having higher education. The effect can also be likened to an unexpected increase in income that takes someone from the bottom half of the income distribution to the middle of the top half. It's not quite winning the lottery, but very satisfying nonetheless. If you calculate this for an entire nation, then the leap in happiness from hosting can easily be worth a few billion euros.

In general in the host countries, older men gained the most extra happiness, presumably because many of them were sitting in front of their television sets with little else to do. Lesser-educated people gained more happiness than better-educated ones. Of all the subgroups we studied, only one (a significant one) did not get any happier: women.

The gain in happiness lasts at least a couple of months, given that the tournaments are played in midsummer and the survey is carried out in the autumn. For World Cups, the gain was quite persistent: even two and four years after the tournament, every subgroup we looked at was still happier than before the tournament. European Championships, though, lifted happiness only briefly. We found no impact on happiness in the host country a year after the Euros.

But if people gain a lot of happiness after hosting a tournament, they lose a little happiness before it. The ritual fuss over whether the stadiums will be ready, whether hooligans or terrorists will invade their country, whether their team will be made to look ridiculous, etc, appears to cause stress. Six years and four years before hosting a tournament, many of the subgroups we studied showed a decline in happiness.

It turns out that hosting doesn't make you rich, but it does make you happy. This begs a question. If countries want to host football tournaments (and American cities want to host major-league teams) as part of their pursuit of happiness, why don't they just say so? Why bother clothing their arguments in bogus economics?

The answer is that politicians have still barely discovered the language of happiness. They talk mostly about money. Anything that serves only to make people happy gets derided with the contemptuous phrase 'feel-good factor', as if politics should be above such trivialities. Only on the political fringes does happiness get any play, such as in the Liberal Party Report of 1974: 'Once the basic needs of food and shelter are met, the individual's greatest satisfactions are to be found in love, trust and friendship, in beauty, art and music, and in learning, none of which are served by the mythology of growth for its own sake.'

However, nobody listened to the Liberals. Most politicians have simply assumed that the real business of government is to make people richer. For one thing, measuring income is easier than measuring happiness. And so, when politicians argue for hosting tournaments, they typically use the language of money. It is almost the only vocabulary they have. John Kay, writing in the *Financial Times* in 2013 about the costs of the London Olympics, remarked: 'A curious puritanism requires politicians to pretend activities intended to make us feel good about ourselves are justified by their contribution to "the economy". The Olympiad was a good party, which cost the British population about £200 per head.'

But it is becoming clear that in rich countries, more money doesn't make people happier. Robert Kennedy was one of the first to see this, remarking in March 1968, three months before he was murdered, that gross domestic product 'measures everything ... except that which makes life worthwhile'.

For a few years before the economic crisis hit in 2008, European politicians did try talking less about money and more about happiness. Whereas Gordon Brown was an old-fashioned 'money' politician, David Cameron started out as more of a new-fangled 'happiness' one. In a speech in 2006, Cameron tried to introduce the acronym 'GWB' – 'general well-being' – to counter the decades-old 'GDP' for gross domestic product.

He said: 'Improving our society's sense of well-being is, I believe, the central political challenge of our times ... Politics in Britain has too often sounded as though it was just about economic growth.' Instead, Cameron wanted politics 'to recognise the value of relationships with family, friends and the world around us'.

It seems that football tournaments create those relationships: people gathered together in pubs and living-rooms, a whole country suddenly caring about the same event. A World Cup is the sort of common project that otherwise barely exists in modern societies. We've seen that the mere fact of following a team in the World Cup deters some very isolated people from committing suicide. If playing in a tournament creates social cohesion, hosting one creates even more. The inhabitants of the host country – and certainly the men – come to feel more connected to everyone else around them. Moreover, hosting probably boosts the nation's self-esteem, and so makes people feel better about themselves.

In the end, the best reason for hosting a World Cup is that it's fun. Brazil's President Dilma Rousseff ought to have been honest and said: 'It'll cost us money, we'll have less left over for schools and roads and poor people, but we all love football and it should be a fun month so it's worth it.' Then Brazilians could have had a clear-headed debate about the true pros and cons of hosting. It's reason-able enough to want to throw the world's biggest party. But you don't throw a party to make money. You do it because it makes you happy.

Hosting even makes politicians happy. Most of their work is frus-trating. You try to get money to build, say, roads, but other politicians stop you. Even when you get the money, it's hard to build the roads because people pop up to object. It's the same with housing or foreign policy or recycling: being a politician is an endless tedious struggle with your enemies.

But it isn't when you want to host a sports tournament. Suddenly, everyone gets on board. While London was bidding for the Olympics, the rower Steve Redgrave pulled an Olympic gold medal out of his pocket during a meeting at the House of Commons, and MPs of all parties began drooling over him. Even going to war doesn't create that sort of unanimous sentiment any more.

The end of ideology – the disappearance of nationalism, social-ism, religion, communism and Fascism from western Europe – has left many politicians with little better to do than to plug sports events using specious arguments. Ken Livingstone wrote when he was mayor of London: 'Crucially, the Olympics will also bring much-needed new facilities: an Olympic-size swimming pool in a city that has just two Olympic pools to Berlin's 19, and a warm-up track that would be turned over to community use.'

Plainly, arguments like these are just excuses. If you want to regenerate a poor neighbourhood, regenerate it. Build nice houses and a train line. If you want an Olympic pool and a warm-up track, build them. You could have built pools and tracks all across London and it would still have beeen cheaper than hosting the Olympics. The only good reason to host an Olympics is that it makes people happy. The politicians behind London's bid did not say so, because when the city was bidding in the early 2000s they hadn't yet discovered the politics of happiness. But they did sense that the voters would reward them for winning the Games.

The eight million Londoners, in particular, have the highest incomes in the European Union, and so would need to receive a fortune in tax rebates to buy the happiness that the Games seem to have brought them.

Puritans might rightly argue that even a rich country like Britain has better things on which to spend money. However, the likely gain in happiness from the Olympics does mean the politicians are canny to give the people bread and circuses. In post-materialist countries like Britain, the maths of hosting and happiness probably stack up.

But it's much less likely that Brazil will get its money's worth in happiness from hosting the World Cup. This is still very much a sub-$15,000 country, where putting more money in people's pockets would make them happier. And like South Africa, it's among the most economically unequal countries on earth. Both countries have a first-world sector of the economy with the money and skills to host a World Cup – but also a third-world sector that desperately needs the fruits of the money and skills. Millions of Brazilians are still stuck in life-diminishing poverty. Some of them have been pushed out of their slums to make way for the World Cup. Like South Africans, they should ask how many homes with running water could have been built for the cost of their new stadiums.

We already know that the World Cup won't make Brazilians richer. It's also probably not the most efficient way to make them happier.

SECTION III

THE COUNTRIES:
Rich and Poor, Tom Thumb, Spain, Ghiddink,
Saddam, and The Champions of the Future

WHY ENGLAND LOSE

BEATEN BY A DISHWASHER

Here is what we wrote in the first edition of this book, which appeared ten months before the World Cup of 2010 kicked off:

When the England team fly to South Africa for the World Cup, an ancient ritual will start to unfold. Perfected over England's 14 previous failures to win the competition away from home, it follows this pattern:

Phase One, pre-tournament: Certainty that England will win the World Cup.

Alf Ramsey, the only English manager to win the trophy, forecast the victory of 1966. However, his prescience becomes less impressive when you realise that almost every England manager thinks he will win the trophy, including Ramsey in the two campaigns he didn't. When his team were knocked out in 1970 he was stunned, and said: 'We must now look ahead to the next World Cup in Munich, where our chances of winning I would say are very good indeed.' England didn't qualify for that one.

Glenn Hoddle, England's manager in 1998, revealed only after his team had been knocked out 'my innermost thought, which was that England would win the World Cup'. Another manager who went home early, Ron Greenwood, said: 'I honestly thought we could have won the World Cup in 1982.' A month before the World Cup of 2006, Sven-Göran Eriksson said: 'I think we will win it.'

The deluded manager is never alone. As England's inside forward Johnny Haynes remarked after elimination in 1958: 'Everyone in England thinks we have a God-given right to win the World Cup.' This belief in the face of all evidence was a hangover from empire: England is football's mother country and should therefore be the best today. The sociologist Stephen Wagg notes: 'In reality, England is a country like many others and the England football team is a football team like many others.' This truth is only slowly sinking in.

Phase Two: During the tournament England meet a former wartime enemy.

In five of their last seven World Cups, they were knocked out by either Germany or Argentina. The matches fit seamlessly into the British tabloid view of history, except for the outcome. As Alan Ball summed up the mood in England's dressing-room after the defeat to West Germany in 1970: 'It was disbelief.'

Even Joe Gaetjens, who scored the winning goal for the US against England in 1950, turns out to have been of German-Haitian origin, not Belgian-Haitian as is always said. And in any case, the US is another former wartime enemy.

Phase Three: The English conclude that the game turned on one freakish piece of bad luck that could happen only to them.

Gaetjens, the accounting student and dishwasher in a Manhattan restaurant who didn't even have an American passport, scored his goal by accident. 'Gaetjens went for the ball, but at the last moment, decided to duck,' England's captain Billy Wright wrote later. 'The ball bounced on the top of his head and slipped past the bewildered Williams.'

In 1970 England's goalkeeper Gordon Banks got a stomach upset before the quarter-final against West Germany. He was OK on the morning of the game, and was picked to play, but a little later was discovered on the toilet with everything 'coming out both ends'. His understudy Peter Bonetti let in three soft German goals.

There was more bad luck in 1973, when England failed to qualify for the next year's World Cup because Poland's 'clown' of a goalkeeper, Jan Tomaszewski, unaccountably had a brilliant night at Wembley. 'The simple truth is that on a normal day we would have beaten Poland 6–0,' England's midfielder Martin Peters says in Niall Edworthy's book on England managers, *The Second Most Important Job in the Country*. Poland went on to reach the semi-finals of the 1974 World Cup.

In 1990 and 1998 England lost in what everyone knows is the lottery of the penalty shootout. In 2002 everyone knew that the obscure, bucktoothed Brazilian kid Ronaldinho must have mishit the free-kick that sailed into England's net, because he couldn't have been good enough to place it deliberately. In 2006 Wayne Rooney would never have been sent off for stamping on Ricardo Carvalho's genitals if Cristiano Ronaldo hadn't tattled on him. These things just don't happen to other countries.

Phase Four: Moreover, everyone else cheated.

The Brazilian crowd in 1950 and the Mexican crowd in 1970 deliberately wasted time while England were losing by keeping the ball in the stands. The CIA (some say) drugged Banks. Diego Maradona's 'hand of God' did for England in 1986. Diego Simeone apparently play-acted in 1998 to get David Beckham sent off, and Cristiano Ronaldo apparently did the same for Rooney in 2006.

Every referee opposes England. Those of his decisions that support this thesis are analysed darkly. Typically the referee's nationality is mentioned to blacken him further. Billy Wright, England's captain in 1950, later recalled 'Mr Dattilo of Italy, who seemed determined to let nothing so negligible as the laws of the game come between America and victory'. The referee who didn't give England a penalty against West Germany in 1970 was, inevitably, an Argentine.

The Tunisian referee of 1986 who, like most people watching the game, failed to spot the 'hand of God', has become legendary.

Phase Five: England are knocked out without getting anywhere near lifting the cup.

The only exception was 1990, when they reached the semi-final. Otherwise they have always gone out when still needing to defeat at least three excellent teams. Since 1970, Bulgaria, Sweden and Poland have got as close to winning a World Cup as England have.

Perhaps England should be relieved that they don't come second. As Jerry Seinfeld once said, who wants to be the greatest loser? The science writer Stefan Klein points out that winning bronze at the Olympics is not so bad, because that is a great achievement by any standards, but winning silver is awful, as you will always be tortured by the thought of what might have been.

England have never been at much risk of that. They won only five of their 18 matches at World Cups abroad from 1950 to 1970, and didn't qualify for the next two tournaments in 1974 and 1978, so at least they have been improving since. The general belief in decline from a golden age is mistaken.

Phase Six: The day after elimination, normal life resumes.

The one exception is 1970, when England's elimination may have caused Labour's surprise defeat in the general election four days later. But otherwise the elimination does not bring on a nationwide hangover. To the contrary, England's eliminations are celebrated, turned into national myths, or songs, or Pizza Hut adverts.

Phase Seven: A scapegoat is found.

The scapegoat is never an outfield player who has 'battled' all match. Even if he directly caused the elimination by missing a penalty, he is a 'hero'.

Beckham was scapegoated for the defeat against Argentina in 1998 only because he got himself sent off after 46 minutes. The writer Dave Hill explained that the press was simply pulling out its 'two traditional responses to England's sporting failure: heralding a glorious defeat and mercilessly punishing those responsible for it, in this case Posh Spice's unfortunate fiancé.'

Beckham wrote in one of his autobiographies that the abuse continued for years: 'Every time I think it has disappeared, I know I will meet some idiot who will have a go at me. Sometimes it is at matches, sometimes just driving down the road.' He added that he kept 'a little book in which I've written down the names of those people who upset me the most. I don't want to name them because I want it to be a surprise when I get them back.' One day they will all get tummy bugs.

Often the scapegoat is a management figure: Wright as captain in 1950, Joe Mears as chief selector in 1958, and many managers since. Sometimes it is a keeper, who by virtue of his position just stood around in goal rather than battling like a hero. Bonetti spent the rest of his career enduring chants of 'You lost the World Cup'. After retiring from football, he went into quasi-exile as a postman on the Scottish Isle of Mull.

In 2006 Cristiano Ronaldo was anointed scapegoat. Only after a defeat to Brazil is no scapegoat sought, because defeats to Brazil are considered acceptable.

Phase Eight: England enter the next World Cup thinking they will win it.

We are not usually this prescient. If we predicted England's experience in South Africa precisely, it's only because over the decades the route map of England's eliminations had become perfectly clear.

In phase one of our sequence, England flew to South Africa expecting to win the World Cup. That wasn't particularly ludicrous: Fabio Capello's team had qualified with more dash than ever before, winning nine out of ten qualifying games.

Phase two was, 'During the Tournament England Meet a Former Wartime Enemy'. Following the 4–1 thumping by the Germans in Bloemfontein, England have now been eliminated by Germany or Argentina in six of their last eight World Cups.

We called phase three, 'The English Conclude That the Game Turned on One Freakish Piece of Bad Luck That Could Happen Only to Them'. This was of course Frank Lampard's shot that bounced inside the German goal without the referee noticing. As Lampard himself had lamented after England's previous elimination, in 2006: 'It seems to be the English way to lose in bizarre circumstances but it wears you down. It gets to the point where you want to tell Lady Luck to f*** off and take her bad sister with her.'

Phase four is, 'Moreover, Everyone Else Cheated'. FIFA should have been using goal-line technology, and the German keeper should have 'fessed up that Lampard had scored.

In phase five, 'England Are Knocked Out Without Getting Anywhere Near Lifting the Cup'. Had they somehow beaten Germany, instead of losing by three goals, they would have then needed to beat Argentina, Spain and Holland.

In phase six, normal life resumed the day after elimination. The British riots broke out in the summer of 2011, not the summer of 2010.

In phase seven, Capello was chosen as the nation's scapegoat. The Italian had raised English hopes by making his players look like world-beaters for two years, before finally pulling off the mask in South Africa to reveal them as the usual losers. Moreover, as a foreigner he made a perfect scapegoat.

The World Cup as ritual has a meaning beyond football. The elimination is usually the most watched British television programme of the year. It therefore educates the English in two contradictory narratives about their country: one, that England has a manifest destiny to triumph, and two, that it never does. The genius of the song 'Three Lions', English football's unofficial anthem, is that it combines both narratives: 'Thirty years of hurt/Never stopped me dreaming.'

There is an alternative universe in which Beckham didn't get sent off, Banks's tummy held up, Lampard's goal counted and so on. In that universe England have won about seven World Cups. Many English people think they would have preferred that. But it would have deprived the nation of a ritual that marks the passing of time much like Christmas or New Year, and that celebrates a certain idea of England: a land of unlucky heroes who no longer rule the world, although they should.

Yet with that failure in 2010, something changed. To adapt T.S. Eliot, humankind can only take so much reality. England's umpteenth disappointment seems to have finally convinced the nation's fans and media to shed the fantasy of manifest destiny. When the understated Roy Hodgson replaced Capello as manager in 2012, he seemed intent on reducing expectations from low to zero. 'It's difficult to say what would constitute "success" at Euro 2012,' he mused at his first press conference. 'I'd like people to cut us a bit of slack.' People did. When his team lost the quarter-final on penalties to a former wartime enemy, Italy, nobody was very surprised.

Finally, the English have become realistic. Perhaps helped by a general decline in national status, they are beginning to realise they are just another country, without any manifest destiny to triumph.

A PERFECTLY DECENT TEAM

Any mathematician would say it's absurd to expect England to win the World Cup. England win just over two-thirds of their matches. To be precise, from 1990 to 2010 (counting from the end of the 1990 World Cup to the end of the 2010 World Cup) England played 224, won 122, drew 57 and lost 45. If we treat a draw as half a win, this translates into a winning percentage of 67.2 per cent. If we then break this down into five four-year World Cup cycles, England's winning percentage has ranged between 65 and 76, except for the 1998–2002 cycle, when it slumped to 60 per cent.

In other words, their performance for most of recent history has been very constant.

Yes, these statistics conceal some ghastly mishaps as well as some highs, but the statistics tell us that the difference between anguish and euphoria is a few percentage points.

On the face of it, winning two-thirds of the time – meaning bookies' odds of 1–2 on – is not too shabby in a two-horse race. Of course, some countries do even better. Brazil's winning percentage is nearly 75 per cent. But against most teams, England is the deserved favourite. In the 1990–2010 period, England's win percentage was eighth best in the world.

The problem comes when we try to translate this achievement into winning tournaments. England's failure to win anything since the holy year of 1966 is a cause of much embarrassment in bars on the Costa del Sol. But next time you are mocked by German or Italian fans, try explaining to them the rules of multiplicative probability.

It is tricky to calculate the exact probability of England qualifying for a tournament, because it requires an analysis of many permutations of events. However, we can reduce it to a simple problem of multiplicative probability if we adopt the 'must win' concept. For example, England failed to qualify for Euro 2008 by coming third in their group behind Croatia and Russia. In doing so they won seven matches, lost three and drew two (for an average winning percentage of exactly 66.66 per cent). They were pipped by Russia, who won seven, lost two and drew three (a winning percentage of 70.83 per cent).

Suppose that to guarantee qualification you have to win eight games outright. Then the problem becomes one where you have to win eight from 12, where your winning probability in each game is 66 per cent. Calculating this probability is a bit more complicated, since it involves combinatorics.

The answer is a probability of qualification of 63 per cent. That means that England should qualify for fewer than two thirds of the tournaments they enter. In fact, from 1970 to 2014 England qualified just over 70 per cent of the time: for eight out of eleven World Cups and seven out of ten European Championships. Given that the number of qualifying matches has risen over time, England's performance is in line with what you might have expected.

The sad fact is that England are a good team that does better than most. This means they are not likely to win many tournaments, and they don't. When we first published this book, we called the British edition *Why England Lose*. Going into the 2010 World Cup, English people often asked us: 'Aren't you worried about your title? What if England win?' We weren't very worried. Later, we changed the title anyway, because it turned out (amazingly) that few English people wanted to buy a book called *Why England Lose*.

Until 2010, the English tended to think that England should do better. The team's usual status around the bottom of the world's top 10 was not good enough. The national media, in particular, felt almost perpetually let down by the team. England were 'known as perennial underachievers on the world stage', according to the *Sun;* their history 'has been a landscape sculpted from valleys of under-achievement', said the *Independent*; while Terry Butcher grumbled in the *Sunday Mirror* in 2006 that 'historical underachievement has somehow conspired to make England feel even more important.'

'Why do England lose?' is perhaps the greatest question in English sport. In trying to answer it, we hear strange echoes from the field of development economics. The central question in that field is, 'Why are some countries less productive than others?' The two main reasons why England lose would sound familiar to any devel-opment economist. So would the most common reason *falsely* cited for why England lose. Here are those three reasons for England's eliminations – first the false one, then the correct ones.

BRITISH JOBS FOR BRITISH WORKERS?
WHY THERE ARE TOO MANY ENGLISHMEN
IN THE PREMIER LEAGUE

When pundits gather to explain why England lose, their favourite scapegoat of the last few years is imports: the hundreds of foreigners who play in the Premier League. Here is Steven Gerrard speaking before England lost to Croatia and failed to qualify for Euro 2008: 'I think there is a risk of too many foreign players coming over, which would affect our national team eventually if it's not already. It is important we keep producing players.'

After all, if our boys can barely even get a game in their own league, how can they hope to mature into internationals? After England lost to Croatia, Sepp Blatter, Alex Ferguson, and UEFA's president Michel Platini all made versions of Gerrard's argument. In 2013 Greg Dyke, the new chairman of the FA, warned: 'In the future it's quite possible we won't have enough players qualified to play for England who are playing regularly at the highest level in this country or elsewhere in the world. As a result, it could well mean England's teams are unable to compete seriously on the world stage.'

These men are effectively blaming imports for the English lack of skills. The reasoning is that our own workers don't get a chance because they are being displaced by foreign workers. Exactly the same argument is often made in development economics. Why are some countries not very productive? Partly because their inhabitants don't have enough skills. The best place to learn skills – such as making toothpaste, or teaching maths, or playing football – is on the job. To learn how to make toothpaste you have to actually make it, not just go on courses to learn how to make it. But if you are always importing toothpaste, you will never learn.

That is why, for over half a century, many development economists have called for 'import substitution'. Ban or tax certain imports so that the country can learn to make the stuff itself. Import substitution has worked for a few countries. Japan after the war, for instance, managed to teach itself from scratch how to make all sorts of high-quality cars and electrical gadgets.

The idea of 'import substitution' in the Premier League has an emotional appeal to many English fans. Britons often complain about feeling overrun by immigrants, and few spots in the country are more foreign than a Premier League pitch on match day. Some clubs have wisely dispensed with Englishmen almost altogether. All told, Englishmen accounted for only 37 per cent of the minutes played by footballers in the Premier League in the 2007–08 season before Croatia's night at Wembley. By the 2012–13 season, only 32 per cent of starters in the Premier League were English. To some degree, *English* football no longer exists.

'It is my philosophy to protect the identity of the clubs and country,' said Platini. 'Manchester United against Liverpool should be with players from Manchester and Liverpool, from that region. Robbie Fowler was from Liverpool. He grew up in that city, it was nice, but now you don't have the English players.'

Imagine for a moment that Platini somehow managed to suspend EU law, and force English football clubs to discriminate against players from other EU countries. If that happened, Platini and Gerrard would probably end up disappointed. If inferior English players were handed places in Premier League teams, they would have little incentive to improve. This is a classic problem with import substitution: it protects bad producers. What then tends to happen is that short-term protection becomes long-term protection.

In fact, however, Platini's entire premise is wrong. If people in football understood numbers better, they would grasp that the problem of the England team is not that there are too few Englishmen playing in the Premier League. To the contrary: there are too *many*. England would do better if the country's best clubs fielded even fewer English players.

You could argue that English players accounted for 'only' 32 per cent of starting players in the Premier League. Or you could argue that they account for a massive 32 per cent of starting players, more than any other nationality in what is now the world's toughest league. The Dutch, Portuguese and Uruguayans dream of accounting for 32 per cent of starters in the Premier League, or indeed in any big league. The English have about 65 to 70 players starting regularly in the world's toughest league. That should be enough to make up a decent squad of 22.

In other words, English players get lots of regular experience of top-level club football. Even if we lump together the continent's three best leagues – the Premier League, Spain's Primera Liga and the Bundesliga – then only Germans and Spaniards play more tough club football.

The experience of playing against the best foreign players every week has probably helped English internationals to improve. Englishmen have had to get better just to stay in their club teams. They now learn about international football every week. Indeed, since the Premier League has become more international, England's performances have improved. The switch from a mostly British league to a mostly foreign one can be dated to 1995, the year of the 'Bosman ruling' that allowed European players to play anywhere in Europe. Let's compare England's performances in the era of a British league, from 1968 to 1992, with their performances since 1998. (We have consciously excluded the World Cup of 1966, which was an anomalous event given that England were playing at home.) In that first 'British' period up to 1992, England reached one World Cup semi-final, in 1990. However, that was an exception. In those years, England reached the quarter-finals of major tournaments only four times in 13 attempts. By contrast, in the 'international' period since 1998, they have reached four quarter-finals in just eight attempts. Moreover, their win percentage at major tournaments jumped from 52 per cent in 1968–1992 to 62 per cent in the 'international' period (counting a draw as worth half a win.) The figures suggest that if anything, the international league has been good for the England team.

In fact, you could argue that in recent years, as the Premier League has got ever stronger, England's players have been playing *too much* rather than too little top-class international club football.

The Premier League is becoming football's NBA, the first global league in this sport's history. So the players earn millions of pounds. So the league is all-consuming, particularly if you play for one of the big clubs, as almost all regular England internationals do. The players have to give almost all their energy and concentration every match. Life is a little more relaxed even in the Bundesliga or Primera Liga, where smaller teams like Mainz or Osasuna cannot afford to buy brilliant foreigners.

Clearly an athlete can't peak in every match. If you are running in the Olympics, you plan your season so that you will peak only at the Olympics, and not before. If you play football for (say) Croatia, and for a club in a smaller league (even in Serie A), you can husband your energy so as to peak in big international matches – for instance, when you are playing England at Wembley.

By contrast, English players have to peak every week for their clubs. In no other country do footballers play as many demanding games a season. Clubs in no other country play as many European games as the English do. Daniele Tognaccini, longtime chief athletics coach at AC Milan's 'Milan Lab', explains what happens when a player has to play 50 tough games a year: 'The performance is not optimal. The risk of injury is very high. We can say the risk of injury during one game, after one week's training, is 10 per cent. If you play after two days, the risk rises by 30 or 40 per cent. If you are playing four or five games consecutively without the right recovery, the risk of injury is incredible. The probability of having one lesser performance is very high.'

So when English footballers play internationals, they start tired, hurting, and without enough focus. Often they cannot raise their game. Harry Redknapp said when he was Portsmouth manager: 'I think England games get in the way of club football for the players now. Club football is so important, the Champions League and everything with it, that England games become a distraction to them.' Moreover, players in the intense Premier League are always getting injured, and their clubs don't give them time to recover. That may be why half of England's regulars couldn't play against Croatia, or why Wayne Rooney has played two successive World Cups while half-fit.

In short, if England wanted to do better in internationals, it should export English players to more relaxed leagues, like for example Croatia's. Indeed, if more young English players spent some learning years abroad, they would probably absorb more international knowledge.

Eriksson understood the problem of English exhaustion. When one of the authors of this book asked him why England lost in the quarter-finals in the World Cup 2002 and Euro 2004, he said his players were tired after tough seasons. Was that really the only reason? 'I would say so,' Eriksson replied. 'If you're not fit enough ... in Japan, we never scored one goal in the second half.'

Ashley Cole, reflecting on the World Cup of 2006, notices the same phenomenon but cannot explain it: 'We had to be honest ... and recognise something was amiss in the second halves. We just didn't know what.' However, some of his smarter teammates did seem to know. Here is Lampard looking back on 2006:

> Throughout the tournament we had suffered in the heat. Our second-half performances were invariably below the standard of the first period and at its worst – against Paraguay in Frankfurt – most of us could barely walk, never mind run, in the latter stages of the match.

This echoes Gerrard's account of the previous tournament: 'The truth was that England were knackered at Euro 2004 ... A long, hard season took a terrible toll.' In 2010 in South Africa, too, England never scored in the second half. Capello later told the FIFA website why he thought England didn't win summer tournaments: 'They're the least fresh of any of the competing national sides, because their league doesn't have a break. It's like when you're driving a car: if you stop halfway to put fuel in then you'll definitely get where you want to go, but if you don't there's always the chance you'll be running on empty before you reach your goal. In my opinion the football played in the first half of the English season is much better than in the second half.'

It is possible to dismiss all these claims of tiredness as self-serving. But if there has to be a single culprit for England's summer failures, we suspect it's more likely to be fatigue than the foreign influx.

In any case, English fans *want* to see teams full of foreign players. Platini wonders whether Liverpudlians can identify with a Liverpool team full of foreigners. Well, they seem to manage. Judging by the Premiership's record crowds despite its record ticket prices, fans still identify enough. England can have an excellent league, or it can have an English league, but it can't have both. Given the choice, fans seem to prefer excellence. In that sense, they are typical consumers. If you try to substitute imports, then, at least at first, consumers have to put up with worse products. They generally don't like that.

THE PROBLEM OF EXCLUSION: HOW ENGLISH FOOTBALL DRIVES OUT THE MIDDLE CLASSES

The Romans built their empire with an army drawn from every part of society. Only when the militia became an elite profession open just to particular families did the empire start to decline. When you limit your talent pool, you limit the development of skills. The bigger the group of people you draw from, the more new ideas are likely to bubble up. That's why large networks like the City of London or Silicon Valley, which draw talent from around the world, are so creative. So is the Premier League.

The problem of English football is what happens *before* our best players reach the Premier League. The Englishmen who make it to the top are drawn very largely from one single and shrinking social group: the traditional working-class. The country's middle classes are mostly barred from professional football. That holds back the national team.

There are many ways to classify which social class someone was born into, but one good indicator is the profession of that person's father. Joe Boyle, with some help from Dan Kuper, researched for us the jobs of the fathers of England players who played at the World Cups of 1998, 2002 and 2006. Boyle ignored jobs the fathers might have been handed after their sons' rise to stardom. As much as possible, he tried to establish what the father did while the son was growing up. Using players' auto-biographies and newspaper profiles, he came up with the list below. It doesn't include every player (asked what Wayne Bridge's dad did for a living, we throw up our hands in despair), but most are here. Another caveat: some of the dads on the list were absent while their boys were growing up. That said, here are their professions:

Player	Father's job
Tony Adams	Roofer
Darren Anderton	Ran removals company; later taxi driver
David Batty	Dustbin man
David Beckham	Heating engineer
Sol Campbell	Railway worker
Jamie Carragher	Pub landlord
Ashley Cole	None given, but in his autobiography he describes 'a grounded working-class upbringing in East London'
Joe Cole	Fruit and vegetable trader
Peter Crouch	Creative director at international advertising agency
Stewart Downing	Painter and decorator on oil rigs
Kieron Dyer	Manager of Caribbean social club
Rio Ferdinand	Tailor
Robbie Fowler	Labourer; later worked night-shift at railway maintenance depot
Steven Gerrard	Labourer (bricklaying, tarmacking, etc.)
Emile Heskey	Security worker at nightclub

Paul Ince	Railwayman
David James	Artist who runs gallery in Jamaica
Jermaine Jenas	Soccer coach in US
Frank Lampard	Footballer
Rob Lee	'Involved in a shipping company'
Graeme Le Saux	Ran fruit and vegetable stall
Steve McManaman	Printer
Paul Merson	Coalman
Danny Mills	Coach in Norwich City's youth academy
Michael Owen	Footballer
Wayne Rooney	Labourer, mainly on building sites; often unemployed
Paul Scholes	Gas-pipe fitter
David Seaman	Garage mechanic, later ran sandwich shop, then worked at steelworks
Alan Shearer	Sheet-metal worker
Teddy Sheringham	Policeman
Gareth Southgate	Worked for IBM
John Terry	Forklift-truck operator
Darius Vassell	Factory worker
Theo Walcott	RAF administrator; later joined services company working for British Gas

Many of these job descriptions are imprecise. What exactly did Rob Lee's dad do at the shipping company, for instance? Still, it's possible to break down the list of 34 players into a few categories:

Eighteen players, or more than half the total, were sons of skilled or unskilled manual labourers: Vassell, Terry, Shearer, Seaman, Scholes, Rooney, Merson, McManaman, Ince, Heskey, Gerrard, Fowler, Adams, Batty, Beckham, Campbell, Ferdinand and Downing. Ashley Cole with his 'working-class upbringing' is probably best assigned to this category, too.

Four players (Jenas, Lampard, Mills and Owen) had fathers who worked in football. Le Saux and Joe Cole were both sons of fruit and vegetable traders. Anderton's dad ran a removals business, which seems to have failed, before becoming a cab driver. Sheringham's father was a policeman. Carragher's and Dyer's dads ran a pub and a social club respectively.

That leaves only five players out of 34 – Crouch, James, Lee, Southgate and Walcott – whose fathers seem to have worked in professions that required more than a basic formal education. If we define class by education, then only 15 per cent of England players of recent years had 'middle-class' origins.

The male population as a whole was much better educated. Of British men aged between 35 and 54 in 1996 – the generation of most of these footballers' fathers – a little over half had qualifications beyond O-level, according to the British Household Panel Study.

English football's reliance on an overwhelmingly working-class talent pool was only moderately damaging in the past, when most English people were working class. In the late 1980s, 70 per cent of Britons still left school aged 16, often for manual jobs. But by then, the growth of the middle classes had already begun. In fact, middle-class values began to permeate the country, a process that sociologists call 'embourgeoisement'. It happened on what used to be the football terraces, which because of high ticket prices are now slightly more middle-class than even the country at large.

Nowadays over 70 per cent of Britons stay in school after 16, and over 40 per cent enter higher education. More and more, this is a middle-class nation. Yet because football still recruits overwhelmingly from the traditional working classes, it excludes an ever-growing swathe of the population. That must be a brake on the England team.

The shrinking of the talent pool is only part of the problem. Until at least the late 1990s British football was suffused, without quite knowing it, by British working-class habits. Some of these were damaging, such as the sausages-and-chips diet, or the idea that binge-drinking is a hobby. 'Maybe in earlier generations the drinking culture carried over from the working-class origins of the players,' wrote Alex Ferguson in his 1999 autobiography. 'Most of them came from families where many of the men took the view that if they put in a hard shift in a factory or a coalmine they were entitled to relax with a few pints. Some footballers seem determined to cling to that shift-worker's mentality ... Also prevalent is the notion that Saturday night is the end of the working week and therefore a good time to get wrecked.'

Of course 'problem drinking' exists in the middle classes too, and of course most working-class people have no issues with drink. However, Ferguson is explicitly describing a traditional working-class attitude.

Furthermore, the working classes tended to regard football as something you learnt on the job, rather than from educationalists with diplomas. It was the attitude you would expect of an industry in which few people had much formal education. The late Ernie Walker, longtime secretary of the Scottish FA, who worked for decades to introduce coaching courses in Scotland, told us that clubs mocked his attempts as 'some new-fangled thing got up by college boys – as if there was shame in being educated'. He recalls that 'coaching' and 'tactics' became 'shame words'. 'People would say, "The trouble with football today is that there is too much coaching." That's like saying, "The trouble with school is that there's too much education."'

It would be crazy to generalise too much about the working classes. There is a strong working-class tradition of self-education. Large numbers of post-war Britons became the first people in their families to go to university. Nonetheless, the anti-intellectual attitudes that the football administrator encountered do seem to be widespread in the English game.

These attitudes may help explain why English managers and English players are not known for thinking about football. When the Dutchman Johan Cruijff said, 'Football is a game you play with your head,' he wasn't talking about headers.

Over the past 15 years these traditional working-class attitudes have begun to fade in British football. Foreign managers and players have arrived, importing the revolutionary notions that professional athletes should think about their game and look after their bodies. Andy Carroll's drinking now marks him out as an exception in the higher reaches of the English game. But one working-class custom still bars middle-class Britons from professional football: what you might call the 'anti-education requirement'.

Most British footballers still leave school at 16. The belief persists that only thus can they concentrate fully on the game. The argument that many great foreign footballers – Ruud Gullit, Dennis Bergkamp, Tostão, Sócrates, Osvaldo Ardiles, Jorge Valdano, Fernando Redondo, Kaká, Josep Guardiola, Andrés Iniesta, etc – stayed in school after 16, or even attended university, is ignored. This is probably because British coaches and players tend to be suspicious of educated people.

It is true that the clubs' new academies are meant to help players keep studying, but in practice this barely happens. A few years ago one of us visited the academy of an English club. It's an academy of some note: two of its recent graduates won their first international caps while still teenagers. But all the boys we met there, bright or otherwise, were sent to do the same single GNVQ in Leisure and Tourism to fulfil the academy's minimum education requirement. Together the boys caused such havoc in class that all the other students had dropped out of the course. It's not that footballers are too busy to study, as they rarely train more than a couple of hours a day; rather, being studious is frowned upon.

Football consequently remains unwelcoming to middle-class teenagers. To cite just one example, Stuart Ford, who at 17 played for England Schools, gave up on becoming a professional because he got tired of listening to rants from uneducated coaches. Being middle-class, he always felt an outsider. He recalls: 'I was often goaded about my posh school or my gross misunderstanding of street fashion. That was just from the management.' Instead he became a Hollywood lawyer. Later, as a senior executive at one of the Hollywood studios, he was one of the people behind an unsuccessful bid to buy Liverpool FC.

Or there was the one-time youth trainee at Oldham Athletic, whose teammates hounded him as an intellectual snob after he walked into the club one day carrying a copy of the *Daily Mail*. He recalls: 'Aside from the club-wide piss-taking, I had Deep Heat rubbed into the lining of my slips. I took so much verbal (and physical) abuse that month that I often wonder what would have happened had it been the *Financial Times*.' This man, incidentally, studied for that same GNVQ in leisure and tourism with several future Premier League players.

Some of the more educated foreign players in the Premier League must view these goings-on with dismay. As they have no assigned place in the British class system, they have a touch more freedom to be intellectual. However, Erik Thorstvedt, Tottenham's Norwegian goalkeeper from 1989 until 1996, does recall bread rolls being chucked at his head when he opened a broadsheet newspaper on the team bus.

If the working classes get little education, that is mainly the fault of the middle-class people who oversee the British schools system. Nonetheless, the educational divide means that any middle-class person entering British football feels instantly out of place.

Many middle-class athletes drift to cricket or rugby instead. Often, this represents a direct loss to football. In most people, sporting talent is fairly transferable until they reach their late teens. Many English footballers, like Phil Neville and Gary Lineker, were gifted cricketers too. Some well-known rugby players took up rugby only as teenagers, when they realised they weren't going to make it as footballers. And in the past, several paragons represented England in more than one sport. Only a few sports demand very specific qualities that can't be transferred: it's hard to go from being a jockey to being a basketball player, for instance. But football competes with other ball games for talent, and it scared away the educated middle classes.

This is particularly sad because there is growing evidence that sporting talent and academic talent are linked. The best athletes have fast mental reactions, and those reactions, if properly trained, would make for high-calibre intellects.

Interestingly, some people inside English football have become aware of the game's class discrimination. Daniel Hargreaves, who works for Everton's academy with the remit to make sure its decisions are evidence-based (the sort of job that didn't exist in English football a few years ago), has spotted the club's tendency to scout mainly in working-class neighbourhoods. 'Traditionally we have core areas where we think we find players,' he says. 'But there's a growing middle class, there are more green spaces in the middle-class areas.' Has Everton operated an unintentional bias against the middle classes? 'I think evidence would suggest that's the case.'

But for now, this class bias helps explain why even though the academies of English clubs are the richest in the world, England doesn't produce better players than poor nations. Instead of trying to exclude foreigners from English football, it would be smarter to include more middle-class English people. Only when there are England players with educated accents – as happens in Holland, Argentina, and even Brazil (Kaká, for instance) – might the national team maximise its potential.

CLOSED TO INNOVATIONS:
ENGLISH FOOTBALL'S SMALL NETWORK

When the internet arrived, many pundits predicted the decline of the city. After all, why live in a flat in Hackney when you could set up your laptop in an old farmhouse overlooking a sheep meadow?

The prediction turned out to be wrong. Cities have continued their growth of the last 200 years, which is why Hackney flats became so expensive. Meanwhile the countryside has turned into something of a desert, inhabited by a few farmers and old people, and used by the rest of us mostly for long walks. It turns out that people still want to live in dirty, overcrowded, overpriced cities. And the reason they do is the social networks. To be rural is to be isolated. Networks give you contacts.

Someone you meet at a party or at your kids' playground can give you a job or an idea. Just as the brain works by building new connections between huge bundles of neurons, with each connection producing a new thought, so we as individuals need to find ourselves in the centre of the bundle in order to make more connections.

Networks are key to the latest thinking about economic development. Better networks are one reason why some countries are richer than others. As it happens, networks also help explain why some countries have done better at football than England. English football's biggest problem until very recently was probably geography. The country was too far from the networks of continental western Europe, where the best football was played.

Once upon a time, England was at the centre of football's knowledge network. From the first official football international in 1872, until at least the First World War, and perhaps even until England's first home defeat against Hungary in 1953, you could argue that England was the dominant football nation. It was the country that exported football know-how to the world in the form of managers. The English expat manager became such a legendary figure that to this day in Spain and Italy a head coach is known as a *'mister'*.

Many English people clung to the belief in England's footballing centrality long after it had ceased to be true. The astonishment each time England didn't win the World Cup ended only with the team's abject failures in the 1970s.

This gradual shift away from British dominance in football echoes the decline in Britain's economic status. The country went from supreme economic power under Victoria to having its hand held by the International Monetary Fund in the late 1970s. Admittedly, in football as in economics, most observers exaggerated Britain's decline. The country's position in the top 10 largest economies was never much in doubt, but in football it became clear by 1970 at the latest that dominance had shifted across the Channel to core western Europe. For the next 30 years, this part of the continent was the most fertile network in football. And Britain was just outside it.

The German World Cup of 2006 demonstrated western Europe's grip on global football. The region has only about 400 million inhabitants, or 6 per cent of the world's population, yet only once all tournament did a western European team lose to a team from another region: Switzerland's insanely dull defeat on penalties by Ukraine.

That summer even Brazil couldn't match western Europe. Argentina continued their run of failing to beat a western European team in open play at a World Cup since the final against West Germany in 1986 (though they did win two of the eight subsequent encounters with Europeans on penalties). Big countries outside the region like Mexico, Japan, the US and Poland could not match little western European countries like Portugal, Holland or Sweden. If you understood the geographical rule of the last World Cup, you could sit in the stands for almost every match before the quarter-finals confident of knowing the outcome.

As we'll discuss in our final chapter, by 2010 the dominance of western Europe was waning slightly. In South Africa, western European countries lost six of their 29 games against teams from other regions. In part, this must have been because the tournament was held outside western Europe. In part, it was because other regions have begun to copy western European methods. Yet even in 2010, first, second and third place all went to western Europeans.

Western Europe excels at football for the same fundamental reason why it had the Scientific Revolution and was for centuries the world's richest region. The region's secret is what the historian Norman Davies calls its 'user-friendly climate'. Western Europe is mild and rainy. Because of that, the land is fertile, allowing hundreds of millions of people to inhabit a small area of land. Moreover, as Malise Ruthven, the scholar of Islam, has pointed out, Europe has 'a higher ratio of coast to landmass than any other continent or subcontinent, and a coastline some 23,000 miles long – equivalent to the circumference of the globe'. No wonder Europeans were the first people to sail the world. Geography has always helped them exchange ideas, inside their continent and beyond. In short, they are networked.

From the World Cup in Germany, you could have flown in two-and-a-half hours to any one of about 20 countries containing about 300 million people in total. That is the densest network on earth. There was nothing like that in Japan at the previous World Cup: the only foreign capital you can reach from Tokyo within that time is Seoul. South Africa, the host in 2010, is even more isolated. And the only foreign capital within two hours' flight of Brazil's biggest city, São Paulo, is Asunción in Paraguay.

For centuries now, the interconnected peoples of western Europe have exchanged ideas fast. The 'Scientific Revolution' of the sixteenth and seventeenth centuries could happen in western Europe because its scientists were near each other, networking, holding a dialogue in their shared language: Latin. Copernicus, Polish son of a German merchant, wrote that the earth circled the Sun. Galileo in Florence read Copernicus and confirmed his findings through a telescope. The Englishman Francis Bacon described their 'scientific method': deductions based on data. England at the time was very much part of the European network.

A typical product of that network was the lens grinder, a crucial new machine in the development of the microscope in the early 1660s. Robert Hooke in London invented a new grinder, which made lenses so accurate that Hooke could publish a detailed engraving of a louse attached to a human hair. But meanwhile Sir Robert Moray, a Scot in London who knew what Hooke was up to, was sending letters in French about the new grinder to the Dutch scientist Christiaan Huygens. Thanks to Moray, Huygens had previously got hold of details of Hooke's balance-spring watch.

Moray and Huygens 'sometimes wrote to each other several times a week', writes the historian Lisa Jardine. Their letters crossed the Channel in days, or about as quickly as mail does now. Meanwhile, in Paris the French astronomer Adrien Auzout was getting copies of some of their letters. So Hooke's breakthroughs were being spread to his European competitors almost instantly.

All this irritated Hooke. But the proximity of many thinkers in western Europe created an intellectual ferment. That is why so many of the great scientific discoveries were made there. These discoveries then helped make the region rich.

Centuries later, football spread the same way. In the nineteenth century the game infected western Europe first, because there it had the shortest distances to travel. Later, the proximity of so many peoples brought the region two world wars. After 1945, western Europeans decided they could live crammed together only under a sort of single government: the European Union. Borders opened, and the region became the most integrated in the history of the world.

Again the best ideas spread fastest here, just as they had in the Scientific Revolution. The region's football benefited. One of the men who carried tactical ideas around Europe was Arrigo Sacchi. His father was a shoe manufacturer in Ravenna, Italy, and the young Sacchi used to accompany him on business trips. He saw lots of games in Germany, Switzerland, France and the Netherlands. 'It opened my mind,' he later said. As manager of AC Milan in the 1980s, he imported a version of Dutch football that revolutionised the Italian game. Or take Arsène Wenger, who while growing up in a village in the French Alsace, near the German border, used to watch the legendary German football programme *Die Sportschau* on Saturday afternoons. He became a fan of the great Borussia Mönchengladbach team, and was generally influenced by German football. Later Wenger took a French coaching course, and came to admire Dutch 'total football'. The point is that he was absorbing influences from all the countries around him. It was easy because they were so close.

Ideas spread even more quickly in European football than in other economic sectors, because football is the most integrated part of the continent's economy. Only about 2 per cent of all western Europeans live in a different European Union country from the one in which they were born, because few companies bother hiring bus drivers or office administrators from neighbouring countries. In some professions, language barriers stop workers moving abroad.

But many footballers do find work abroad, largely because TV advertises their wares to employers across Europe. And so most of the EU's best players have gathered in the English, Spanish and German leagues, and meet each other on weekday nights in the Champions League. This competition is the European single market come to life, a dense network of talent. There's always much debate about the superiority of one football model over another – the Bundesliga versus the Premier League versus the Spanish league and Italy's Serie A – but the real point is the intensity of competition inside Europe, on the field and in the boardroom. That forces the big clubs constantly to strive for improvements.

The teams in the Champions League can draw talent from anywhere in the world. Nonetheless, an overwhelming majority of their players are western Europeans. With the world's best footballers and coaches packed together, the world's best football is constantly being refined here.

The best football today is Champions League football, western European football. It's a rapid passing game played by athletes. Rarely does anyone dribble, or keep the ball for a second; you pass instantly. It's not the beautiful game – dribbles are prettier – but it works best. All good teams everywhere in the world now play this way. Chris Anderson and David Sally showed in their book *The Numbers Game* how statistically alike the top European leagues are. Whether in the English Premier League, Serie A, the Bundesliga or Spain's premier division, the average team completed similar numbers of passes per game, of similar lengths, and had comparable numbers of shots and corners. In all four leagues, the average game produces somewhere between 2.5 and three goals. The differences between these nations 'are cosmetic, shallow', the authors conclude. 'If it was not for the shirts, you would not be able to tell them apart.' All four leagues are producing western European football.

Even the Brazilians adopted the Champions League style in the 1990s. They still have more skill than us, but they now try (and often fail) to play at our pace. Brazil has been losing dominance in football even as it got richer because it is excluded from the knowledge networks of western Europe. It has struggled to work out that slow dribbling rarely beats fast passing.

Western Europe has discovered the secret of football. More precisely, a core group of western European countries has: namely five of the six nations that in 1957 founded the European Economic Community, ancestor of the European Union. (We'll leave out the sixth founding nation, the pathetic minnows Luxembourg.) West Germany, France, Italy, Holland and even Belgium don't all play in exactly the same style. Holland and Italy, say, are rather different. But they all adhere to the basic tenets of rapid collectivised western European football. Here are some results from the period 1968–2006:

- ⚽ The five core countries won 12 European Championships and World Cups between them.
- ⚽ The countries at the corners of Europe – the Brits, former Soviet bloc, Balkans, and Scandinavian nations north of the Baltic Sea – between them won one: Greece's European Championship of 2004 was delivered by a German coach.
- ⚽ Europe's only other trophies in this period went to Denmark and Czechoslovakia. Denmark enjoys an utterly permeable border with the five core countries. Czechoslovakia was the only eastern European country to win anything in this period.

Countries separated from the core EU – either by great distance, or by poverty, or by closed borders under dictatorships – often underperform in football.

In the vast land mass running from Portugal in the southwest to Germany in the northeast, and including Croatia and Bosnia just east of Italy, every country of more than 2 million inhabitants qualified for the World Cup 2014. The nations that didn't make it were on Europe's margins: the Scots, Irish and Welsh, all the Scandinavians, the Turks and most of Europe's eastern edge. The countries at great distance – and it can be a distance of the mind, rather than geographical distance – are often out of touch with core European football. Many countries on the margins have traditionally had dysfunctional indigenous styles of football. The Greeks, for instance, dribbled too much. The Brits played mindless kick-and-rush.

Again, this is explained by theories of networks. If you are on the periphery, as the British were until recently in football, it's harder to make new connections, because you have to travel further. Worse, those not on the periphery see you only as a second-best connection. You are the end of the line, not the gateway to a new set of connections. That's why foreign countries stopped hiring English coaches or even English players. As a result, the people on the periphery become more and more isolated and insular. The Ukrainian manager Valeri Lobanovski was a genius, but during the days of the Soviet Union he was so isolated that when a Dutch journalist came to interview him in the mid-1980s, Lobanovski pumped him for information about Dutch footballers. Spain, to some degree, had the same problem under Franco. 'Europe ends at the Pyrenees,' was the saying in those days.

Gradually isolation becomes your mindset: after a while you don't even *want* to adopt foreign ideas anymore. Anyone who has spent time in England – particularly before 1992 – has witnessed this attitude. Isolation can lead you into your own blind alleys that nobody else appreciates. For instance, the long refusal of English players to dive may have been an admirable cultural norm, but they might have won more games if they had learnt from continental Europeans how to buy the odd penalty.

Happily, the era of British isolationism has now finished. The era began on Sunday, 3 September 1939, when the country's borders closed at the outbreak of the Second World War. In football, that isolation deepened when English clubs were banned from European competitions after the Heysel disaster of 1985. They lost what modest network they had.

Between 1990 and 1994, however, British isolation began to break down: English clubs were readmitted to European competitions, new laws enforced free movement of labour and capital within the EU, and Eurostar trains and budget airlines connected Britain to the continent. London turned into a global city. Nowadays southern England, at least, belongs to core Europe, just as it did during the Scientific Revolution.

The end of isolationism meant the end of English football managers managing England or the best English clubs. You wouldn't appoint a Frenchman to manage your baseball team, because the French don't have a history of thinking hard about baseball. And you wouldn't appoint an Englishman to manage your football team, because the English don't have a history of thinking hard about football. After Graham Taylor in his time as England manager unintentionally discredited kick-and-rush, the English embraced EEC football. The FA hired a manager drawn from Italian football, Sven-Göran Eriksson.

At this, the *Daily Mail* lamented, 'The mother country of football, birthplace of the greatest game, has finally gone from the cradle to the shame.' It was a wonderful statement of 'English exceptionalism': the belief that England is an exceptional football country that should rule the world playing the English way. However, the obvious statistical truth is that England is not exceptional. It is typical of the second-tier football countries outside core western Europe.

The numbers strongly suggest that England needed foreign knowledge. From 1990 to 2011 England had two foreign managers and seven English managers, including two caretakers

(Wilkinson and Peter Taylor). On every measure the foreigners won hands down:

	Games won	Win percentage (draw = half a win)	Qualifications for tournaments
Foreign managers	62%	73%	5/5
English managers	49%	64%	4/6

Eriksson should be remembered as the great qualifier: for the first time since the 1960s, he ensured that England consistently made it to the major tournaments. But foreign managers have also performed slightly better at the final tournaments themselves: Eriksson and Capello's England teams never lost at the group stages, and reached three quarter-finals and one round of 16. By contrast, the English managed one semi-final (at home at Euro 96), one appearance in the last 16, and two exits in the first round.

Quite clearly, foreign managers have outperformed with England. This is not merely because Eriksson and Capello had a 'golden generation' of players to work with. Many of the same men who played well for the foreigners performed abysmally for Steve McClaren and Kevin Keegan. It's painful to imagine how well England might have achieved if the FA had stopped discriminating against foreigners decades earlier. In the same way, British cycling and cricket have recently become world-class by stealing foreign ideas. In tennis, Andy Murray in 2013 became the first male Briton to win Wimbledon since 1936, largely because as a teenager he had taken himself off to an academy in Barcelona. (If only some English footballers had made the same move.)

When it comes to England's football coaches, it may sound odd that a foreign passport can make such a difference. After all, you might think that England's players these days have enough foreign experience of their own. They play with and for and against foreigners at their clubs every week. Michael Owen, the first England international to play his entire professional career after the Bosman ruling, told us that he had grown up a 'European' rather than a purely English footballer. Surely players like him no longer need foreign managers?

Why they do was best demonstrated that miserable night against Croatia. A team of Englishmen led by an Englishman played like caricatures of Englishmen. Gerrard in particular was a remarkable sight, charging around in the rain at top pace, hitting impossibly ambitious passes, constantly losing the ball. He played like a headless chicken, or like an English footballer *circa* 1988.

For Liverpool, Gerrard usually plays like a European sophisticate. He has mastered the international, globalised style of top-class modern football. The problem against Croatia was that there wasn't a foreigner on the field or the bench to check him. When things began going badly, he shed that cosmopolitan skin, returned to childhood, and played like an Englishman of old. He and all the other England players had grown up until about the age of 20 playing an only slightly diluted version of English football. Because of that upbringing, national football cultures continue to exist. That's why England still need a foreign manager to correct their flaws.

Other peripheral countries from Greece to Japan soon followed the English example. Importing know-how from the core EEC turned out to be an excellent remedy for the problem of isolation, which makes it even odder that in 2006 England did an about-face and appointed Steve McClaren, who had never even worked abroad. The FA didn't realise that England, as a recovering isolationist, still needed foreign help. Rooney, for one, seems to have known better. Here he is in his autobiography, damning the newly appointed McClaren with faint praise: 'But he's a good coach, always smiling. I'm glad he's got the job. I think he was the best Englishman available.'

By hiring Capello to succeed McClaren in 2007, the FA was accepting the need for continental European know-how. The Italian was like one of the overpaid consultants so common in development economics, flying in on business class to tell the natives what to do.

His job was to teach the English some of the virtues of western European football. To cite just one of those virtues:

A GAME LASTS 90 MINUTES

Habitually, English footballers charge out of the gate, run around like lunatics, and exhaust themselves well before the match is over, even if they aren't hung-over.

You see this in England's peculiar scoring record in big tournaments. In every World Cup ever played, most goals were scored in the second halves of matches. That is natural: in the second half players tire, teams start chasing goals, and gaps open up on the field. But England, in their last seven big tournaments since 1998, scored 27 of their 43 goals in the first halves of matches. Their record in crucial games is even starker: in the matches in which they got eliminated from these tournaments, they scored eight of their nine goals before half-time. In other words, England perform like a cheap battery. This is partly because they play in such an exhausting league, but also because they don't seem to have thought about pacing themselves.

Italians know exactly how to measure out the 90 minutes. They take quiet periods, when they sit back and make sure nothing happens, because they know that the best chance of scoring is in the closing minutes, when exhausted opponents will leave holes. That's when you need to be sharpest. In the World Cup of 2006, typically, Italy knocked out Australia and Germany with goals in the final three minutes.

England has already bought Italian know-how. In Hodgson, it deliberately chose a coach who had spent most of his career abroad. Now all it needs to do is include its own middle classes, and stop worrying about foreigners in the Premier League, and it will finally stop underachieving and perform as well as it should do. Hang on a moment: who says England underachieve?

SHOULD DO BETTER: ARE ENGLAND WORSE THAN THEY OUGHT TO BE?

That England underachieve is usually taken for granted in the British media. After all, the team haven't won anything since 1966, and sometimes don't even qualify for tournaments. Clearly that is not good enough for 'the mother country of football, birthplace of the greatest game'.

But are England really underachievers? Or is it just that the English expect too much of them? To answer this, we first need to work out how well England should do *given their resources*.

Before we are accused of looking for excuses, let's consider what is and isn't possible. A five-year-old can't win the 100-metre finals at the Olympics, and neither can a 70-year-old. You aren't going to have a career in the NBA if you are only five foot tall, and you'll never cox Oxford in the Boat Race if you are six foot eight. It is very unlikely that you will have a career in show-jumping if your parents earn less £20,000 per year, you probably won't win a boxing match if you've never had any training as a boxer, and you won't have a shot at being world chess champion unless you can persuade a team of grand-masters to act as your seconds. Genetics are still just about beyond our control; training depends partly on our own effort, but partly on the resources that other people give us.

What is true for the individual is also true for the nation. During his tenure an England football manager cannot easily (a) increase the size of the population from which he will have to draw the talent, (b) increase the national income so as to ensure a significant increase in the financial resources devoted to developing football, or (c) increase the accumulated experience of the national team by very much. (England played nearly 800 games from their first game in 1872 until 2000, and currently play around a dozen games per year, so each extra game doesn't add much to the history.)

Yet in any international match, these three factors – the size of the nation's population, the size of the national income and the country's experience in international football – hugely affect the outcome. It's unfair to expect Belarus, say, to perform as well as much larger, more experienced and richer Germany. It is fairer to assess how well each country *should* perform given its experience, income and population, and then to measure that expected performance against reality. Countries like Belarus or Luxembourg will never win a World Cup. The only measure of performance that makes any sense for them is one based on how effectively they use their limited resources. The same exercise makes sense for England too, if only as a check on tabloid hysteria: do England really under-perform given what they have to work with?

In absolute terms England are about 10th in the world. But we want to know how well they do in relative terms – not relative to the expectations of the media, but relative to English resources. Might it be that England in fact *overachieve* given the country's experience, population and income?

To work this out, we need to know the football results for all the national teams in the world. Luckily, we have them. There are a number of databases around of international matches, but one of the best is maintained by Russell Gerrard, a mathematics professor at Cass Business School in the City of London. By day Russell worries about mathematical ways to represent the management problems of pension funds. For example, his most recent paper is snappily entitled 'Mean-Variance Optimization Problems for the Accumulation Phase in a Defined Benefit Plan'. It concerns, among other things, Lévy diffusion financial markets, the Hamilton–Jacobi–Bellman equation and the Feynman–Kac representation. As you might expect, Russell has been meticulous in accumulating the football data, which took him seven years of his life. His database runs from 1872 to 2001, and includes 22,130 games. We have now updated it to cover all international games up to 2012.

RUSSELL GERRARD: BRILLIANT FOOTBALL DATABASE

Later in the book, we will crunch Russell's data to discover which is the best football country on earth, and which punches most above its weight. But here, let's limit ourselves to a sneak preview of where England stand.

The distant past is of limited relevance. Let's therefore concentrate on recent history, the five World Cup cycles from 1990 to 2010. This was by no means a golden age for England. The country didn't even qualify for the European Championship of 2008 or the World Cup in 1994, and its best moment in these two decades was the lost semi-final at Euro 96. As we've already seen, England played 224 matches in these 20 years. It won 54 per cent of them and drew 25 per cent, for a 'win percentage' of 67 per cent (remember that for these purposes we treat a draw as half a win). That is near the middle of their historical range.

We want to see how much of a team's success, match by match, can be explained by population, wealth and experience. However, 'win percentage' is not the best measure of success, because any two wins are not the same. We all know that a 1–5 away win against a certain someone is not the same as a tame 1–0. To put it another way, if England play Luxembourg and win only 1–0, it's more likely that the Luxembourgeois press will be in ecstasy than the *Sun*.

Instead, we chose goal difference as our measure, since for any match we expect that the greater the difference between the two teams' population, wealth and experience, the greater will be the disparity in scores. (Of course, a positive goal difference tends to be closely correlated with winning.)

We then analysed Russell's database of matches using the technique of multiple regression. A reminder: multiple regression is the mathematical formula for finding the closest statistical fit between one thing (in this case success of the national team) and any other collection of things (here experience, population and income per head). For each international match you simply input the population, income per head and team experience of the two nations at that date, and in seconds you get a read-out telling you how sensitive (on average) the team's performance is to each factor. We will also take account of home advantage for each match.

Collecting the data is usually the toughest part. We have assembled figures for the population, football experience and income per capita of 163 countries. We will unveil our findings about the other 162 countries later in the book. Here, we will just focus on England and their supposed underperformance.

We ran our regression, and immediately made several discoveries about international football. First, home advantage alone is worth a lead of about two-thirds of a goal. Obviously that is a nonsense if applied to single game, but think of it this way: playing at home is like having a goal's head start in two out of every three games.

Second, having twice as much international experience as your rival is worth just over half a goal a game. In fact, experience turns out to matter much more than the size of your population, which is why the Dutch, Swedes and Croats do better at international football than very large but inexperienced China or India. The finding suggests that experienced Scotland should win rather more than they have been recently.

Having twice your opponent's population is worth only about one 10th of a goal. Having twice the GDP per head is worth about as little. In other words, although being large and rich helps a country win football matches, being experienced helps a lot more.

It should be added that our estimates are statistically very reliable. Not only is there not much doubt that these factors matter, but there is little doubt about the size of the effects. It is these effects that make the first rounds of World Cups fairly predictable.

However, much still remains unexplained. Experience, population and income per head combined explain only just over a quarter of the variation in goal difference. That is good news: if we could predict outcomes perfectly by just these three factors there would not be much point in watching World Cups at all. Nonetheless, the fact that these three factors explain so much tells us that, up to a point, football is rational and predictable.

For now, we are only interested in England. Are its resources so outstanding that it should do better than merely ranking around 10th in the world?

First, let's look at experience. England is one of the most experienced countries in football. It played 889 internationals between 1872 and the end of the 2010 World Cup. According to our data, only Sweden played more (923). However, England's much-vaunted history is not worth much against the other leading football nations, because most of them have now accumulated similar amounts of experience. Brazil, Argentina and even Hungary had all played more than 800 internationals by 2010. When it comes to our second variable, national income, England scores high, too. It is usually one of the richest of the serious football countries. Where it falls short is in size. What often seems to go unnoticed is that England's population of 53 million puts it at a disadvantage to the countries it likes to measure itself against in football. Not only is Germany much bigger, with over 80 million inhabitants, but France has 66 million and Italy 60 million. Among the leading European nations, England is ahead only of Spain (47 million). So in football terms, England is an experienced, rich, but medium-sized competitor.

Then we ran the numbers. We calculated that England, given the country's population, income and experience, 'should' score on average 0.19 goals per game more than their opponents.

To get a feel for how this works, consider England's performance at the World Cup of 1998. England played Tunisia, Romania, Colombia and Argentina, all on neutral ground, so there was no 'home ground' effect. Facing Tunisia in their opening game, England had a population five times larger, a GDP per head four times larger and two times more international experience than their opponents. That combination gave an expected goal difference of one goal in England's favour. In the event, England won 2–0 and so did better than expected.

Against Romania, England had the advantage of twice the population, five times the income per head and a bit more experience (other countries have been playing football for longer than we sometimes like to think). All this gave England an expected advantage of about half a goal. England's 2–1 defeat meant that they underperformed by 1½ goals.

Next, England played Colombia, with a slight advantage in population, four times the income per head and double the experience. The package was worth an advantage of almost an entire goal (you start to see how the Tom Thumb World Cup might be organised) but again England overperformed, winning 2–0.

Then came Argentina: that goal, that sending-off, that disallowed header and that penalty shootout. (If you are under 16, well done for reading for this book, and now go ask your parents what we're talking about.) Should England have done better? Well, they had a slight advantage in population over Argentina, double the income per head, but about equal experience – going into that day, England had played 750 international matches and Argentina 740. Putting all that together, England's total advantage was minute. A fair score would have been a draw, which is exactly what happened after 120 minutes. Pity about the penalties.

Our model allows us to re-examine every game ever played. The glorious uncertainty of football means that there are many deviations from expectations. However, if we average the difference between expectations and results for each country, we get a picture of whether any national team systematically overperforms or underperforms relative to its resources.

Our finding: England in the 1990–2010 period outscored their opponents by 0.87 goals per game. That was 0.68 more than we had predicted, based on the country's resources. In short, England weren't underperforming at all. Contrary to popular opinion, they were overperforming by two-thirds of a goal per game. It might be argued that England weren't winning the all-important games (perhaps because of tiredness in the final stages of major tournaments), but the fact is that losses are rare events. And as we'll show, England's overperformance has been getting even better in recent years.

As an example of this overachievement, let's take England's games against Poland. England played them 10 times between 1990 and 2010, winning seven and drawing three, with a goal difference of plus 12. Over the period England's population was about 25 per cent larger than Poland's, its income per head about two and a half times greater, and its international experience about 20 per cent more. These should have contributed to a positive goal difference of about one half, one, and one half, respectively, or a total of plus two over the 10 games. So England's goal difference of plus 12 was 10 goals better than you might have expected. That is not too shabby.

Later in the book we will reveal our global table for relative performance from 1990 to 2010: a ranking of the teams that did best relative to their countries' experience, income and populations. For now, we'll just say that England came in 17th out of 163 countries. This in itself is a leap forward in recent years. When we did the same calculation in earlier editions of this book, covering performances from 1980 to 2001, England came in only 67th out of 189 countries. It has risen in the last decade from a group of moderate overachievers, including countries such as Russia, Morocco, Ivory Coast and Mozambique, to a level of overachievement comparable to the likes of Honduras, Croatia, South Korea and Italy. Like England, all these teams scored about 0.6 to 0.8 goals per game more than they 'should' have, given their populations, income and experience.

However, England doesn't benchmark itself against Honduras or Morocco. It's more interesting to see whether England overperforms 'more' than the teams it sees as its rivals: the best countries in the world. Here's a ranking of the game's giants, plus England, based on how many goals per game each scored above expectations in the 1990–2010 period:

OUTPERFORMANCE (IN GOALS PER GAME)

1	Brazil	1.486	6	Netherlands	0.906
2	Spain	1.196	7	Portugal	0.863
3	Germany	0.978	8	France	0.797
4	Czech Republic	0.954	9	England	0.681
5	Argentina	0.949	10	Italy	0.605

It turns out that England's overachievement – though large compared with almost all other countries on earth – isn't very good when you class them beside the giants of the game. Still, England overachieved more than Italy, even though the Italians won a World Cup in this period and England didn't.

Our conclusion: England do just fine. They perform even better than expected, given what they have to start with. All they need to bring home some trophies is better timing – they must win fewer friendlies and more World Cup semis – and a few million more inhabitants. Consider the England–Germany semi-final at Euro 96. Both countries had similar levels of experience, and by 1996 Germany's lead over Britain in income per capita had slipped to only about 10 per cent. However, according to our analysis, England's home advantage (worth about three-quarters of a goal in this match) was partly wiped out by Germany's much larger population. That made the expected goal difference only about 0.50 in favour of the English home team, not far short of the draw that materialised in open play. In the end Gareth Southgate missed his penalty in the shootout and England lost.

Overall in the 1990–2010 period, England played Germany nine times. England won three and lost six (once on penalties). Their goal difference over the nine games was minus one. Given Germany's slight lead in GDP per head in these years, but particularly given

England's shortage of people, that is almost exactly the goal difference we would have predicted. The '30 years of hurt' shouldn't be a mystery.

If Britain keeps letting in immigrants, and if the German population drops by millions as predicted, and if English football finally enfranchises the middle classes, then that same match at Euro 2032 might have a different outcome; though given everything we know about life, possibly not.

England simply should not expect to be world-beaters. As so often, Jamie Carragher in his autobiography gets it right:

> The psychology of our international game is wrong. England ought to be embracing the idea of being the underdog on the world stage ... We should be revelling in the image of the plucky outsider trying to unbalance the superpowers of Argentina and Brazil, while matching the French, Germans and Italians.

Still, it is true that over its history, England could have got luckier. A better penalty here, a stronger goalkeeper's stomach there, Darren Anderton's shot rolling home in extra time against Germany at Euro 96 instead of hitting the post, and it could all have been different.

What we see here is partly the enormous role of luck in history. We tend to think with hindsight that a team that did well in a particular tournament was somehow always going to do well, and a team that lost was doomed to do so. The winner's victory comes to seem inevitable. This is a common flaw in the writing of any kind of history.

But in fact, inevitable victories hardly ever happen in football tournaments. Perhaps the only recent case was Brazil at the World Cup of 2002. Just how dominant they were dawned on a leading European club manager a few months after the final. This manager was trying to sign Brazil's goalkeeper, Marcos. The player visited the club and did some physical tests, in which he didn't perform particularly well. Never mind, thought the manager, the guy won the World Cup. So he offered Marcos a contract.

At two o'clock that morning, the manager was awoken at home by a phone call. It was Marcos's agent.

The agent said, 'I'm sorry but Marcos won't sign for you.'

The sleepy manager said, 'All right, but why not?'

Then the agent confessed. A couple of years before the World Cup, Marcos had broken his wrist. It had never healed properly. But his old club manager, Luiz Felipe Scolari, became manager of Brazil and put Marcos in the team. Suddenly Marcos was going to a World Cup.

Every day at the tournament, the agent explained, Marcos was in pain. He could barely even train. In matches he could barely catch a ball. Every day Marcos told himself, 'I really must tell Scolari about my wrist.' But he could never quite bring himself to. So he went on, day by day, until he found that he had won the World Cup. Brazil were so superior that they won the World Cup with a crocked goalkeeper.

However, such dominance is very rare. Normally the differences between teams in the final stages of a World Cup are tiny. The difference between an England team being considered legendary or a failure is two to three games, each generally decided by a single goal, in two years.

After all, the difference between making a World Cup and spending the summer on the beach can be just a point. Sometimes it's a point that you lost by hitting the post. Sometimes it's a point garnered by a rival in a match you didn't even play in.

Once you're at the World Cup, the difference between going home ignominiously in the first round and making the semi-finals is often a matter of a few inches here or there on a couple of shots. The greatest prize in the sport hinges on a very few moments. Jonathan Wilson puts it well in his *Anatomy of England*: 'One moment can shape a game, and one game can shape a tournament, and one tournament can shape a career. Football is not always fair.' Wilson points out, 'One of the major problems of international football: that there is so little of it, huge conclusions are drawn from individual games.' As Wenger has noted, European championships are over in three weeks, and any team in a league can be top of the table after three weeks.

In those short tournaments, England have probably been unluckier than most. Over lunch in London in October 2013, the FA's chairman Greg Dyke, who has spent a lot of time asking people in the game why England lose, told us: 'There's another argument. The guy who owns Brentford [the club Dyke supports] is Matthew Benham, right? He's very rich. He's made all his money gambling on football. He employs top-quality graduates, maths graduates. All they do is study football around the world. He does everything on statistics. Everything is on probabilities. He says, the single biggest factor why England haven't done well is because they've been unlucky.'

Luck is particularly important in World Cups, we interjected.

'And also,' said Dyke, 'the number of times you're knocked out on penalties.'

Of the 10 tournaments in which England played from 1990 to 2012, they exited six on penalties.

Dyke continued: 'He [Benham] says you can alter the chances of winning or losing on penalties, but not by a lot. So if the luck had gone the other way, his argument is that we'd have won one or two of those and we wouldn't be sitting here having this conversation.'

Yet there we were, having this conversation.

There is a similar issue with luck in major-league baseball, notes Michael Lewis in *Moneyball*: 'The season ends in a giant crapshoot. The play-offs frustrate rational management because, unlike the long regular season, they suffer from the sample size problem.'

Lewis means that because there are so few games in the play-offs – because the 'sample size' is so small – random factors play an outsize role in determining the winner. It's the same in football World Cups, and even more so in European Championships. Football fans celebrate the 'miracle' of Denmark winning Euro 92, but given that there were only eight teams in the tournament, it wasn't a miracle at all.

Most fans understand that luck matters, even if they construct a post-fact story about the tournament that makes either the false breasts or the turnips seem fated from the start. But our data point to an even scarier truth than the existence of fluke: namely, that there is barely any difference between 'brilliant' and 'terrible' England teams. It looks suspiciously as if England for almost all their history – at least before Capello arrived – have been more or less equally good.

This may sound hard to credit. Fans feel strongly about the qualities of managers and players. There have been periods of national optimism, and national pessimism, associated with the view that the England team is either strong or disgraceful.

But in fact, watching England play has resembled watching a coin tossing competition. If we focus on outright victories, then England on average win just over 50 per cent of their games; the rest they either draw or lose. So just as a coin has half a chance of landing heads, and half tails, England in the average game have about half a chance of winning and half of not winning. We assigned a '1' for each win and '0' for a loss or a draw, and examined the sequence of England's 400 games from 1972 to 2007.

Before we discuss this sequence, let's look at coin-tossing. If you tossed a coin 400 times, you would expect on average to get 200 heads and 200 tails. However, there is no reason to think that the outcomes would alternate (heads, tails, heads, tails ...). Sometimes you will get sequences of a few heads, sometimes a few tails. Crucially, though, there would be no relationship at all between the current coin toss and the last one. If you toss a fair coin there is always a 50/50 chance of heads, whatever sequence has occurred up to this point. There is no statistical correlation between current coin tosses and past coin tosses, even if the average of any sequence is always around 50 per cent.

Here is our finding: England's win sequence over the 400 games is indistinguishable from a random series of coin tosses. There was no predictive value in the outcome of England's last game, or indeed in any combination of England's recent games. Whatever happened in the last match appeared to have no bearing on what will happen tonight. The only thing you could predict is that over the medium to long term, England would win about half their games outright. We have seen that the outcome of matches can be largely predicted by a country's population, income and experience. However, this only explains the *average* outcome. In other words, if England were smaller, poorer or less experienced, it would have a lower percentage of wins, but the sequence of these wins would still be unpredictable.

To make sure that our finding was right, we constructed a few random sequences of ones and zeros to see if they looked like England results. Often we found more apparent correlation in our random sequences than in England's results.

Contrary to all popular opinion, it may be that the strength of the England team has barely ever changed (which would make the entire apparatus of punditry attached to the team instantly redundant).

The chart opposite shows the win percentage of the England team from 1950 to 2013 (again counting draws as worth half a win). Apart from a few moments in the 1950s it has not risen above 70 per cent, and it has never fallen below 67.5 per cent. The overall picture is one of steady but extremely slow decline, punctuated by two eras of exceptional performance. One of those eras was the late 1960s, when England were world champions. The other period of clear improvement began in the early 2000s and continues today.

On the whole, though, very little has changed over 60 years. A star player might fade or retire, but in a country of 53 million people, there is always someone coming up who is near enough his level as to make almost no difference. Over the long term, the three key factors that determine a country's performance are very stable. The British economy may have boomed in the 1990s, and is now dropping down the global wealth rankings, but measured over the last

England win percentage 1950–2013

century Britain has always been one of wealthiest nations in the world. Equally, its share of the football population changes only glacially. And while the England team gains experience, so do its main rivals. The only key factor that changes is home advantage. Given that playing at home is worth a lead of two-thirds of a goal per game in global football, it's little wonder that England won the World Cup in 1966. The rest of the time, England generally feature in the global top ten, regularly beat weak countries, and fall two or three hurdles before the finish of major tournaments. That is a fair reflection of the nation's demographic and economic muscle (even if most people see someone richer and more powerful when they look in the mirror).

In short, England's performances in good or bad times have been much the same. It's just that fans and media have sought to see patterns where none exist. Nick Taleb, the financial investor who wrote *The Black Swan: The Impact of the Highly Improbable*, famously explained that we are constantly fooled by randomness. In neuroscientific terms, our rational brains are egged on by our emotional brains to find patterns even when there aren't any. In the end, the best explanation for the short-term ups and downs of the England team has been randomness.

THE CAPELLO EFFECT

At least, that was true before Capello's reign. There is some reason to believe that Capello changed something during his four years in charge. Contrary to popular belief, and despite the national joy when he resigned in February 2012, it does appear that England under him were better than they had ever been before. This is exactly what you would have expected, if he imported the latest continental know-how.

As we've seen, Capello was the nominated scapegoat for the World Cup of 2010. But it is unfair to judge him on just four matches, played at a time when England were suffering their ritual end-of-season fatigue. (Capello's star, Rooney, had been squeezed like a lemon by Manchester United that spring.) Taking Capello's English years as a whole, from 2008 through February 2012, his results stand out:

ENGLAND'S GREATEST-EVER MANAGER

Manager	P	W	D	L	%Won	Win%*	F	A	G diff	G game
Capello	42	28	8	6	0.667	0.762	89	28	1.452	2.119
Ramsey	112	67	28	17	0.598	0.723	212	97	1.027	1.893
Greenwood	55	33	12	10	0.600	0.709	93	40	0.964	1.691
Eriksson	67	40	15	12	0.597	0.709	128	61	1.000	1.910
pre-war	225	136	38	51	0.604	0.689	641	293	1.547	2.849
Venables	24	12	9	3	0.500	0.688	35	14	0.875	1.458
Hoddle	28	17	4	7	0.607	0.679	42	13	1.036	1.500
Winterbottom	138	77	33	28	0.558	0.678	369	192	1.283	2.674
Robson	95	47	29	19	0.495	0.647	154	60	0.989	1.621

Taylor, G	38	18	13	7	0.474	0.645	62	32	0.789	1.632
Mercer	7	3	3	1	0.429	0.643	9	7	0.286	1.286
Revie	29	14	8	7	0.483	0.621	49	25	0.828	1.690
McClaren	18	9	4	5	0.500	0.611	32	12	1.111	1.778
Keegan	18	7	7	4	0.389	0.583	26	15	0.611	1.444
Wilkinson	2	0	1	1	0.000	0.250	0	2	-1.000	0.000
Pearce	1	0	0	1	0.000	0.000	2	3	-1.000	2.000
Taylor, P	1	0	0	1	0.000	0.000	0	1	-1.000	0.000
Grand Total	922	521	220	181	0.565	0.684	1993	913	1.171	2.162

*Including draws as half a win

Most obviously, Capello's winning percentage of 76 (counting draws as half a win) is higher than anyone else's (and 15 per centage points above his immediate predecessor, McClaren). As we've noted earlier, in no other four-year period from 1978 to 2007 did England's winning percentage rise above 68 per cent. Capello also won a higher proportion of games outright than any of his predecessors. True, he had the good luck of coaching in the aftermath of the breakups of the Soviet Union and Yugoslavia. There are now far more weak little countries in European football, the likes of Slovenia and Kazakhstan, whom England generally beat. But the previous five regular England managers enjoyed the same advantage, and none of them has stats to match Capello's.

What's also noticeable is how freely his teams scored. They beat their opponents by an average of 1.45 goals a game, nearly half a goal better than the typical modern England manager. Scoring was easier for pre-war England sides and for Walter Winterbottom's teams in the immediate postwar period, because many international sides in those days were rubbish: in May 1947, for instance, Winter-bottom's England won 0–10 away to Portugal, not a result that England have threatened to match since.

Hodgson started even better than Capello. By the time his England had beaten Poland 2–0 at Wembley in October 2013 to qualify for the World Cup in Brazil, Hodgson's win percentage after 22 games was 77 per cent – fractionally above Capello's, and the highest in English history.

Admittedly, his team then lost two straight friendlies to dilute his numbers. We are still fairly confident that Hodgson's boys will fly home from Brazil in tears. That's only to be expected. The difference with past World Cups is that English fans now expect it too. It has taken nearly 50 years of hurt, but the fantasy of manifest destiny has finally been discarded.

THE CURSE OF POVERTY: WHY POOR COUNTRIES ARE POOR AT SPORT

When Didier Drogba was five, his parents put him on a plane in the Ivory Coast and sent him to live with an uncle in France. The six-hour flight, alone with his favourite toy, passed in a blur of tears and tissues.

About a decade later Drogba's father lost his job at a bank in the Ivory Coast, and the family moved to a suburb of Paris, where they were reunited with their exiled son. Eight Drogbas ended up living in a flat about 10 metres (33 feet) square. 'A very large wardrobe, really,' Drogba recalled in his autobiography. 'Hard. Very hard. Even enough to drive you crazy.' The flat was cold, and his little brothers were so noisy that he couldn't concentrate on his schoolwork. 'Luckily, my father had allowed me to start playing football again.'

There is a myth that poor people are somehow best equipped to make it as sportsmen. A cliché often used about them is that sport is their 'only escape route from poverty'. The poor, supposedly, are figuratively 'hungrier' than the rich. If they are black, like Drogba, they are sometimes thought to have greater genetic gifts than white people. And the evidence that poor people excel at sport seems to be in front of our eyes. England is not the only national football team dominated by players from lowly backgrounds. France since the 1990s have generally fielded a majority of non-white players, and few Brazilian internationals are sons of corporate lawyers either. Most of the world's best footballers started life poor: South Americans like Diego Maradona, who as a toddler almost drowned in a local cesspit, Africans like Samuel Eto'o, who appear to support hundreds of people back home, or European immigrants like Zlatan Ibrahimović or Zinedine Zidane, who grew up in some of the toughest neighbourhoods on the continent. Drogba's childhood was only slightly more Dickensian than most. The origins of American basketball players and football players are mostly lowly too. The best preparation for sporting greatness seems to be a poor childhood.

And yet it is not. The facts show that the world's poor people and poor countries are worse at sport than rich ones. It is true that poorer immigrants in rich countries often excel at sport, but the reasons for that have nothing to do with skin colour or 'hunger'.

Let's look at poor countries first. The vast majority of countries on earth are firmly excluded from sporting success, simply because they are poor. This becomes apparent in a simple exercise to discover which country is the world's best at sport, and which country is best for its size.

To find the best countries, we combined the historical results from many major international sporting events: the summer and winter Olympics, World Cups in several sports, and the most popular individual sports. For some sports the data go back more than a century; for others, only a couple of decades. For all sports, we took November 2013 as the end-point.

Our methodology is not perfect. We started with the men's World Cups in biggish sports that have seldom or never featured at the Olympics. We ranked the top five countries in these sports, based first on the number of world titles they won, and in case of ties, on finishes in the final four. We gave the best country in each sport five points, the second four, the third three, the fourth two, and the fifth one. There is no need to read the rankings for every sport, but here are the detailed points tallies for those who are interested:

RUGBY UNION: TOP 5 COUNTRIES

1	New Zealand	5	4	England	2
2	Australia	4	5	France	1
3	South Africa	3			

CRICKET: TOP 5 COUNTRIES

1	Australia	5	4	Pakistan	2
2	India	4	5	Sri Lanka	1
3	West Indies	3			

Baseball was trickier. Historically the US dominates the sport. However, it traditionally sends amateurs or minor leaguers to the World Cup. The US ranks only third all-time in the tournament. But we used our judgement to rank it as the world's best country in baseball, producing this ranking:

BASEBALL: TOP 5 COUNTRIES

1	US	5	4	Colombia	2
2	Cuba	4	5	South Korea	1
3	Venezuela	3			

Basketball is an Olympic event. However, as the world's second-most popular team game it deserves additional input in this quest. We therefore added the results of the basketball World Cup. Again, the US rarely fields its best players, and historically ranks second behind Yugoslavia. But using common sense we placed the US first here, too, producing this ranking:

BASKETBALL: TOP 5 COUNTRIES

1	US	5		3	USSR/Russia	3
2	Yugoslavia/Serbia & Montenegro	4		4	Brazil	2
				5	Argentina	1

Favouring the US in baseball and basketball did not affect the outcome of our quest.

The only women's world cup we counted was football. Women's football is an Olympic event, too, but far more popular than most other women's team games, and therefore it seemed to merit more input. The rankings for women's football:

WOMEN'S FOOTBALL: TOP 5 COUNTRIES

1	US	5		4	Japan	2
2	Germany	4		5	Sweden	1
2	Norway	3				

We also assessed popular individual sports that have seldom or never been represented in the Olympics. We rewarded countries for triumphs by their citizens. In tennis we counted men's and women's Grand Slam tournaments – tennis being a rare sport in that it is played widely by women. We used only results from the 'Open era' starting in 1968, when tennis became very competitive.

MEN'S TENNIS: TOP 5 COUNTRIES

1	US	5		4	Spain	2
2	Sweden	4		5	Switzerland	1
3	Australia	3				

WOMEN'S TENNIS: TOP 5 COUNTRIES

1	US	5		3	Australia	3
2	Germany/West Germany	4		4	Belgium	2
				5	Yugoslavia/Serbia	1

In golf we used the results of the men's majors:

GOLF: TOP 5 COUNTRIES

1	US	5	3	South Africa	3
2	Britain (including all four home countries)	4	4	Australia	2
			5	Spain	1

In cycling we counted victories by citizens of each country in the Tour de France, a more prestigious event than the World Championship. We didn't count doped winners like Lance Armstrong who were later stripped of their titles:

CYCLING: TOP 5 COUNTRIES

1	France	5	4	Italy	2
2	Belgium	4	5	Luxembourg	1
3	Spain	3			

In motor racing we chose the most prestigious competition, Formula One, thus discriminating against the US, which prefers its own races. Again, we counted world championships by citizenship. The rankings:

MOTOR RACING: TOP 5 COUNTRIES

1	Britain	5	4	Argentina	2
2	Germany	4	5	France, Australia Austria and Finland	1 each
3	Brazil	3			

We did not include the world cups of popular sports like volleyball and ice hockey, because these are Olympic sports, and so we will assess them through their role in the Olympics' all-time medals table. Boxing was too hard to assess, as there are various rival 'world championships'. We also excluded the athletics World Cup. Athletics is copiously represented at the Olympics, and for most of the history of its World Cup, the entrants have been entire continents rather than single countries.

Clearly the summer and winter Olympics deserve to carry more weight in our quest than any single world cup. In the London Games of 2012, medals were awarded in 26 sports. Many of these, such as archery or kayaking, are played by very few people. Still, because of the event's profusion of sports and its prestige, we gave the summer Games 10 times the weighting of world cups in single sports. So we gave the top country in the all-time medals table 50 points rather than 5 points for a single world cup. Because the whole planet competes in the Olympics – unlike, say, in baseball or cricket – we rewarded the top 10 rather than five countries in the all-time medals table. The ranking:

SUMMER OLYMPICS: TOP 10 COUNTRIES

1	US	50	6	France	8
2	USSR/Russia	40	7	East Germany (GDR)	6
3	Germany	30	8	Sweden	4
4	Italy	20	9	China	2
5	Britain	10	10	Norway	1

We gave the winter Olympics three times the weighting of a world cup. Because few countries play winter sports, we rewarded only the top five in the all-time medals table:

WINTER OLYMPICS: TOP 5 COUNTRIES

1	USSR/Russia	15	4	Germany (including West Germany)	4
2	Norway	12	5	Austria	3
3	US	9			

Finally, the football World Cup. Football is an Olympic sport, but it is also the planet's most popular game. We gave its world cup six times the weighting of world cups in other sports, and rewarded the top 10 countries in the all-time points table. The ranking:

FOOTBALL WORLD CUP: TOP 10 COUNTRIES

1	Brazil	30	6	Spain	5
2	Germany	24	7	France	4
3	Italy	18	8	Netherlands	3
4	Argentina	12	9	Uruguay	2
5	England	6	10	Sweden	1

We then totalled up all the points. Here are our top 23 sporting countries on earth:

TOTAL POINTS ACROSS ALL SPORTS AND OVERALL RANKING

1	US	89	11	Spain	11
2	Germany (including West Germany)	72	12	Sweden	10
3	USSR/Russia	58	13	East Germany, Belgium and South Africa	6
4	Italy	40			
5	Brazil	35	14	Yugoslavia/Serbia & Montenegro and New Zealand	5
6	Britain	27			
7	France	19	15	Austria, India and Cuba	4
8	Australia	16			
9	Norway	16	16	Netherlands, West Indies and Venezuela	3
10	Argentina	15			

The winner, the US, deserves particular praise given that we omitted two of its favourite sports, gridiron football and NASCAR, because nobody else plays them. Germany, in second place, would have got closer to the American total if we had credited the united country with East Germany's Olympic medals (and forgotten all the male growth hormones that went into winning them). The USSR/Russia in third place can be slightly less pleased with itself, because it won most of its points when it was still a multinational empire. Britain was fourth when we first calculated this table in 2006, but has since dropped to sixth, despite the London Olympics.

Australia in eighth place did brilliantly given that we ignored its prowess at its very own version of football, 'Aussie Rules'. Brazil was the best developing country by a very long way, and not just thanks to football. It has also diversified successfully into basketball and Formula One. India (1.2 billion inhabitants, 4 points for cricket) and China (1.3 billion, 2 points for the summer Olympics) were the biggest flops per capita. The Arab world combined got zero points.

But which country is world champion per capita? To find out, we worked out how many points each country scored per million inhabitants (taking their population figures for 2013). That produced this top 10 of overachievers:

TOTALS

1	Norway	3.19
2	Luxembourg	1.88
3	New Zealand	1.14
4	Sweden	1.05
5	United Germany (excluding the GDR's Olympic medals)	0.88
6	Australia	0.79
7	Italy	0.66

8	Uruguay	0.59
9	West Indies*	0.58
10	Belgium	0.54

* Or the nations that together supply almost all West Indian cricketers, namely Jamaica, Trinidad and Tobago, Guyana, Barbados and Antigua

Heia Norge: Norway is the world's best per-capita sporting nation. Its lead is so big that it would most probably have won our sporting Tom Thumb trophy under almost any scoring system – even, say, if we had halved its points for the winter Olympics. This is a country where at a state kindergarten in suburban Oslo in mid-afternoon, among the throng of mothers picking up their toddlers, someone pointed out to us an anonymous mum who happened to be an Olympic gold medallist in cross-country skiing. Norway won more points in our competition than all of Africa or Asia (excluding Oceania) put together. We could even have omitted the winter Olympics –

almost a Norwegian fiefdom – and the country still would have finished sixth in our efficiency table.

But the main thing the top of our rankings demonstrates is the importance of wealth. Our efficiency table for sports bears a curious resemblance to another global ranking: the United Nations' human development index. This measures life expectancy, literacy, education and living standards to rank the countries of the world according to their well-being. We found that a nation's well-being is highly correlated with its success in sports. Try to guess which country topped the UN's rankings for human development in 2012: *Heia Norge*, again.

New Zealand and Australia, third and sixth in our sporting rankings, were sixth and second for human development in 2012. Sweden, fourth in the world for sports, was joint seventh for human development. Germany was fifth in sport, fifth in human development. The only poorer nations that sneaked into our sporting top ten were Uruguay and the West Indian nations. However, even these poor cousins were all classified by the UN as 'very highly' or 'highly' developed countries except Guyana, whose development was 'medium'. Generally the most developed countries also tend to be best at sports.

The case of Norway shows why. It's Norwegian government policy that every farmer, every fisherman, no matter where he lives in the country, has the right to play sport. And Norway will spend what it takes to achieve that. Just as supermarkets have sprouted all over Britain, there are all-weather sports grounds everywhere in Norway. Even in the unlikeliest corners of the country there's generally one around the corner from your house. Usually the changing-rooms are warm and the coaches have acquired some sort of diploma. A kid can play and train in a proper team for well under £100 a year, really not much for most Norwegians. Almost everyone in the country plays something. Professor Knut Helland of Bergen University, who has written a book on Norwegian sport and media, notes that Norway has the biggest ski race in the world with about 13,000 participants. 'I'm taking part in it myself,' he adds. When the European Commission studied time use in European countries in 2004, it found that the Norwegians spent the most time playing sport: on average, a whopping 13 minutes a day. People all over the world might want to play sport, but to make that possible requires money and organisation that poor countries don't have. Money buys sporting trophies.

After we published the first edition of this book, Chris Anderson, a political scientist at Cornell University in the US, and later co-author of *The Numbers Game*, riposted that we placed undue weight on wealth. In his paper, 'Do Democracies Win More?', Anderson analysed all football World Cups from 1950 to 2006. The key to winning wasn't so much wealth, he argued, as democracy.

That may well be true. Wealth and democracy tend to correlate very closely. Almost all rich countries (leaving aside a few oil states in the Middle East) are democracies. That makes it tricky to separate the effects of wealth from the effects of democracy. Anderson might well be right that democracy contributes more than wealth to winning football games. (Note also that in making our case, we were looking at many sports rather than just football.) Most democracies are good at providing resources to their citizens, and resources include good football pitches and coaches. It's impossible to say whether Norway is good at sport because it's rich, or because it's a democracy. Rather, being rich and democratic are usually part of the same thing.

However you measure it, poor countries are generally poorer at sport. It's no coincidence that China won nothing at sport before its economy took off, and that it topped the medals table at the Beijing Olympics afterwards. Most African countries barely even try to compete in any sports other than football and a few track events. And the best place to find out why the world's poor do worse than the world's rich is South Africa, where some very poor and very rich neighbourhoods are almost side by side, separated only by a main road or a golf course.

South Africa is the one African country to score any points at all in our sporting table. Yet it owes almost all those points to an ethnic group that makes up less than 10 per cent of the country's inhabitants: white people.

Only about 4.6 million of the 51 million South Africans are white. Nonetheless, whites accounted for 14 of the 15 players in the Springbok rugby team that won the World Cup in 1995, and 13 of the 15 that won it in 2007, as well as all five South African golfers who have won majors and most of the country's best cricketers. If we treated white South Africa as a separate country, then its six sporting points would have put it in third place in the world in our sporting efficiency table. That is entirely predictable. South African whites were nurtured under apartheid on almost all the resources of the country.

The national teams of South African whites now dominate their respective sports. Since the end of apartheid, the country's mostly white cricket team and the mostly white Springboks have been among the best in the world. Non-white South Africa's national team does less well. At the time of writing, in January 2014, the 'Bafana Bafana' football team, sometimes known at home as the 'Banana Banana', are 54th in FIFA's rankings, well behind Panama, Scotland and the Cape Verde Islands.

Even that represents quite a big rise in recent years. The Bafana just missed qualifying for the African Nations Cup of 2012, having failed to figure out that they needed to beat rather than draw with Sierra Leone in their last qualifying game. (The scenes of the Bafana wasting time in the final minutes to preserve the draw would have been hilarious were they not a terrible reflection on the state of maths teaching in South Africa.)

Here are five vignettes to explain why black South Africa and other poor nations fail at sport:

YOU ARE WHAT YOU EAT

JOHANNESBURG

Steven Pienaar, Everton's South African midfielder, has the frame of a prepubescent boy. There's hardly a European footballer as reedy as he is. But in South African football his body type is common. Frank Eulberg, a German who spent about five minutes as assistant coach of the Kaizer Chiefs, South Africa's best team, says that when he arrived at the club, 16 of the players were shorter than 1.75 metres (5ft 9in). 'I sometimes thought, "Frank, you're in the land of the dwarves."'

Most likely, Pienaar is reedy because he grew up malnourished and without much access to doctors. He was born in a poor Coloured township in 1982, at the height of apartheid, when almost all money and healthcare went to whites. Growing tall is not just a matter of what you eat; when children become ill, their growth is interrupted, and because poor children tend to get ill more often than rich ones, they usually end up shorter.

Most of the players who represented South Africa in 2010 were born in non-white townships in the 1980s. And so the ghost of apartheid bugged the Bafana at the World Cup. One reason South Africans are so bad at football is that most of them didn't get enough good food. There are big strong black South Africans like Lucas Radebe and Aaron Mokoena, but not very many of them.

Apartheid, based on the bogus ideology that races are different, ended up creating white, black, 'Coloured' and Indian South Africans who really were like separate peoples. The whites on average tower over the blacks. No wonder the cricket and rugby teams are so much better than the Bafana. 'Well, they have their moments,' laughs Demitri Constantinou.

This descendant of Greek immigrants, an exercise scientist at Wits University in Johannesburg, directs FIFA's first medical centre of excellence in Africa. When we met, he was running a project with the South African Football Association to help develop young footballers. Constantinou's team tested the health of all the players selected for SAFA's programme. In a Woolworths tearoom in one of Johannesburg's posh northern suburbs, among white ladies having afternoon tea, he says, 'The biggest issue was nutrition.' Is malnutrition one reason why African teams perform poorly at World Cups? 'I think yes. And I think it has been overlooked as a possible cause.'

Hardly any players in the latter stages of the World Cup of 2006 were shorter than about 1.73 metres (5ft 8in), Constantinou notes. 'There is a minimum height.' If a large proportion of your male population was below that height, you were picking your team from a reduced pool. Conversely, though he didn't say it, one reason that Norway and Sweden (two of the three tallest countries in the world) excel at sport is that almost all their male inhabitants are tall enough. They are picking their teams from a full pool.

A BEAST INTO A TOOTHPICK

CAPE TOWN

George Dearnaley is a big ruddy white man who looks like a rugby player, but in fact he was once the Bafana's promising young centre-forward. Dearnaley never got beyond promising, because when he was in his early twenties his knee went. He didn't mind much. He spoke a bit of Zulu, and had studied literature and journalism at college in Toledo, Ohio, and so he joined the football magazine *Kick Off*. He became its publisher as well as the author of an excellent column.

Over an English breakfast in a Cape Town greasy-spoon near the *Kick Off* offices, Dearnaley reflected on the Amazulu team in Durban where his career peaked. Seven of his teammates from the Amazulu side of 1992 were now dead, out of a squad of about 24. Dearnaley said: 'One guy died when his house exploded, so that was probably a taxi war or something. But the rest must have been AIDS. One player, a Durban newspaper said he was bewitched. A six foot four [1.93m] beast of a man, who was suddenly whittled down to a toothpick.'

Constantinou says it's quite possible that a fifth of the Bafana's potential pool of players for 2010 carried the HIV virus. Not many people now remember Emmanuel 'Scara' Ngobese, once a South African 'dribbling wizard', who died aged 28 in a Johannesburg hospital on 11 May 2010, a month before the World Cup kicked off. His cause of death was given as 'tuberculosis'. Scara won the league with Kaizer Chiefs in 2005, and played once for the Bafana. How many South Africans who could have played in 2010 were dead instead?

THE DARK SIDE OF THE MOON

SANDTON, JUST OUTSIDE JOHANNESBURG

It was quite a step for Danny Jordaan to organise a World Cup, because until he was 38 he had never even seen one.

The chief executive officer of the FIFA World Cup 2010 grew up a million miles from the world's best football. Being in South Africa under apartheid was not quite like being on the moon, or being in North Korea, but it was almost as isolated. South Africa was the last industrialised country to get television, in 1976, because the white government was afraid of the device. Even after that hardly any blacks had TV sets, and FIFA did not allow its World Cup to be broadcast in the apartheid state. So the first time Jordaan saw a World Cup on television was in 1990.

The country's isolation continued even after that. As far as most South Africans were concerned, international football still might as well have been happening on Mars. Jordaan says, 'South Africans played on their own. We thought we were so smart. That's why when we played our first competitive match against Zimbabwe [in 1992], every South African knew we were going to hammer Zimbabwe. But Zimbabwe had this little player called Peter Ndlovu. Nobody knew Peter Ndlovu. By half-time it was 3–0 for them. That was the first entry into international football. That really shook this country.'

As late as 1998, when South Africa entered its first World Cup, large swathes of the population assumed that the Bafana would win it. After all, everyone knew that their native style of 'tsamayas and shoeshine' – essentially, doing tricks on the ball while standing around – was just like Brazilian football but better. The Bafana did not win the World Cup.

Black South Africa was isolated twice over: first by sanctions, then by poverty. However, isolation – a distance from the networks of the world's best football – is the fate of most poor countries. Their citizens can't easily travel to Italy or Germany and see how football is played there, let alone talk to the best coaches. Some can't even see foreign football on television, because they don't have a televi- sion. And only a couple of the very best players in these countries ever make it to the best leagues in the world.

One reason why poor countries do badly at sport – and one reason why they are poor – is that they tend to be less 'networked', less connected to other countries, than rich ones. It is hard for them just to find out the latest best practice on how to play a sport.

Playing for national teams in Africa hardly lifts the isolation much. Most poor, isolated African countries compete only against other poor, isolated African countries. At best, they might encounter the world's best once every four years at a World Cup. No wonder they have little idea of what top-class football is like.

'THE ORGANISERS. IT'S THE BIGGEST PROBLEM'

LONDON

For mysterious reasons, in 2006 someone decided that the Bafana should play their annual charity match, the Nelson Mandela Chal- lenge, not in the magnificent 78,000-seat FNB Stadium just outside Johannesburg, but more than 5,000 miles away at Brentford's Grif- fin Park.

On a grey November London afternoon the day before the game, the Bafana were in their grey-coloured three-star hotel on the outskirts of Heathrow Airport. In the lobby were flight crews, travelling salesmen and cheery men in green-and-yellow tracksuits hanging with their entourage: the Bafana Bafana. Their opponents, the Egyptians, who were also staying in the hotel, had congregated in the bar. Apparently Egypt were furious. They had been promised a five-star hotel, and a match fee that had yet to materialise.

Pitso Mosimane, the Bafana caretaker manager – a big, bald, bullet-headed man – was also hanging around the lobby. Mosimane complained that African coaches never got jobs in Europe. He gestured towards the bar: 'The coach of Egypt, who won the African Cup of Nations. Don't you think he could at least coach a team in the English first division?' Then Mosimane went off for pre-match training at Griffin Park.

Minutes later he was back at table. 'That was quick,' someone remarked. 'No, we didn't train!' Mosimane said. Nobody had bothered telling Brentford the Bafana were coming, and so the field wasn't ready for them. Now they would have to play the African champions without having trained on the pitch. 'And I'm carrying players who play for Blackburn Rovers and Borussia Dortmund, and you know? We're laughing about it.' Mosimane jerked a thumb towards four men in suits drinking at the next table: 'The organisers. It's the biggest problem. This wouldn't happen with any other national team.'

He was wrong. Organisational mishaps are always happening to national teams from poor countries. There are stories of African countries simply forgetting to enter World Cups. In most sub-Sahara African national teams that do make it to a World Cup, players and officials have a ritual dispute over pay about a week before the tournament. In 2002 Cameroon's dispute got out of hand, whereupon the squad made a brief aeroplane odyssey through Ethiopia, India and Thailand before finally landing in Japan four days late. Jetlagged and confused, they were knocked out in the first round. In 2006

Togo's players spent much of their brief stay at the country's first-ever World Cup threatening to go on strike because of their pay dispute. They worried that after the tournament was over, Togo's federation might never get around to paying them. Eventually FIFA sidestepped the federation, paid the players' bonuses directly, and told them to play or else, but it is little wonder that the team lost three matches out of three.

To win at sport, you need to find, develop and nurture talent. Doing that requires money, know-how and some kind of administrative infrastructure. Few African countries have enough of any of them.

'COLOURED' BEATS 'BLACK'

THE CAPE FLATS

If you stand on Table Mountain at night and look down at Cape Town, you will see a city of lights. Next to the lights are the railway tracks. And on the far side of the tracks are 'black spots': Coloured townships without lights. These are the rainy, murderous Cape Flats, where most of South Africa's best footballers grew up.

Benni McCarthy, South Africa's record goalscorer, comes from the Cape Flats. So does the man just behind him on the scoring charts, Shaun Bartlett. So does Benni's old mate Quinton Fortune, for years a loyal reserve at Manchester United.

The key point is that according to the racial classifications of apartheid, still tacitly used by South Africans today, none of these players is 'black'. They are 'Coloured': a group of generally lighter-skinned people, mostly derived from the lighter African tribes of the Cape, though some descend from Asian slaves and mixed white–black liaisons. Less than 10 per cent of South Africans are Coloured, while about three quarters are black. However, Coloureds often make up as much as half the Bafana side. Pienaar and the striker Delron Buckley, for instance, are from Coloured townships in other parts of South Africa. This density of Coloured talent is a legacy of apartheid.

Under apartheid, the Coloureds were slightly better off than the blacks. They had more to eat, and more opportunities to organise themselves. In the Coloured Cape Flats, for instance, there were amateur football clubs with proper coaches such as you might find in Europe. Not so in black townships, where a boys' team would typically be run by a local gangster or the shebeen owner, who seldom bothered much with training.

To the irritation of many South African blacks, the Bafana have been a largely Coloured team for much of their history since 1992. The blacks are simply too poor to compete within their own country, let alone with Europeans. Even in the simplest game, the poor are excluded by malnutrition, disease and disorganisation.

That leaves one thing unexplained. Why is it that so many of the best European footballers – Zidane, Drogba (officially an Ivorian but raised in France), Ibrahimović, Wayne Rooney, Cristiano Ronaldo – come from the poorest neighbourhoods in Europe?

It cannot be that boys from the ghetto have an unquenchable hunger to succeed. If that were so, they would do better at school and in jobs outside football. There must something about their childhood that makes them particularly well suited to football. That reason is practice.

Malcolm Gladwell, in his book *Outliers: The Story of Success*, advanced the '10,000-hour rule'. This is a notion from psychology, which says that to achieve expertise in any field you need at least 10,000 hours of practice. 'In study after study, of composers, basketball players, fiction writers, ice-skaters, concert pianists, chess players, master criminals,' says the neurologist Daniel Levitin in *Outliers*, 'this number comes up again and again ... No one has yet found a case in which true world-class expertise was accomplished in less time.'

The 10,000-hour rule has since been questioned by academics in various fields. It may indeed not apply in very physical sports like running or jumping, where somebody with the perfect genes can become world-class without much training. However, in a highly skill-based sport like football, Gladwell's essential point is correct: practice makes perfect.

In football, it is the poorest European boys who are most likely to get the most practice. They tend to live in small apartments, which forces them to spend time outdoors. There they meet a ready supply of local boys equally keen to get out of their apartments and play football. Their parents are less likely than middle-class parents to force them to waste precious time doing homework. And they have less money for other leisure pursuits. A constant in footballers' ghosted autobiographies is the monomaniac childhood spent playing non-stop football and, in a classic story, sleeping with a ball. Here for instance is Nourdin Boukhari, a Dutch-Moroccan footballer who grew up in an immigrant neighbourhood of Rotterdam, recalling his childhood for a Dutch magazine:

> I grew up in a family of eight children ... There was no chance of pocket money ... I lived more on the street than at home ... And look at Robin van Persie, Mounir El Hamdaoui and Said Boutahar. And I'm forgetting Youssef El-Akchaoui. [Like the other players Boukhari mentions, El-Akchaoui became a professional footballer.] Those boys and I played on the street in Rotterdam together. We never forget where we came from and that we used to have nothing except for one thing: the ball.
>
> ... What we have in common is that we were on the street every minute playing football, day and night. We were always busy, games, juggling, shooting at the crossbar. The ball was everything for me, for us. We'd meet on squares ...

By the time these boys were 15, they were much better players than suburban kids. The importance of practice also explains why blacks raised in American ghettoes are over-represented in basketball and American football.

But it would be misleading to say these European footballers grew up 'poor'. By global standards, they were rich. Even in Cristiano

Ronaldo's Madeira, Rooney's Croxteth or Zidane's La Castellane, children generally got enough to eat and decent medical care. It is true that Cristiano Ronaldo grew up in a house so small that they kept the washing machine on the roof; but in black South Africa, that washing machine would have marked the family out as rich. Beside the 10,000-hour rule, there is another rule that explains sporting success: the $15,000 rule. That's the minimum average income per person that a country needs to win anything. There is only one way around this: be Brazil.

TOM THUMB: THE BEST LITTLE FOOTBALL COUNTRY ON EARTH

In 1970, when Brazil won their third World Cup, they got to keep the Jules Rimet trophy. The little statuette of Nike, then still known as the Greek goddess of victory, ended up in a glass case in the Brazilian federation's offices in Rio de Janeiro. One night in 1983 the trophy was stolen, and was never seen again.

However, the point is that everyone agrees that Brazil deserves the Jules Rimet trophy. The five-fold world champions are undoubtedly the best country in football history. Our question here is a different one: which country is best taking into account its population, experience and income per capita? If Brazil are the absolute world champions, who are the relative ones, the biggest overperformers? That overachieving country deserves its own version of the Jules Rimet trophy – call it the Tom Thumb. And which countries are the worst underachievers relative to their resources? Along the way we will have to consider several impressive candidates and make some judgement calls before coming up with our winner and loser.

* * *

First of all, if we are dealing with statistics, we have to construct our arguments on the basis of large numbers of games played. There have only been 19 World Cups up to 2010, and most of these involved hardly any countries from outside Europe and Latin America. So crunching the numbers from World Cups might at best tell us something about the pecking-order among the long-established large football nations. But when the difference between, say, Argentina's two victories and England's one comes down to as little as the hand of God, or the difference between Italy's four and France's one to a pre-match pep talk given by Benito Mussolini to the referee in 1934 and a comment by Marco Materazzi about Zidane's parentage in 2006, then the statistician needs to look elsewhere.

Happily, since national teams play a lot of games, we have plenty of data. As in chapter 16, we will rely on Russell Gerrard's remarkable database of matches, which we have updated to 2012.

The number of international matches has soared over time. Between the foundation of FIFA in 1904 and the First World War the number rose quickly to 50 per year. After 1918, growth resumed. By the eve of the Second World War, there were more than 100 international matches a year. But this was still a world dominated by colonial powers, and only with the independence movement after the war did international competition mushroom. In 1947 there were 107 international matches; by 1957 there were 203; by 1967, 308. Few new countries were founded in the next two decades, but the number of international matches continued to rise thanks to the jet plane, which made travel less of a pain and more financially worthwhile. In 1977 there were 368 international matches; in 1987 there were 393. At that point the world seemed to have reached some sort of stable equilibrium.

But then the Soviet Union broke up into 15 separate states, and Yugoslavia collapsed. The new countries flocked into FIFA. At the same time the commercial development of football meant that cash-hungry national associations were keen to play lucrative friendlies.

In 1997 there were 850 international games, more than double the figure of a decade before. Since then growth has slowed but not stopped altogether, reaching a figure of 923 in 2007.

If we concentrate on just the 20-year cycle from the end of the 1990 World Cup to the end of the 2010 World Cup – the post-Cold-War era – a list of the most successful teams features the usual suspects. Let's rank the top 10 countries by the percentage of games won, or, given that around one-third of matches are draws, by the 'win percentage' statistic calculated by valuing a draw as worth half a win.

TOP 10 NATIONAL TEAMS BY WIN PERCENTAGE, ALL GAMES 1990–2010

	Team	Played	Won	Draws	Win %	Goal diff
1	Spain	195	0.656	0.215	0.764	1.272
2	Brazil	296	0.615	0.240	0.735	1.311
3	France	213	0.577	0.277	0.716	0.939
4	Germany	226	0.606	0.199	0.706	1.040
5	Argentina	236	0.576	0.246	0.699	0.839
6	Netherlands	192	0.552	0.281	0.693	1.010
7	Italy	200	0.525	0.310	0.680	0.690
8	England	193	0.528	0.295	0.676	0.865
9	Portugal	185	0.535	0.276	0.673	0.903
10	Czech Republic	156	0.571	0.199	0.670	0.904

The top few teams are much as you would expect. Spain – as we'll discuss in the next chapter – has been the world's leading football nation for a surprisingly long time. And even in a 20-year period when Brazil tried to reinvent its national style of play, its win percentage was almost 75 per cent. That equates to bookmakers' odds of 3 to 1, or about as close as you can get to a sure thing in a two-horse race.

If we look at Brazil's performance over time, some interesting insights emerge. Here are the team's results by decade:

BRAZIL: THE DISASTER OF 1950 AS THE START OF SOMETHING BEAUTIFUL

Decade	P	W	D	L	F	A	Win%*
1910s	15	6	4	5	28	24	0.533
1920s	24	10	4	10	35	34	0.500
1930s	22	14	1	7	60	49	0.659
1940s	43	23	7	13	127	68	0.616
1950s	96	62	18	16	229	100	0.740
1960s	115	78	16	21	275	134	0.748
1970s	101	65	27	9	188	62	0.777
1980s	117	73	28	16	222	83	0.744
1990s	166	108	38	20	366	137	0.765
2000s	157	96	36	25	323	118	0.726

*Including draws as half a win

Viewed in the light of history, it's little wonder that Brazil lost at home to Uruguay in the World Cup final of 1950. The Brazilians simply weren't that good then. Their hubris at that tournament had no historical basis. It was only later in the 1950s that Brazil turned into football's superpower. Indeed, in the fifty years since then the team's performance has been strikingly consistent: Brazil's winning percentage (counting draws as worth half a win) hovered between 73 per cent and 78 per cent in each of the last six decades. If you had to pick a particular golden age, it would probably be 1964 to 1985, but our main finding is great stability of performance, even in the supposedly fallow 20 years after 1970. World Cups, as we have seen, usually turn on a couple of crucial matches, which in turn are usually decided by one goal each. The pundits then investigate these crucial matches for meaning, when in fact the best explanation of the outcome of such a tiny sample of games might be chance. The broader story of Brazil in the last 50 years is consistent excellence. Still, if Brazil is going to remain at the top, it will probably need to plug into the western European knowledge networks. In recent World Cups the Brazilians have sometimes looked ponderous against the best European teams. They ought to consider the revolutionary step of hiring a Western European manager. If Brazil can combine the world's best players with the world's most advanced tactics, the result could be scary.

There's just one other finding of note. Brazil perform better in World Cup years. They win about 5 per cent more often in years with a World Cup, and the difference is statistically significant. That sounds counterintuitive: after all, the team would tend to face tougher competition in those years. However, the sordid truth is that most of the time, Brazilian internationals coast a little. They don't raise their game for qualifiers against Bolivia or Nike-inspired friendlies against Asian countries. In these off-years, weary stars sometimes cry off claiming injury, and agents sometimes finagle places in the team for players who need a foreign transfer. But in a World Cup year, when everyone is playing for his place, Brazil are at their best.

You might think that 1990 to 2010 was a time of decline for Argentina. After all, in these years the country never even reached the World Cup semi-finals, whereas in 1986 and 1990 it had won a World Cup final and then lost another only on a dubious penalty. Yet in fact the 1980s – the decade of Diego Maradona's greatness – was match for match the worst decade in Argentina's football history. The country's winning percentage slumped to a miserable 53 per cent:

ARGENTINA'S RESULTS: WHERE IS THE MARADONA EFFECT?

Decade	P	W	D	L	% Won	Win %*
1902–1910	20	12	4	4	0.60	0.70
1911–1920	64	30	12	22	0.47	0.56
1921–1930	77	40	20	17	0.52	0.65
1931–1940	44	29	6	9	0.66	0.73
1941–1950	50	37	8	5	0.74	0.82
1951–1960	79	51	12	16	0.65	0.72
1961–1970	81	33	24	24	0.41	0.56
1971–1980	114	60	30	24	0.53	0.66
1981–1990	95	33	35	27	0.35	0.53
1991–2000	130	74	35	21	0.57	0.70
2001–2010	127	77	26	24	0.61	0.71

*Including draws as half a win

But for his 'hand of God' in 1986, Maradona might have gone down in history as a brilliant underperformer, much like his contemporary Zico. Argentina's uneven performances during Maradona's era, as well as his rather sporadic club career, underline a difference between him and his little successor: Maradona never provided weekly brilliance the way Lionel Messi has. On the other hand, genius may in part be the ability to perform when it matters most.

In any case, Argentina's relative failure in his era probably wasn't Maradona's fault. The team's results seem to track the country's economic fortunes: in the 1980s, both declined.

Until well after the Second World War, Argentina was one of the richest countries on earth. Indeed, in the 1940s it exported beef to a starving Europe. No wonder that decade was also its best in football. But later Argentina became, in the words of Maradona's former teammate Jorge 'El Filósofo' Valdano, 'the world's first undeveloping country'. The 1980s were the 'lost decade': average income shrank from $7,500 per head in 1980 to $5,700 in 1990.

The past 20 years have been a rollercoaster for the Argentine economy, but ultimately a great success in that income per head has risen to nearly $16,000 in 2010. That represents almost a trebling of real income since 1990. Admittedly there was a terrible recession around 2001, when the banking system collapsed, and Argentina devalued its peso and defaulted on its debts. Yet for much of the time since then, the economy has grown at close to 10 per cent a year. Some economists are predicting a new Armageddon, but it hasn't come yet.

It's notable that, as the economy has bounced back, so has the football team (though admittedly not in the knockout stages of World Cups). Argentina's winning percentage has shot back up to 70 per cent in the 20 years since 1990, a level it had previously reached only in the good old 1950s. Returning to that standard was quite an achievement. Since the 1950s football has become a global sport, and many new countries have joined the race for supremacy. The international game today is more competitive than ever, and Argentina's comeback deserves a compliment.

The Czech Republic and Portugal, too, warrant particular praise for making our top 10 of most successful football teams. Each country has only 10 million inhabitants, compared with the 47–82 million of the large European nations and Brazil's 178 million. Some readers may also be surprised to find England in the top 10, given England's false reputation as 'notorious underachievers'.

Pace Brazil and Argentina, one thing our top 10 tells us is that Europeans have dominated international football. The continent provides eight of the 10 best countries. We have seen that this is partly thanks to Europe's unmatched knowledge networks. Those networks rest on tradition: European nations are generally older and have played international football longer than the rest of the world. It may also help that until very recently, control of global football largely remained in Europe. FIFA makes the rules of the game from a posh suburb of Zurich, and although western Europe has only 6 per cent of the world's population, it hosted 10 out of 19 World Cups up to 2010. (A mark of how power in football is shifting is that the region might now have to wait decades before hosting another.)

But tradition does not in itself secure dominance. If it did, then British companies would still dominate industries like textiles, ship-building and car making. Dominance is transitory unless producers have the resources to stay ahead of the competition. The key resource in football is talent. Generally speaking, the more populous countries are more likely to have the largest supply of talented people. We have also seen that rich countries are best at finding, training and developing talent. In short, it takes experience, popu-lation and wealth to make a successful football nation.

The easy bit is recognising this. The hard work is assembling the data to answer our question: Which countries do best relative to their resources of experience, population and wealth?

Thankfully, Russell's data can help us with the issue of experi-ence. He has recorded every single international game in history. With his list, we can measure the cumulative number of games a country had played up to any given date. We have seen that the most experienced football countries had played more than 700 interna-tional matches up to 2000. Pedants might dispute some of the exact numbers – identifying international games is often a judgement call if we go back more than 50 years, when arrangements could be quite informal – but even if our figures were off by 5 per cent, it wouldn't significantly affect the statistical analysis.

We also have data on each country's income. The measure typic-ally used is gross domestic product. GDP is the total value of all goods and services bought and sold within an economy. (It includes imports and exports but excludes income from assets owned over-seas and profits repatriated to foreign countries.) The best sources for GDP figures are the Penn World Tables, produced by the Center for International Comparisons at the University of Pennsylvania, which has estimates of GDP for 167 countries between 1950 and 2011. To measure the economic resources available to each person, it divides GDP by population. Admittedly, there are all sorts of finicky issues involved in making comparisons across countries and across time, not to mention worries about measurement error and statistical reliability. Nonetheless, these data are the best we've got.

Now we run the multiple regressions that we described in chapter 16. Our aim is to find the connection between goal difference per game and our three key inputs – population, wealth and experience – while also allowing for home advantage.

After all these pyrotechnics, we can make another ranking. But this time we can compensate all the world's national teams for that trio of factors beyond their control: experience, population and income per head.

THE TOP TEN OVERACHIEVING NATIONAL TEAMS IN THE WORLD, ALLOWING FOR POPULATION, WEALTH AND EXPERIENCE, ALL GAMES 1990–2010

Team	Played	Won	Draws	Win %	GD	OP
1 Brazil	296	0.615	0.240	0.735	1.311	1.486
2 Spain	195	0.656	0.215	0.764	1.272	1.196
3 Iran	225	0.516	0.280	0.656	0.969	1.019
4 Germany	226	0.606	0.199	0.706	1.040	0.978
5 Iraq	157	0.414	0.287	0.557	0.573	0.962
6 Czech Republic	156	0.571	0.199	0.670	0.904	0.954
7 Argentina	236	0.576	0.246	0.699	0.839	0.949
8 Netherlands	192	0.552	0.281	0.693	1.010	0.906
9 Portugal	185	0.535	0.276	0.673	0.903	0.863
10 Mexico	362	0.486	0.243	0.608	0.721	0.839

The final column of the table is the one to notice. It shows what you might call each country's 'outperformance': the gap between the goal difference it 'should' have achieved against opponents given its national resources and experience and what it actually did achieve (listed in the penultimate column). Brazil, the most over-achieving country in football according to this table, scores nearly 1.5 goals per game more than you would expect judging by its resources. All our top 10 scored on average about a goal per game more than their resources would predict. Of our original 'absolute' top 10, Brazil, Spain, Germany, Argentina, the Czechs, the Dutch and the Portuguese all survive in this 'relative' top 10. It turns out that these countries aren't merely very good in absolute terms. They are also overachieving relative to their resources. As for Mexico, we suspect its presence in the top 10 is only because it spends so much of its time playing Caribbean islands, tiny Central American countries and Canada. Viewed from Mexico City, even the US is a soccer superpower. The Mexicans would win a lot fewer games (and would sink in our rankings) if they were moved into the South American confederation.

There are only two big surprises in our top 10 of relative over-achievers: Iran and Iraq. For a start: kudos to the Iranians. The international sanctions don't seem to have had much impact on their football. They qualified for the World Cup of 2014, and if they now start to open to the world they could get even better.

But the stunner, for us, is Iraq. The years from 1990 to 2010 – two Gulf Wars, massacres, sanctions, Saddam, near-civil war – were not happy ones for Iraqis. Nonetheless, over 20 years it scored nearly a goal a game more than you would expect given its resources.

It did so even while under the thumb of Saddam's family, which loved sports. Each April, Baghdad celebrated Saddam's birthday by hosting the 'Saddam Olympics'. You might not have caught these on Sky but as late as 2002, with Baghdad's Russian–Iraqi Friendship Society as sponsor, Iraq attracted athletes from 72 countries. And not many people know that Baghdad was also bidding to host the real Olympics in 2012 before events intervened.

Saddam left control of the national football team to his bestial son Uday. A playboy and pervert, who walked with a limp after an assassination attempt, Uday motivated his players by threatening to amputate their legs if they lost. One former international reported being beaten on the soles of his feet, dragged on his bare back through gravel and then dipped in raw sewage so that his wounds would be infected. Some players spent time in Abu Ghraib prison. After Kuwait came to Baghdad in 1981 and won, one of the ruling family's helpers beat up the referee, who was then 'driven hurriedly to the airport and put bleeding on a plane out of the country', writes Declan Hill in his book on global match fixing, *The Fix*.

Stories like these from Iraqi defectors prompted FIFA to send a committee to Iraq to investigate. The Iraqis produced players and coaches who swore blind that it was all lies. FIFA believed them, and so the Lions of Mesopotamia were allowed to keep on collecting prizes.

Only when American troops entered Baghdad in 2003 did they find the prison Uday maintained in the basement of Iraq's Olympic headquarters. It featured 'a rack and a medieval torture device used to rip open a man's anus', writes James Montague in his *When Friday Comes: Football in the War Zone*.

But despite everything, under Saddam the Lions of Mesopotamia were the strongest team in the world's largest continent. Though they had to play on neutral ground for much of Saddam's reign due to the war with Iran, they qualified for the World Cup of 1986 and for three Olympics. As Iraqi supporters used to chant (often while firing bullets into the air), 'Here we are Sunni – yah! Here we are Shiite – yah! Bring us happiness, sons of Iraq!' Even Kurds supported the Lions. Montague calls the team 'arguably the last symbol of national unity left in Iraq'. Only from the 1990s, as Saddam's regime became even more isolated and brutal, did Iraqi football decline. Its win percentage from 1980 to 2001 was still a magnificent 67 per cent; in the turmoil from 2002 to 2012, it dipped to a merely impressive 55 per cent.

All this may be a case of people immersing themselves in football because it was their only form of public expression. Huthyfa Zahra, an Iraqi artist who now produces football-themed 'pop art' from the safety of nearby Abu Dhabi, says: 'Even during the wars, in the Nineties, there were bombs above us, and we were playing in the streets. Because we didn't have anything to do.'

Why were the Lions so good under Saddam? Zahra is surprised to hear that they were. 'We are much better now,' he replies, 'because the players play without fear now. If you don't feel comfortable, you can't play.' He points out that since the fall of Saddam and Uday, Iraq's Lions have finished fourth in the Athens Olympics and won the Asian Cup of 2007. Iraqis may now finally be getting the chance to devote most of their energies to football. The American writer Nir Rosen reported in 2010:

> On my trips to Iraq in years past, I made a habit of scanning the walls of Baghdad neighbourhoods for bits of sectarian graffiti, spray-painted slogans that were pro-Mahdi Army, pro-Saddam, anti-Shiite or pro-insurgency. This time, however, there were almost none to be found; the exhortations to sectarian struggle had been replaced with the enthusiasms of youthful football fans: now the walls say 'Long Live Barcelona'.

Still, the presence of both Iran and Iraq in the top five of our 'over-achievers' table does illustrate the problem of comparing national teams from different continents. It is hard to imagine that either country would have done all that well against the other teams in the top 10. In fact, they have hardly ever played against the global big boys (neither Saddam's nor Mahmoud Ahmadinejad's boys got many invitations to play friendlies at Wembley). Mostly, Iran and Iraq beat Middle Eastern and Asian countries.

Furthermore, GDP statistics for poorer countries outside Europe (especially countries in the midst of war or sanctions) are notoriously unreliable. In general, there is more 'noise' in all the data for countries outside Europe, meaning that we struggle to pick up the influence of the factors we are interested in. It's like listening to a radio with poor reception: the meaning of the words becomes hard to make out.

It therefore makes more sense to focus on Europe alone. Europe is a more homogeneous place than the world as a whole, meaning that differences, especially in incomes and experience, tend to be smaller. Secondly, the data is better: Europeans have been collecting it for longer, and they have a relatively long history of transparent recordkeeping (though there are some very dodgy European statistics). Lastly, most of the world's dominant teams are grouped together in Europe, playing against pretty much the same set of opponents. It all adds up to a fairly accurate picture of how well each European team performs.

Let's first rank the best European teams on their absolute performance, without taking into account their population, experience or GDP. Taking only those games played between European teams (i.e. eliminating games where at least one team comes from outside Europe), here is the 'absolute' top 10 ranked by win percentage.

TOP 10 EUROPEAN TEAMS BY WIN PERCENTAGE, GAMES BETWEEN EUROPEAN COUNTRIES 1990–2010

	Team	Played	Won	Draws	Win %	Goal diff
1	Spain	151	0.623	0.232	0.738	1.298
2	France	157	0.592	0.274	0.729	0.955
3	Italy	166	0.542	0.295	0.690	0.729
4	Germany	159	0.585	0.208	0.689	0.925
5	Croatia	134	0.552	0.269	0.687	0.657
6	Netherlands	146	0.534	0.274	0.671	1.014
7	Czech Republic	135	0.570	0.193	0.667	0.911
8	Portugal	156	0.519	0.282	0.660	0.827
9	England	140	0.507	0.300	0.657	0.864
10	Romania	161	0.503	0.248	0.627	0.634

Bunched at the top are the four European superpowers of modern times: Spain, France, Italy and Germany. Very impressively, the Croats are only the tiniest notch behind them. For the most part, a knowledgeable fan would have been able to predict the European top 10 (with the possible exception of Romania).

However, things become more interesting after we correct for population, experience and GDP. Now a new picture emerges. We find that in Europe, home advantage boosts the home team by a little under half a goal per game, compared with two thirds of a goal in global football. Experience also counts for less in Europe than in the world in general, though it remains the most important of our key variables in winning football matches. Having twice the experience of your opponent gives you an advantage of about 30 per cent of a goal per game. By contrast, population and GDP count for more in European football than they do in global football. Having twice the population of the opposing country is worth a quarter of a goal per game in Europe. Having twice the opponent's income per capita is worth about one goal every six games. So the factors in order of importance are – 1: Playing at home.2: Experience. 3: Population. 4: GDP.

The European efficiency table (the first of its kind, as far as we know) may be the most telling we have, so let's rank every team for which we have data:

OVERACHIEVERS: RANKING OF EUROPEAN NATIONAL TEAMS, CORRECTING FOR POPULATION, WEALTH AND EXPERIENCE, ALL GAMES BETWEEN TWO EUROPEAN OPPONENTS 1990–2010

	Team	Played	Won	Drawn	Win %	Average goal difference per game	Overachievement: Actual minus expected goal difference
1	Spain	151	0.623	0.232	0.738	1.298	1.185
2	Czech Republic	135	0.570	0.193	0.667	0.911	1.010
3	Netherlands	146	0.534	0.274	0.671	1.014	0.957
4	Portugal	156	0.519	0.282	0.660	0.827	0.888
5	Croatia	134	0.552	0.269	0.687	0.657	0.840
6	Romania	161	0.503	0.248	0.627	0.634	0.769

7	France	157	0.592	0.274	0.729	0.955	0.745
8	Serbia & Montenegro	61	0.361	0.328	0.525	0.426	0.687
9	England	140	0.507	0.300	0.657	0.864	0.668
10	Sweden	170	0.494	0.265	0.626	0.671	0.622
11	Germany	159	0.585	0.208	0.689	0.925	0.615
12	Italy	166	0.542	0.295	0.690	0.729	0.504
13	Denmark	162	0.469	0.259	0.599	0.451	0.439
14	Bulgaria	136	0.419	0.250	0.544	0.257	0.439
15	Republic of Ireland	119	0.420	0.353	0.597	0.412	0.346
16	Norway	155	0.458	0.290	0.603	0.568	0.341
17	Greece	169	0.491	0.231	0.607	0.325	0.257
18	Poland	178	0.421	0.253	0.548	0.157	0.156
19	Ukraine	127	0.386	0.307	0.539	0.071	0.151
20	Switzerland	132	0.409	0.273	0.545	0.242	0.098
21	Turkey	157	0.369	0.287	0.513	0.025	-0.006
22	Israel	137	0.358	0.277	0.496	0.073	-0.017
23	Bosnia-Herzegovina	80	0.350	0.175	0.438	-0.238	-0.037
24	Slovakia	126	0.333	0.262	0.464	-0.143	-0.043
25	Russia	133	0.459	0.286	0.602	0.586	-0.066
26	Montenegro	20	0.250	0.400	0.450	-0.250	-0.130
27	Belgium	121	0.355	0.264	0.488	-0.058	-0.139
28	Finland	146	0.301	0.281	0.442	-0.144	-0.163
29	Hungary	159	0.327	0.220	0.437	-0.189	-0.202
30	Slovenia	124	0.306	0.258	0.435	-0.258	-0.211
31	Belarus	112	0.268	0.232	0.384	-0.393	-0.218
32	Latvia	151	0.272	0.205	0.374	-0.444	-0.247
33	Georgia	128	0.242	0.203	0.344	-0.570	-0.290
34	Albania	124	0.242	0.250	0.367	-0.565	-0.351
35	Lithuania	147	0.286	0.190	0.381	-0.524	-0.360
36	Austria	114	0.316	0.237	0.434	-0.263	-0.399
37	Iceland	111	0.261	0.216	0.369	-0.523	-0.558
38	Moldova	119	0.218	0.227	0.332	-0.882	-0.569
39	Armenia	93	0.140	0.215	0.247	-1.172	-0.895
40	Cyprus	133	0.271	0.165	0.353	-0.947	-1.061

41	Estonia	165	0.139	0.242	0.261	-1.309	-1.212
42	Azerbaijan	107	0.112	0.234	0.229	-1.542	-1.252
43	Kazakhstan	52	0.058	0.212	0.163	-1.462	-1.306
44	Malta	146	0.096	0.151	0.171	-1.829	-1.921
45	Luxembourg	110	0.045	0.127	0.109	-2.164	-2.715

Again, the most important number is in the last column: each country's 'relative goal difference'. It turns out that all the leading European nations – Spain, France, Germany, Italy and England – overachieve relative to their already considerable resources. These are large, well-connected countries, all of them richer than the European average. They should do well, but they are doing even better than expected. Against European opponents, each scores at least half a goal per game more than its resources would predict.

In Eastern Europe, Croatia, Romania and Serbia/Montenegro (when they were still together) have overachieved. It's no coincidence that these are all among the best-connected eastern European countries. Prague before communism was an unmistakably central European city, with many ties to Germany and Italy. Very soon after the fall of communism the Czechs had restored networks with their western neighbours. Croatia and Serbia spent the communist era in the most open communist country, Yugoslavia, which among other things sent many footballers to western clubs. And Romania was an outlier in the Soviet bloc, always resistant to the USSR's control. After the fall of the Ceaucescu communist regime, the country's Latin-derived language helped it network with western countries with similar languages.

Now that we've reviewed all the evidence, who gets the Tom Thumb trophy – the poor, small, inexperienced man's Jules Rimet – for the relatively best team on earth? Which country does best allowing for experience, population and income? Well, one day we'd like to see this played out on grass. Let's have a World Cup in which teams start with a handicap, settled by a panel of econometricians chaired by Professor Gerrard. But until that great day comes, all we have is our model. Clearly the Croats, Czechs, Iranians and Portuguese have done wonders with their modest resources. However, the country that stands out most given what it has to work with is Iraq, even taking into account its easy Asian schedule. If the country ever achieves normality, then watch out, world.

Only one great question remains: which is the relatively worst team on earth? The figure below shows the worst underperformers relative to their population, income and football experience.

WORST UNDERPERFORMERS, 1990–2010, ENTIRE WORLD (OF 116 TEAMS WITH MORE THAN 100 GAMES PLAYED)

	P	W	D	Win %	GD	U*
Luxembourg	116	120	0.050	0.142	0.121	-2.371
Malta	115	158	0.114	0.152	0.190	-1.921
Estonia	114	195	0.169	0.246	0.292	-1.158
Cyprus	113	140	0.271	0.179	0.361	-1.141
Armenia	112	106	0.160	0.217	0.269	-1.076
Azerbaijan	111	132	0.167	0.235	0.284	-1.042
Sri Lanka	110	102	0.235	0.235	0.353	-0.881
Venezuela	109	192	0.240	0.234	0.357	-0.867
Swaziland	108	112	0.205	0.295	0.353	-0.830
Benin	107	109	0.220	0.220	0.330	-0.811

*Underperformance: actual minus expected goal difference

Luxembourg is the shocker. The country of just over half a million people ought to be bad at football, but in fact it's much, much worse than it should be. That seems surprising. It's sandwiched amidst some of the best football nations on earth. If you judge by the map, Luxembourg is smack in the middle of the western European knowledge network. But networks are never simply geographical. Nobody in football wanted to network with Luxembourg because the country was too small to support a decent league or to produce many good players. Top-class foreign coaches and players were never spotted at the Jeunesse Esch grounds passing on their know-how. Admittedly, the nation's dry spell of 15 years without a win ended with Paul Koch's legendary last-minute penalty save against Malta in 1995, but even after that the Luxembourgeois hardly hit the heights. In 2001 Joel Wolff, secretary-general of the country's FA, confessed to us in a world exclusive interview: 'Let's say that we have arrived at a relative nadir.' Whenever managers recited the verity, 'There are no more minnows in international football,' they were forgetting Luxembourg.

Happily, the country has improved a touch in recent years. There was the legendary 2–1 triumph over mighty Albania at home in 2011, and the 3–2 slaying of Northern Ireland in 2013. Still, looking at our period of study, we give Luxembourg the *Soccernomics* award for the relatively worst football team on earth.

MADE IN AMSTERDAM: THE RISE OF SPAIN AND THE TRIUMPH OF EUROPEAN KNOWLEDGE NETWORKS

**On the chilly Johannesburg evening of 11 July 2010, we of
Soccernomics genuinely thought we might be within five
minutes of deciding the World Cup final.** In extra time at Soccer
City, Holland and Spain were still tied 0–0. Simon, sitting in the
media stand, was barely watching the game any more. Instead, he
was rereading on his laptop the pdf file that we had sent the Dutch
camp that morning. The file's author was Ignacio Palacios-Huerta,
the economics professor featured earlier in this book, who in 2008
had given Chelsea an analysis of Manchester United's penalty-
takers for the Champions League final.

This time Ignacio, working day and night, had given Holland an
analysis of the Spanish penalty-takers. (True, Ignacio has a Spanish

passport, but as a Basque he was perfectly happy to see Spain lose.) With a penalty shootout looming in Johannesburg, the pdf suddenly made compelling reading. For instance, Ignacio had predicted that Xavi and Andrés Iniesta, as right-footed players who didn't usually take penalties, would probably hit their kicks to the right of the Dutch keeper Maarten Stekelenburg. And Fernando Torres almost always kicked low. Against him, Stekelenburg would need to go to ground fast. 'It's a report we can use perfectly,' the Dutch goalkeeping coach Ruud Hesp had emailed us that morning. Now it looked as if we might be about to help the Dutch win the World Cup. Alternatively, if our advice was wrong, we might be about to help them lose it.

Just then, down on the field, Cesc Fàbregas found Iniesta unmarked, as if in some childhood training session on the sunny fields of Barcelona's academy. Iniesta fired home. Simon closed the pdf and began writing his match report.

For all our best efforts, Spain's win was about as inevitable as victories in World Cups get. The country once derided as eternal losers had not merely become world champions; they were also the best team in the world. (Many world champions are not.) In fact, Spain had probably been best in the world for nearly a decade before 2010. Then, in 2012, they completed an unprecedented triple of European title, world title, European title. This Spain was arguably the best national team ever. Crucially, the country owed its triumph in large part to its location in interconnected western Europe. The rise of Spain is the perfect example of our network theory: why the countries of western Europe still rule football.

Spain hadn't always been so connected. General Francisco Franco, Spain's fascist ruler from 1936 until his death in 1975, had isolated the country from the rest of Europe. Jimmy Burns, the Anglo-Spanish writer born in Madrid in 1953, recalls in his *When Beckham Went to Spain*:

... Spain was virtually a closed economy. I spent part of my childhood between England and Spain, smuggling things from
London to Madrid, never the other way round – clothes, gramo-
phone records, books and magazines. While England seemed
to be very much part of the world, Spain even to my young eyes
struck me as something of a world of its own, where kids of my
age all seemed to be taught by either priests or nuns ...

The cosmopolitan Real Madrid of Burns's childhood, studded with
imported stars like Alfredo di Stéfano (from Argentina), Ferenc
Puskás (Hungary) and Raymond Kopa (France), was very much the
exception in Franco's Spain. Few foreigners wanted to join lesser
clubs in this poor country, and those who tried to come were often
blocked. For most of the 1960s Spain officially only let in foreign
players of Spanish descent. In fact many Latin American players
invented Spanish ancestors to get in – one Argentine claimed his
father had come from 'Celta', which isn't a town at all but the name
of the club in Vigo – but even these imports didn't transform Spanish football. There weren't many of them, and they mostly weren't
very good. Nor did Spanish players of the Franco era go abroad to
learn new tricks.

Spain's isolation in those years was usually reflected in the
national team's results. Though the country won the European
Championship at home in 1964, in the period before western
Europe made its great leap in football know-how, for the next
40 years the Spaniards did almost nothing in international
tournaments.

What saved Spain's football was the country's opening to
Europe and the world. Spanish isolation began to break down in
the last years of Franco's life. In 1973, just after Spain reopened
its borders to foreign footballers, FC Barcelona imported the great
Dutchman Johan Cruijff. It is possible to draw a direct line between
Cruijff's arrival in Barcelona, and Spain's victory in Johannesburg
37 years later.

Signing Cruijff had not been easy. Franco's regime often obstructed Spanish companies from making foreign payments, and Barcelona ended up having to register the player as a piece of agricultural machinery. In another mark of the isolationist climate of the time, an elderly Barça director lamented to the club's secretary Armand Carabén: 'A Dutchman in the Nou Camp! What's the world coming to? This is pure madness. A man from the land of butter comes to the land of olive oil. Does nobody understand that even if he plays nicely, his stomach will be a mess within four days?'

But Cruijff was more than just stomach and legs. Possibly more than any other great player, he was brain, too. He was a philosopher of football, and the most important thing about football, for Cruijff, was the pass. He could (and often did) spend hours talking about the pass. You never passed into a team-mate's feet, he lectured, but always a yard in front of him, to keep the pace in the game. While the first man was passing to the second man, the third man already had to be in motion ready to receive the second man's pass. Cruijff talked people silly about the pass.

In the early 1970s he and Barcelona's Dutch manager Rinus Michels introduced Spaniards to a form of Dutch 'total football'. The two men had arrived at just the right time. Besides opening to the world, Spain was then beginning its long economic rise. Cruijff played his last game for Barcelona in 1978, but Spain would hear from him again. Much later, he would bring his ideas on football back to Catalonia. They would provide the underpinnings first of the great Barça sides, and eventually of the Spanish world champions of 2010.

Cruijff had planned to retire as a player after leaving Barcelona. However, he lost his money in a series of ill-advised ventures, most notably a pig farm, and had to start playing again. After a spell in the North American Soccer League, he finished playing at Ajax in 1984. He stayed in Amsterdam, and a year later became manager of the club that he had first entered in the early 1950s as a toddler from down the road. As manager he went to the fields where Ajax's boys' teams played, fields that had practically been his backyard, and said that everything had to change. Years before Cruijff transformed Barcelona's academy, he transformed Ajax's.

Everything he did there was the sum of a lifetime's thinking about football. Cruijff once said that before he was 30, he had done everything on instinct; but after 30, he began to understand why he did it. No longer would Ajax's youth teams aim to win matches, the club's new manager told a surprised set of volunteers. From now on, the only purpose of the youth teams would be to turn talented boys into adult stars. That meant, above all, creating two-footed players who were masters of positional play and the pass. The boys in Ajax's academy would spend much of their time playing passing games, especially Cruijff's favourite, six against three. Cruijff's long-time assistant Tonny Bruins Slot recalled in the Dutch magazine *Voetbal International* in 2011: 'Making triangles, getting a numerical advantage in midfield, speed of action in a small space, putting pressure on an opponent: everything was in there.'

For Ajax's boys' teams, even matches became practical classes. Sometimes kids were put in older age groups, where they could no longer get by on natural brilliance or speed and had to develop guile, too. Often the coaches deliberately played boys out of position. 'That began with [Dennis] Bergkamp,' said Bruins Slot. 'He was a wonderful attacker anyway and the right-back in the under-18s just wasn't good enough. So we put Dennis in that position for a while. He managed it with his fingers in his nose [a Dutch phrase meaning without any trouble]. Also, Dennis could now put himself inside the mind of a defender, which would be useful to him as a striker. That was a success, so we began to do it more often.'

Cruijff was always looking for lessons from other disciplines. An opera singer was brought in to teach Ajax's players how to breathe. In winter, when pitches were frozen, the boys attended lectures: a great female table tennis player taught them how to deal with stress; a groundsman told them how to look after their kit; and a one-time promising youngster who had never made it explained where he had gone wrong.

Cruijff ran a red thread through the entire club, from the youngest boys' 11 to the first team. Every Ajax team in every age group played the same 4-3-3 formation as the great Holland and Ajax teams of the 1970s. (Cruijff said that only with 4-3-3 could every zone on the field be occupied.) When the opposition's left-back had the ball, Ajax's players from the under-eights to the first team knew exactly which positions they had to occupy to press him. When the outside-right from the under-18s made his professional debut, he felt entirely at home. That's one reason why Cruijff happily threw kids into big European games: the 17-year-old Bergkamp turned a Swedish full-back and part-time policeman inside out one night, and returned to school in Amsterdam the next day.

And partly, it was simply that Cruijff was a born teacher. One of us, Simon, experienced it directly. When I interviewed the great man in his Barcelona mansion in 2000, he rose from his sofa and taught me how to kick with my left foot. 'Look,' he demonstrated, 'whether you kick with your right or left, the point is that you are standing on one leg. And if you stand on one leg, you fall over. So you need to adjust your balance, and the only way to do that is with your hand, your arm.' And he kicked an imaginary ball with his left foot, flinging out his right arm. Simon's left foot improved instantly.

Cruijff left Ajax in 1988 after yet another row, and stayed away until 2011, when he returned to the club as a director and spiritual godfather. However, Ajax's youth academy has always stuck to the Cruijffian model. It works. Over the last 20 years, homegrown Ajax players (including foreigners who joined the club as teenagers) have included Bergkamp, Edwin van der Sar, Frank and Ronald de Boer, Edgar Davids, Clarence Seedorf, Patrick Kluivert, Nwankwo Kanu, Zlatan Ibrahimović, Maxwell, Steven Pienaar, Christian Chivu, John Heitinga, Rafael van der Vaart, Wesley Sneijder, Nigel de Jong, Jan Vertonghen and most recently the Dane Christian Eriksen, who joined Tottenham in 2013. The CIES Football Laboratory in

Lausanne, Switzerland calculated in 2014 that Ajax had produced more footballers currently with top-division European clubs than any other club in Europe: 69 players, three more than Partizan Belgrade in second place.

In 1995 a largely homegrown Ajax team had beaten Milan in the Champions League final, with 18-year-old Kluivert scoring the winner. A few months later Simon visited Amsterdam to find out how the world could copy Ajax's model. After all, football progresses largely through international copying. Co Adriaanse, the then head of Ajax's youth academy, sat in the metal container that was his office and scoffed: 'It's not a recipe for pancakes! Other clubs don't have a club style. They don't start with kids at eight years old. They don't have the quality. And there's no continuity.'

Indeed, not even Arsène Wenger at Arsenal has managed to replicate Ajax's recipe. Something is lacking. In Wenger's years in London since 1996, Arsenal's youth teams have produced very few future stars: Ashley Cole (already nearly 16 when Wenger inherited the club), Fàbregas (16 when Wenger nabbed him from Barcelona), Gaël Clichy (nearly 18 when he came to London from France) and most recently Jack Wilshere.

Only one club has learned Ajax's recipe: Barcelona. No wonder, because Cruijff carried the recipe across in person. It's the perfect case-study of intra-European knowledge transfer. When the Dutchman moved from Amsterdam to the Nou Camp as head coach in 1988, he did something that few Barça coaches had ever done before: he went to the fields where Barcelona's youth teams played. There he saw a skinny kid in central midfield hitting perfect passes. 'Take that boy off at half-time,' he told the boy's coach. 'Why?' asked the coach. 'Because I'm putting him in the first team,' said Cruijff. The skinny kid, whose name was Pep Guardiola, spent a decade in Barcelona's first team. From 2008 to 2012 Guardiola managed the Spanish, European and world champions. He once said: 'Johan Cruijff taught me the most. I worked six years with him and learned a terrific amount.'

Guardiola was only the latest in a line of Cruijffians in the Nou Camp. His predecessor, Frank Rijkaard, was an Amsterdammer and an Ajax man. Rijkaard got the Barcelona job on Cruijff's recommendation despite having recently been relegated from the Dutch premier division with Sparta Rotterdam. Louis van Gaal, Barcelona's coach from 1997 to 2000, was also an Amsterdammer and Ajax man, though he had absolutely not got the job on Cruijff's recommendation. Van Gaal had played for Ajax in the early 1970s at the same time as Cruijff, but only in the second team. Van Gaal appears to have harboured a jealousy of Cruijff ever since. Though the personal feud between the two men has amused Dutch fans for years, both of them think almost exactly the same about football. When Van Gaal came to Barcelona, he cemented the club's veneration of the pass. He advanced the careers of great passing kids like Xavi and Iniesta. Van Gaal and later Rijkaard didn't always win on the field, but they continued the transfer of Dutch know-how to Catalonia that Cruijff had begun in 1973.

When Guardiola became Barcelona's head coach, he updated and perfected Cruijffism. How this works was explained to us in 2009 by Albert Capellas, then coordinator of Barça's youth academy. We met Capellas over beers in a Swiss hotel bar. A couple of weeks later, he was giving us a tour of the 'Masia', or farmhouse, the unlikely headquarters of Barça's academy until the little brick building with the sundial on the front was finally closed in 2011.

The day we visited the Masia, in October 2009, you could simply walk in off the street. There were no guards. Inside you got a coffee and a friendly welcome at the bar. It felt like the house of a large Catholic family. A delivery-man stopped by and carried an enormous ham into the kitchen. There was a room with foosball and billiard tables, but when we visited they were covered, because the boys in the Masia had to study for school. The doors to the garden were open, to let the sun flood in. In the garden stood a sculpture of a female body, which must have provoked the odd stray thought among the Masia's all-male residents.

From the upstairs windows of the Masia, you could look out on to the Nou Camp. You could almost touch it here. The boys of the Masia actually slept in the stadium; the little farmhouse had got too small to house them.

But that morning, nine months before the World Cup in South Africa kicked off, the Masia still felt as cosy as the canteen at Ajax's old home, the now destroyed little De Meer stadium. Both places resembled neighbourhood cafés, where men gathered for fellowship and coffee. Part of Ajax and Barcelona's secret is that they are local clubs, run by largely the same bunch of local men for decades. These locals are interested in the talented kids of today, because in ten years' time, when the kids will be in the first team, the locals expect still to be around.

When the staff sat down to explain how the Masia worked, you felt as if you were being transported back to Amsterdam in 1985. For a start, said Capellas, Barça's youth teams all played the same 4-3-3 as the first team. When the opposition's left-back had the ball, Barça's players from the under-eights to the first team knew exactly which positions they had to occupy to press him. When the outside-right from the under-18s made his professional debut, he felt entirely at home. That was one reason why Barcelona happily threw kids into big games: Iniesta, Xavi and Lionel Messi were all playing regularly in the world's biggest stadium while still in their teens.

There were a lot of things the Masia didn't worry about. Until players reached their mid-teens, said Capellas, 'we don't think about competition, or not so much'. As at Ajax, boys' matches were treated as practical classes. The Masia didn't care about size either. Nobody minded that Messi and Iniesta were short. Capellas said: 'If he's small or if he's tall, for us that is not important. We don't test for physical capacities. We are always thinking about the technical and tactical capacities of each player.' The players barely ever did fitness training without the ball. Even speed was of limited relevance. Guardiola, a slow runner, had moved the ball fastest.

Nor did the boys train much. Ninety minutes a day was enough, Capellas told us. Schoolwork took up much more of their time, because like Ajax, Barcelona knew that most of its players would never turn pro. This was not a ruthless corporation. 'We treat our 50 boys like our family,' said Pep Boade, Barça's grizzled old chief scout, and this didn't appear to be cant. Many youth academies are ruled by militaristic brutes, but Barça's coaches sounded like traditional Catholic mothers. When a boy was cut from the Masia, sometimes his rival would cry from guilt at having been better. Capellas said: 'Messi and Iniesta don't live here any more, but this is their home, they come by to eat; if they have a problem they come to talk to us, as they would to a mother or father. For us they are not stars. It's Leo, it's Bojan, it's Andrés. Andrés is humble. We say: "You are a good man, you are an incredible person, don't lose your values."'

In one regard, though, the Masia was hyper-professional. What mattered to Barça, as to Ajax, was passing. Both academies fetishised the pass. Football, to Cruijff, was about making passing 'triangles' on the pitch. If a player could do that, Cruijff picked him. That remains Barça's principle. Capellas recited the mantra: 'Always the players must find triangles.' Training, then, is a deep study of passing.

To pass, or to stop the other team from passing, you also need to know exactly where to be. The average player has the ball for only 53.4 seconds a match (according to Chris Carling, the English performance analyst at Lille in France), so any player's main job is to occupy the right positions for the other 89 minutes and 6.6 seconds. The boys in the Masia spent a lot of time playing four against four, with two touches of the ball allowed, and with three 'joker' players who join whichever team has the ball. You win this game by being in the right position: football as a sort of chess, rather than football as physical combat. In the sun of the Masia, just as at Ajax's youth complex De Toekomst ('The Future'), where the chill wind sweeps in off the highway, some great future players spent the mornings of their youth making Cruijffian triangles.

Our tour of the Masia ended in the dining room, where in late morning you could already smell a tasty lunch. 'Home cooking,' Capellas noted. On the plain, whitewashed walls were pictures of Masia teams past. Capellas and Boade found the picture from 1988, with an absurdly skinny young Guardiola. Two other boys in the photo later became his assistant coaches at Barça. One of them, Tito Vilanova, would succeed him as head coach in 2012 before resigning a year later because of throat cancer.

Guardiola was another part of the Masia's secret. The academy produced the boys; he sent them onto the field in the stadium next door. Capellas said: 'When we play Real Madrid's youth teams, we are equal. Don't think Real doesn't have good youth players.' Yet Real's boys rarely make the first team, because Madrid keeps buying stars. By contrast, Guardiola, like Cruijff, was a man of the club who knew exactly what was cooking in the Masia, even in the second-string youth teams.

'You have to have someone up there who says, "Go in,"' said Capellas. That was easy when the kid is as good as Messi or Iniesta. But Guardiola had done the same with Pedro, not an obvious star, and he stuck him in the first team. In the sun outside the Masia, Capellas used his foot to draw a circle on the ground: Guardiola had gone from the Masia to the first team and then recruited from the Masia again. The circle was round, said Capellas.

Barça have been lucky, the club's then chief executive Joan Oliver admitted to us in 2009. 'Yeah, good fortune exists always in the world, in every kind of industry. It's not possible always to guarantee that we will have a Messi or an Iniesta or a Xavi from the academy. Perhaps you could not get the best player of the world from your academy, but we get six, seven first-team players.' That is not to mention Masia exports such as José Reina and Mikel Arteta.

FROM THE MASIA TO JOHANNESBURG

In short, once Spain's isolation had been lifted in the last years of Franco's regime, Barcelona began building a style based on know-ledge transfer from Amsterdam. Eventually Spain adopted this made-in-Amsterdam game. At Euro 2008 and again at the World Cup in South Africa, the Spaniards often looked as if they were still making their triangles at morning practice at the Masia. They passed the ball up and down like little men filling in a crossword puzzle at top speed. Whenever they went 1–0 up, they simply made sure the opponent never got the ball again. The World Cup final was the 44th straight game in which Spain had won after scoring first. Everyone knew exactly how the men in red played, yet it was impossible to beat them because they had become Cruijffian masters of the pass.

Spain became a great football nation because it joined European knowledge networks. This might sound like too neat a theory – the sort of thing you get when you let academics loose on something as mysterious and intuitive as football. Luckily, though, the facts seem to match our theory. Let's look at Spain's results, decade by decade:

THE RISE OF SPAIN

Decade	P	W	D	L	% Won	Win %*
1920s	32	23	4	5	0.72	0.78
1930s	25	13	5	7	0.52	0.62
1940s	19	8	6	5	0.42	0.58
1950s	44	20	13	11	0.45	0.60
1960s	60	28	13	19	0.47	0.58
1970s	59	29	18	12	0.49	0.64
1980s	103	49	28	26	0.48	0.61
1990s	98	57	26	15	0.58	0.71
2000s	128	91	25	12	0.71	0.81

*Including draws as half a win

We'll take the 1920s as an illustration of what this table shows. Spain won 23 of their 32 matches in the decade, or 72 per cent. They also tied four games. If we count a draw as worth half a win, then Spain's total winning percentage for the decade was 78. That figure in the last column for each decade is the most telling one. It provides the best measure of Spain's success decade by decade.

The table demonstrates how closely Spain's footballing success tracks the country's integration with Europe. In the 1920s, before the civil war of the 1930s, Spain performed very well. But then isolation descended under Franco. From the 1930s through the 1980s, Spain's winning percentage hovered around a disappointing 60. The team was winning about half its games, and drawing another quarter. That European Championship of 1964 was an anomaly. The broader story was that a poor, shut-off Spain was struggling to access the world's best football know-how. Spain's football history in these sorry decades was summed up in a phrase by Di Stéfano, the Argentinian turned Colombian turned Spanish international: 'We played like never before, and lost like always.'

But in 1986 Spain joined the European Union – a sort of formal entry into European networks. Soon afterwards, the Spanish national team improved sharply. We have seen that a country's success at football correlates with its wealth. And Spain from the 1980s was growing richer fast. In the 1960s and 1970s its income per capita had been stuck at about 60 per cent of the average of the core 15 member nations of the EU. In the 1980s and 1990s Spain began to catch up. The Barcelona Olympics of 1992 nicely captured the rise: the Games showcased a 'new Spain', and a young Spanish football team guided by 21-year-old Pep Guardiola won gold.

Yet during this period the Spaniards continued to be mocked in international football as 'notorious underperformers'. Like England, they just couldn't match the big nations in big tournaments. However, the criticism was wrong. Even in these 'bad' decades Spain was already overachieving, given its modest resources of people and wealth. It was simply not big or rich or connected enough to expect to match the leading nations in football.

Let's take the relatively recent period from 1980 to 2001. For Spain this was a fallow era: failure in a World Cup hosted at home, and no performance of note save an appearance in the final of Euro 1984, which is remembered chiefly for goalkeeper Luis Arconada's fumbling of Michel Platini's free-kick.

In absolute terms Spain's winning percentage (counting ties as half a win) of about 66 per cent in that period ranked it somewhere near the bottom of the global top ten, around the same level as England. But we want to measure Spain's relative performance: how it achieved relative to its resources.

First, let's look at experience. By 2001, Spain had played 461 internationals in its history. That itself is a marker of isolation. We've seen that, according to Russell's data, Sweden by 2001 was the most experienced country in international football, with 802 internationals. England, Argentina, Hungary, Brazil and Germany (including West but not East Germany) had all played over 700 each. Spain – cut off for so many years – lagged.

When it comes to our second variable, wealth, Spain still fell short of most of its rivals. In the 1980s and 1990s it was significantly behind Germany, France, England and even Italy.

And Spain's population was small. When people complain that the country underperforms, they usually mean it does worse than the giants of international football. Well, no wonder, given that Spain is much smaller than they are. Not only did Brazil in 1990 dwarf Spain's then population of 39 million people, but so did Germany, France, Italy and even that other 'notorious underachiever' England.

We calculated that Spain, given its population, income and experience in the 1980–2001 period, 'should' have scored on average 0.3 goals per game more than its opponents. But Spain did much better than that: it averaged nearly 0.6 goals more than expected. Of the teams that played at least 100 games in this period, Spain was the eighth best overperformer in the world. The country was an overachiever long before it began winning prizes. Until very recently, it just wasn't quite big or rich or experienced or lucky enough to win anything.

Consider for instance its record against Italy in those years. Over the period Spain's population, income per head and international experience were on average about 30 per cent inferior to Italy's. Given that, we would have expected Spain's goal difference to be about minus two over its four games against Italy. Instead Spain overachieved, notching a win, two ties and a defeat with a goal difference of zero.

In short, Spain's bad times were not bad at all. It always was overachieving. But in the last 20 years or so, even taking into account the recent economic crisis, Spain's resources have improved. Since joining the EU, the country's average income has risen to about three-quarters of the core EU's average. Its population has grown to 47 million. Spain has also become fully networked in Europe. Its best footballers now experience the Champions League every season. A richer, more populous, more experienced and more networked Spain became first a serious contender and finally (thanks to its continued overachievement) the best team on earth.

Wealth, size and integration have translated into goals. In the 1990s Spain's win percentage (still treating draws as worth half a win) shot up to over 70 per cent. In the 2000s it was over 80 per cent, with Spain losing just 12 per cent of its games. From 2000 to 2009 the country won 71 per cent of its matches outright, a long-term performance about as good as any other national team's since international football took off in the 1930s. Brazil never managed it. Even the all-conquering Italy of the 1930s won just 70 per cent of its games that decade. Spain had become a great team long before it won titles. Here is Wayne Rooney in his autobiography describing a Spain–England friendly in 2004, a time when the Spaniards were still considered eternal losers:

Spain had been taking the mickey, passing the ball back and forth, and showboating, which upset me. When that happens, you have to try and break up your opponents' passing game by getting stuck into them, tackling hard and quickly. Perhaps I overdid it because I was so frustrated, but we couldn't get a kick of the ball. Not nice.

Of course, the emergence from isolation cannot by itself explain Spain's success. Intangibles matter too – the sudden emergence of several great individuals like Xavi and David Villa, for instance. Spain was the only team at the 2010 World Cup with as strong a personnel as the best club teams. No other country in the tournament fielded 11 players who were starters at big clubs. Spain was massively over-performing in relation to its size and wealth, but that overperformance was possible only because of the end of isolation. Nor has the crash of 2008 hurt the Spanish team. Despite the recession, the collapse of property prices and unemployment of over 20 per cent, Spain has remained networked with the rest of Europe.

It was wonderfully appropriate that the Spaniards sealed their rise in a World Cup final against their mentor country. This was the Cruijff versus Cruijff final. Probably for the first time, both teams in football's biggest game were, in their origins, the product of one man. It was a triumph of intra-European knowledge transfer. That night in Johannesburg, the old Amsterdammer living in Barcelona must have felt like the proud father of twins – albeit that the Dutch twin behaved like a fratricidal delinquent.

Seven of the 14 Spaniards who played in the match had spent time in the Cruijffian Masia; seven of the 14 Dutchmen had come from Ajax's Cruijffian academy. One of those seven Dutchmen, Eljero Elia, had never even made it into Ajax's first team. Khalid Boulahrouz and André Ooijer, who sat on the Dutch bench that night, were also rejects of the Ajax academy. When even your dropouts are staffing the second-best national squad on earth, you are doing pretty well. Not as well as the Spaniards, though. Had Spain been able to field just one other product of the Masia – and when the Argentine Messi was a boy the Spaniards had begged him to play for their national youth teams – FIFA could have dispensed with the World Cup altogether and simply handed Spain the trophy at a quick ceremony in Zurich.

The Holland–Spain final was best understood as 'Jungian mirroring', summed up David Winner, author of *Brilliant Orange: The Neurotic Genius of Dutch Football*. 'Holland's path to the world title is blocked by the more authentic version of their better selves. It is now Spain who play Dutch football.' That is how Cruijff saw it too. 'I thought my country would never dare to play like this and would never give up its own way of playing,' he said after the game.

> Even without great players like in the past, a team has its own style. I had the wrong end of the stick … They didn't want the ball. And unfortunately, and it's hard to say so, they played dirty. So bad that they really should quickly have been down to nine men. Then they made two such mean tackles that I felt the pain myself. This nasty, vulgar, hard, closed game that wasn't watchable and was barely football any more – yes, with that they could trouble Spain. They played anti-football.

But perhaps Holland had to, because Spain were now better at football. The Dutch had taught the Spaniards how to play, just as in the Eighty Years' War between the Netherlands and Spain (1568–1648) the Dutch had sold arms to the Spaniards. In Johannesburg Holland paid for it.

CORE TO PERIPHERY: THE FUTURE MAP OF GLOBAL FOOTBALL

On a snowy night in Amsterdam, a dozen or so Dutch football writers and ex-players have gathered in a flat in the dinky city centre. Guus Hiddink walks in, and grabs someone's shoulders from behind by way of greeting. Growing up with five brothers gave him a knack for the right matey gesture. (Hiddink appears to be equally relaxed with women, and his cohabitation with his then mistress in Seoul shocked Koreans.)

The evening starts with a football quiz, at which the future manager of Chelsea, Russia and Turkey performs indifferently. Then there is food and football talk until the early morning. Though Hiddink is the senior figure at table, he never tries to dominate. He likes telling stories – about his former player Romario, or his old teammate at the San José Earthquakes, George Best – but when others interrupt he is just as happy to lean back in his chair and listen. He is a solid, soothing, jowly presence. 'You can feel he's at ease,' Boudewijn Zenden, one of his former players, told us, 'so if he's at ease, the others are at ease. He creates this environment where you feel safe.'

Hiddink – a great success as coach until 2008, less so in his declining years – has a special place in the latest stage of football's history. In the twenty-first century, he became one of the world's main exporters of football know-how from western Europe to the margins of the earth. We saw in chapter 16 that from about 1970 to 2000, the six founding members of the European Economic Community dominated football thinking and won almost all the game's prizes. These countries perfected what you might call the EEC style: a fast, physical, collectivist football.

But then these countries began exporting their expertise. Hiddink and other Dutch, German, French and Italian expat managers established themselves in Hiltons and westerners' compounds around the planet. In the last few years they have helped several new football countries – Russia, Australia, South Korea, Turkey and Greece to name a few – catch up with the managers' own native countries. It's because of men like these that England will not be the best football country of the future. Hiddink's native Holland appear even more thoroughly doomed. On the new map of football, which Hiddink helped to draw, his own country will shrink to a dot.

FROM THE BACK CORNER TO THE WORLD

Born in 1946, Hiddink grew up close to what was then just becoming the epicentre of global football knowledge. He is the son of a village schoolteacher and Resistance hero from a small town in the Achterhoek, or 'Back Corner', about 5 miles from the German border. The Back Corner is wooded and quiet, one of the few empty bits of the Netherlands, and on visits home from stints in Seoul or Moscow, Hiddink enjoys tootling along its back roads on his Harley Davidson Fatboy. 'Pom-pom-pom-pom-pom,' he goes, puffing out his cheeks to mimic the motor's roar.

He grew up milking cows, ploughing behind two horses, and dreaming of becoming a farmer. But Dutch farms were already shedding labour, and he became a football coach instead. At 19 he took an assistant's job at the Back Corner's semi-professional club, De Graafschap, where his father had played before him. He then made an unusual career move: from coach to player. The head coach, seeing that his young assistant could kick a ball, stuck him in the team, and thus began a 16-year playing career.

The handsome, round-faced, wavy-haired playmaker was too lazy and slow for the top, yet he was present at a golden age. The Dutch sides of the 1970s shaped Hiddink. Holland, playing what foreigners called 'total football', a new kind of game in which players constantly swapped positions and thought for themselves, reached two World Cup finals. Dutch clubs won four European Cups. Off the pitch, Dutch players of Hiddink's generation would answer foreign journalists' questions with sophisticated discourses in several languages. For a keen observer like Hiddink, the players' constant squabbles provided object lessons in how to keep stars just about functioning within a collective.

Dutch football's renown at the time helped even a second-rate player like Hiddink find work abroad, with the Washington Diplomats and the San José Earthquakes. 'I was Best's roommate,' says Hiddink, enjoying the quirky American word, and he mimics himself fielding the phone calls from Best's groupies: 'George is not here. George is sleeping.'

It was the start of a world tour whose recent destinations have included South Korea, Australia, a suite in a five-star hotel in Moscow (where, according to the president of the Russian FA, he spent a fortune ordering cappuccinos from room service) and Istanbul. Hiddink got the Koreans playing the best football in their history at the World Cup of 2002, the Australians playing their best in 2006, and the Russians at Euro 2008.

True, he then failed to take the Russians to the World Cup of 2010 and the Turks to Euro 2012. There are signs that after passing sixty he has lost some of his drive. Moreover, once almost all countries began trying to acquire western European know-how, he lost some of his first-mover advantage. Nonetheless, Hiddink and other expat western European coaches like him are helping to shift power in football from their own region to the rest of the world. It's no coincidence that this is happening just as economic power shifts in the same direction.

1889–2002: OFF THE PLANE WITH A LEATHER FOOTBALL

Football seems to have a quality that enables it eventually to conquer every known society. The first wave of exporters of the game were Victorian British sailors, businessmen, missionaries and colonial officers. In 1889, to cite a typical story, the 21-year-old Englishman Frederick Rea disembarked on the island of South Uist off the west coast of Scotland to work as a headmaster. A couple of years later two of his brothers visited, carrying with them a leather football. Within two decades the game had conquered South Uist. Shinty, a stick sport that had been played there for 1,400 years, 'was wiped like chalk from the face of the island', wrote Roger Hutchinson in the British football journal *Perfect Pitch* in 1998, 'supplanted, like a thousand of its distant relatives from Buenos Aires to Smolensk, by a game almost as young and innocent as Frederick Rea himself'. Today football is the dominant sport on South Uist. It conquered because of its magic.

Victorian Britons spread the game to continental Europe, Latin America and bits of Africa. However, for a century Asia and North America remained almost immune. Contrary to myth, football took a long time to become a global game. What people called the 'World Cup' should until the 1980s have been called 'the Euro–Latin American Duopoly'. Though most people on the planet lived in Asia, the continent's only representative at the World Cup of 1978 was Iran. Even in 1990 the British Isles had more teams at the World Cup (three) than all of Asia combined (two). Many Asian countries still barely knew about football. When that year's World Cup final was shown on Japanese television, there was a surprising studio guest: the baseball player Sadaharu Oh. 'Mr Oh,' he was asked during the match, 'what is the difference between sliding in baseball and in soccer?' In Australia, too, soccer was then still marginal. Johnny Warren, an Australian international and later TV commentator on the game, called his memoirs *Sheilas, Wogs and Poofters*, because, according to Australian myth in the years before Hiddink landed there, those were the three core elements of the national soccer public.

But by 1990 the so-called 'third wave of globalisation' was under way. Increased world trade, cable television, and finally the internet brought football to new territories. Roberto Fontanarrosa, the late Argentine cartoonist, novelist and soccer nut, said: 'If TV were only an invention to broadcast football, it would be justified.'

Suddenly the Chinese, Japanese, Americans and even many urban Indians could see football's magic. They saw it even more clearly than the people of Uist had a century before. Football by now had the prestige of being the world's biggest sport, and everyone wanted a piece of its fans' passion. Football is often mocked for its low scores, but precisely because goals are so scarce, the release of joy is greater than in other sports. When the former goalkeeper Osama bin Laden visited London in 1994, he watched four Arsenal matches, bought souvenirs for his sons in the club shop, and remarked that he had never seen as much passion as among football supporters.

Just then football was capturing the last holdouts. On 15 May 1993, Japan's J-League kicked off. The next year China acquired a national professional league, and in 1996 the US and India followed. The new marginal countries began to hire European coaches who could quickly teach them the latest in football.

By the turn of the millennium, Hiddink was an obvious candidate for export. He had won the European Cup with PSV Eindhoven, had managed clubs in Turkey and Spain, and had taken Holland to the World Cup semi-final in 1998. After he passed 50, he felt his ambition begin to wane. Never a workaholic to start with, the boy from the Back Corner had by now proved himself. He had met with triumph and disaster and treated those two imposters just the same. He had gone from villager to cosmopolitan. He had fallen in love with golf. Football was becoming just a hobby.

He took a break, and in 2001 popped up in his first missionary posting, as manager of South Korea. As part of the globalisation of football, the country was due to co-host the 2002 World Cup with Japan. South Korea had played in several World Cups before, but had never won a single match, and in 1998 had lost 5–0 to Hiddink's Holland.

When Hiddink landed in Seoul, history was beginning to work in his favour. Like many emerging nations, the South Koreans were getting bigger. Thanks to increased wealth, the average height of a South Korean man had risen from 1.63 metres (5ft 4in) in the 1930s to about 1.73 metres (5ft 8in) by 2002. That meant a bigger pool of men with the physique required to play international football. In an interview during a Korean training camp in the Back Corner, a year before the World Cup, Hiddink told us he'd caught Koreans using their smallness as an excuse in football. 'But I won't allow that,' he added. 'I won't let them say beforehand, "They're a bit bigger and broader, we're small and sad." And gradually, I notice that some of our players are big too, and know how to look after themselves.' The 'height effect' was also quietly lifting many other emerging football countries, from China to Turkey.

But the Koreans had other problems. The Dutch psychological quirk had been squabbling. The Korean disease, as Hiddink soon discovered, was hierarchy. In Korean football, the older the player, the higher his status. A 31-year-old veteran international was so respected that he could coast. At meals, the group of older players would sit down at table first, and the youngest last.

Whereas Dutch players talked too much, Koreans were practically mute. 'Slavishness is a big word,' Hiddink said that day in the Back Corner, 'but they do have something like: "If the commander says it, we'll follow it blindly." They are used to thinking, "I'm a soldier, I'll do what's asked of me." And you have to go a step further if you want to make a team really mature. You need people who can and will take the team in their hands.' Hiddink wanted autonomous, thinking, 'Dutch' players: a centre-half who at a certain point in the game sees he should push into midfield, a striker who drops back a few yards. He was teaching the Koreans the Dutch variant of the EEC style.

Hiddink said of his players: 'Commitment is not their problem. Almost too much. But if your commitment is too high, you often lose the strategic overview.'

Hiddink had started out in Korea by kicking a couple of the older players out of his squad. He made a young man captain. He asked his players to make their own decisions on the field. 'That makes them a bit freer, easier,' he said. Shortly before the World Cup, he brought back the jilted older players, who by then were pretty motivated.

However, the educational process in Korea was always a two-way one. During his 18 months in the country, Hiddink learnt a few things himself. Already during his stints in Turkey and Spain, he had begun freeing himself from the national superiority complex that pervades Dutch football: the belief that the Dutch way is the only way. In Holland, football is a thinking man's game. When the Dutch talk about it, the concepts to which they always return are '*techniek*' and '*tactiek*'. '*Passie*', or passion, was a quality they associated with unsophisticated footballers from unsophisticated countries, like England. In Korea, Hiddink learnt that it was actually pretty important. Even when speaking Dutch he tends to describe this quality with the English word 'commitment', perhaps because there is no obvious Dutch equivalent.

He had also learnt what every successful missionary knows: respect the native way of life, or at least pretend to, because otherwise the natives won't listen to you. That afternoon in the Back Corner he said, 'I don't go to work on the culture of the country. I just leave it, I respect it. I only do something about the conditions that they need to perform on the pitch. And of course there are a couple of things off the field that do influence that.'

At the 2002 World Cup the Koreans played with a fervour rarely seen in football. Helped by bizarre refereeing decisions, the country from football's periphery reached the semi-final.

Korea had craved global recognition, and Hiddink delivered it. His autobiography in Korean reportedly sold more than 160,000 copies in the first month of publication. Altogether in 2002, 37 books with Hiddink's name in the title appeared in Korean, most of them in the self-help genre. In the Back Corner, Korean tour buses made pilgrimages to the Hiddink ancestral home. Soon after the World Cup, the man himself dropped by to visit his octogenarian parents. 'Well, it wasn't bad,' admitted his father. 'Coffee?'

2002–2004: THE PERIPHERY TAKES OVER INTERNATIONAL FOOTBALL

During that World Cup of 2002, other peripheral football countries were emerging too. Japan reached the second round, the US got to the quarters, and Korea's conquerors in the match for third place were Turkey, which hadn't even played in a World Cup since 1954.

We said in chapter 16 that a country's success in football correlates strongly with three variables: its population, its income per capita, and its experience in international football. For Turkey, as for many other emerging countries, all three variables were improving fast.

From 1980 to 2001, Turkey were the second-worst underperformers in European football. They scored a full goal per game fewer than they should have done given their vast population, their decent experience in international football, and their admittedly low incomes.

But just as that period was ending, the Turks were improving. It is no coincidence that the country went from being a pathetic football team to occasional contenders at the same time as it grew from a mid-sized European state into the continent's third-most populous nation. Turkey had 19 million inhabitants in 1945, double that by

1973 and over 80 million by 2013. In Europe, only Russia and Germany have more. While Turkey's population grows, most European countries are losing people. Add several million Turks in the diaspora, and the youth of most Turks, and the country starts to rival even Germany in its football potential. And Turkey is just one of many developing countries whose population is fast outstripping those of rich countries.

At the same time Turkey's economy was booming, and it was using some of the new money to import football knowledge. In chapter 16 we had measured a country's football experience by how many matches its national team had played. However, there is a shortcut to gaining experience: import it. This process began for Turkey in June 1984, when West Germany got knocked out of the European Championship. The Germans sacked their coach, Jupp Derwall. That year he joined Galatasaray, and began to import the EEC style of football into Turkey.

Derwall and other German coaches (as well as the Englishman Gordon Milne at Beşiktaş) got Turkish players actually working. They also introduced the novel idea of training on grass. Turkish television began showing foreign matches, which introduced some Turkish viewers to the concept of the pass.

Before Derwall's arrival, the average Turkish footballer had been a selfish midget dribbler. Derwall shipped German-born Turks into Galatasaray. The German Turks were bigger than Turkish Turks, thanks to a better diet, and they trained like Germans. Admittedly, soon after arrival in Istanbul they were exposed to the sultanesque harem lifestyle of many Turkish footballers, and their game deteriorated, but it was a start. Diaspora Turks – from Germany, France, but also the Londoner Colin Kazim-Richards at Euro 2008 – have continued to give Turkey a fast track to European football know-how. No other national team in Europe includes as many players who grew up in other European countries.

In 1996 Turkey qualified for their first major tournament since 1954. Though they didn't score a goal or register a point at Euro 96, they were judged to have done quite well. They have since reached two semis and a quarter-final at major tournaments.

Despite a fallow period after 2008, globalisation has improved Turkish football. In the 1990s Turks came to the realisation – as every marginal country needs to – that there is only one way to play good football: you combine Italian defending with German work ethic and Dutch passing into the EEC style. ('Industrial football,' some Turks sulkily call it.) In football, national styles don't work. You have to have all the different elements. You cannot win international matches playing traditional Turkish football. You need to play EEC football.

Both Hiddink's experiences and Turkey's point to an important truth: in football, 'culture' doesn't matter much. Turkey may well have had 'a different culture, a different approach, a different way of life', as the French grandee Giscard d'Estaing said when he drafted the European Union's failed constitution, but it didn't stop the Turks in football. Cultures are not eternal and unalterable. When they have an incentive to change – like the prospect of winning more football matches, or perhaps the prospect of getting richer – they can change.

Turkey was only one of many countries brave enough to jettison its traditional football culture. Most countries on the fringes of Europe had dysfunctional indigenous playing styles. The ones on the southern fringe – Greece, Turkey, Portugal – favoured pointless dribbling, while the British and Scandinavians played kick-and-rush. Gradually they came to accept that these styles didn't work.

Nobody did better out of abandoning their roots and adopting EEC football than Turkey's friends across the water, the Greeks. The Greek national team had traditionally played terrible football in front of a couple of thousand spectators. During foreign trips, their camp followers – friends, journalists and miscellaneous – would hang around the team hotel drinking espressos with players until the early morning. When Greece somehow made it to the World Cup of 1994, they ended up regretting it. At their training sessions outside Boston, an outfield player would stand in goal while the others blasted shots into the bushes. They spent most of the tournament travelling the East Coast of the US to receptions with Greek–Americans, though they did find time to be thrashed in three matches. In 2002 Greece gave up on the Greek style and imported a vast chunk of experience in the person of an ageing German manager, Otto Rehhagel.

The Rhinelander was the prototype post-war West German collectivist. He had grown up a healthy drive across the border from Hiddink, amid the ruins of post-war western Germany. An apprentice housepainter and bone-hard defender, Rehhagel was brought up on the 'German virtues' of hard work and discipline. As a coach in Germany for decades, he aimed to sign only collectivist, EEC-type players whose personality had been vetted by his wife over dinner in the Rehhagel home. Everywhere he tried to build an organisation. Sacked as manager of Arminia Bielefeld, he sighed: 'At least thanks to me there is now a toilet at the training ground.' On later visits to Bielefeld with other clubs, he always enquired after his toilet.

Rehhagel quickly rooted out Greece's cult of the soloist, introduced EEC football, and took the team to Euro 2004 in Portugal. There he went around saying things like, 'Now that I am coaching Greece, I want to make one philosophical statement. Please write it down: Man needs nothing more than other people.' Banal as this sounded, it must have resonated in post-war West Germany. Certainly the Greek players, who pre-Rehhagel never seemed to have heard of collective spirit, had begun preaching the notion in many languages. 'We was very good organised,' said Zisis Vryzas after Greece beat France in the quarter-finals. Angelos Charisteas, the reserve at Werder Bremen who would become the highest scorer of Euro 2004, eulogised: 'We have a German coach, he has a German mentality, and we play like a German team.' In fact, Greece had made the same journey as Turkey: from midget dribblers to boring EEC football thanks to German coaching.

Rehhagel himself called it 'learning from European football'. At the time, becoming 'European' – code for becoming organised –

was the aspiration of many marginal European countries, in football and outside. Just as these countries were joining the European Union, they were absorbing EEC football. The final of Euro 2004 pitted Greece against another recently marginal country. The Greeks beat the Portuguese 1–0 thanks to another header from Charisteas, who soon afterwards would be a reserve again at Ajax. It turned out that with merely half-decent players, a good EEC coach and time to prepare, almost any marginal country could do well.

2005-2006: EVEN AUSTRALIA

In this new climate, the best EEC coaches could pick their posts. Hiddink received many offers to take teams to the World Cup of 2006, but he chose the most marginal country of all: Australia.

In 1974, while Hiddink was still absorbing total football in the Back Corner, Australia had qualified for its first World Cup as Asia's sole representatives. The Socceroos of the day were part-timers, and some had to give up their jobs to go to Germany. The German press was particularly interested in the milkman-cum-defender Manfred Schaefer, who had been born in Hitler's Reich in 1943 and emigrated to Australia as a child refugee after the war. At one point in the tournament West Germany's striker Gerd Müller asked him if he really was an amateur. Well, Schaefer proudly replied, he had earned $4,600 by qualifying for the World Cup. 'That's what I earn a week,' said Müller.

The Australians achieved one draw in three matches at the World Cup. 'However,' writes Matthew Hall in his excellent book about Australian soccer, *The Away Game*, 'their thongs, super-tight Aussie Rules-style shorts and marsupial mascots endeared them to the German public.'

In the next 30 years, soccer sank so low in Australia that the country's soccer federation was sometimes reduced to filming its own matches and giving them to TV channels for free. Australian club football was punctuated by weird vendettas between Balkan ethnic groups. Only in 1997, during the new wave of globalisation, were the Socceroos of 1974 publicly honoured in their own country.

Then, in 2005, Hiddink landed with a mission to teach EEC football. First he gathered the Australian team in a training camp in his native Back Corner. His first impression: 'What a bunch of vagabonds. Everyone came in wearing a cap, or flip-flops. One had on long trousers, another shorts, and another Bermuda shorts. I said, "What is this?" "Well, that's how we live." "Hello, but you probably play like that too."'

Hiddink spent Australia's first training session in the Back Corner watching his new charges fly into each other like kamikaze pilots. 'You don't have to chase these guys up,' he remarked. After half an hour he stopped the game. When the players' cries of 'Come on, Emmo!', 'Hold the ball, Johnno!', 'Let's go!' and the streams of 'Fucking' had finally faded, Hiddink asked them to shout only when a teammate was in trouble and needed coaching. That would improve everyone's vision of play, he said. The game resumed in near silence. It was Australia's first baby step towards EEC football.

Just as he had with the Koreans, Hiddink was turning the Australians into Dutch footballers. That meant giving them the intellectual discipline needed for the World Cup. The Australian way was to train hard, play hard, but then relax with late-night beers in the hotel bar. Hiddink wanted the players thinking on their own about their jobs. Working hard wasn't enough. Since the Australians already had 'commitment' and *passie*, Hiddink was teaching them to think like Dutchmen. The Socceroos tended to run to wherever the ball was. Hiddink forbade them from entering certain zones. In EEC football, doing the right things is always better than doing lots of things.

He had noticed at the Confederations Cup of 2005, shortly before he took over, where the Socceroos had lost all their three games and conceded ten goals, that all four Australian defenders would often stay back to mark a single forward. That left them short elsewhere on the pitch. No semi-professional Dutch team would be so naïve.

Hiddink was surprised that the Australians were so willing to listen to him. They understood that they had a chance to learn the EEC style from the man himself. Hiddink had always excelled in dealing with difficult characters: Romario, Edgar Davids, or the Korean Ahn Jung-Hwan. He knew just how to touch them. But the Australians, he admitted, were 'zero difficult'.

Except perhaps Mark Viduka, Australia's best but not its most committed player. Hiddink recalled later: 'He came in with, "Oh I'd like to go to a World Cup but it's going to be difficult. We've never made it and I'm not fit."' Hiddink sent the Socceroos' physiotherapist to work with Viduka at his club, Middlesbrough. This didn't merely get the player fit. It made him feel wanted. Hiddink also made Viduka his captain, to make sure he would be inside the tent pissing out rather than outside pissing in.

It was striking how quickly the Socceroos learned EEC football. Once again, 'culture' seemed to be no obstacle. In November 2005, only a couple of months after Hiddink had started part-time work with them (he was also coaching PSV at the other end of the globe), they beat Uruguay in a play-off to qualify for the World Cup. Suddenly the *Melbourne Herald Sun* found itself wondering whether Aussie Rules football could survive as the dominant sport in Australia's southern states. Already more Australian children played soccer than Aussie Rules and both rugby codes combined.

The newspaper's worries appeared justified when a few months later, just before the World Cup of 2006, an Australia v Greece friendly drew 95,000 people to the Melbourne Cricket Ground. In no city in Europe or Latin America could such a game have drawn such a crowd. Australia had also just become approximately the last country on earth to acquire a national professional soccer league.

And then Hiddink led the Socceroos to the second round of the World Cup of 2006. Great crowds of Australians set their alarm clocks to watch at unearthly hours. Soon after the Socceroos got back from Germany, Australia launched its own (disastrous) bid to host a World Cup. What had happened on Uist over a century before is now threatening to happen in Oz. A century from now, Aussie Rules might exist only at subsidised folklore festivals.

2006–2009: HIDDINK TO GHIDDINK IN A MOSCOW HOTEL SUITE

After Australia, Hiddink could have had almost any job in football. In an ideal world, he would have liked to manage England. Of all the world's marginal football countries, England had the most potential because it was rich, large and had recently rejoined the network of core countries.

Hiddink also relished the specific challenges of managing England. He had the psychological expertise to inspire tired multi-millionaires. He loved dealing with difficult characters; Wayne Rooney would be a cinch for him. And he would have improved the thinking of a team that had everything but intellect. As a lover of the bohemian life, he would have been happy in London, and his girl-friend would have been an hour from her beloved Amsterdam. But Hiddink couldn't bear the thought of British tabloids crawling over his family, and so he decided to spread his EEC know-how to Russia instead.

Like England, Russia had always been at a remove from the best western European football know-how. The country didn't have much of a tradition. The excellent Soviet side of the 1980s had been mostly Ukrainian. But now, after communism, Russia's door to the west had opened slightly. There was potential here.

Admittedly the country's population was collapsing rather than growing, as Russian men drank themselves to death. However, when Hiddink took the job the Russian economy was moving the right way. In the decade from 1998, Russian income per capita nearly doubled. The country's new oil money bought Hiddink's brain. (Oil in general has become one of the dominant financial forces in modern football.)

As in Korea, Hiddink's job was to force his players to be free. Traditionally, Russian footballers had the 'I only work here' demeanour of *Homo sovieticus*. They feared their coaches as much as they feared the mafiosi who stole their jeeps. They shoved safe sideways passes into each other's feet, because that way nobody could ever shout at them. There was *zaorganizovannost*, over-organisation.

Ghiddink, as the Russians call him, joked with his players, relaxed them. As a 'punishment' in training, a player might have a ball kicked at his backside, while the rest of the squad stood around laughing. The times helped: this generation of Russian players could not remember the USSR. Armed with iPhones and SUVs, they had left the periphery and joined the global mainstream.

As he had in Korea, Hiddink practically ordered his players to think for themselves, to give riskier passes, to move into new positions without him telling them to. Marc Bennetts, author of *Football Dynamo: Modern Russia and the People's Game*, said: 'It's as if he's beaten the Marxism-Leninism out of them.' At Euro 2008, Russia's hammering of Ghiddink's native Holland was the ultimate triumph of a marginal country over a core one. It also provided the almost unprecedented sight of Russian footballers having fun. They swapped positions and dribbled, knowing that if they lost the ball no one would scream at them. After the game, their best player, Andrei Arshavin, muttered something about 'a wise Dutch coach', and cried.

Russia lost in the semis of Euro 2008 to another former marginal country, Spain. By then, after 22 years in the European Union, Spain was so networked that it didn't even need a foreign coach to win the Euros.

Spain, Russia and Turkey, another semi-finalist at Euro 2008, were all beneficiaries of the spread of football know-how to marginal countries. When all countries have about the same football information, and converging incomes, the countries with the most inhabitants usually win. Three of the four semi-finalists at Euro 2008 (Russia, Germany and Turkey) had the largest populations in Europe.

The rise of the periphery is now upsetting football's traditional order. We've noted that western European teams lost six matches to nations from other regions at the South African World Cup, compared with only one (on penalties) in Germany in 2006. The old ruling countries now have to keep learning tactically to stay on top. The Spaniards, Germans and Dutch have. They constantly exchange knowledge with each other.

But in the long term, even that might not be enough to save small core countries like Holland, Denmark or the Czech Republic. Their populations and economies are almost static, and they have exported their football knowledge. What made them unique between 1970 and 2000 was their network. Now that that has expanded to include much of the world, they are probably doomed.

2014–?: THE PERIPHERY WINS THE WORLD CUP

Until the late 1990s the cliché in football was that an African country would 'soon' win the World Cup. Everyone said it, from Pelé to Walter Winterbottom. But it turned out not to be true, mostly because although African populations were growing, their incomes remained too low to import much good football experience. A better tip for future World Cups might be Iraq. If the country remains halfway stable, it's likely to do even better than it did in its years of madness. However, the best bets for the future are probably Japan, the US or China: the three largest economies on earth, which can afford good European coaches, where potential footballers have enough to eat and don't get terrible diseases.

There are already omens of their rise. Both the US and Japan reached the last 16 of the South African World Cup, and were unlucky not to go further. The US has the most young football players of any country, and its Major League Soccer is expanding fast; Japan plans to host the World Cup again by 2050 and win it; China topped the medals table at the Beijing Olympics. Already these countries are starting to dominate female football: in the women's World Cup final of 2011, Japan beat the US; in the Olympic final the following year, the US beat Japan. In the women's game, where no country has much experience, big rich nations win.

In men's football too, the US, Japan and China are fast closing the experience gap. They have overtaken the Africans en route to the top. In the new world, distance no longer separates a country from the best football. Only poverty does.

AFTERWORD:
THE BEST OF TIMES

'Absolutely crazy,' commented Jürgen Klinsmann, coach of the US national team, after Real Madrid paid Spurs a reported £85 million for Gareth Bale in 2013. 'I think that all those huge transfers – I don't know if you can justify that stuff any more. It's kind of out of control,' Klinsmann told the BBC.

He was expressing a broadly felt disquiet: that football's transfer fees, debts, wages, ticket prices, spoiled players and general hype have got out of hand. Many people have argued that the 'football bubble' is bound to burst, just as the American housing bubble did after 2006. Jim Spence, writing about English football's ticket prices on the BBC website in 2011, contributed some other metaphors: 'If football's elastic snaps, the game will be caught with its trousers down very soon, charging these kinds of prices ... Football has to be careful not to cut its own throat and see that lifeblood drain away to leave a lifeless corpse.'

We disagree. We don't think there is a football bubble. We do think the game has never had it so good, but we also think it will have it even better in years to come as football continues to conquer the world. Like it or not, we expect leading players to become even more 'overpaid' and the game even more overhyped in future.

Not long ago, there was very little money in football. By the 1970s, most western Europeans had acquired TV sets (except in Spain, where in 1970 only 28 per cent of households had one). However, they hardly ever used those TVs for watching football.

Europe's state broadcasters of the day barely screened the game. In most countries it wasn't possible to watch regular league competition, week in, week out. European sponsors weren't very interested in football, and so almost the only people putting money into the sport were the ones showing up at the weekend at their local club's rundown stadium. In 1974, the total income of all of European professional football was probably somewhere around £90 million (a bit over $200 million). That made it a slightly bigger business than American major-league baseball ($153 million) or the US National Football League ($172 million), but it was a little amoeba compared with Hollywood. In 1974, total box-office receipts for the movie industry in the US alone were $1.9 billion.

But then something changed. Over the last 30 years, sport has been the fastest-growing segment of the entertainment business, and football has been the fastest-growing sport.

This is mostly thanks to TV. When rights to live broadcasts of the English Football League were first sold, in 1983, they fetched just £2.5 million a year. However, in the early 1990s the multi-channel era reached Europe. TV moguls like Rupert Murdoch and Silvio Berlusconi used some of the new channels to show football. It rapidly became clear that even the most popular soap operas – which for decades had glued entire nations to the sofa – couldn't get a fraction of the audience commandeered by the biggest football matches. Moreover, the soaps' scriptwriters couldn't write fast enough to generate enough material to fill the schedules.

Football clubs became de facto producers of TV content. That changed the game. When you're on television every week, you have to smarten yourself up. Rundown stadiums full of misbehaving fans no longer cut it. It's no coincidence that the refurbishing of English stadiums and the first sale of the rights to satellite TV happened almost simultaneously in the early 1990s. In the new TV era, with smarter stadiums, hooliganism has declined across most of western Europe. Since 2002, the build-up to the World Cup has no longer been overshadowed by angst about thugs.

On the field, too, the violence has been taken out of the game. In the past, being a creative player was a hard life. In 1966 Pelé limped out of the World Cup; in 1983 Diego Maradona had his time at Barcelona ruined by an assault by Andoni Goikoetxea ('The Butcher of Bilbao'); and in 1992 Marco van Basten's career was effectively ended by injuries at the age of 28. But in the TV era, the authorities began to crack down on thuggish defending. Before the World Cup of 1998, FIFA actually made the tackle from behind a sending-off offence. These curbs have freed creative players. In our day, Lionel Messi, Cristiano Ronaldo and Zlatan Ibrahimović have been able to thrill fans week in, week out for years, almost untroubled by injuries or fear.

With a better spectacle on offer, and stadiums more comfortable, no wonder clubs in the best leagues began charging more for tickets. No wonder, too, that in the 2000s viewers beyond Europe began switching on to European games. A club like Manchester United started life as a club in Manchester. It soon became a club in England, later a club in Europe, and today it is a global club.

Football is now, by a large and constantly growing margin, the planet's favourite game. There was a landmark moment in 2009, when the Champions League final overtook the Super Bowl of American gridiron football as the world's most watched sporting event: 109 million viewers versus 106 million, according to the Futures Sport + Entertainment consultancy. Even in the Canadian prairie town of Edmonton, crowds took over downtown to celebrate Barcelona's victory over Manchester United. Football – notably European football – is inheriting the globe. That's why movie stars nowadays want to hang out with footballers, rather than vice versa.

Not even the economic crisis has stunted the game's rise. Even after 2008, European clubs kept growing their revenues by 5 per cent a year, against the tide of almost every other business. By 2012, European football had become a much bigger industry than any of its American competitors:

Sector	Annual revenues in $billions
European football	24.6
US cinemas	10.8
NFL	8.8
US Major League Baseball	7.5

It's in the context of football's current revenues that we must see its current debt. In 2013 European clubs owed a cumulative €7.7 billion (about £6.4 billion), according to UEFA. That's a lot more than they owed a decade ago – but now they have a lot more money to pay it with.

The football economy is not a bubble, because its higher spending is funded by higher revenues. Madrid could afford to pay £86 million for Bale because from 1997 to 2013 its revenues had jumped six-fold to €521 million. With all that money in the game, of course players are earning enormous salaries and becoming spoiled. These are the problems of success.

It's perfectly reasonable to make a moral critique of the new football. You can say: 'I remember the time when my local team consisted of local boys earning the same sort of wages as most people in our town. I don't like the moneyed football of today.' That's fair enough. You can still find the old local football if you drop down a division or two, but perhaps you still want to go to Arsenal or Manchester United and find everything more or less as it was in 1974, and you can't. It's reasonable to resent that. After all, most of us like football because it connects us with our childhood. It's also perfectly reasonable to think that football should not have been commercialised. But it's illogical to jump from a moral preference ('I dislike the new football') to an economic prediction ('This is a bubble that's going to burst'). You might loathe today's big football, but the probability is that it will only get bigger.

Back in the 1960s, the football agent Ken Stanley told his client George Best: 'Think about what football will be like when it's truly a world game. Think of the size of America. Think of every boy in Africa having a team shirt and a ball at his feet. Think about China and Japan and the rest of the Far East. There are billions of people out there, George. The game is still growing. They'll be watching you on television in Peking and Calcutta before long.'

For all the global growth we've seen in the last decade, Stanley's prophesy is only just starting to come true. The Premier League, in particular, is working hard at tapping new markets. Kevin Alavy, the managing director of the Futures Sport + Entertainment consultancy whom we met earlier in the book, says that often the Premier League enters a new territory by offering itself on free-to-air TV. That's what it did in eastern Europe, across the former Soviet Union, and more recently in Indonesia. Until a few years ago, hardly any of the 247 million Indonesians knew football. But given the chance to watch top-class English games on TV for free, many switched on. In recent years, says Alavy, 'Typically Indonesia has been the number one market by TV audiences for the Premier League.' Once Indonesians were hooked, the Premier League gave them a new TV rights deal that offered them far less free football.

Using these methods, says Alavy, 'Football now touches all countries without exception. That is different to 20 years ago.' However, he adds, football still has great scope for global growth. The game has only just begun to penetrate the world's four most populous countries, China, India, the US and Indonesia, which between them account for about 45 per cent of humanity.

In China and India, says Alavy, fewer than 10 per cent of the population 'really, really cares about football'. The Premier League currently earns only about three cents in TV rights per Chinese person, compared with about $56 per Singaporean, according to the business website sportingintelligence.com. That's room for growth. Then there are the large economies of Japan, Canada and Australia, where football is also growing fast. One measure of the unrealised potential is that the Premier League still earns more from TV rights inside the UK (about £3 billion total from 2013 to 2016) than in the rest of the world put together (about £2.2 billion).

Those proportions won't stay that way for long. And all of European football will keep tapping away at those new overseas markets. One prediction: in the next few years, the Champions League will grow its global TV audiences by admitting the champions of countries such as the US, China and Japan. These teams will replace the Polish or Dutch champions, or the Italian number three. The problem of travel will be solved by making the non-European teams play their three European games back to back. And their home audiences will switch on in the millions.

Pessimists warn that people might well watch more football, but stop paying for it. After all, consumers now illegally download much of their music for free, so why not Arsenal v Chelsea? Already, with a bit of internet savvy, you can watch plenty of games online. However, the consultancy PwC, in its report 'Outlook for the Global Sports Market to 2014', is reassuring. It says: 'Research and indeed the experience of pay-TV broadcasters with exclusive sports content confirm that people are prepared to pay for additional value.'

Better, for the first time ever, viewers no longer need a TV to watch football. Increasingly, they can choose their platform: cellphones, tablets, Xboxes. That means they can watch on the train, in the pub, or during lunch break at the office. Already, most young viewers watch games with a 'second screen' up, so that they can chat with fellow-fans on Twitter or Facebook. Within a couple of decades, technology should make the viewing experience even more fun: if you want, you will have holograms of players running around your living-room.

In thirty years' time, when European stadiums are packed with Asian fans paying £300 for their tickets, we may well look back and say: 'Can you imagine that in 2013 you could get in to a game for £70 and have money left over for a pie?' Or perhaps by then everyone will be watching US soccer instead.

ACKNOWLEDGEMENTS

Dozens of people helped make this book possible. We would like to thank Peter Allden, Dave Berri, Joe Boyle, Edward Chisholm, Dennis Coates, Bastien Drut, Rod Fort, Bernd Frick, Brian Goff, Jahn Hakes, Pauline Harris, Brad Humphreys, Paul Husbands, Kristján Jónsson, Kai Konrad, Dan Kuper, Markus Kurscheidt, Mike Leeds, Ben Lyttleton, Wolfgang Maennig, John McMillan, Roger Noll, Andrew Oswald, Holger Preuss, Skip Sauer, Philip Soar and Lia Na'ama ten Brink.

We got ideas and information from Kevin Alavy, Rob Baade, Vendeline von Bredow, Carl Bromley, Tunde Buraimo, Pamela Druckerman, Russell Gerrard, Matti Goksoyr, Adam Kuper, Hannah Kuper, Kaz Mochlinski, Ignacio Palacios-Huerta, Ian Preston, Antoinette Renouf, Andreas Selliaas and Paul in 't Hout; from Benjamin Cohen, Jonathan Hill, Mark O'Keefe and Alex Phillips at UEFA; and from David O'Connor and Andrew Walsh at Sport+Markt (now part of Repucom).

The following were fantastic collaborators: Kevin Alavy, Wladimir Andreff, Giles Atkinson, Tunde Buraimo, Luigi Buzzacchi, David Forrest, Filippo dell'Osso, Pedro García del Barrio, Steve Hall, David Harbord, Takeo Hirata, Tom Hoehn, Georgios Kavetsos, Stefan Késenne, Tim Kuypers, Umberto Lago, Stephanie Leach, Neil Longley, Susana Mourato, Susanne Parlasca, Ian Preston, Steve Ross, Rob Simmons, Ron Smith, Tommaso Valletti and Andy Zimbalist.

At HarperCollins, Jonathan Taylor had faith in the book before we had even written it, and was a thoroughly supportive presence throughout. Steve Dobell was a most literate copy-editor and Steve Burdett has saved us from many errors over the years. Katherine Patrick got us publicity, and Rory Scarfe, Peter Sherrott and Nick Canham masterminded the publication of subsequent editions without ever getting too irritated with us.

We also want to thank all the interviewees quoted in the text.

SELECT BIBLIOGRAPHY

BOOKS

Anderson, Chris and David Sally. *The Numbers Game: Why Everything You Know About Football Is Wrong*. Viking, London, 2013

Andreff, Wladimir, and Stefan Szymanski, eds. *Handbook on the Economics of Sport*. Edward Elgar, Cheltenham, 2006

Andrews, David L. *Manchester United: A Thematic Study*. Routledge, London, 2004

Ball, Phil. *Morbo: The Story of Spanish Football*. WSC Books, London, 2001

Bellos, Alex. *Futebol: The Brazilian Way of Life*. Bloomsbury, London, 2002

Bennetts, Marc. *Football Dynamo: Modern Russia and the People's Game*. Virgin Books, London, 2008

Biermann, Christoph. *Die Fußball-Matrix: Auf der Suche nach dem perfekten Spiel*. Kiepenheuer & Witsch, Cologne, 2009

Bose, Mihir. *The Spirit of the Game: How Sport Made the Modern World*. Constable & Robinson, London, 2011

Burns, Jimmy. *Hand of God: The Life of Diego Maradona*. Bloomsbury, London, 1996

Burns, Jimmy. *When Beckham Went to Spain: Power, Stardom and Real Madrid*. Penguin, London, 2004

Carragher, Jamie. *Carra: My Autobiography*. Corgi Books, London, 2009

Cole, Ashley. *My Defence: Winning, Losing, Scandals and the Drama of Germany 2006*. Headline, London, 2006

Dobson, Stephen, and John Goddard. *The Economics of Football*. Cambridge University Press, Cambridge, 2001

Drogba, Didier. *"C'était pas gagné"*. Editions Prolongations, Issy-les-Moulineaux, 2008

Epstein, David. *The Sports Gene: What Makes the Perfect Athlete*. Yellow Jersey Press, London, 2013

Exley, Frederick. *A Fan's Notes*. Yellow Jersey Press, London, 1999

Ferguson, Alex. *Managing My Life: My Autobiography*. Hodder and Stoughton, London, 2000

Ferguson, Alex. *My Autobiography*. Hodder and Stoughton, London, 2013

FIFA TMS Global Transfer Market 2012. FIFA TMS, Zurich, 2013

Foot, John. *Calcio: A History of Italian Football*. Fourth Estate, London, 2006

Gerrard, Steven. *Gerrard: My Autobiography*. Bantam Books, London, 2007

Ginsborg, Paul. *A History of Contemporary Italy*. Penguin, London, 1990

Gopnik, Adam. *Paris to the Moon*. Random House, New York, 2000

Hall, Matthew. *The Away Game*. HarperSports, Sydney, 2000

Hamilton, Aidan. *An Entirely Different Game: The British Influence on Brazilian Football*. Mainstream Publishing, Edinburgh, 1998

Hamilton, Duncan. *Immortal: The Approved Biography of George Best*. Century, London, 2013

Hill, Declan. *The Fix: Soccer and Organized Crime*. McClelland & Stewart, Toronto, 2008

Holt, Richard, and Tony Mason. *Sport in Britain, 1945–2000*. Wiley-Blackwell, London, 2000

Hopcraft, Arthur. *The Football Man: People and Passions in Soccer*. Aurum Press, London, 2006

Hornby, Nick. *Fever Pitch*. Indigo, London, 1996

Kapuʼsciʼnski, Ryszard. *The Soccer War*. Vintage International, New York, 1992

Kok, Auke. *1974: Wij waren de besten*. Thomas Rap, Amsterdam, 2004

Kolfschooten, Frank van. *De bal is niet rond*. L.J. Veen, Amsterdam/Antwerp, 1998

Lampard, Frank. *Totally Frank*. HarperSport, London, 2006

Lewis, Michael. *Moneyball*. W.W. Norton & Company Ltd., New York, 2004

Lever, Janet. *Soccer Madness*. University of Chicago Press, Chicago, 1983

Mandela, Nelson. *The Long Walk to Freedom*. Abacus, London, 1995

Montague, James. *When Friday Comes: Football in the War Zone*. Mainstream Publishing, Edinburgh, 2008

Mora y Araujo, Marcela, and Simon Kuper, eds. *Perfect Pitch 3: Men and Women*. Headline Book Publishing Ltd, London, 1998

Nieuwenhof, Frans van de. *Hiddink, Dit is mijn wereld*. De Boekenmakers, Eindhoven, 2006

Norridge, Julian. *Can We Have Our Balls Back, Please? How the British Invented Sport and Then Almost Forgot How to Play It*. Penguin, London, 2008

Oliver & Ohlbaum Associates and Fletcher Research. *Net Profits: How to Make Money out of Football*. Fletcher Research, London, 1997

Orakwue, Stella. *Pitch Invaders: The Modern Black Football Revolution*. Victor Gollancz, London, 1998

Peace, David. *The Damned United*. Faber and Faber, London, 2006

Rooney, Wayne. *My Story So Far*. HarperSport, London, 2006

Silver, Nate. *The Signal and the Noise: The Art and Science of Prediction*. Allen Lane, London, 2012

Simons, Rowan. *Bamboo Goalposts: One Man's Quest to Teach the People's Republic of China to Love Football*. Macmillan, London, 2008

Szymanski, Stefan. *Playbooks and Checkbooks: An Introduction to the Economics of Modern Sports*. Princeton University Press, Princeton, 2009

Szymanski, Stefan, and Tim Kuypers. *Winners and Losers: The Business Strategy of Football*. Penguin, London, 1999

Szymanski, Stefan, and Andrew Zimbalist. *National Pastime: How Americans Play Baseball and the Rest of the World Plays Soccer*. The Brookings Institution, Washington, DC, 2005

Taylor, Peter. *With Clough by Taylor*. Sidgwick & Jackson, London, 1980

Tomkins, Paul, Graeme Riley and Gary Fulcher. *Pay as You Play: The True Price of Success in the Premier League Era*. GPRF Publishing, Wigston, 2010

Turnbull, John, Thom Satterlee & Alon Raab (eds). *The Global Game: Writers on Soccer*. University of Nebraska Press, Lincoln, 2008

Varley, Nick. *Parklife: A Search for the Heart of Football*. Penguin, London, 1999

Vergouw, Gyuri. *De Strafschop: Zoektocht naar de ultieme penalty*. Uitgeverij Funsultancy, Antwerp, 2000

When Saturday Comes. *Power Corruption and Pies: A Decade of the Best Football Writing from 'When Saturday Comes'*. Two Heads Publishing, London, 1997

White, Jim. *Manchester United: The Biography*. Sphere, London, 2008

Wilson, Jonathan. *Inverting the Pyramid: A History of Football Tactics*. Orion, London, 2008

Wilson, Jonathan. *The Anatomy of England: A History in Ten Matches*. Orion, London, 2010

Wortmann, Sönke. *Deutschland. Ein Sommermärchen: Das WM-Tagebuch.* Kiepenheuer & Witsch, Cologne, 2006

Zirin, Dave. *A People's History of Sports in the United States.* The New Press, New York, 2008

ARTICLES AND RESEARCH PAPERS

Anderson, Christopher. 'Do Democracies Win More? The Effects of Wealth and Democracy on Success in the FIFA World Cup'. Paper presented at the Annual Meeting of the Midwest Political Science Association, Chicago, 2011

Baade, R. 'Professional Sports as Catalysts for Metropolitan Economic Development'. *Journal of Urban Affairs* 18, no. 1 (1996): 1–17

Berlin, Peter. 'Playing by the numbers'. *Financial Times*, February 1, 1992

Feenstra, Robert, Robert Inklaar and Marcel P. Timmer. 'The Next Generation of the Penn World Table'. 2013. Available for download at www.ggdc.net/pwt

Gabaix, Xavier. 'Zipf's Law for Cities: An Explanation'. *Quarterly Journal of Economics* (MIT Press) 114, no. 3 (August 1999): 739–767

Hicks, Joe, and Grahame Allen. *A Century of Change: Trends in UK Statistics Since 1900.* House of Commons Library Research Paper 99/111. London: House of Commons Library, December 1999

Hirshleifer, J. 'The Paradox of Power'. *Economics and Politics* 3 (1991): 177–200

Kavetsos, Georgios, and Stefan Szymanski. 'National Wellbeing and International Sports Events'. *Journal of Economic Psychology* 31, no. 3 (April 2010): 158–171

McGrath, Ben. 'The Sporting Scene: The Professor of Baseball'. *New Yorker*, July 7, 2003

Palacios-Huerta, Ignacio. 2003. 'Professionals Play Minimax'. *Review of Economic Studies* 70, no. 2 (2003): 395–415

Peeters, Thomas and Stefan Szymanski. 'Financial Fair Play in European Football'. *Economic Policy* (forthcoming 2014)

Peeters, Thomas, Victor Matheson and Stefan Szymanski. 'Tourism and the 2010 World Cup: Lessons for Developing Countries'. *Journal of African Economies* (forthcoming 2014)

Szymanski, Stefan. 'Income Inequality, Competitive Balance, and the Attractiveness of Team Sports: Some Evidence and a Natural Experiment from English Soccer'. *Economic Journal* 111 (2001): F69–F84

Szymanski, Stefan. 'A Market Test for Discrimination in the English Professional Soccer Leagues'. *Journal of Political Economy* 108, no. 3 (2000): 590–603

Tapp, A. 'The Loyalty of Football Fans – We'll Support You Evermore?' *Journal of Database Marketing and Customer Strategy Management* 11, no. 3 (April 1, 2004)

Tapp, A., and J. Clowes. 'From "Carefree Casuals" to "Professional Wanderers": Segmentation Possibilities for Football Supporters'. *European Journal of Marketing* 36, no. 11 (2002)

Taylor, Matthew. 'Global Players? Football, Migration and Globalization, c. 1930–2000'. *Historical Social Research* 31, no. 1 (2006): 7–30

MAGAZINES

Hard Gras (Netherlands)

Johan (Netherlands, now defunct)

Voetbal International (Netherlands)

So Foot (France)

INDEX